God: An Itinerary

God: An Itinerary

Régis Debray

Translated by Jeffrey Mehlman

VERSO

London • New York

Liberté • Égalité • Fraternité
RÉPUBLIQUE FRANÇAISE

This book is supported by the French Ministry for Foreign Affairs as part of the Burgess Programme, headed for the French Embassy in London by the Institut Français du Royaume Uni.

Ouvrage publié avec le concours du Ministère français chargé de la culture – Centre national du livre. This book is published with the support of the French Ministry of Culture – Centre national du livre.

This edition first published by Verso 2004
© Verso 2004
Translation © Jeffrey Mehlman 2004
First published as *Dieu, un itinéraire*
© Éditions Odile Jacob 2001

1 3 5 7 9 10 8 6 4 2

Verso

UK: 6 Meard Street, London W1F 0EG
USA: 180 Varick Street, New York, NY 10014–4606
www.versobooks.com

Verso is the imprint of New Left Books

ISBN 1–85984–589–4

British Library Cataloguing in Publication Data
Debray, Régis, 1941–
   God : an itinerary
   1. God – History of doctrines
   I. Title
   291.2′11
   ISBN 1859845894

Library of Congress Cataloging-in-Publication Data
Debray, Régis.
   [Dieu, un itinéraire. English]
   God : an itinerary / Régis Debray ; translated by Jeffrey Mehlman.
   p. cm.
   Includes bibliographical references.
   ISBN 1-85984-589-4 (hardcover : alk. paper)
   1. God – History of doctrines. I. Title.
   BT98.D3513 2004
   202′.11–dc22
                                             2003027791

Typeset in Sabon by YHT Ltd, London
Printed in the UK by The Bath Press

Contents

This journey would not have been possible without the encouragement of all those who tirelessly agreed to answer my questions, frequently inspiring me to reformulate them in the process. I would like to thank in particular Father Jean-Michel de Tarragon, prior of the convent of Saint-Étienne in Jerusalem and editor of the *Revue biblique,* along with his Dominican brothers on Nablus Road; Simon Claude Mimouni of the Section des Sciences Religieuses at the École pratique, and editor of the *Revue des études juives*; as well as Professor Maurice Sachot of the Université Marc-Bloch in Strasbourg, a specialist on late Antiquity.

Father Olivier de la Brosse, prior of the Dominican Convent of Saint-Honoré, and, in another domain, Anne-Hélène Hoog, of the Musée d'art et d'histoire du judaïsme, were equally willing to guide me to precious sources of information.

May they all forgive my errors of interpretation and accept this expression of my gratitude.

1 A Reader's Guide

*To meditate in the face of this formidable
question mark is, in our opinion, the duty of
every mind. Whence this book.*
(Victor Hugo, *Dieu*)

For a quarter of a century now, the objective study of religion has been markedly in advance of religious awareness, including agnostics' awareness of the common stock of legends. The dates, places and heroes of the biblical saga, as they have been transmitted to us by our grandparents, the catechism, bestsellers or mere rumour, no longer have currency with most scholars. Abraham, 'our common father', 1750 BCE; Moses, 1250 BCE; the exodus from Egypt, Mount Sinai, Joshua and Jericho; David and Solomon's Temple; the New Testament as opposed to the Old: such are the clichés, the almost instinctive beliefs that the best-educated even among believers have taken to calmly dismantling.[1] The gap that has, as a result, opened up between the image bequeathed to us of our origins and what archaeology, epigraphy and exegesis currently allow us to understand of them by no means pits faith, on the one hand, against objective inquiry on the other. In the French-speaking world, the pioneers of patient investigation and positive knowledge are to be found, to a large extent, in monasteries and congregations, among pastors and monks; whereas in lay or atheistic circles a kind of nostalgic inertia holds sway (the cultivated being by no means the least credulous). Factual precision and intellectual rigour may choose to pitch their tent among Dominicans and Jesuits, those experts on Judaism and Islam of times past. Consider, for example, the French Biblical and Archaeological School set up at the Dominican monastery of Saint-Stephen in Jerusalem, or the works of the *Revue biblique*, whose publication it has overseen for the past 108 years. Such is the paradoxical reversal of values to which we have been brought by a poorly understood (and, in the long run, suicidal) secularist policy banning the teaching of religions in our public schools. In the face of the rising tide of illiteracy, are we actually intent on making tomorrow's monasteries the last refuge of the spirit of the Enlightenment? (*a*)

If I find myself addressing the merely curious reader, it is not with the ambition –

---

[1] Here I am referring to the turn (some would say the earthquake) prompted in particular by the efforts of two researchers: Thomas L. Thomson (*The Historicity of the Patriarchal Narratives: The Quest for the Historical Abraham*, Berlin: De Gruyter 1974) and John Van Seters (*Abraham in History and Tradition*, New Haven, CT: Yale University Press 1975).

far from it – of bridging that gap. To be a popularizer, one must first be an expert. And an expert who has assimilated the innumerable specialized analyses whose synthesis (and whose synthesis alone) would enable one to escape the customary correlation between inflated titles and the impoverished developments they generally introduce. Although I have been concerned with questions of religion for more than twenty years, I have neither the pretension nor the requisite skills that might allow me to undertake such a task (I can read Greek and Latin, but neither Hebrew nor Aramaic, and certainly not hieroglyphics or cuneiform). For me it would be sufficient to throw off the yoke of convention, moving from received ideas to more considered points of view. (b)

To this end, my point of departure has been an initial sense of astonishment: on the Earth's surface and in the density of the ages, our heavenly Father is seen as a strange and somewhat disconcerting Being. No doubt belief is natural for the only animal that knows it is going to die. But it is so unnatural to 'believe in God' that many civilizations we still remember, and the most refined among them at that, were able to live and die without having the slightest notion of a Creator at once omnipotent and sufficiently solicitous to sidle up and whisper in our ear. Only the prophetic religions endowed with a putative founder (such as Moses, Zarathustra, Mani or Mohammed) have entertained so bizarre a conception. Its epidemic spread has diverted our attention from the infinitesimal and random events that serve to trigger things. Those 'small insignificant truths' that Nietzsche, in *Human All Too Human*, pitted against the 'great beneficent errors'. And it is to them that I would like to return, with a view to grasping what proved simultaneously so adventurous and so fertile in so unwonted an acquisition. Not in order to debate the existence of God for the upteenth time, but in order the better to understand how the only carnivore to practise voluntary fasting succeeded in generating his very humanity.

Is our 'great question mark', then, a matter of course or a huge mystification? Please forgive us for not having the slightest idea. It will suffice for our purposes to maintain the register of His transitions and about-faces. That He appeared in times past to certain errant individuals called prophets is a fact for which we have documentary evidence. That certain highly strung and warlike peoples followed in their footsteps, and got something out of doing so, is a second. That the believing biped was then propelled from Jerusalem to Byzantium by way of Rome, from Mecca to Córdoba, and from Europe to America in order to destroy and rebuild, to immolate himself and to massacre, in all sorts of incursions, conquests, colonizations and holy wars, is still a third. And so on. I shall leave those more inspired than I am to determine which of the two, God or the kamikazi, is the generator of the other. The effects are verifiable, the ultimate Cause unfalsifiable. I shall restrict myself to the manifest level in order to situate the paths along which God's fire managed to be transmitted from the desert to the city. A somewhat cavalier investigation, and necessarily so, but one conducted as close as possible to the surface of things, at the very level of residues, signals and archives. I shall not plunge into the depths of time in order to retrieve 'things hidden since the foundation of the world', some dormant unspoken reality couched in the recesses of Scripture whose exhumation would supply us with the key to the future. I will humbly attend to flora and fauna, shapes and materials. To the work of irrigation and storage. To question the Invisible One with naked eyes, on His ways rather than His words, is to choose the ascertainable as our guiding thread even as we attempt to avoid the delusions of interpretation. While attempting not to seduce Him into saying what we perhaps already know from other sources. Without wanting to compete with those latter-day ventriloquists who generously bestow on the history of religion the privilege of endorsing their own petty or grand secret (vital energy, the murder of the Father, sacrificial violence, etc.) without regard for facts, dates and places. Remembering all the while the film-maker Robert Bresson's line: 'The supernatural is the natural precisely rendered.' If I have an ambition, it is to answer as soberly as possible a childlike – and, in its triviality, frequently deferred – question: how is it that the Absent One, born in the desert three thousand years ago, is still with us? And that hundreds of millions of men (who no longer travel by donkey or camel, but in trains and planes) continue to go off to meet Him, in pilgrimages, sacrifices or feasts, mosques, churches or synagogues?

For He was not always there, above our heads or in our hearts. There was a time, a very long time, during which He was nowhere to be seen; and another, quite recent, in which that void was duly registered or alleged. The original nomenclature remains, but the Being so called does not have the same mode of existence in the year 500 BCE, 400 or 2001 CE, in Hebron, Byzantium or Boston.

יהוה ΘΕΟΣ DEVS DIEU GOD

Same name, same person? In detaching it from the procedures and institutions that produce and reproduce it, we have *ontologized* the sacred (Mircea Eliade) lest we be obliged to *historicize* it. For the happiness of being able to take shelter within a closed totality, given once and for all in the reassuring form of the identical. In order to make do without taking our *Deus ex machina* down into the machine room, and charting the interruptions and twists of the main road. Israel's Lord of Hosts is not the Christian God of love and intimacy, who in turn is not the impersonal cosmic energy of New Age theology. If the 'I am that I am' had been His last word, Yahweh would have remained immutable in the general flux. But the long-term perspective reveals just how far His Uniqueness is from Simplicity. It is the meandering advance of His complications that will be our focus in these pages. In order to extricate the circumstances of a birth, the bifurcations of an itinerary and the costs of a survival. In the West alone, a limited, circumscribed expanse of civilization, which happens to be ours. That division, or confession of incompetence, is admittedly arbitrary and even somewhat scandalous, since it leaves aside Islam (which was 'Western' more than once, establishing itself in Seville and licking the walls of Vienna). In Christianity itself, the division between West and East makes sense only as of the second millennium, with the schism over *filioque*.[2] Our Incomparable One comes to us from the East, like Europa, daughter of Agenor, King of Phoenicia, where Zeus, disguised as a bull, came to carry her off to Greece. But reference to the Arabo-Islamic East (our knowledge of which is second-hand) will be only lateral, at least in the present volume. The narrowness of the expanse traversed is openly admitted.

Which is, at the same time, to say what ought not to be sought here: anything on the order of 'Science and Faith, convergence or antagonism', and even less 'Ethics and the Ten Commandments, the limits of permissiveness'. I will not be wondering whether or not the universe bears witness to some finality; whether there is room alongside scientific method based on observation and reasoning, and after quantum theory and Gödel, for some other order of reality accessible through intuition and awareness; whether the logic of *how*, that of science, allows for a logic of *why* alongside it, one to which religions speak; whether or not what we know today about the universe authorizes us to posit an intelligent Plan; whether the invention (or discovery) of a single God was the result of a lamentable blunder or a stroke of genius; whether more good than evil, or the reverse, has resulted from the invention (or the discovery) of Good and Evil. These are all honourable and intriguing questions. I reserve the right not to offer an opinion on them (or to do so as little as possible, since no one is perfect).

Concerning monotheism, everything has been said – and its opposite. That it is a humanism, and a form of barbarism. A liberation, and a plague. The cure for our malaise, and a substitute neurosis. A kind of operatic duet, with alternating voices, has been composed on this theme. I choose not to get involved in that particular confrontation. Neither to stigmatize, with the sons of Zarathustra and the bacchante, social conformity, hatred for the body, misogyny, and the murderous Manichaeism of societies that have adopted the lamentable notion of poisoning life with an overbearing and incomparable Male; nor, with the sons of Levinas and Hannah Arendt, to vaunt the ethical universal, the emergence of the idea of a Law superior to Nature, the tonic separation of the temporal from the spiritual, which saves us from deifying our Caesars and submitting to the *fait accompli*. A dialogue of the deaf between neopagans and neobiblicists. Let it be noted that the thesis and the antithesis can simultaneously be true: the divine pharmacy, like every other, has its ambivalence. *Pharmakos*, as is well known, means both elixir and poison. No need to break swords, once again, over a familiar theme.

Nor will these materials serve as a supplement to the sociology of religion, however instructive it may be in other contexts. The accomplishments and merits of that

---

[2] In 1054, the Greek Eastern Church split from the Latin Church, rejecting the proposition that the Holy Ghost stemmed from the Father 'and the Son'.

discipline (since Max Weber) have been immense, but they have kept the theological question itself, prudently sidestepped, at a friendly distance. 'Our investigation goes up to the threshold of the mysteries', said Gabriel Le Bras, the founder of religious sociology in France, quite naturally refusing to allow his 'science to get involved with the supernatural'. I will be criticized for pretending to breach the action of grace with observations that will surely be qualified as 'positivistic', but that is precisely the division of labour I would wish to unsettle. There is not, on the one hand, a 'tormented history of religions' and, on the other, a great immobile secret, incapable of transformation. An Absolute resembling an *objet trouvé*, definitively indefinable, before which would parade, like so many prisms or coloured lenses, different 'communities of reception', 'forms of sociability' and 'modes of membership'. There is not, on the one hand, 'grounded in truth and authority', an untouchable Founder, and, on the other, the stuff of graphs and statistical inquiry, since they are subject to critical examination, religious practices and institutions. There is not an ideal or real Invariant, in relation to which believing communities would be so many modes of approach, externalized as sources of influence, ways of speech, styles of presence. To seek to acclimatize the Absolute to a modernity that dreams of taking its distance is one thing. It is undoubtedly good for His deputies to know the audience they are addressing and in what language, better adapted to their living conditions, they can be most persuasive. 'Acculturate the message to a different world,' is the advice given by experts in homiletics, in order *to talk about God differently*. To attempt to think a God who is metastable, unpredictable and always *different* from Himself, but about whom, out of laziness, we continue to talk in *the same language* partakes of a wholly different register.

When it comes down to it, far from wanting to disconcert, we shall quite simply be taking the Lord literally. To Moses, who asks Him: 'Show me your glory, I pray,' He replies: 'No, I shall show you only my footsteps. You cannot see my Face, for no man shall see me and live' (Exodus 33: 20). Even then, one must agree to look at God's back close-up, to follow at His heels, walking in His footsteps, like a simple investigator. Without attempting to play advocate or prosecutor. And even less examining magistrate. We shall be content to take notes, to photograph marks. Neither for nor against – one God rather than another, or none at all. This indirect pursuit, this genealogy of the externalities of the divine, might have been called a *technohistory* if *techno*, debased by usage, meant something else, embraced something broader than the *mechanical*. It will be a question in these pages of the *mediations of God*, in the full sense of the term, which considerably exceeds the various ways He has undertaken to mediate Himself. Beyond means of access and distribution, groupings of believers come into play, since enrolments govern organizations, which in turn endow them with life. The documentary sciences will thus not be sufficient for a study of the Eternal as a phenomenon of transmission, which is, to be sure, subject to a material history of signs and their supports, and remo-

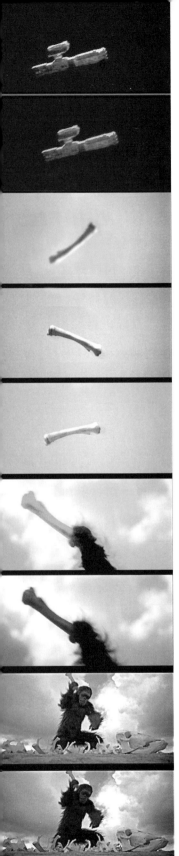

delled by successive materialities, but always by way of populations, Churches and communities. I have thus preferred the neologism *mediology*. This original mode of investigation is concerned not with a realm of reality, the media, but with a realm of relations. It helps to disentangle and to characterize the correlations between our 'higher social functions' (religion, art, ideology, politics) and our procedures of memorization, displacement and organization. Let us say: between what is most ethereal and most trivial.

To bring technology and theology into contact will appear grotesque or pathetic, so profoundly do the terms clash in our hoary lexicon. Like the mechanical and the mystical, the accidental and the essential. The first term concerns matter, the second spirit? A simplistic division. There are intellectual technologies – and our procedures of annotation are among them; as for theology, it requires an argumentative craft, a mastery of the mechanics of discourse (as Saint Thomas mastered the rhetoric and logic of Aristotle). Let us summarize the meaning it would be prudent to give the word: the opposite of 'natural' or innate. We shall qualify as 'technical' every behaviour or performance that is not included in our genetic programme. Natural language, as it is aptly called, is not in itself a technique, since every normally constituted infant has a competence for speech that is realized in time without any special apprenticeship. We are all born with a tongue and a larynx, but clay and cuneiform inscriptions, paper and pen, are 'extra'. The proof that such an 'extra' is optional is that 'societies without writing' exist, whereas no ethnographer, be it in deepest Amazonia or New Guinea, has ever encountered a culture that is mute. That writing is a technique is something that was already understood by the Sumerians, its inventors: 'If oral language is a gift of the gods,' they said, 'writing is a human creation.'

Along with numerous others – those, in particular, who have learned from the prehistorian Leroi-Gourhan – I accept that it was the gift of the prosthesis that constituted the humanity of man, who became human by externalizing his faculties in a process of objectification without end (without finish or aim). The subject is constituted as human with and in the object. Technical invention, which inserts the other in the same, allows for the *cumulative succession* called 'culture'. It ceaselessly provokes new worlds, and as Stanley Kubrick suggests in a grippingly emblematic visual (the opening of *2001: A Space Odyssey*), there is a continuity between a femur-cudgel thrown into the air by a palaeoanthropic ape and a

2001: A Space Odyssey, Stanley Kubrick, 1968,
MGM Productions

space rocket at takeoff. God appeared midway in that ascending trajectory, and to inquire into that sublime innovation is first of all to resituate it there in its place. By unpacking the ages it compacts. By unpleating a toneless monosyllable, restoring its volume and depth.

Technology has no less invented man than the obverse, and the Creator Himself cannot claim exemption from that interplay. Just as we change behaviour every time we change our social or technical surroundings, God has changed His *mind* with every change of armature. It is the decisive incidence of insignificant gadgets and apparatuses, apparently unworthy of His glory, that I would like to bring to light. The hypothesis should not be termed 'demystifying'. Perhaps it does no more than put Providence back in its place. Take a pair of binoculars and stand at the window. It is through the small end that you will discover the landscape. In the large – and official – one, you will see only your own face reflected back at you: zero information.

To talk about quadrupeds, baked clay, wheels and roads, alphabets, pixels and bytes may appear offensive, indeed degrading. Wrongly so, in my opinion. I regard as counterproductive the received division between high and low, treasure and mere equipment. It seems to me, for instance, that our Beaux-Arts (fine arts) are singularly diminished by turning their back on Arts et métiers (arts and crafts). The sanctuary on one side and the eco-museum on the other? Such enervation through mutual enucleation replaces art with fakery and tools with gadgets. There thus emerge from commentary on the Scriptures informed by neither archaeology nor ethnography a host of phantom religions, derelict like so many virtual basilicas from which the objects of the cult, which account for the daily texture of the liturgy, have been removed: chalice, paten and ciborium, wafer, wine and oil, not to mention the eucharistic fixtures and the altar-stone. These spawn places of faith without faith, unsuited for consecration and fit only for tourism. Why separate 'wheelbarrows and hoofs' from mysteries and dogmas? Wheat and grapes from the Eucharist? The mystical can be deciphered in material dispositions, just as the Trinity can be discovered in a stained-glass window, and the heavenly Jerusalem in the architectural plan of a basilica. In the long run, metaphysics does itself no good in scorning its own physics. In repeating too often that science is concerned with *how* and religion with *why*, we have allowed the *how* of the *why* to sink into obscurity. The consideration of the accoutrements of theology which I propose to undertake in what follows should not, for all that, surprise the faithful of a Church that was born while setting the table for a shared meal, and for which the very term *ekklesia* embraces both a building and a mystical body. We should remember the two meanings of *misericordia*: God's compassion for the sinner and the wooden corbel allowing the officiant in his stall to rest his buttocks. Bodies think, and things do too. Let us allow God to rejoin His site; let us align cathedral vaults with storage vaults. The pulpit is the centre of the Protestant temple because it is a Church of speech. The altar is the centre of the Catholic chapel because it is a Church of sacraments. *'Ecclesia materialis significat ecclesia spiritualem.'*

'Inanimate objects, have you then a soul / Which clings to our soul and forces it to love?' Let us try to shake off the false modesty of *naive spiritualism* (as opposed to the original variety, which was in no way spectral or vaporous) imprinted in our mental habits by the binary lexicon inherited from Hellenic dualism (being and accident, form and matter, soul and body, etc.). The Semites favour the notion of the psychosomatic unity of the human being. We shall follow them rather than the Greeks, while taking care to reconnect object to subject, the practical to the symbolic, and the useful to what is deemed worthy of worship. Those pairs of terms do not constitute a zero-sum game, in which everything that is accorded to exteriority would be taken away from interiority. The two terms exist solely in the relation that unites them. A bit of etymology. From the Latin *anima* come, in a single breath, both the French *âme* (soul) and *animal*. And *spiritual* comes from *spirare*, to breathe, *respirer*, or to activate mouth and lung. Spirit blows a breath of life into our nostrils. And we should be suspicious of any *Dictionary of Spirituality* that fails to contain an article on zoology. As though sheep, donkey and camel were of no significance in the genesis of the biblical God. As though Christ in his majesty, on the tympanum of our cathedrals, were not escorted by a biped and three animals, his evangelists. The allegories are medieval but promising. Let us hope for a series of studies of the role of lentils, biscuits, sticks, jugs, sandals and backaches in the discovery of the Almighty.

Without Him, in any event, the face of the Earth would not be what it is. Neither Israel nor Christendom nor Islam. And the whole of the West would not follow, with bated breath, a conflict that concerns, in the last analysis, no more than 50,000 square kilometres and a few million people. Hypereffects demand a hypercause: such is our first reflex. This dates from scholasticism. God is the cause of the world, and every cause comprises, to an eminent degree, the perfections possessed by its effect. We have learned from Darwin that more can emerge from less, and from Henri Poincaré that 'small differences in initial conditions can engender very large ones in final phenomena'. In relation to their effects, initial conditions may appear ludicrously trivial and unworthy of attention. A tornado in Texas? A beating of wings above the Amazon jungle. It may not seem serious, but meteorologists tell us that in fact it is. It is a residual bit of magical thinking that leads us to assume that a thing's origin need be at least equal in volume and dignity to the thing itself. Pascal has already thrown Cleopatra's nose in the face of our solemnity. There are some very curious trivialities that change everything, in an unpredictable manner. The study of God's own trivia is not, in my view, a way of diminishing Him but, rather, of deploying anew, at new cost, the spiritual question. While relinquishing a simplistic view of causality.

'At new cost'? By rolling the projectors back from front-stage to the wings and machinery of the divine production; by receding from the Law to the Tablets of the same name – a bit like the idiot who, when the Chinese sage points out the moon, stares at his finger. By observing Heaven at its most down-to-earth. By shifting our focus from opus to operation, from downstream up, placing the emphasis not on what is written and worth reading, but on how it has been written, with and on what, to what end and in accordance with what strategy. This wish to ally ourselves with things, what the poet Ponge called *le parti pris des choses*, breaking with the cultural idiom of recent decades, requires a kind of *askesis* or suspension of our habits: renouncing the nobility of hermeneutics, the nobility laid claim to by philosophers dedicated to the interpretation of the world as language. The order of meaning exceeds that of discourse. And words do not exhaust events. My aim is not to provoke a sacred text into interpreting itself, but to find out how such things as the sacred, a text, and traditions of reading come to be. It is not a matter of unpacking the implicit meaning of canonical Scripture, but of finding out why a canon was necessary and what logic is implicit in the act of separating, among documents of equal consistency, texts said to be canonical and suited for liturgical reading (because they are imbued with authority) from their apocryphal equivalents, which are said to be abusive and heretical.[3] To take an eminently respectable example, my perspective is precisely the opposite of that of Paul Ricœur and his splendid meditations 'between philosophy and theology'. Which is to suggest not a contradiction, but – such is our hope – a complementary source of understanding.

The dream would have been to move a mirror along the road from source to delta, from Mesopotamia to the 'global village'. In order to observe the tracks left behind by the Great Rambler. Longitudinally, from the swamps of Sumeria to the shores of the Pacific; and down the centuries, from oil-lamp to our 'Son et Lumière' extravaganzas. Were it possible to film the Invisible One, it would quickly be seen that He has not come down to us in the state in which He began. His trip has transformed Him. The operator of the shuttle extracts his percentage from whatever it is he chooses to shuttle, which would not exist without him. Where have we ever seen a self-mobilizing idea, moving on its own through space and time? Nothing here below is transmitted of itself, self-propelled without cost or wear and tear. Mathematics is conveyed by schools and qualified teachers; music by conservatories and interpreters; painting by museums and art critics. God by holy books and communities of prayer. Here too, no doubt, the genealogy and current difficulties of the Everlasting will not be illuminated without relinquishing scholastic definitions of God as cause of Himself, *ipsum esse subsistens* – the pure act of existing. Philosophers have defined Him as a Being 'absolute, necessary, without cause, simple,

---

[3] See Simon C. Mimouni, *Le Judéo-Christianisme ancien: Essais historiques* (Paris: Cerf 1998).

infinite, immutable and unique' – Father without father, son of no one. Floating unimpeded in His headway like a hydroplane atop its cushion of air, the Holy Spirit. In French, 'the Holy Spirit *se répand*: spreads *itself* through the world'. How was that? A Word *se fait entendre*: allows *itself* to be heard. The active reflexive participates in magical thinking (the refusal of whose facility gives us mediology). We shall ask instead: whose Word is it, and subject to what system of acoustics? Through what channels? In which translation? With which spokesmen? And in accordance with which ceremonials, originating where? The Creator, it emerges from an unbiased account, proceeds by way of a conjoining of the inert and the animate. He requires material and personnel. If a transcendental Being is to survive His own birth, He needs *organs* and *tools*. A *spiritual organism* (family, nation, church, sect, etc.) and a *mnemotechnical apparatus* (scrolls, books, effigies, figures, etc.). Their articulation alone ensures a *viaticum* (from *via*, the path or road) For nothing traverses the centuries, not even the extra-chronological time of the Everlasting, without travelling gear. How have eighty generations of Jews managed to subordinate themselves to a Yahweh intent on strict observances? How have Christians submitted to their incomprehensible trinitarian God? And Islam to its unimaginable Allah? Such is the enigma of all that wills its persistence and perseveres, all that does not die with mortals. A search for the beginning of enlightenment leads us to explore the *underpinnings of perseverance*, their *sui generis* meshing of signals and rituals. Religions and doctrines have been depicted from the waist up in the noble history of ideas; yet they progress on two legs. If one leg happens to buckle, the keepers of the Tradition are on the alert, at the side of the road, armed with stretchers. It takes so little for public exposure to ensue.

'Do this in remembrance of me.' The act of retaining, repeating what has been eradicated, is at the heart of every cult. But how does one transform a past into a present? First of all, by substituting for a venerated *being*, alleged to be a saint or a hero, an ancestor or an ally, a solid and visible *thing*, a written or constructed memorial – say: some *organized matter*, or OM (stela, slab of stone, cross or mound). Yet if the relic does no more than persist in its materiality, an inert mass among others, without serving as an occasion for ceremonies, pilgrimages and visits, with flowers and flags, its religious coefficient (for rallying or assembling) will be nil. Now a series of periodically renewed acts of homage, *pedibus cum jambis*, presupposes a calendar or means of computing time, observances or obligations – say: a somewhat authoritarian administration of customs. This in turn requires a *materialized organization*, or MO – family, college, fraternal organization, party, church or state. The conjoining of the two, external memory and internal memory, is neither automatic nor guaranteed. Consider an altogether banal example. The Mur des Fédérés in Père-Lachaise Cemetery in Paris, site of the crushing of the Commune, was invested in 1900 and 1950 with a measure of the socially sacral which had vanished by 2000. The Wall is physically intact, with its plaques and memorial slabs. What are missing are the speakers and wreaths. Because in the interim, the Workers' Movement, the engine behind the transmission of the myth of the Commune and of a certain vision of the future, disappeared. No more May Day liturgy, no more will, no more energy. When the 'living stones', believers or militants, dry out and crumble, the stones themselves regress from relics to mere residues. Museums have begun to fill up as churches have gradually emptied out. And a church, too, can turn into a museum. How many monasteries have become concert or exhibition halls?

I do not claim, to be sure, to *exhaust* all the senses of the divine idea, but only to *describe* its metamorphoses, extracting from the shadows its underpinnings and externalities. And perhaps one day that long series of avatars will come to be ordered into a sequence of questions addressed to its impedimenta: who transmits the divine, to whom, where, how and under what constraints? Who received the Word as a charge – a people, a clergy, the family, a multinational community? Where will it seek out its interlocutors, and what will it ask them to do? By privileging or banning which mode of expression – images, or text alone? In what kind of space, and with what temporal depth? The traditions of Judaism, Catholicism, Protestantism and Islam do not supply the same answer to these questions.

Let us forget acronyms and schemata, and turn to history and geography. But before surprising the Everlasting *in statu nascendi*, stimulated by His milieu and liberated by His medium, let us begin by seeing precisely what place He came to occupy in the endless procession of human beliefs.

BOOK I
Coronation

2 An Endpoint Called Origin

Veritas filia Temporis.
(Bernard de Chartres)

In the evolution of the species and of beliefs, our solitary God is a latecomer. How are we to explain the fact that the Creator lagged so far behind His Creation? And that Genesis, the Book of beginnings, was added on towards the end of the sacred patchwork? The fact is that monotheism, the slow decanting of polytheism, is a result, not an initial given. Mediodependent, the Eternal One could not move any faster than the history of our means of deposition and locomotion – and the music of civilizations begins in a rhythm that is slow. God was obliged to predate His birth announcement in order to make up for lost time. We have projected His pure essence, which was codified later than we think, back to the beginning of history. All of which is normal. In any and every process, what we baptize 'origin' is usually its point of completion.

An Eternal Father who is younger than His progeny? Comparative chronologies bear witness to this bizarre circumstance. We His children are ancient in relation to our Creator, who may be august but is a late bloomer. He is, at best, six thousand years old; *Homo sapiens* is between fifty and a hundred thousand years old. The two millennial timelines unfurl in polite ignorance of each other, which avoids the embarrassment of a confrontation. The fact that the Eternal intervened *in extremis* in the adventure of the species, as the curtain was falling, and not in just any setting (between the two horns of a warm and fertile 'crescent', shortly after the domestication of quadrupeds) no longer raises – and habit is a help here – any uncomfortable questions. 'Why so long after original sin? Why the Son of God in Bethlehem and not elsewhere?' certain curious Christians wondered in times past in relation to the Redeemer. The theologian reduced them to silence: 'God's free will makes the most insignificant details of the Saviour's birth entirely appropriate.'[1] Revelation is His prerogative. He alone decides and disposes. Amen. But that begging of the question makes the problem the solution.

Currently, the separation of an 'australopith' branch from the simian trunk is assumed to have taken place 3.6 million years ago, and the branching off of *Homo erectus* at 1.7 million years. The symbolic function, attested to by painted figures and burial sites, appears in the middle Palaeolithic (between 100,000 and 35,000 BCE), and monotheism assuredly not before the middle Bronze Age (2000 to 1550 BCE). In our holy book (the rhapsody of interpolations that the translators of Alexandria, known as the Seventy, called 'the books', *biblion* in Greek), the years are counted in hundreds. The timescales on high and here below, as we shall see, are so out of phase that the articulation of one agenda with the other surpasses the imagination – for our greater convenience. Such is the psychosocial advantage of a partitioning of faculties, disciplines and histories, sacred and profane: to spare oneself the embarrassment of seeing the year zero of salvation coincide approximately with the year 100,000 of the sinner. The delay in revelation is a matter of

---

[1] *Dictionnaire de théologie catholique*, VII, 2, p. 1472.

such little concern that the *where* and *when* of God scarcely interest researchers, assured as they are of the scientificity conferred on them by lab coat, laboratory and high-tech cabling.

God's Belated Media

Invoke Heaven as a witness? We should be wary: the reflex no longer pays. The Most-High has very recently changed His address. No doubt He remains light, fire and flame (French *Dieu* has the same root as *dies,* day in Latin), but the ignition takes place in our heads. Single photo emission computed tomography (SPEC) cameras have recently taken a 'photograph of God' (*sic*). By injecting a radioactive tracer into the cerebral blood supply of meditating Tibetan Buddhists and praying Franciscan nuns, two American neurophysiologists, Andrew Newberg and Eugene d'Aquila, have at last succeeded in localizing the Ungraspable: in our upper rear parietal lobes, both right and left. The neuronal bases of mystical ecstasy being thus identified, in normal conditions, for subjects suffering from neither epilepsy nor intracranial tuberculoma, it follows, according to our cognitive scientists, that the 'human brain was genetically conceived to encourage religious beliefs'. The inventors of neurotheology summarize their discoveries concerning the 'neurology of transcendence' under a reassuring title: 'Why God Won't Go Away: Introduction to the Biology of Belief'.[2]

Respect for scientific progress aside, one fails to see why He who caused from on high so many perturbations down below (in public order, in the exercise of intelligence and the instinct of conservation in the case of individuals) should not produce a reasonable share in our brains. At the very least. This revelation – God? an electrochemical flash – far from closing the debate, gives it new momentum. With the *where* circumscribed – specifically in the parietal lobes in charge of relations of causality – the *when* only becomes more enigmatic. Neurons, not clouds? The atmosphere is billions of years old, our cerebral machinery, millions; the Eternal, thousands. Since the neuronal connections of the believer were stabilized a hundred thousand years ago, with the invention of the first funeral rites, we may wonder what precisely deactivated the 'God genes' or the biological imperative to find a higher sense to things during our long animistic (or idolatrous) night.

Let us give a less naive turn to the objection. That man, with or without endomorphines, may have a generic and genetic competence for the supernatural (as he has for uttering articulate sounds) is a more than plausible hypothesis. There are human groups that are more or less taciturn, more or less 'materialistic', but no ethnologist has as yet discovered an aphonic society, nor one that abandons its dead

[2] Andrew Newberg and Eugene d'Aquila, *Why God Won't Go Away: Brain Science and the Biology of Belief* (New York: Ballantine 2001).

on the ground, for its bones, like an animal's, to be scattered (the state of total agnosticism, like that of the deaf-mute, being taken as a limit-case or an individual anomaly without probative value). It remains to determine why, in sum, Neanderthal man deposits his deceased in a ditch, in a foetal position; Celebesian man installs them in vertical position on a balcony atop a cliff studded with niches; and we on their backs, in a coffin, without the slightest nourishment; why one ethnic group speaks an agglutinative language and a neighbouring group an isolating one; why the cerebral cortex of a Roman happened to bond with divine Epicurus and that of Blandine of Lyon with our Saviour; while the Indian neuron prefers Ganesha the elephant and the Japanese neuron Maitrega, plump of belly, presiding on his throne over the Heaven of the sated. Our cerebral architecture no more accounts for those significant discriminations than the hardwiring of our nerves does for our various grammars. To engage the concrete means articulating the invariant with its variations, the neurochemical givens of the religious animal (Jews and Muslims, Chinese and Turks, endowed with the same dendrites and neurotransmitters) with the fractures of the Annals, the striations of the Atlas of spiritualities.

Constructing a model for the variants neglected by a dominant biologizing perspective remains the Holy Grail of anthropologists. Their effort has been to simultaneously distinguish and co-ordinate the innate and the acquired, what persists and what changes, the scenario of the genome and the hidden design of the centuries. That ideal compass – which would indicate both physiological invariant (the hominid family of primates) and historical variation, and which would allow us to measure *sociotechnical variables*, in step with the tools that the human species has gradually acquired – is not yet at our disposal (so far as we know). The teaming up of biochemists and historians of mentalities not, to all appearances, being in the immediate offing, we are obliged to make do with whatever means happen to be available in our effort to understand why there have been so many distractions, so many swerves on the part of the Creator (if one is a believer), or in our neurotransmitters (if not). We are assured that the Almighty, for our greater good, will, then, never *disappear*, but why was it that He *appeared* so late?

Let us open the Bible. One week to create the heavens and the earth through the utterance of a few key-words – light, water, grass, star, animals, man – and then millions of weeks without a word – or any effort to make Himself known. Without revealing his exploit – or His blunder. Elohim took His time. The revelation by the Demiurge of a planet four million years old to His favourite creature, the opportunistic and omnivorous predator of the savanna, who happened to have more than a million years behind him himself (if we are to judge by the first stone tools), that He was the author of his days barely six thousand years before (according to the Hebrew calendar, 5,762) does not appear to indicate a particular hurry. Indifference? Disgust? Or the quest for a sensational intervention on the part of a particularly alert *Deus ex machina* (the one who descends from the theatre rigging in Act V, Scene 6)? That God did not deem *Homo habilis* and *Homo erectus* worthy of receiving the information is understandable. Their cranial capacity was modest (600 cm^3). But what of the Neanderthal occupying Asia and Europe from 100,000 to 35,000 BCE, who had the same brain as we do, spoke, buried his dead, and believed in the beyond? Are signs of maturity, of receptiveness, as considerable as mastery of fire (500,000 BCE), the invention of ceramics (6000 BCE) and the calendar (3000 BCE) to be regarded as negligible? Why wait for Abraham before entering the plot in His own name in the form of a familial contract: 'I shall establish my covenant with you, and your race after you, from generation to generation'? A contract renewed later on with Moses, under the name of Yahweh, and on explicitly national grounds. Such would be the Event, the authorities tell us, which divides the course of the ages in two. During which epoch did the caesura come? Traditional datings (until quite recently) placed the departure from Egypt, which went unmentioned by the Pharaoh's administration (just as the bureaucracy of Rome retained no trace of Jesus), as far back as the thirteenth century before our era (the period of the Ramessides, in fact of Ramses II himself). In terms of the anthropological record, the Old Testament tells of overwhelming changes, but at the very last moment. Moses was just this morning. The caesura in the poem? Its ending.

Why does the great Clockmaker's clock lag so far behind the timepiece of the species when the inverse would have been more plausible? Why did *Homo sapiens* manage to set up viable societies in many points on the globe over the course of tens of thousands of years without referring to an Only One? Since I am dwelling on this question, I shall offer a blunt reply at the outset (I shall have time to refine it). The Covenant? A written charter enacted between *transhumant or itinerant shepherds* (in a wilderness setting) and a *scriptor* perched on high (God, with His finger). No shepherds without grazing, and no grazing without the taming of beasts. Sheep (in Iraq, around 9000 BCE) and goats shortly thereafter were the first domesticated species (after dogs, to be sure). Then, in due course, came oxen, horses and donkeys (between 6000 and 3000 BCE). Herbivorous animals live in groups, a circumstance that facilitates the activities of herdsmen and dogs, but they do not make the transition from the wild to grazing on their own. The temporality involved would take us into agroalimentary history. As for the wandering, it partakes of that poor cousin of History known as the history of transport, whose turning points coincide more or less with those of the history of communications (the first known outline of a cart, with hollowed-out wheels, appears on a tablet from Uruk, the Iraqi city from which the first written tablets come). Wheeled vehicles appear on the banks of the Nile and the Euphrates towards the end of the fourth millennium. The twofold transition from pictographic to phonetic signs and from simple sledges, made of branches, to carts drawn by oxen or donkeys (and by horses as of 2000 BCE) is directly implicated in our subject. It should be recalled that a transcendent Invisible Being, by definition, can be neither sculpted nor drawn, and that it is migration by caravan that confers its full use value on a portable Sacred Name (since the traditionally sedentary can do without it). So long as the 'featherless biped' (a mammal not at all pampered by nature and biologically premature by birth) had not attained cruising speed – below, that is, a threshold of minimal domestication of space and time – the idea of an abstract God, whether true or false, was not utterable. Non-pertinent. A hunter-gatherer would not have been able to conceive it because he was able to survive without it.

To anticipate: God is essentially unthinkable without writing and secondarily so without the wheel, which together reduce by several degrees man's dependence on natural space (the wheel) and natural time (writing). Belated is the Only One because belated were those prostheses affecting certain ways of circulating and memorizing, which were themselves dependent on quite specific ecosystems. The All-Powerful did not, one fine morning, on a peak in Sinai, discover an opportunity to reveal Himself in His eternity. It was a certain political usage conferred on technical innovations that gave to monotheism its consistency and necessity. The various panoplies of the inventive primate have their own *tempo* (which has been extremely rapid since the Industrial Revolution, but was still rather slow following the neolithic revolution). Man may descend from the simian [*singe*], but God descends from the sign [*signe*], and signs have a long history. The technogenesis of transcendence is a phase to be resituated in the technogenesis of man, a process that continues, in full view, and whose inception goes back to the first incised stones, that is, to the early Acheulean carvings, in Africa, 1.4 million years ago (700,000 in France). That moment, which we may call miraculous, is that of a stunning act of technopiracy which married pastoral nomadism to alphabetical script. It was not biologically determined in so far as nature does not require any manchild to pass through such a state. A structured human group is viable without livestock and an alphabet. And in fact, humanity lived, dreamed and invented without them for most of its existence. Adam, who talked and walked, did not know how to count or write or saddle a mule.

The Indispensable Illusion of the Origin

When it comes to the Judaeo-Christian God, we find it hard to break with the habits of imperial thought, in which a certain serene theocentrism serves to cloak an ethnocentric bias. A culminating and central God strikes us as the point of origin of an irreversible liftoff specific to civilized humanity once the threshold of 'primitive' religions has been cleared. Or, better still, as a mental reserve, a common ground subtending the full gamut of regional and local divinities. Thus we read in the *Dictionnaire de théologie catholique*: 'Biblical revelation indicates to believers that at the beginning there existed not animism but a pure monotheistic religion. The polytheisms of Antiquity and modernity are but its degraded forms.'

That conviction of chronological anteriority receives more than a little support from the superstitious reverence that surrounds the very notion of a Source. The Perfect Being predisposes us to it by His very nature. 'The conception that in the beginning of all things is to be found what is most precious, most essential' was characterized by Nietzsche as a bit of 'metaphysical sleight of hand'. How might one exorcize the chimera of the Origin at the summit of metaphysics in the figure of a God who is nothing less than Origin become Being? How escape the idea that in His infancy is to be found His purest essence? Is not the return to sources, the quest for a primordial emanation, in every domain, the hope for a moment of self-rediscovery, allowing us, in a flash, to glean identity in all its freshness, the barely emergent secret of what we have subsequently become, and of what we have lost in the process? Is that not the heady charm of Genesis and the Creation? Creationism is no longer deemed appropriate in the natural sciences (even if one in two Americans continues to believe in it, and the American President wants to reinstate it in public education in order to counterbalance the pernicious effects of Darwinism). But it is a strain for us to admit that the Creator *ex nihilo* of the world was not created *ex nihilo*. He through whom time came to be ought to be strictly atemporal; He who decompressed space ought not to occupy any. To admit that the Heavenly Father did not spring fully armed from a cloud would be tantamount to imagining a Most-High lacking in exalted birth – and something adventitious, incongruous or accidental in his emergence. A solitary God of modest origins? Whose upper-case initial would be woven of lower-case stories? In order to escape the Origin, a teleological myth by which the end commands the inception, and to ward off the consolatory play of mirroring recognitions, Foucault proposed using the word *provenance* (*Herkunft* instead of *Ursprung*). The term is an incitement to

> retrieve beneath the singular aspect of a character or concept the proliferation of events through which (thanks to which, against which) it came to be formed. To follow the complex channels of a provenance is, on the contrary, to maintain what has occurred in the dispersion specific to it, to locate accidents, infinitesimal deviations ... ; it is to discover that at the root of what we know and what we are, there is not the inner truth of being, but exteriority and accident.[3]

The 'provenances of God'. The phrase is less impressive than 'the origins' – in which the plural softens the ontological pre-emption of becoming, but none the less reduces the singular randomness of the event. There was a time when geographers were obliged to resign themselves to the fact that the Nile and the Loire, in their majesty, do not have one source but *various* sources, which are, moreover, erratic

[3] 'Nietzsche, la généalogie, l'histoire', in *Hommage à Jean Hyppolite* (Paris: PUF 1971), p. 153.

and shabby of aspect to boot. Theographers may well be constrained to do the same: renouncing the Origin as a great lost secret. One is not born God, solemnly; one becomes Him, through ruse and tenacity.

If it be true – and, we believe, understandable – that the 'third chimpanzee' is and remains a religious mammal (a quality not attributed to the pygmy chimpanzee and the common chimpanzee), there can be no question of identifying the diffuse and universally confirmed sentiment of the sacred, holy or 'numinous' with a belief in the 'God of our fathers'. There is nothing in monotheism of a founding and generic principle destined, from the outset, to conquer the entire planet. As though God had been owed us, like a dormant idea sheltered deep within our genetic capital, which would suddenly awaken humanity as it emerged from its infancy (or perhaps in its adolescence, after a somewhat frolicsome childhood). One can speak to a corpse, converse with him through prayer and offerings, deposit ample nourishment in his tomb, without positing an Omnipotent Being keeping loving watch over all men. All that took place long before Our Lord, and might well take place long afterwards. The reflex that consists of investing death with a vital message, in order to alleviate the trauma of a demise, does not imply any particular theology. No correlation between God and the beyond. The Eternal does not guarantee His adepts individual survival – which His faithful can do without; and paradises are not inherent in His concept. To maintain that 'the first person to intervene in a spiritual sense is God' is to forget nothing less than the sun, ancestors, spirits and Great Pan – that is, nine-tenths of the journey. It is to forget the unicorn of Lascaux or the half-animal, half-human sorcerer of the grotto of the Three Brothers. It is to mock the future, pre-history, and societies without writing. Need we recall that from the Magdalenian to the Roman, or from Lascaux to the Rome of Saint Peter, there are more than fifteen thousand years, while only two thousand five hundred years separate us from the return from Babylon? The time from the fertility cults to the worship of the *imperator* is at least ten times as long as that between the master of lightning bolts and thunder, a Yahweh still relatively close to Indo-European Jupiter, and Voltaire's resplendently indifferent deity, the Grand Architect of the Freemasons, to whom it is perfectly useless to address one's prayers or sacrifice a lamb (*de minimis non curat praetor*).

Might monotheism, then, be a kind of terminal skid, a parochial lurching off course? Seen from India or China, through the density of millennia, that provocative image might turn out to be simple fact. It is from the perspective of Euro-America that the God of the 'Western Republic' – imposed, with or without their consent, on Indian America and black Africa – appears as *primus inter pares*, endowed with rights of seniority *vis-à-vis* the 'idols' of the periphery. The primacy of an origin, or of an end, depending on whether history be teleguided by what precedes or what follows it, but one which makes short shrift of the contingencies of the middle. And just as the historian in a Christian world is tempted to erect Christianity as the standard of measurement to which allegedly inferior cults (which may never even have heard of the term 'religion') are referred, we have made of our Western hierarchy the legal standard for all others in terms of both values and development. For it pleases us to shape the randomness of the planet's deities to a finalistic evolutionary scheme. And just as the slow perfecting *ad majorem gloriam hominis* of the animal realm leads to *Homo sapiens*, so we see the divine dynasties ascend towards a supreme encounter *ad majorem gloriam Dei*. Prior to the *Ens perfectissimum*, there would be nothing but a thicket of more or less abominable absurdities, narrowing itself down, sifting itself out over time, each generation of gods improving over the previous one in a kind of selection of the fittest, which eliminates the weakest at each rung of the ladder and ends with a final masterpiece: our Eternal Father. This teleguiding by the end makes short shrift of the variety of geographical settings (the advantages of a God selected by the desert becoming disqualifications in the tundra or tropical forest).

A modest history, then, for an immodest God, concerning whom it should be recalled – in view of His origins, and statistically as well – that He is neither the lowest common denominator of extant pantheons nor the key, or coda, of the symphony of human beliefs. Even at present, a majority of the species lives under the influence of non-theological religions, such as Confucianism; and in the historical heart of Christendom, new modes of spirituality, and even clergies themselves, are quietly divesting themselves of their theological assets. Moreover, if it was His destiny to crown the 'progress of the human mind' (in Rousseau's phrase), our personal God, speaking secretly to our souls, would have come to us from Greece, India or China, civilizations significantly more 'advanced', endowed with sciences, astronomy and geometry, art and town planning – all of which were unknown, and for good reason, to an arid and rudimentary culture of the desert. The late modernity which is ours offers ample evidence of the vanity of linear schemes inherited from the nineteenth century, which posit as a succession – by way of analogy from secular progressivism to the sacred, as though they were modes of economic production – the stages of animism, totemism, polytheism, and finally monotheism. But the facts are more stubborn than our spontaneous ideology of evolution. Postmodern Japan remains largely animistic, even somewhat shamanistic (in the case of Shintoism). In the postindustrial West, Buddhism – a religion without God but abounding in deities (and aspiring to Wakefulness, a state close to divinity) – currently occupies the place that has been vacated. And within the syncretistic elites of our deregulated social patchwork, who knows whether the Buddha will not one day take the place of Jesus, who is five centuries his junior? Nothing, to paraphrase Aragon, is ever definitively the Lord's, 'neither his strength nor his weakness nor his heart, and when he pretends to open his arms, his shadow is that of a Cross …'.

On Anachronism as a Means of Conquest

Let us now change register and consider the limited expanse of time known as monotheistic, on whose outskirts may be found 'the first and most ancient anthology of testimony concerning the Word of God'.[4] 'The Law and the Prophets', as the Holy Scriptures were known during Jesus' time. In the readjustment of humanity's pivotal dates currently under way, God and 'art' have known inverse fates: there has been no end to the rejuvenation of the former and to the ageing of the latter. Around 1950, Lascaux embodied the beginning of the world's art, fixed in the ancient Magdalenian Age, around 1500 BCE, and was centred in Europe. Our most recent discoveries indicate that 'art' (engraved on rocks or painted on slabs) first appeared in Africa, and that even in Europe, we are obliged to move things back 15,000 years (the stencilled hands of the Cosquer cave, near Marseille, are 27,740 years old, and the mammoths of Chauvet 31,000). The chronology of the Bible, during the same period of time, has followed the opposite path, moving forward. In the light of available documents, the era of the Patriarchs ('Abraham, Isaac and Jacob') has lost its antiquity, and the current consensus is that the figure of Abraham took shape, at the earliest, a thousand years after his alleged existence. A second unexpected revision concerns genealogy. Observing that neither Abraham nor Isaac is mentioned in the most ancient texts, which speak only of Jacob, whereas the other two appear in later compositional strata, a number of eminent biblical scholars have advanced the idea that the order in which they are mentioned inverts the chronological order.

With the exception of a stele marking the victory of Pharaoh Merneptah (thirteenth century), the first – rather vague – indication of what would become the Hebrews, mentioned in passing in a long enumeration of vanquished peoples ('Israel is vanquished, and its seed along with it'), and despite a very belated assimilation (which is not incorrect but vague) between 'apiru' and 'Hebrew' on a cuneiform relic discovered at Tell el Amarna, we possess no extra-biblical information concerning the world of the Bible before the eighth century. For that entire period, signs, objects and stones are completely silent. Up until that point there is no overlap between the Babylonian, Assyrian and Egyptian annals and what is indicated in the literary monument. Afterwards, to be sure, there is. Concerning the dynasty of David (end of the eleventh century) we possess an inscription that is difficult to read (the Dan stele). The Siloé inscription (end of the eighth century) confirms what we are told about Ezechias, king of Judah (716–687). It is, in fact, around the eighth century that literature joins up with archaeology with the Lakkish *ostraca*[5] and Sennacherib's annals, which mention the siege of Jerusalem under Ezechias in 701 ('he was locked up in Ursalimmu, his royal city, like a bird in a cage'). As for

---

[4] Introduction to *Traduction oecuménique de la Bible* (1988 edn), p. 11.
[5] Pottery fragments.

Jericho, one is hard put to see how it could have been conquered by Joshua in the thirteenth century, since its destruction goes back to about 1550. Jericho existed, to be sure, but Joshua? 'An emblematic figure' is the conclusion of a number of specialists.

As for Moses, the poignant showdown between Charlton Heston and Yul Brynner provides an enchanting image at which Egyptologists are inclined to smile. One is hard put it to envisage the immigrant chief of a tribe being received in the holy of holies of the greatest empire (comparable to the America of today, in terms of power and influence) by the master of the world. How are we to assume, moreover, in a society so heavily bureaucratized, in which the slightest event is recorded, that an entire army, with the living god Ramses II at its head, could disappear into the Red Sea without a single written document or image having taken note of it? Could the greatest national catastrophe in three thousand years of recorded history not have left a trace? Moses, or Mosis, is the flexional ending of an Egyptian patronymic (like Amosis), and the civilization, atmosphere and phraseology of Egypt have undeniably coloured the composition of the first chapters of Exodus (just as the aura of American popular culture pervades the inventions, customs and names of peoples on its periphery), but it is currently impossible to date the episode from the Ramesside period (1308–1087), as has been done until quite recently. It would be quite possible, on the other hand, for a son of Israel, having settled in the Delta, to have found his inspiration, a number of centuries later, in a well-known ceremonial cartoon of sorts, featuring the Battle of Qadesh, which pitted Ramses II against the Hittites, and in the course of which some of the Hittite chariots are said to have been engulfed in a swamp. A famous battle (of uncertain result, both camps proclaiming victory), which figured in a bas-relief, seen by all, on the monumental pylons of the Ramesseum of Thebes. Was it a transposition of a popular narrative and visual reference, with a switch of protagonists? Such is the thesis, convincing in its abundance of details, of Bernard Couroyer. The author (but there may have been several)

> thus inserted his people in a framework that he knew quite well. Concerning the past, he opted to echo the tradition according to which Jacob and his people had been forced by famine to leave their land and settle in a more fertile region, the north-eastern region of the Delta. 'The Israelites were fruitful and prolific; they multiplied and grew exceedingly strong, so that the land was filled with them' (Exodus I: 7). That growth would have alerted the authorities, who would have issued decrees intended to reduce the proliferation of these foreigners. These would have been followed by a series of vexations – which may have seemed a form of slavery, although that particular vexation seems not to have been imposed on the Israelites. No doubt some were occasionally requisitioned, as were the peasants of Egypt, and perhaps more frequently than they, for several more or less long and onerous tasks, but these did not constitute

actual slavery. Such tasks, moreover, were an obsession of Egyptian peasants themselves .... One can understand that such a situation ended up exhausting the Israelites and that they may have implored God to take them out of the country in which their ancestors, in former times, had found refuge .... But how was one to get them out? ... A military expedition with Pharaoh's troops would in fact have been necessary: the infantry, it goes without saying, but also his most rapid weapon, the chariots, with the sovereign in the lead. Now the expedition in the year V of Ramses II entailed precisely such a mobilization, which was visible on the reliefs. Whoever reported on that fragment of the Exodus would have adapted what he may have seen of the Battle of Qadesh to the requirements of his narrative. For him it was not a matter of recounting a battle but, rather, a pursuit that was destined to fail through the intervention of God and His envoy. Just as Pharaoh had been punished for retaining the Israelites, so was he to have been for chasing them to bring them back to Egypt. Now at whatever point one chose to cross it, the Egyptian border at the time was constituted by a body of water. It would engulf the royal retinue, much as the Orontes had done for the chariots rallying against the Hittite fortress.[6]

To summarize: something on the order of a collective departure did indeed take place (not 603,550 men, as we read in Numbers I: 46, but, rather, a few hundred). *In illo tempore* (since the hypothesis leaves the dating open ... until Cleopatra). That migration was magnified and legitimated by being couched as a chronicle, inserted into an accredited narrative mould – better still, conceived in terms of the officially endorsed visual reference of the superpower in command.

The motley collection we call the Bible, following an error in translation (*the books, biblia* in Greek, having been rendered in Latin by a feminine singular), as it was constituted as a corpus by the Doctors of the Law assembled at Jamnia in Palestine around the year 90, is divided into three sets: the Law, the Prophets, and the Writings. The Law or Torah groups the five books of the Pentateuch (a Greek term meaning the five vessels containing the corresponding scrolls): Genesis, Exodus, Leviticus, Numbers and Deuteronomy. The Prophets group the early prophets (Joshua, Judges, Samuel and Kings) and the later (Isaiah, Jeremiah and Ezekiel, in addition to the twelve 'minor' prophets, so called because their books are short). The Writings group the Psalms, poems that are sung – in praise, prayer and instruction – and texts that were incorporated belatedly, such as the Book of Job, the Song of Songs, and Chronicles.[7] The succession of utterances is given (more or less) as the course of things. The beginning of the Book tells the beginning of the

---

[6] Bernard Couroyer, 'L'Exode et la Bataille de Kadesh', *Revue biblique* 97 (1990), pp. 321–58.
[7] Both the Hebraic and Protestant canons exclude such deuterocanoncial 'writings' as Judith, Maccabees, Wisdom, Baruch, Jeremiah's Letter, etc.

world (Genesis) and is followed by the encounter with the only God (Exodus), then the tribulations of the chosen people, its distress and its glories. The book most often published, read and glossed, our MetaBook, derives its aura from being a source of both information and a faith, the annals of a people and the Word of God. It has a dual value: horizontal (as the chronicle of a localized history) and vertical (as the unveiling of a supernatural design). On the one hand, the epic narrativization of a national itinerary, issuing in a picturesque saga; on the other, the promotion to universality of a number of quite specific events, which have been turned into the stuff of every man's prayers. Two stories for the price of one, the profane and the sacred each drawing support from the other. Yet the more the elements of the file have been examined, the more the theological has come unglued from the historical. The creative virtue of the fantastical, and the efficacy of symbols, deserve to be admired all the more for it. The Bible is not 'false' (except from the perspective of our historicist illusions). It is performative.

Memory before History

The fact that Isaiah never read Genesis, and that David knew nothing of the Sabbath, is not something that comes spontaneously to mind. It is none the less what follows from the gap between the unfolding of history and the form in which it was finally couched. The Prophets were 'closed' before the Law ('nothing was actually written before the eighth century BC,' says Jean-Michel de Tarragon). The first trumpet blast of monotheism dates from the return from the Babylonian exile (522, after the liberating edict adopted by Cyrus). Fragments of it may be observed after the occupation of the northern kingdom, Samaria (721 BCE), with Isaiah as harbinger of disaster. The affirmation resonates as an act of defiance on the part of the exiles, a small minority of the influential – officers, scribes and ironsmiths – directed towards the natives of Judah, who had been left behind and whom they suspected of being lukewarm in their commitment. For Ezra, the reformer returning from exile and said to have proclaimed the Law, those who stayed in the country were adversaries to be convinced, quasi-foreigners on whom it was deemed salutary to inflict the punishment of yielding to the will of a muscular, but trustworthy, God. Which might necessitate a symbolic re-education. Just as the kingdom of France in its formative phase gave itself, under the Capetians, founding heroes, turning a brutal soldier, Clovis, into a saint, and an illiterate, Charlemagne, into a guiding light, the small southern kingdom, centred on Jerusalem, isolated and encircled, had already begun to constitute a gallery of ancestors worthy of its anxieties and its perils. Nebuchadnezzar's destruction of the Temple and the Babylonian exile, which confirmed all previous fears, gave new stimulus to the *ex post ante* invention of a 'reparative' past, one commensurate with the current disasters and capable of giving them meaning. The Exodus would consequently be the projection of a return to an ardently desired and deserved homeland. Similarly, the image of the Tablets of the Law, both support and content, probably stems from Babylonia, where legislation tended to be quite advanced (the Hammurabi Code). It is not surprising that an Assyriologist (Father Marcel Sigrist) was able to recognize the very disposition of the Persian army in the disposition of the column led by Moses, with flag (*degel*) in the lead. Clearly, Yahweh, master of the people and the cosmos, like the Flood and the Tower of *Babel* (from *Babylon*), are elaborations that were modified in the course of the four centuries between the 'Persian period' and the revolt of the Maccabees (167 BCE). It was when Ezra was authorized – indeed, incited – by Cyrus and his administration, who encouraged the self-government of subject peoples to enact a body of duly recorded domestic laws, in order to restore order to Jerusalem (rebuilt by Nehemiah), that Judaism truly acquired consistency. Exegetes claim that the Old Testament, in all probability, dates from the Hellenistic period (starting with Alexander, around 330), with several passages revealing a Greek influence. 'In Genesis, the narrative of origins evokes the beginning of Ovid's *Metamorphoses*', as Étienne Nodet, for example, notes.[8]

It will be understood that ever since Abraham, or even Moses, the exalting figure of a monotheistic Hebrew, alone against the world, is on the order of a pious image. The Israel of the Kings (and Judges) was monolatrous, if not openly polytheistic (allied with Baal, Astarte, Hadad, the god of storms, or Yarakh, the moon god). A *monolator* is someone who chooses a preferred god while admitting the existence of his rivals. A circumstance admitted by the first commandment: 'Thou shalt have no other gods before me .... Thou shalt not bow down before them and thou shalt not serve them.' Yahweh reveals Himself to Moses as a jealous god, which He would not be if He were the only master on board. 'Only' *for whom* is precisely the question. Only for Israel is one thing, called 'henotheism' (in which a people chooses a god in preference to others for itself alone). Only *in itself* and absolutely is quite another. In this regard, the first undeniably monotheistic prophet was Deutero-Isaiah, a contemporary of Cyrus and Pericles, in the sixth century BCE. Only with him does the affirmation of self become, in the case of Jehovah, a negation of the others: 'There is no other god beside me, a righteous God and a Saviour, there is no one beside me' (Isaiah 45: 21). The misperception, for us, stems from the fact that we put Genesis before Deuteronomy, because we trust the table of contents. The endpoint of a long itinerary, studded with intermittences, is thus hypostasized, in our minds, as a simple and luminous point of departure – Moses on Sinai.

Monotheism spontaneously predated itself; such was the genealogical imperative. The struggle for primacy and the struggle for priority were one. Lineage is tantamount to a credential in a world in which nothing can be simultaneously both recent and venerable. Chronology is the argument from authority *par excellence*, the most effective means of subjecting newcomers or ancients said to be such to the needs of

---

[8] Étienne Nodet, *Essai sur les origines du judaïsme* (Paris: Cerf 1992), p. 288.

the cause. We predate in order to be the mightiest, and the mightiest is he who can show his neighbours (and himself) that he was there before the others, in the lap of the Primordial, as close as possible to the Origin. Thus do we produce, man or god, under pressure, with whatever means are at hand, the requisite certificates of pre-existence. Our surprise is far from negligible when we learn from specialists of historico-critical exegesis that Abraham was a petty southern hero promoted in rank and seniority by a team of intelligent editors. Or that the two Tablets of the Law were 'forged' after the Exile, in place of the two statuettes of El and his wife Asherah lodged side by side in the original Ark. But this is a constant in the history of nations as of sciences ('the precursors are those who come afterwards', as Georges Canguilhem used to say). The object of transmission – in this case, the Covenant established upon leaving Egypt between the only God and His only people – does not pre-exist the process of its transmission. It is its itinerary that makes of a discourse what it is. A petty chieftain of a local clan (Joshua or Abraham) is elevated to the sublime; a zero or two are added to a small troop (three thousand Judaeans, according to Jeremiah 52: 28, had been deported to Babylon in 597, and fewer than a thousand in 587); a two-bit king (Solomon) is exalted; a crisis (the break between North and South) is minimized; the peripheral is declared central, or the reverse, in accordance with the imperatives of the moment. With utter good faith, the tradition invents what it claims to convey; and, better still, it authenticates what it utters by effacing its very act of utterance (the medium always conceals or cancels itself as the condition of its performance). The metamorphosis (or reformulation of actual more or less mediocre givens) fulfils a *vital function* for the community which is both its subject matter and driving force, speaker and utterance. The rewriting of the past is dynamic, orientated towards the future. Its role is to endow the present with meaning by offering a focus of desire to a community with reason to doubt its future. This is why every episode of Scripture (whose composition is spread over seven or eight centuries) speaks the language of the century in which it was written, not that of the time in which it is alleged to have taken place. In all narratives of a performative bent (which include national, tribal and familial legends), the way in which things are told tells us far more about the mental categories and historical situation of the narrator than about those of its protagonists. This way of reading, moreover, provides a plausible method for establishing dates. During which era and for whom might the story of Adam and Eve, expelled from Paradise for disobeying the Almighty, be most eloquent? For the exiles of Babylon, expelled from Jerusalem, after 587, for disobeying their natural leaders, the prophets (who did not hesitate to treat kings with insolence). For which period can we make sense of the strange itinerary of Abraham, who leaves from the East, rejoins the West via the North, descends into Egypt, and finally backtracks into Canaan? When it was necessary to reunite the Jewish communities of Egypt with those that remained in Mesopotamia, around a central holy land, after the return authorized by Cyrus (538).

To transmit is not to remove, on demand, from a desk drawer called heritage or collective memory, some document which happens to be already there, a magical scrawl deposited by the ebb and flow of centuries. It is, rather, to inject a measure of novelty into the old, imparting patina to what we invent and allure to what we inherit. A functional blurring of lines. Literary forgery does not stem from a will to deceive, nor from mere inventive talent, but from an instinct for preservation: lest the group's imagination career into despair, or meaninglessness, it is obliged to re-elaborate its reality. Lying to oneself rather than dying is preferable to the other way round. Inasmuch as 'a people without legends is condemned to die of cold', the retroactive construction of origins is part of the thermal effort indispensable to the maintenance of a human group. What establishes its cohesion is the mental sharing of an origin and a destination. The Bible has magnificently fulfilled its role as a communitarian matrix by *fabricating an origin in order to invent a destination.* Avoiding dissolution requires that the present 'fix' the past with a glue that neutralizes dissemination. In that sense, the origin is something that is far too important to be abandoned to registrars and historiographers. It is an asset of memory, to be administered by a family council. Inner cohesion and the capacity for initiative: what is at stake in the origin/destination matrix affects vital integrity in a way that is too fundamental for a search for documents to play any role in it. Such a search is all the less pertinent in that it is jarring to the very idea of an origin that one might capture it in a chronicle, in real time, at a stage concerning which no one would be in a position to say what it is the origin *of*. The crucial moment is always left 'blank'. From this it follows that a transmission is successful when the fabrication is no longer visible. In this respect, the Old Testament is a consummate masterpiece. The invention of history, attributed to Herodotus and the Greeks, does scant justice to ancient Israel, which, by blurring the boundaries between the dreamt and the experiential, ended up forging a single people out of a scattering of tribes. It is not exceptional for the scientific examination of the supernatural to be experienced by its adepts as an aggressive act ('we are being stripped of our past'). So great is our need for a plumb-line that the very individuals who venerate Moses for freeing us from taboos and the Golden Calf have made of him an untouchable idol on whom it is forbidden to lay hands. This is a human reflex. Lucretius the materialist congratulates Epicurus for emancipating us from fear of the gods, and in the process erects an altar to divine Epicurus. Our incoherence is every bit as robust as our paranoia.

The Tenacity of Clichés

It is by flexing its joints, at the cost of several minor aches for our vanity, that we can rid ourselves of those mental cramps that frequently affect the traditional history of religions (whose popular version duplicates, in this respect, the orthodox one). And, in particular, the way in which the monotheistic epic is taught: the myth of the founder (in this case, Moses); the figure of the Event, revelation or bedazzlement, crystallized in a series of occurrences 'on that day' (the flight from Egypt, the burning bush, Sinai); and the radical break with the past (in this case, polytheism) which is the underlying theme.

Moses no more 'founded the Jewish religion' than Jesus 'founded the Christian Church'. The expression 'founder of the Jewish religion', which Freud adopts for his own purposes in what he confidentially and knowingly characterized as a 'historical novel' (in his correspondence with Arnold Zweig), is aberrant three times over. The idea and the word *religion* are imported, since they come from a later (Latin and Roman) source. In a world in which everything, including economy and finance, is religion, there is no separate religious domain. Worshipping Yahweh is part not of a creed or doctrine, but of a mode of existence: of cooking, washing, raising children, urinating, and so on. *Judaism* is similarly a retroprojection. The term appears, fleetingly, only in the second century BCE, along with *Hellenism* ('Judaism' is of Greek origin). Finally, the *one* (religion) has something self-sufficient and exclusive about it, as though the partisan of Yahweh were considering denying the gods of his neighbours – a claim which, in the traditional chronology, surfaced a thousand years before Moses.

Without the first of the Prophets – it is, none the less, still possible to read here and there – without the Lawgiver and the Liberator, the Pentateuch would not exist. It is even, with the exception of Genesis, his autobiography (in which the author, *in fine*, writes up his own death). Without him, there would be no Decalogue, no mobile sanctuary, no Judaean priesthood (which Moses invested in his brother Aaron, under God's command). The celebratory writings which assure us of all this come more than half a millennium after that fabled man – of unknown origin and bereft of a burial plot. They date from a period in which – with the Temple destroyed, the king blind and in prison, and the country occupied – an intelligentsia of exiled priests had excellent reasons to ascribe a compensatory superhero to itself as paterfamilias. In a pastoral people, shepherds are king, but there is not, need it be said, any historical trace of a shepherd prince of that stature, a figure who emerges from an amalgamation of ancient legends (dating, it would appear, from the time of the Assyrian hegemony over Syria–Palestine, the birth and childhood of Moses replicating those of Sargon, the legendary founder of the Assyrian Empire). Moses, a cultural compromise, no doubt as much a product of fantasy as Jonah (and why admit that one is a fiction and not the other?), is, like Abraham, the result of a synthesis. And, as a result, not exempt from contradictions (he who commanded 'Thou shalt not kill' murdered an Egyptian in his youth). Such 'figures' appear to be political transactions elevated to heroic dignity, with the plausible aim of reconciling and federating hostile or quarrelsome tendencies or territories (the enemy kingdoms of North and South). Abraham would thus be a local figure from Hebron, promoted as eponymous hero following the city's annexation by Idumea, as a token of commonality offered to the population of the South by the people of Jerusalem.

The fact that Abraham was reputed to have his grave in Hebron, in the cave of the Patriarchs, tends to support this interpretation.

It was not Abraham and Moses who invented Judaism, but the other way round (as with Jesus Christ and Christianity). The prophets Ezekiel, Hosea and Zachariah do not mention the hero of Sinai, whose role is increasingly exalted with the passage of time (the Talmud will give him a leading role, at the beginning of our era). Nor do David and Solomon, who were by no means ingrates, make any allusion to Abraham. These figures, who are fundamental for us, are absent from the whole of the historical period. The Judaeans did not go on pilgrimages to Mount Sinai, whose renown did not exceed the limits of Exodus. The Byzantine monastery of Saint Catherine chose it as its site only in the sixth century of the present era, for a Marian cult (its location owing more to the verifiable existence of a spring at the foot of Gebel Mousa than to any divine presence at the summit). As a monk told us: 'Even with God at the top, if there is no water at the bottom, there is no monastery.' From the perspective of theology, everything would be given at the inception, the water *and* God. And just as Scripture transmutes ideals into events, and theology into chronology, it also realizes collective types as individual persons, bearing patronymics (Antiquity does not tolerate anonymity). Such is the mainspring of parable: concretize the abstract, and personalize the group. The times demanded that every technique have an inventor (Thoth or Daedalus), and every city a founder. But monotheism, like writing and metallurgy, was, in actual fact, a group effort (more akin to the martial arts than to philosophy).

And a *long-term* one. The 'on that day, the Eternal caused the children of Israel to leave the land of Egypt' is a rhetorical compaction. The monotheistic storm, streaked with lightning, seems to have been an extremely slow rise to power, marked by breakthroughs and relapses, a circumstance betrayed, in its way, by the dilated and repetitive temporality of the founding narrative. There was no D-Day enacting a leap from barbarism – in which animal-faced gods demanded their daily ration of human flesh – to the sanitized and quasi-philological cult of a Word couched in script. In the world of the Canaanites, which precedes and survives, the divine is trivial, commonplace, polymorphous; and atheism, in the strict sense, unthinkable ('impiety' is blasphemy, not godlessness). In that patchwork of minute principalities, each kingdom carves out for itself a protective god, whose warrior or political talents are symbolically appropriated by the population in a classic exchange of goods and services (taxes paid to the temple, appropriate prayers). The god's name, incorporated as a root into the patronymic of the *gens*, is a national identity card. This was, and in part remains, the case for Yahwism, a local cult among ten others. Monarchical Israel had its ethnic god, just as the Moabites had Chemosh and the Edomites Qos. Such gods and men were contiguous, rubbing up against each other in a restricted space. Seven nations shared what might be called Greater Palestine under Assyrian domination: Phoenicians, Samaritans, Philistines,

Ammonites, Moabites, Edomites and, finally, Judaeans. Each had its couple of divinities, male and female. There were rivalries between such powers, annexations, fusions, dynastic alliances, just as there were between the populations themselves. Yahweh was a participant in that political game; He implemented the constitution of a unified whole, which was pursued with some fanfare within existent power relations and by every available means: military conquest, cultural osmosis, or marriage between houses (David marrying a vintage Jebusite, Bathsheba).

After 722, the retreat to Jerusalem of refugees from the fall of Israel, the northern kingdom (which contained ten of the twelve tribes), precipitated the unification of the two stocks through a fusion of the Elohist schools of the North with the Yahwists of the South. And it was around this time that fragments and strata of writing were mixed and recombined, splicing the traditions attributed to Moses (the South) and David (the North). This pact engendered the figure of a *federating Superpower* which sublimated and authorized what would currently be called a struggle for national independence, by simultaneously facilitating the assimilation of the most recent arrivals and differentiating them from neighbouring aliens. In sum, the divine oneness would be the result of several centuries of strategic approach, pursued obliquely and implicitly (intelligently). Freud detected in the constructions of material reality specific to religions 'a psychology projected on to the external world'. This might be completed, if it is indeed the case that public life is made out of personal psychology, by another formula: 'a politics below projected on to a world above'. There is nothing astonishing about this, since we are dealing with a collective organizer as unrivalled as God.

God made neither the revolution nor, as the 'Internationale' has it, *tabula rasa* of the past. The subversive is rather a restorer who recycles scraps and plasters over cracks. Polytheism, in its polymorphous approach to the divine, is more monotheistic than we might think, and monotheism is always more polytheistic than it would have us believe (the One is sought in the multiple, and multiplicity survives in the One). The slow emergence proceeded by a series of dislodgings, on the basis of a religiosity structured like a sequence of nestings, in which each culture gradually chooses and develops the best element (the one that suits it best). The *Elohim*[9] of Jerusalem prolongs and sublimates the Canaanite *El* (same root), as illustrated by the Ugaritic case. Monotheism might thus be called a converted monolatry. 'The Hebrews', according to Jean-Michel de Tarragon, who cites documents in support, 'are converted Canaanites who continue to venerate their ancestral deities even as they begin to adhere to a new cult imported from the South, Yahwism.' And he adds, drawing from onomastics: 'With matters developing towards the absorption of the characteristics of local deities by the national god of the Hebrews, the latter ended up taking on certain of the names or epithets of those deities. Such was the case with Elohim, formed from the common name El, the designation of the

---

[9] God's most frequent name in the Bible, the plural of Eloah, but functioning as a singular.

supreme god of the Canaanites of the region that would become Israel and Judah.'[10]
Our One and Only began His career as leader of a group or chair of a meeting, like a
commonplace Marduk or Amon-Ra, like all the 'I the Supreme' figures of the sur-
rounding area. For a long time He was married; His partner and spouse was called
Asherah (figurines of nude goddesses have been discovered in sixth-century ruins in
Jerusalem). He had His central, but not sole, sanctuary (there are temples in Tell es-
Seb, on the Elephantine Isle in Egypt, in Arad); His steles and His bronze serpent,
His sacrifices, His burnt fats, and His incense. One dressed Him, woke Him in the
morning, and laid Him down at night; one fed Him – like the others. Jeremiah, as
we shall see, had good reason to lash out at the reign of idols, to which Deuteronomy intended to put an end (between 550 and 520), by banning, for example, the
erection of *asherim* (carved stakes representing a goddess), which were Canaanite
fertility symbols.

There is thus a continuity from the Akkadian *Il-aba*, the father-god worshipped
by Sargon, to the Canaanite *Il-ib*, and then to 'our Father who art in Heaven'. A
continuity from the Ugaritic hymn to the Judaic psalm, from the Song of Songs to
the Egyptian love chant, and from psalm to gospel. A continuity from the baptismal
water to the Red Sea, and from the Old Testament to the New (the break between
the two being a fairly late Christian initiative). Rituals tell us more than dogmas
about underlying persistences, and the unwitting gestures of the faithful pay tribute
to a magico-religious heritage that may make our scholars blush. Adjacent to the
temple of Solomon lay a primitive slaughterhouse for the killing of goats, oxen and
sheep prior to the 'barbarous' exhibition of liver and lung. Yahweh is no longer an
animal-headed god, but He still demanded, over a period of centuries, His quarters
of meat and His pint of fresh blood, as did His elders. Ancient Judaism had by no
means worked its way free from the system of agricultural and animal offerings that
everywhere regulates exchanges between earth and heaven, and which is itself
modelled on the payment to the sovereign of a tribute in kind. The Semitic rituals
thus took over from the Canaanite ones, which themselves took over from the
Assyrian ones (as is the case for their respective systems of writing, which emerge, so
to speak, out of each other).

Where the biographer of God discovers a film, the hagiographer isolates photos.
The historian brings back to the surface the fade-ins (and -outs) that disorientate the
theologian's scissors. We speak of a 'Judaeo-Christian' world where a long-range
view would delineate an Assyrio-Canaano-Judaeo-Christianity unfurling towards us
by way of the biblical surge. As soon as we take a little distance from that ongoing
creation, the entirely literary contours of the latest arrival tend to lose their dis-
tinctness. Every denomination appears to be a denial of kinship, or the flaunting of
an exclusiveness which its genesis denies. It thus has every reason to arrogate to

[10] Jean-Michel de Tarragon, 'Le Panthéon, les cultes cananéens et la Bible', *Le Monde de la
Bible*, no. 110, April 1998.

itself an ostensible and clearly indicated zone of sovereignty. Here, the sanctified; beyond, the impious. Here, the Judaeans; there, the Samaritans. The map of eras and areas – once the various obediences have carved out, at swordpoint, their own fiefdoms in opposition to all others – protects us from the depressing (because banalizing) vision of lakes of fluctuating borders, borrowings, slippages and reuses which end up pouring new divinity into old bottles. An abrupt division into domains helps us to conceal the rather monochromatic backdrops of what each of us takes to be the colours of his or her soul. The distribution of spiritual flags is not merely a matter of vanity. It is quite possible, as we shall see further on, that the delimitation of the territories of life, however brutal and obscene it may seem to us, has something essential to tell us about our desperately animal aspirations towards divinity (c).

3 High Atop the Dune

In the wilderness, prepare ye the way of the Lord.
(Isaiah 40: 3)

Between mortals and the Eternal there is a mediating physical milieu: desert or wilderness, the traditional setting of theophanies. Moses, Jesus or Mohammed, our prophets, be it with the Exodus, the Temptation, or the Hegira, were all 'pilgrims of the sands'. Aridity cures us of idols. The 'true God' is opposed to the false as the desolate is to the overpopulated, the mineral to vegetation. On this basis, Renan concluded, somewhat hastily: 'The desert is monotheistic'. In point of fact, that is the case only if the Bedouin knows how to read. Let us not attribute to the geographical incubator the virtues of literal insemination. There is an ecology of the divine, indubitably, but the desert is but a place of passage, and what allows it to be traversed is a mastery of signs. For access to transcendence lies not in the immensity of things, but in their miniaturization.

God has the history of man begin in a verdant space, and He ends it in a holy city, Jerusalem. Between the two, He placed the desert, lest we lose track of Him. Abraham leaves the city, Ur, an industrious metropolis, much as Moses leaves palaces for encampments. On each occasion He drives his elect to a stony world before revealing Himself to them. 'I will lead you to the desert and speak to your heart' (Hosea 2: 16). That whispering in the ear is not for the well-to-do. The Eternal irrupts by way of a wasteland for caravans, 'antisocial' fringes, outskirts where institutions collapse and taxes are not levied. In which plunderers, cattle thieves and reprobates roam. This abrupt God of the borders is repelled by circumlocutions and preciosity. He lacks the ever-changing demeanour of the courts and bazaars. The desert tells its truth to man; it is not hypocritical, like the city. Hence His predilection for those grey zones in which urban and nomadic creatures rub elbows, the no-man's-land between sands and fertile plains, subdesert regions in which small livestock, sheep and goats, are free to graze. The gilded filth of our current surroundings would prefer to forget that foundational austerity. The servants of the cult have set up shop alongside Cain, whose name appears with the first city. He, however, roams among the dunes, alongside Abel, with the impoverished. The first to invoke the name of Yahweh was Enoch, son of Seth, rival of Cain the builder of cities, who was himself too urbanized to be pure. *Allah akhbar*, at present, is the humble shack demanding to be acknowledged by the skyscrapers, the holders of grazing rights demanding recognition by the holders of stock options.

The Desert Refrain

Whether in Hebrew, Aramaic or Arabic, He has designs on the – discreet, emaciated – wearers of sandals. He puts His trust in the halfbreeds of the margins, not in the pot-bellied or the sedentary. Abraham the donkey-driver and Mohammed the camel-driver, nephew and son-in-law of caravaneers. Roamers and migrants by trade, each of them. Freemen, like all herd owners, free to wander as they wish.

Attributing to the soil a capacity for elevation that belongs, no doubt, to the feet alone, Renan, in his *History of the People of Israel* (1887), derived the idea that the 'desert is monotheistic; sublime in its immense uniformity, it reveals to man first of all the idea of the infinite, but not the sentiment of unflaggingly creative life that more fertile climes have imparted to other races. That is why Arabia has always been the boulevard of the most exalted monotheism.' There is nothing mechanical in this, to be sure, and the desert of the Spirit is as much a figure of style as a physical reality. But it was indeed in the arid steppe, pocked with strange boulders, between cliffs of red granite, at the abrupt peak of a *djebel* cut through with fissures and jutting rocks – the 'hierophantic' mountain compounding exponentially the ascensional virtue of the desert – that the Tablets of the Law are alleged to have been given to Moses. In the heart of Sinai, the 'vestibule of the desert', a minor Araby on the flank of Africa. An undoubtedly a posteriori localization, but a revealing one. A period of abnegation and testing, the Desert serves as a refrain for dissidence, for monotheistic *desertion*. To be Godsick is to be stricken with the desert. The appeal of purity – inseparable from a hatred for the impure metropolis, that of Ezekiel and Jeremiah for Babylon and Tyre. Forty years for the Hebrews after their departure from Egypt. Forty days of fasting for Jesus grappling with Satan (Moses, too, had spent forty days and forty nights, alone with God, at the Sinai summit). Mohammed's flight to Medina. Akhenaton the Egyptian (the pharaoh in whom Freud saw the prototype of 'Moses the Egyptian') had also been obliged, it is said, to leave Thebes, his waterfront metropolis, to make his way to the desolate plain of Tell El Amarna in the upper Nile. Aton was voiceless, deaf like the sun, and monolatry is not monotheism. But his case allows us to see a first indication of the negative theology of the One God. Nothingness opens on to everything. The city closes man in on himself; the desert opens him up to the Other. The polytheist prefers the vegetal, embellishments and valleys; his despiser prefers the mineral, abrupt canyons, limestone cliffs limned with geological phantasmagoria. The mountain, which is the desert on high for people of the plain, offers a variant of that ageless affinity evidenced in more clement climates. (It has been measured by sociologists: in the French Alps, religious observance increases as a function of altitude.) Our Carthusians have their 'desert' in the foothills of the Alps. For in a temperate country, one can place one's Sinai in the snow, provided that it be set apart, combining sterility and steepness (like the Musa and Mount Moses, which have to be climbed by a ladder carved into the rock).

One goes down into the city, but one ascends to the desert. An ascendant theology – which goes from History to Spirit. *Burn, Babylon!* Monotheism is not monolithic, and there are different types of desert wildernesses. Ice, salt, steppe, sand, Saharan erg ... . What remains is the common *midbar* ('desert' in Hebrew), the shared archetype, the 'lesson of the desert' which enjoins one to burn one's boats by turning one's back on all idolatry. Dust thou art, and to dust shalt thou return. You will be

*'Gathering of
Protestants in the
Wilderness',
eighteenth-century
engraving,
Bibliothèque
Nationale de
France*

buried in the earth, and on your grave, in fidelity to the Books, we shall deposit not flowers of life but a few small stones. Jewish cemeteries continue to pay homage to that past, with their pebbles piously perched on engraved slabs. The Prophet is a *vox clamans in deserto* – summoning the agglomeration of the lowlands to run the supreme risk (*anachoresis*, like *anabasis*, is to pass from a lower to a higher level). The 'inner man' is to rise up against his *alter ego*, social man, a pure mineral that has been corrupted. The constancy of the prestige enjoyed by Distance. Carmelites and Franciscans refer to the site of their meditative retreats as the 'desert', and the Protestants of France have their museum of the desert. Every year, on the first Sunday in September, in the heart of the Cévennes, they hold their 'desert assembly'.

Thus the Afrikaaners' Great Trek in 1835, when they chose exile from the coast to the high Veld behind their charismatic leader (Piet Retief), with their wagons (*laagers*) their cattle, and their Bible. Thus the exodus of the Mormons in 1847 behind Joseph Smith, along the Mormon trail, towards the Utah desert, where they would found, far from the Gentiles, Salt Lake City. Trying ascents towards the Kingdom, through the unknown, in which those hallucinating the Great Return confront locusts, epidemics, thirst and despair – so many collective ordeals, proof by suffering. There is no 'awakening' or regrounding of monotheism that has failed to seek its 'desert palm' (the Christian symbol crowning the three nails of the Cross and the profile of a camel). Every 'revivalism' takes up the pilgrim's staff towards the hinterland, in quest of rediscovering the arid. All of which enables one, it may be noted in passing, to transform a persecution into a secession, or a political defeat into a moral victory. Is God the vitamin of the sacrificial victim, the celestial alibi for terrestrial courage, casting the keys of the Kingdom on the other side of the mountain in order to force those who live here to make their way through the pass and go and look elsewhere, at whatever cost? Such would be the ruse of the Only God. What counts is the break with Sodom and Gomorrah, the back turned on compromise, on the thunderous din of the city, in which absence can no longer be heard, and the chaos of images and sounds stifles the voice of the essential.

A quest for solitude .... Yahweh raised Israel in the silence of the desert, which is where Christ leads God's own resistance-fighters, those 'athletes of faith', an extreme sport, who were the Fathers of the desert and anchorites. Saint Anthony, patron saint of *hermits*, and Saint Pachomius, the author of the first rule regarding *cenobites* (monks living together), took off for Upper Egypt – the former for an extreme form of isolation, the latter to order the finances of a community. In the first centuries, one went to the desert, the wilderness, much as one goes into rural dissidence – in order to escape the tax-collector and the judge; and little separated the rebel from the saint, or the bandit from the monk ('anchoretism' could refer to either adventure). In the course of the fourth century, the new man referred to by Saint Paul took on the emblematic form of the divine outlaw. It was in the loneliness of the wilderness that the Second Coming of Christ was awaited, that Kingdom of Heaven announced by the prophets, into which those who have renounced the kingdom of false appearances (the virginal, the lean, the penitent) will enter first. Those who outpace history through asceticism and prayer. For the blessed become godlike, or at least angelic, through emaciation by hunger and thirst, becoming skeletal and diaphanous, traversed by grace like a windowpane. 'Pneumataphoric' is the Greek term: bearing and borne by the spirit, the divine afflatus. They become shadows in order to escape our theatre of shadows, outstripping the grave by becoming sepulchral before their time. The anchorite wants to die to the world, but to a world slated to die this very evening. For the Day of the Lord comes like a thief in the night, so one must not sleep like the others (Paul, 1 Thessalonians 5: 2). He will descend from Heaven, preceded by the Archangel and the Trumpet of God. And we will be carried off into the Clouds .... And thus it is reasonable to become mad. To gain time in order to stew in caves and cloisters, preparing for the beyond through fasts, prayers and mortification. To anticipate the heavenly city in a community that *already* obeys God alone, the monastery. Thus did our Cluniac, Cistercian, Carthusian and Benedictine orders (among others) find their models in the Solitaries of the East. Who themselves, no doubt unwittingly, retread the steps of the Essenes of Qumran. Our monasteries: deserts in the depths of valleys, miniature Sinais, grouped at the foot of the 'high house'. We retain within us a slim hope of returning to dryness, to refuges perched in some extreme locale: peaks, grottos, isles

– Cappadocia, Lérins, Mount Athos, Saint Catherine, or Monte Cassino. And in these unencumbered sites, once the high walls of the monastery have been breached, the tourist of God, the distracted or agnostic passer-by, enters into a present without future or past, an extratemporal world, braced by canonical hours, rhythmically ordered by the liturgy, an immobile time in which the dead are no longer opposed to the living, and the hurried man of day becomes a contemporary of the first cenobites.

The Divine Ecosystem

To every niche its God. The Judaeo-Christian is not sylvan. The forest encourages sacred panics (since it is off-limits), but it is a realm of telluric and pagan wonders, those of tales, charms and potions. Mystery abounds, but a bit too much to induce the decisive decanting. The woods are Wagnerian and entrancing, imbued with legends, but their abundance stifles the mystical with myths. The fantastic creatures of the underwood have not broken with the realms of fauna and flora. A nature sublimated into Rhinegold, but nature none the less. More magical than religious. A romanticism of the underbrush, almost neolithic. The forest has certainly served as a wilderness, metaphorically, for a number of recluses of the medieval West, who have carved out their clearings and built their sanctuaries at a remove from all else (thus did Sainte-Foy de Conques originate, deep in a forest of thieves). There one returns to a kind of spiritual wild state, pitted against all institutions. But if we examine a historical map, we perceive that the Great Other has shown up solely in the realms of Absence, which constitute an environment less uniform than abstract. He is repelled by the lower plains, the marshlike approaches to rivers, estuaries, the depths of valleys. He is introduced from above, far from stifling corners and deltas – upstream, not down, from the rivers. He prefers virgin heaths, remote isles, exemplars of limitlessness. Where nothing separates heaven from earth. Where man, exiled from his familiar contexts, is revealed to be naked, almost superfluous, insignificant. Monotheism has a preferred landscape, which is repelled by the picturesque and all forms of the exotic. That mineral and lunar milieu (Arabia Petraea is not the Sahara), that geology from before the Flood, is more than a supporting surface. It is the first hero of the monotheistic romance.

Deprivation/transcendence [*dépouillement/dépassement*] Monochromatic/monotheistic. Like a rhyme, a visual echo from eye to mind. A resonance between two incommensurables, the seen and the conceived. Like a pink harmony streaked with gold, between horizon and orison (prayer), a horizontal vertigo and abyss from above. On that raw crust, 'the heavens are telling us the glory of God', as well as the inanity of human vainglory, the comedy of potentates: every Empire shall perish .... Negativity made palpable. A décor without adornment or pomp, which impels the wanderer to sense the insufficiency of his being, and the unbreachable distance between his nothingness and the whole; neither garlands nor capitals, nothing that prettifies. The gods of Antiquity were slightly indolent aesthetes. They might latch on to a spring, a hedge, or a tree. There is nothing for a God of the desert to latch on to except the wind. What could be more likely to induce us to forget the petty boundaries of the former gods (for the pagans of Antiquity, the boundary itself was sublimated into the god Terminus) than those great spaces so refractory to division? Nothing in common with the rustic tranquillity of the Romans. There is nothing Virgilian in the desert of the believers, which is risk, insecurity and poverty.

That God should prefer hostile landscapes, extreme temperatures and the harshness of stones is the sign of a passage to the limit. Is there not something 'inhuman' in the infinite? But beyond the infinity of grains of sand, is there not a more intimate bond between that thankless environment and the notion of an absolute Leader: that of Toynbee's 'challenge and response'? Life in the desert is a challenge for humans in that it is more random and precarious than elsewhere. There are blows of fate, abrupt shifts of climate, quarrels between clans, bandits behind the dunes. One is on the lookout for manna, and water from the rock. Pastoral – as opposed to agricultural – economy distances tribes and families from each other, each one requiring a space in order to find sustenance. God is our first defence against anxiety, and the aspiration to mutual assistance and agglomeration ('synagogue', *beit ha-Knesset*, means 'house of assembly') is felt where anxiety is most pronounced, where the centrifugal pressures are most threatening – prickly and perpetually dissatisfied tent leaders, rebellious factions and jealous subfactions. The anarchical pangs afflicting desert societies inclined to violent sentiments summon up in reaction the Great Federator capable of restitching a human fabric more exposed than elsewhere to impairment – indeed, to tribal dislocation. A sagacious observer of the microsocieties of Arabia before the era of oil, at the beginning of the nineteenth century, noted that the Islamization of the Bedouins, 'the most miserable and proudest of men', intervened precisely when tribal bonds began to slacken. 'Religious pressures begin to appear in a world in decomposition. They act by substitution.'[1] Such is the immemorial *I-give-so-that-you-give* of patronage societies ('I am faithful to You; in exchange, You protect me'). The God that is One would thus be the ultimate recourse against internal division. And His proclaimed uniqueness a way of declaring oneself unique and unassimilable by the powers that be. Our Gods are not compatible; don't try to annex us.

In point of fact, in the Old Testament, the desert is as magnetic as it is repellent. It is charged with ambivalence: the punishment of Adam and the salvation of Moses, a

---

[1] Robert Montagne, *La Civilisation du désert, Nomades d'Orient et d'Afrique* (Paris: Hachette 1947), p. 204.

place of trial and a space of temptations, near the *Sheol*, the shadowy domain of the dead. Never indifferent: it revives or induces death. It is the chaos before the creative act, before the rains of the third day, before the well-irrigated Garden of Eden. It is also the dust to which man will return *in fine*. In which demons, jackals and serpents loiter .... Jesus will be obliged to make his way there for a final purgation, the terminal confrontation with the Enemy. People of the desert have an unconscious fascination for rites involving water – baptism, sprinkling of holy water, benediction. The Bedouin's paradise is an oasis, a garden of shade and fresh water, where one can eat and drink one's fill. One is purified by the lustral spring, fortified in one's faith by the sand. No doubt the nordic West will replace Saint Anthony's desert with the ocean of Saint Brendan, wandering from isle to isle over the Irish Sea. But there may be, in that love–hate, a sequel to the phobias specific to the Mesopotamian cradle. The cities between the two rivers were constructed against the desert, its treacheries and its plunderers. In the Epic of Gilgamesh, Enkidu, the man of the desert, symbolizes the savage. A repugnance for aridity is understandable in centralized empires, surrounded by walls and dykes, strengthened by their efforts at irrigation and the careful taming of their overflowing rivers. And that hoary mistrust has affected their hostages. Adam is a practitioner of agriculture. 'Elohim took the man and put him in the Garden of Eden to till it and keep it' (Genesis 2: 15). His burden will be to defeat the reticence of the land, to push back bramble and thorn, which will return in force after the error. Malediction. 'When you till the ground, it will no longer yield to you its strength; you will be a fugitive and a wanderer on the earth' (Genesis 4: 12). So be it. But Adam will have two sons by Eve. Cain, the elder, will be a tiller of the soil (such is the Assyrian precedence when it comes to legitimacy). Abel, the younger, will be a shepherd. A traditional hierarchy. The innovation is that Yahweh, an anticonformist, will bestow His grace on the second-born, and not on the farmer. 'In the course of time Cain brought to the Lord an offering of the fruit of the ground, and Abel for his part brought of the firstlings of his flock, their fat portions. And the Lord had regard for Abel and his offering, but for Cain and his offering he had no regard' (Genesis 4: 3–5). Between farmers and cowboys, Yahweh made his choice. A nod signalling that salvation will come by way of the nomad, the messiah of the borderlands, disturbed–disturbing (the opposite of 'work–family–fatherland')? The descendants of Cain (a word meaning smith, an accursed craft, in Hebrew) will always find it in their interest to leave their enclosures to escape the curse. The farmer has goods to protect and, consequently, arms, bronze and iron. And from enclosure will come violence and avarice. Behind the fruits of the earth there will soon surface the bad fat of the cities, glutinous envy, the domesticity from which the man of God must tear himself to go towards music (David's harp, Orpheus' lyre). Just as one flees the table of the obese in order to follow a diet, like a Long March. For deliverance, in the beginning, comes not from humus but from *transhumance*. The energizing dream is not of a place, but of a tearing away from every individual place. Every time the Hebrew 'relaxes' in the city, his God will have to send him off to the place of his ordeal. The people of the Spirit cannot stay put.

The Pastoral Model

In Hebraic chronology, stays in the desert are fairly short. They are evoked in Exodus and Numbers, before the entry into Canaan. But those episodes have not been magnified by chance. The passage through the desert corresponds to an actual experience, but it is emblematic above all of an access to transcendence by breaking with the city, which encloses man in on himself, much as a woman does. The desert (*midbar* in Hebrew) is masculine in gender, and the city, in Semitic languages, is feminine. The City is a woman, and Babylon the prostitute, 'inebriate with the blood of the saints', 'mother of the debauched and the abominations of the earth', 'the great city clothed in fine linen, purple and scarlet, gleaming with gold, precious stones, and pearls' (Apostles 18: 16). No cajoling women in the sands, nor anything comely at all. There one is shielded from all seduction, delivered over to the sole glory of the everlasting God. As through an inversion, the Prophet exalts *askesis*, distrusting milk and honey, and the Canaan towards which he advances. Not without premonition, since overly long halts are a trial for faith. When the wanderer opts for indulgence, settles in, his election goes awry.

Yahweh chooses Abel because they are of the same race, each of them a shepherd. Zones in which to range have priority, in their view, over lands to be cultivated. Every people creates gods in its own image. A people of fancy talkers gives itself an Olympus ringing with eloquence and disputation. A people of herdsmen gives itself, as an instrument of cohesion, a great celestial herdsman, represented on earth by herdsmen of flesh and bone, prophets or monarchs, Moses and David. The pastoral metaphor of supreme powers was current in the ancient societies of the region, Egypt and Assyria. The Hebrew people appears to have systematized the metaphor, which was suited to shepherds of small flocks. God is the shepherd of His people. His mission is to gather, to prevent the scattering of the flock. He has promised pasture to His sheep (the Holy Land), but the fold comes after the flock, which must first be guided and saved, by attending to its nourishment and safety with punctilious compassion. Yahweh is to man as man is to his animals, in a relation of benevolent domination. He has absolute authority, but He must not abuse it. Oxen and donkeys are to benefit from a weekly day of rest; a goat must not be slaughtered on the same day as its calf; and an animal fallen under the weight of its burden must be assisted in getting up. The Hebrew does not like hunting, and would surely not tolerate, as Catholics do, bullfights. God chose Moses on the basis of a good deed, when he saw him bringing back on his shoulders a lost lamb, weakened by thirst. 'Because you showed compassion for a member of your flock, you will lead my flock, Israel.'

The abandonment of hunting-gathering for techniques of herding 'dates' the

Revelation by inscribing it in material cultures somewhere between the invention of ceramics and that of the harness-yoke. The domestication of space began with that of animal species. Dogs were first (as may be seen in graves) – in the upper Palaeolithic, between 70,000 and 40,000 BCE. This facilitated hunting, and thus survival. The Neolithic, towards 12,000 BCE, domesticated the wild ass, capridae and bovidae, at the same time as the first fruit trees were grown. And it was with the domestication of the one-humped camel on the Arabian steppe, at the end of the second millennium before Christ, followed by the acclimatization of the horse, that pastoral nomadism was able to extend its domain to all of Arabia and North Africa. Prior to the Bronze Age, a delocalizable and transcendent God – adapted, consequently, to transhumance, the seasonal moving of livestock – was not possible, for lack of herds and saddles. Similarly, pastoral monotheism could not appear just anywhere on the earth's surface, but only where vegetation was neither too abundant nor too sparse.

The Father, we have seen, was simultaneously the desert and a reaction to the desert – its son, but a rebel. He represents the optimal solution for zones of intermediate challenge. Neither too much nor too little. When the challenge of the physical milieu is too great (say, in the Sahara or Greenland), where nature offers nothing (or just about), the response is impossible or rather poor. When it is too weak – in Oceania, for example, where nature offers everything – the reactive impulse is lacking. The rule of median difficulty is also valid in the domain of communications. Too much distance to be traversed discourages mobility. The same holds when there is not enough. This is why the overly facile valley of the Nile, an oasis-corridor two thousand kilometres in length, turned out to be inadequate. Too easy to traverse by the fluvial highway. The Nile is navigable after the first falls, as it is from downstream up thanks to a very specific wind. Aquatic transport, whether maritime or nautical, is more rapid and less costly than transport over land. Thus the Egyptians proved inventive when it came to river travel, but not to locomotion on land. The 'builders of the pyramids' hauled blocks of granite, quartz rock or sandstone, weighing nearly a hundred metric tons. They dragged them towards the Nile by sledge (even after the appearance of the wheel), from which barges would take them to the work-yards, hauled to the sites on curved wooden billets. Well-irrigated silt allowed the blocks to slide, with ropes pulled by hundreds of men. Such formidable ingenuity had no use, it would appear, for beasts of burden. The wheel is not of Egyptian origin. It comes from the steppe. It was the Hyksos, speaking a Semitic language, barbarians who came from the North via the Eurasian plains, who brought them the horse and, towards the eighteenth century BCE, the wagon drawn by horses harnessed to a shaft by means of a yoke. The Egyptians had sufficient technical mastery to invent the wagon, but they did not have an overwhelming need for it, since river travel sufficed. Use of a horse and wagon is indispensable only on hard flatlands. The chariots of the Pharaohs stemmed from the confiscation of a foreign technology, adapted by the importer as a means of retaining mastery over outlying desert regions, and occasionally going on to counterattack (raids and counter-raids). The ancient Hebrews, on the other hand, were constrained to invent a duly equipped means of land travel when they were forced to leave the Delta to traverse the wilderness lying between the Red Sea and the Mediterranean, a desert that is far from easy (without being unpassable), neither too narrow nor too vast. A challenge of precisely the right degree. Roland de Vaux, in this context, would talk about an 'attenuated Bedouinism'. The true Bedouins were the nomads of the Arabian desert. The semi-nomad, at the periphery, was a herder of sheep, not camels.

A pastoral God is, in any event, a God of movement, for whom displacement is more than a go-between. Time–distance has a substance. A holy person is ambulatory by destination; Jesus, the Life and the *Way*; his adept, 'a stranger sighing as he walked' (Saint Augustine); and God, 'a road for life' that is without end. 'God is my horizon,' says the Christian. 'He is never my prey.' *Homo viator* and wandering Jew claim that the voyage has more genius than the place. This makes for a traveller who never stops travelling, like Abraham and Moses. And for good reason, if a shepherd who stays where he is exhausts his pasture; his flock is obliged to move on lest it render nature sterile, and drought is an even greater incentive to migration. Driving cattle on long journeys requires beasts of burden and draught animals as well. Which is to say that a Super-shepherd God needs at his disposal legs and paws in great quantity. For subsistence as well as for war. Sandals can easily become conquerors' boots, since when one has the means of mobility, one has those of expansion as well. Expansionism rhymes with monotheism, understood as a pursuit of pastoral nomadism by offensive means. The map of its historic conquests, at the time of the first millennium, signalled the relentless anonymous expansion of nomadic horsemen over the flatlands of the ploughmen. Was not the fate of Islam in its early days linked to the movements of merchants? Every surge of monotheism can be chronologically correlated with a population shift in the Fertile Crescent. Barbarian invasions, tribal displacements, deportations. Despite – or because of – its hieratic propensities, Egyptian culture, the product of an all-too-stable empire (thirty-five centuries without disruption) with excessively solid defences, in which the architect Imhotep was exalted, was not propitious, on its own terrain, to the perspectives of despair or nostalgia. Anaxagoras said: 'Man thinks because he has a hand.' To which we would add: 'and he believes because he has two feet.' If our sciences are daughters of the sedentary position, our various mysticisms stem from our mobility. As do our wars.

Animal Distinctions

There are hoofs, and then there are hoofs. There is the noble and the vile, the pure and the impure, the rapid and the slow. There exists a hierarchy of vehicles specific to pastoral societies, in which degrees of animal mobility dictate a scale of social dignities and individual sources of pride. It is, moreover, according to mode of locomotion – walking, flying, crawling or swimming – that the ancient Hebrews divided animals into four major categories: quadrupeds, birds, reptiles and fish. Among the first, beasts that carry or transport enjoy higher social consideration than draught animals, because they guarantee independence and freedom of movement. At the top of the Bedouin pyramid are the great camel-drivers, because they are the most mobile (a camel can get by drinking only every three days). Then come those who raise sheep (more demanding when it comes to water, they inhibit movement). They territorialize. At the bottom are the bovines, which require proximity to cities and rivers, and make of the herdsman something on the order of a farmer (it being dishonourable to work the land). Above the camel, which deserves a genealogical tree in its double capacity as cargo-ferry (up to three hundred kilograms of useful weight) and racing frigate, stand the rider and his mare, the mount of princes, the insignia of power and wealth. But there are no horses in Genesis (they appear only after Exodus). The stallion, steed and mare remained for the Hebrews a sign of foreign domination or imported luxury, which was the case during their glory years.

Nor does the camel get much of a mention in the Old Testament, even though it is more animal-sensitive than the New (six hundred mentions versus twenty-nine). Classified as an impure animal, it is mentioned only once in the Pentateuch (with a few random and probably anachronistic allusions in Genesis) – no more than the sacred Egyptian cat prowling about in the temples of the false gods. The reason is simple: the Israelites had only donkeys at their disposal, which gave them a rather limited range of action, preventing them from moving too great a distance, in the Negev, from previously charted oases (reported in Numbers 33). The donkey and the domesticated wild ass – fierce and disagreeable specimens of the horse family – link the world of the Bible with ancient Sumeria (which possessed neither camels nor horses). 'Abraham arose early, saddled his donkey, and took with him his son Isaac ... .' The patriarch was as stubborn as a mule. Yahweh will go as far as to bequeath the gift of speech to Balaam's ass, so that it might recognize Yahweh's angel, standing before it on a path dug between the vines. On the road, the ass saw God's emissary, whom the magician Balaam could not see. And so he beat the ass with his staff without knowing whom he was dealing with (Numbers 22: 25–35). More than the lamb, more than the dromedary of the New Testament magi, the symbolic animal of the Jewish odyssey is no doubt the first beast of burden (and harness) to be known. It appears in Mesopotamian bas-reliefs, and as early as the first Egyptian dynasties (at the same time as the reindeer in subpolar tundras). The donkey is the preferred mount of our God, and the animal He trusts. Together they make their way up the sacred mountain; together they stop in the great animistic forest. In any event, their place (neither God's nor the donkey's) is not in a peasant economy of the market-gardening type, whether Chinese or Japanese in style. The Bedouin's donkey will remain the friend of the poor, of children, and of those who are down on their luck. It will carry Mary, and save Jesus during the flight into Egypt. It gave him its trough as a cradle in the stable (see our Christmas manger). Jesus could not make his entrance into Jerusalem on horseback, symbol of war and victory, suggesting haughtiness and pride. He mounted a donkey, sweet and humble obstinacy. To denounce the ass's colt is a sacrilege. This may be why Victor Hugo, with his mediological genius, exalted the evangelical role of the donkey as celestial emissary. *L'Âne* was the title he gave to his plea in favour of God, a remonstrance to the scientifically minded atheists (written in 1856, published in 1886). His original title was *L'Épopée [The Epic] de l'Âne*: 'And I said to myself: donkey, you must persist ... .' Francis Jammes's poem 'La Prière pour aller au paradis avec les ânes' [Prayer to Go to Heaven with the Asses] is not a child's fantasy, but a mark of wisdom and a tribute from the New Covenant to the Old. For the Carmelite fathers, a hermit living freely in the desert earns the title of donkey – whose dignity he has attained.

There is a mystical zoology. In the West as in the East, every messianism has its mascot, which is also its preferred means of land travel. The Messiah is 'multi-modal' (the expression currently used for combinations of rail, highway, and sea transport). 'Christ is ram, lamb, bull and goat,' says Saint Augustine (*Sermon* XIX). But sacrificed as a lamb and reappearing as a heavenly lamb, Jesus will always remain the '*agnus dei* who takes away the sins of the world'. Joined by saddle and staff, the three monotheisms are differentiated by and as the donkey, the lamb and the horse. Abraham, Jesus, Mohammed. To each his honoured vehicle, which turns into allegory. The donkey is obstinate: Jewish memory. The lamb inspires tender-ness: Christian love. The horse conquers: holy war. The expansion of Islam, before the modern era, stopped where the horse could no longer go. In Africa, in the eleventh century, it descended to the southern limits of the Sahel, but was unable to penetrate tropical forests, where the equestrian was obliged to backtrack.

A Pathology of the Desert: Theocracy

The dark forest is the locus classically assigned to the barbarian and the terrifying – such was Germania for Rome. The desert has a *sui generis* ferocity that is less visible, more inward. It is intransigent like the Truth, the immoderate love of which bears the name, for sceptics, of fanaticism. Truth is one, runs the adage, and error is multiple. It is not surprising, in the mind of those who have been made pure, that the desert should preach truth and the city error. Tolerance, said Locke, is the principal Christian virtue – not without a dose of optimism, but with some basis, since Christianity is a monotheism diffracted, made more supple, by cities. Its urbanity is revealed by (among other things) the variety of its authorized sources, reflecting the plurality of its first implantations. Even after the Church had separated the wheat from the chaff, in order to obtain a single canon – a selection initiated at the end of the second century and actually ending only in the sixteenth, with the Council of Trent – there still remained, from that prodigious sifting, four versions of the Good News. Four Jesuses, according to Saint Luke, Saint Mark, Saint Matthew and Saint John. Matthew's Jesus was an educated Jew who was quite punctilious on matters of genealogy. Mark's, the oldest, was a simple man of the people, close to children. Luke's was a man of elegance and refinement; John's a great illuminate, who was never a child. To each his Christ. Without counting the 'apocryphal' or hidden Gospels, which were in fact excluded, not recognized by orthodox Christians (such as some of the Gnostic manuscripts of Nag Hammadi, discovered in 1945). The games of the One with the many had no currency in the cities. Having retrenched to the 'fortresses of the pious', sects could devote themselves with impunity, and without needless friction, to the 'ardent love of God'. Did not the Essenes, a community of iconoclastic and misogynistic ascetics, leave Jerusalem and its priestly corruptions for barracks of limestone and salt? When the One no longer has any neighbours in sight, He is promoted into the All. This leads to the morbid law of the Same, which makes the other an enemy and a stone Buddha sacrilegious. Destruction by explosives, expulsion of the impious, and everyone on his knees. As for the desert, pluralism's foremost enemy, we may say that it is a place of spiritual ebullition and cultural suffocation.

The Mediterranean valley is divided. Favourable to vernacular cults, with a certain lack of curiosity about the beyond, the Greeks and Romans had no knowledge of the infinite; they were not 'Faustians', did not go up to mountain peaks. Horizons were closed. What they loved were well-defined limits (Hermes was also the god of enclosures). The divine patchwork was already there in the landscape, and their mythology, composed of bits and pieces, was not there to unify but, on the contrary, to demarcate (and instil respect for) differences of place (d). With its mosaic of orchards, groves and windward isles, rustic Greece diversified its goddesses, counterbalancing one divinity with another, even managing to elude, according to Dumézil, the Indo-European mould of three functions (harvesting, warring, praying). Its Zeus was polymorphous, and his numerous colleagues owe more to fiction than to ideology. Eminently sociable, each existing relative to the others, they are defined by that very relation. Within the Pantheon, a system of ambivalent complicities and jealous oversights, Hestia thwarts Aphrodite, and Zeus himself comes up against Fate, which is loftier than he is. Olympus practises a separation of powers à la Montesquieu, with dramatic – but non-tragic – quarrels. That divine tribunal seems to be imbued with a genuinely liberal scepticism (so much so that the gods of Homer died laughing upon learning that only one of them was real). On high, they coexist without excluding one another; down below, they gamble, place bets and withdraw them, without too much acrimony. The bosom of Abraham is harsher and less welcoming. The Andalusian exception of two or three centuries, under the Ommayad dynasty of Córdoba, during which Mozarabic Christians, Jews and Muslims lived together peacefully (from the tenth to the thirteenth century), proves the rule: when it comes to 'people of the Book', that state of grace is the exception.

There is a political mentality specific to the desert, which is precisely a refusal of the political, an ignorance of the state, and a rejection of civil law. A curious mix of rebellious individualism, refractory to all constituted authority, and extremely strong tribal solidarity. The nomad has a sense of property, but not of boundary. The border is elastic as a function of the forces there assembled. God has to be able to strike anywhere. A sovereignty without borders, supereminent and supernational, leaves humans with neither recourse nor refuge. This circumstance lends itself to cruelty no less than to hospitality, to homicide no less than to sacrifice (two sides of the same coin). The Jealous One of the desert considers it a crime to deny Him, and Islamic law punishes apostasy and blasphemy with death. 'If God does not exist, all is allowed,' feared Dostoevsky, who saw in this eclipse the quasi-official pro- mulgation of a generalized right to murder. As if he himself had been a guarantor of sweetness and respect for life. Pious America, the Western country in which God is most present, on pediments and in hearts, is also the last to retain the death penalty (e). Need we recall the massacres that He who will not tolerate being compared to others is capable of instigating? At the sight of the Golden Calf, Yahweh demands of His faithful that they kill 'brother, friend, and neighbour' (Exodus 32: 28). Three thousand corpses, a modest initiation into such matters. A single superpower, over Heaven and Earth, is no less fertile in formidable criminal initiatives than a dozen average ones or a hundred petty ones.

Absolutism against fetishism. Vandals against idolators. The correction of an evil does not produce only good. Whence the repetitive and ecumenical scenario: urban folk worship statues; along come the people of the desert and hack them to pieces – whether it be Moses, Calvin and his sectarians, who decapitated stone virgins and saints with axes, or the last of the Taliban, all breakers of idols in the name of Scripture.

The God-inflamed of every nationality and obedience continue to set up residence in the drylands of Iran, Afghanistan, Arizona, the Brazilian sertão. The negative space of separation attests to an effort of inner purification. The desert remains an ideal site for chosenness, simplicity and *askesis*. The danger of the stony, however, is less the hallucinatory rumination of 'onliness' than an assurance of immediacy. A direct relationship with the Almighty, without any interposition of mediation. Without chiaroscuro, clouds or seasons. A variety of local traditions allows the Absolute several entries and fluctuating boundaries. Which is not the case for the Book that says everything about everything (Bible or Koran). The Prophet is a Bedouin who has arrived directly in the city of caravans, Mecca, without having passed through the cultivation of 'thankless and degrading' fields, a relativizing culture of multiple crops allowing for a margin of error. Truth on this side of the enclosure, error beyond.

But the deepest link between the distress of the desert and intolerance is a throbbing sense of insecurity. This is not intrinsic to monotheism. Hinduism, a superb poly-theism, is no less subject to it when it feels itself invaded, jostled by Islam; nor is Buddhism itself, as we have seen quite recently in Sri Lanka, with its priests in arms. Every collective belief will tend towards fanaticism as soon as it sees itself threa-tened with disappearance, minority status, or siege. Intolerance, like deception, is the weak man's weapon against the strong, that of the periphery against the centre. And polite indifference towards those other than oneself is the surest indication of a position of hegemony. It is easy to respect those from whom one no longer has anything to fear. At present (or until recently) the West preaches tolerance *urbi et orbi* all the more so by virtue of the fact that its power base is not under threat – at least for now. For tolerance, the supreme good, is first of all a luxury, dependent on power relations. Al Andalus (711–1492) dominated its periphery. The Islam of Granada could turn a smiling face to all. That of Kabul is hateful. When Chris-tianity itself felt insecure, it set up the Inquisition as a 'rampart of the faith', invented crusades and pogroms. No religion, no civilization, is immune to hatred of the other, and those who preach concord today brandished lightning-bolts only yesterday. If we may be allowed to correct Claudel: there are no houses for intol-erance, there are tents. More solid constructions are for afterwards. When canvas metamorphoses into brick. As soon as the camel gives way to the Cadillac (and the coal of Judaea to the oil of Arabia).

Raids are fatiguing, it's true. Which is why the city-dweller should not exaggerate the perils of the desert. The last word, for the Bedouins, is not given to the camel-driver or the horseman, but, rather, to the profitable market trader in the street, or in the 'international community'. How is one to resist the shimmering of cascades and the carpets of greenery? The day comes when the starving man fords the river and assimilates into the Empire. When the cock's crow from the other side of the camp resounds; when the tent posts give way to wooden beams, and brick replaces wickered reeds at the entrance as a protection from the cold. A victory of the cock over the falcon. The stock-breeder settles down. The sect becomes a church. Cain sets up shop. God returns to the city. The bishop triumphs over the monk errant, and the prior over the hermit. After the God-mad individual, the monastery – an infinitely paradoxical institution, since it derives from 'monk', *monos*, a lone man. As though the solitary, wherever he be, were obliged, whether he likes it or not, to found a community. As though every ascent to silence were already resonant with the peal of a bell. At the end of the desert, a new city. '*Desertum civitas*' was the oxymoron invented by Saint Jerome in order to encompass that paradox, the flow of solitaries to a common refuge. He who flees the city will sooner or later found another.

Establishment here below does not come without a certain renunciation. So that we may wonder whether monotheism *stricto sensu* is not an impossible wager, if for no other reason than that no man can wander indefinitely in solitude. One cannot walk one's entire life in the light: the unlimited has its limits. Or rather, we may wonder whether monotheism is viable in the long term, whether it must not, one day or another, gradually rejoin its polytheistic adversary – from the *most* Catholic to the *least* Wahhabite. Whether the round trip (or the cohabitation between plain and valley) does not form a coherent system despite all the stresses and strains, given the demands of subsistence. Because the city remains pivotal for stock-breeders, who are obliged to have animals, men and goods pass through it. We are dreaming if we imagine a desert in its pure state, a self-sufficient and viable pastoral state, without agricultural and urban life serving as both commercial outlet and source of relaxation. On camel or on horseback, nomads still need to buy and sell. They need watering places, stopping points, markets, established feast-days – and holy places. Abel lived off Cain, who, all things considered, could have done without a parasite. The shepherd's ultimate dilemma is to disappear or yield – that is: accept the boundary.

The desert is therefore an untameable promise of absoluteness. Moreover, there is no true desert (where the biomass equals zero); there are only relative deserts, covered by a more or less thick layer of living matter. Similarly, monotheism in its pure state will never be more than the regulating idea of Onliness, to which He tends as best He can, without attaining terminal mineralization. Like the anchorite of the first centuries, entirely orientated towards an Apocalypse he would never see. While waiting for Godot, one is, nevertheless, obliged to live, and come to terms with the flowers.

The Natural Selection of Memories

With the 'end of the nomads', rock humbles itself before humus, but at least retains what it wrought. Sand, like ice, keeps our agenda better than mud and moss. It stores the archives of humanity. Rejected by the builders of churches and temples, since the political translation of faith is exercised in and through the city: after the prophets, the kings. Does the desert succumb? Archaeologists will be its avengers. It has its ghosts: our God is one of them. Egypt, Syria, the North of Iraq – these form our *chronothèque*, the reservoir of traditions from which the West draws on its deposits of memory, from sarcophagus to the Book of the Dead, from the sphinx to the settling of the War of Qumran. Such is the dependence of symbol on support, and support on climate. In the physicochemical laboratory of 'sustainable development', what better 'preparation' for an 'experiment'? How might one form a culture without transmitting? And what is transmission if not the extracting of a stock from a flux, a permanent residue from a biodegradable substance, a hard body from a soft one? If not the extracting from a sack of stinking viscera a streamlined solid made impermeable to bitumen? Just as the polar ice-cap keeps a register of four hundred thousand years of climatic change, and the Alpine glacier can return a body intact after ten thousand years, hot sand embalms what it engulfs. It accomplishes naturally what the Egyptians did through a technique: separating flesh from bones, dehydrating what was likely to putrefy (removing the brain and entrails, desiccating the rest to the natron) and wrapping (with a kilometre of linen strips). It purifies by making hard. As a rule, the wind of the centuries – by which we should understand insects, mushrooms and microbes – effaces cultures without monuments. Desiccation preserves. Clay, for example, is dried in the sun or baked in an oven in order to make tablets or slabs on which cuneiform is incrusted. The Egyptians, more pampered by nature, harvested papyrus growing in the swamps, which, like rag paper later on, needs water, a good deal of water. Paper mills would subsequently be set up in Europe on riverbanks, and God, at the end of the Middle Ages, would make magnificent use of an irrigated support, but He was, in the beginning, a product of dehydration. He would travel far, over plains, prairies and copses, borne by the papyrus reed and, much later, by paper, brought to Europe from China by the Arabs. Yes, the God of the desert resists monsoons quite well – and Indonesia, the world's leading Muslim country, beats all records for rainfall. But would the Only One have been able to weather outrage and storm without first being freeze-dried in writing?

Consider the effect of substrates and climates on the official records. When it comes to recording the 'human heritage' in writing, there are supports that should be avoided. We are far more familiar with the coins, sarcophagi and mosaics of the ancient Christian, Ethiopian or Byzantine world, for instance, than with its wall-paintings, which have decomposed. Or take the ancient East. The Mesopotamians were a potential counterweight to the Egyptians, and even though they had no knowledge of each other, the two civilizations were almost equally significant. Time and humidity decided otherwise. For raw brick is more perishable than diorite, alabaster, or speckled granite. The Sumerian inventions appear to have come earlier, specifically for systems of writing, but the Egyptian variants outstripped them over time. Our philosophers evoke the Egyptian god and inventor of writing, the notorious Thoth, with his ibis or baboon head, but the god Nabu, his Mesopotamian counterpart, is not anthologized or the stuff of dissertations. The subsistence of minds and the resistance of materials. Sumer, a well-appointed swamp on the lower basin of the Tigris and Euphrates. 'Man is a fallen god who remembers' ... his caves and sand-hills far better than his coastlines and swamps. Egypt offers far more to *see*, with its colonnades, cartouches and multicoloured panels. Mesopotamia, which is grayer, offers above all matter *to read*, with its millions of tablets. The handicap of cuneiform in relation to the comic strip, of the scholar in relation to the fantasist (it being difficult to resist almost any vaguely pharaonic fabulation). Egyptomania never encountered a countervailing Assyriomania, and from Vivant Denon to Howard Carter, the discoverer of Tutankhamun, by way of Champollion and Mariette, our Egyptologists have provided endless delight to the readers of popular journals, whereas our Assyriologists are relegated to the austere precincts of the Académie des inscriptions et belles-lettres. There was indeed Griffith's *Intolerance*, with its cardboard Babylon. But *Cigars of the Pharaoh, Mysteries of the Great Pyramid, Cleopatra Servant of Eros*, and a series of Cecil B. DeMille or King Vidor triumphs have continued to dominate the competition.

Among other explanations, the following should not be forgotten: the inhabitants of the shores of the Euphrates built in brick; those of the banks of the Nile built in stone. Already in their day, the ziggurats (our Tower of Babel) were crumbling beneath the alternation of rain and sun, and had to be periodically reconstructed by a political power. The pyramids can remain standing with or without a Pharaoh; and their outline is ever more striking on the posters of our travel agencies, so much does our compulsion to travel need those rare forms that bear witness and never budge. The documentary depths of the sands rise at the horizon of our urban clutter, even as camel-drivers and caravans vanish from sight, and the attraction of the unchanging grows even as our own archives evaporate. Charter flights and researchers favour Upper Egypt, where the remains have lasted better than in the Delta, with its perennial problem of alluvial excess. The posthumous revenge of the dry over the humid. Palms make life more beautiful; thorns make it longer.

The flowering of signs and forms that brighten up the earth's crust, from east to west, may be viewed from the perspective of 'transmission', as so many offerings of meaning, pleasure and dream submitted to the juries of posterity – which retain not the most eloquent, but the most resistant. Such resistance is more dependent on materials than we might think. The conquerors who burned the cities of Assyria unwittingly rendered them a considerable service, since the fire baked and hardened the clay tablets, which were converted into reusable materials for the reconstruction of new temples and palaces, to the great delight of our archaeologists. Who, as a result, have better documentation concerning periods of war in the interfluvial region than for periods of peace, in which scribes eventually threw their tablets on to the rubbish heap, where they slowly decomposed. But fire and pillage were fatal for papyri, which lightened the archive while making it more fragile. Along with, at the end of the process, the following paradox: a historian today has better documentation for the twentieth century before than for the third century after Christ, when papyrus had already replaced clay as a support for inscription.

In this Darwinism of memory, an arid climate confers precious advantages on those favoured by posterity (which can, at any moment, downgrade a winner who has ceased to please). Consider other spiritual advances, in other latitudes, which, for lack of anything better, were obliged to confide themselves to 'ôlei' – dried, polished palm leaves which, in the south of India, received Vedic (and then Bud-dhist) writings. This material is exceedingly sensitive to humidity and insects. Northern India and Russia, lands of forests, made use of birch bark, which was hardly any better. Little has reached us intact.

For its sacred texts, Hinduism banned any support of animal origin. That rejection does it honour, but proved counterproductive in the long term. The Hindus who respected their domestic animals too much to eat their flesh, then dry their skin in the sun (from which process our vellum and fine parchments come), took serious risks for the future. Had medieval Europe been vegetarian, the thought of Antiquity would have eluded us to a large extent, and there would have been no humanities, or even humanism. For in our civilization, where it is not stuffed into jars in the depth of caves, like the Dead Sea Scrolls or the Nag Hammadi Codex, papyrus is not a suitable support, for reason of humidity. It disintegrates (but less than leather). The Graeco–Roman texts that have reached us are those that managed to be transcribed in time from papyrus to parchment (cowskin or sheepskin are expensive, but trustworthy materials, which 'retain' better than any vegetable matter).

The tropics, with their all-too-precarious museums – think of the French Antilles – have a problem with granaries, and not only because their inhabitants are tem-peramentally more akin to grasshoppers than to ants. A hygrometric constraint, aggravated by cyclones, which utterly decimates all remains, wood or clay, season after season. What is valid for substrates is valid for texts. The miracle of desic-cation. Describing the 'dry style', Valéry noted that it 'traverses the centuries like an incorruptible mummy'. Sentimentally tearful or hydrated prose, but we realize it only afterwards – moulders in the space of a generation. Just as in seaside towns, facades which face the sea directly peel and crumble, while their counterparts on the heights still retain their attractiveness. Advice to Prometheus: avoid tropical cli-mates; too much of the *now* [*maintenant*] is difficult to maintain.

All human collectives have *their* memory; some derive a history from it; very few succeed, by interesting their neighbours in it, in making history. If one is to go beyond the fold, 'leaving a trace' is not enough. Incising a support, to be sure, is where one begins. The depositing of archives. But in order to turn a depository into a springboard, it has to be reactivated from generation to generation by way of teaching and rituals, indispensable devices for making it reascend the slope towards nothingness. It is the insertion of a collective soul (the expression of a transindivi-dual body) into a heritage of traces that allows the addition of (social) recognition to the (physical) persistence of a past via a *tradition*. To infuse a stock of letters, marks or volumes with life requires the invention of an *orthopraxis*, a system of familial or communitarian liturgies capable of opening to the future a legacy of symbols that a solitary, cerebral, scholarly deciphering would soon reduce to the silence of a ves-tige. The Amarites, the Jebusites (inhabitants of ancient Jerusalem) and the Amalekites had a history, but they did not perform an act of memory. They did not leave their imprint on our present. What they may have left to be deciphered or voiced was not remodelled, reshaped by heirs, be they putative or not. Nothing but an obscure abyss, an excavation site. But we keep the Bible perennially at hand on our bedside table. From the region's entire shadowy protohistory, in all its amorphousness, from which so many prototypes and archetypes have come down to us, only a single version, the Old Testament, has emerged. A single interpretative framework. The source which is the standard reference for any Westerner. We may imagine how a refugee from one of the neighbouring peoples subjugated and eventually engulfed by the 'children of Abraham' might have reacted upon reading it. Those unfortunate tribes would certainly confront us with an entirely different perspective on the first millennium before Christ, but to lack a legend is also to lack dignity, so that until the end of time the West will have, for Goliath, the eyes of David.

4 Alphabetical Liftoff

*Civilization, or at least the history
of humanity, rests on papyrus.*
(Pliny the Elder, around 70 CE)

*We have no knowledge of a purely oral society possessing a notion of the Eternal.
Between myth and poetry, those two sibling rivals, the God of Revelation makes
His initial appearance as spoken word, but that word takes on force of law over
time solely by virtue of the Letter. Writing is the manufacture of the only God.
Anyone who fails to exile himself from the visible will not encounter the Invisible,
and writing in its most advanced state, the alphabet, harbours for us this theological
virtue: it encourages mental detachment from the world of the senses, and abstracts
the Absolute from his circumstances. And when the letter is deposited on papyrus, it
– writing – can be circulated from top to bottom of the tribe. This diverting of a
means of recording quantities into a lever of transcendence was to engage the God
of psalms on the treacherous paths of the written, where an ambush awaited Him in
the guise of formalization and argumentation, the precursors of critical reason.*

The exile to Babylon was thus, for the universal Master, a narrow escape. The names of Ezekiel and the second Isaiah signed the call to unity issuing from (or provoked by) physical dispersion. With the sanctuary in ruins, it became necessary to find a substitute amenable to performance of the traditional rites, which had become unperformable. The elevation of the material to the symbolic was the result not of a deliberate decision, but of a *fait accompli*. It was imposed by the brutal withdrawal of matter constituted by the dismantling of customary practices, following the foreign invasion. *Nolens volens,* that cleansing required the exiles and deportees to invent a dematerialized and unlocalizable altar. A task managed by the Judaean intelligentsia in Babylon, concluding that the majority of the population, having remained behind, at home, continued to grow amid sinister compromises with the ambient pluralism (a majority which it will feel obligated, after the return, to re-educate or restore to sobriety). The Torah will be the temple without the Temple: what is left when there is a desire not to forget anything, and everything is in ruins.

Even so, it was necessary for the flower of the dissolved community, bearing its soul on its sandals, to dispose of the effective means of dematerialization. It is at this juncture that the technical factor crucially intervenes: writing and its support. Catastrophe is the mother of monotheism, and the alphabet is its father.

Words are Discreet

In the history of civilizations, it was a turning point: the sacred without spectacle. Keep on moving, there's nothing to *see*. The Hebrews are an ancient people of the east. And yet, in the Louvre's Department of Oriental Antiquities, it is as though the kingdoms of Judah and Israel had never existed. The visitor moves through the Mesopotamian, Iranian and Middle Eastern rooms – where nothing is found to evoke Saul or Jeremiah. The visitor is surprised. Is it not generally accepted that the West has three sources: Jerusalem, Athens and Rome? Of the latter two we have a plethora of tangible testimony. The first is far more sparing: neither statuary nor panelled painting. The non-existence of a 'Jewish Room' in the most beautiful museum in the world poses a problem. This may be interpreted as a form of tribute. The institution of the museum is not a relevant medium for Judaic transmission.[1] Israel, like every great nation, has had (since 1965) its museum of art and archaeology. It contains ritual objects specific to the various polytheistic cults of ancient Palestine (scythes, sculpted vessels, statues of Venus, sarcophagi, figurines

Interior of the Shrine of the Book in Jerusalem, Photo: David Harris

of Astarte, etc.). Monotheism has its museum, which lies alongside it: the Shrine of the Book, whose cupola is in the form of the neck of a jar striking in its whiteness. In the basement are the Dead Sea Scrolls, biblical and apocryphal manuscripts on copper, leather and papyrus, and nothing else. Rows of blue and black characters in Old Hebrew, Aramaic and Greek. The Judaic – in which the quest for meaning absorbs the search for beauty, and which is not distinguished, like the pagan world, by its architects and sculptors – is transmitted through recitations, gestures and rituals, not by way of the plastic or the iconographic. This opting for discretion increases the chance for longevity: here it is impossible to shunt one's 'obligation to memory' off on to some expiatory contraption or identity-based mausoleum charged with alleviating the bad conscience of the amnesiac. Not that a literal heritage is immaterial. In His Onliness, He finally triumphed over his rivals, Marduk and Amon-Ra. They lie congealed in our museums, whereas He continues to mobilize millions of believers – in the streets. In explaining this 'miracle', we would do well not to lapse into *naive spiritualism*, evoking an undefined victory of spirit over matter. Matter is defeated by matter, as evil is by evil. The refusal of forms and volumes would have been fatal were it not that inner memory had succeeded in externalizing itself in the shape of letters, materializing itself in *ostraca* and scrolls, the antidotes of bronze and wood, making itself into a *trace*. Polishing, scratching

---

[1] See Laurence Sigal, *Discours à la Fondation du judaïsme français* (27 June 2000).

and inscribing are still varieties of handiwork, with their corresponding corporeal techniques. A labour requiring, depending on the era, appropriate instruments (stylus, chisel, qalamus, brush, goose-quill, metal penpoint, etc.) and primary materials (copper, silver, papyrus, parchment, paper, etc.). The being-there of God – namely, Scripture – would not exist as an imperceptible perceptible, 'as a being bereft of corporality and none the less objective' (Hegel), without the operation consisting of exteriorizing the interior and spatializing vocal utterances in order to imbue them with timelessness. Without that artisanry and those materials, the Tablets of the Law, shattered by their bearer (who was given to intemperate outbursts), would never have been able to find a facsimile, and the memory of the iconoclast Moses would have been lost in the sands without either biography or destiny.

An example of what separates orality from writing. In the Fertile Crescent, during the two millennia before Christ, population transfers were common currency, with invasions and changes of dynasty punctuating the ongoing 'ethnic cleansing'. Trapped between two colossi, local populations of moderate size suffered many a deportation. The Hebrew people is the only one of them to have transcended, by way of graphic transmutation, its misfortune into a Value. If we may compare the incomparable: the Gypsies, of Christian – but oral – culture, with neither museum nor *thesaurus,* without scriptural accumulation, underwent the Nazi genocide – but without either documenting or interpreting it. From that human and national catastrophe, they failed to derive a quasi-supernatural (and in any event refoundational) meaning – nothing comparable to the Shoah.

The Semitic world, in brief, was to bequeath two fundamental gifts to humanity: God and the alphabet. Which remains, in whatever language it is translated, the aleph-bet, the a and b of the Hebraic abecedarium. We Latins benefited from it by way of Phoenicia, which transferred it to the Greek world around 1000 BCE. The two innovations are linked by an intimate and necessary bond. The fact that the most ancient biblical writings date from after the invention of the alphabet – the system of notation through which all signs that do not correspond to elementary sounds of the spoken language vanish – is testimony to the fact that without the alphabet, a metaphysical delayed-action bomb, there would be no God. They grew up together. Without, in the beginning, occupying much space. For a long time Yahweh was a local god among others, 'who had credit in the mountains, and none at all in the valleys' (Voltaire), and writing, in Mesopotamian society, was a mercantile activity among others. It took more than a millennium for each of them to climb the rungs of the hierarchical ladder. A gradual sifting, rather than a series of thunderbolts. Bedazzlement by the burning bush is a flattering image. But there was no genius who discovered writing, the way others were to discover America, one fine morning at the end of the fourth millennium, in the Sumerian city of Uruk, which is today Warka, in the south of Iraq. It was a meandering process, with tunnels and re-emergences. What was sown in Sumer flourished a thousand years later in Byblos, and subsequently bore fruit in Hebron. Medium and message, throughout, gave each other a hand, refining each other as they went. No one, strictly speaking, has proprietary rights on God, or, for that matter, on the alphabet. Neither patent nor inventor. The deceptive facilities of signatory flourish and newsflash had to yield at this juncture to the labour of the sign and the patience of things. Jesus the Son would be accorded, after the fact, a date of birth, but on what date of what calendar are we to affix the birthday of the Father and of cuneiform?

Saying and Reading

Objection, Your Honour. The Prophet is a crier, not a public scribe. The vociferator of God does not say: 'Read, O Israel', but 'Hear, O Israel'. And when indeed does the Book talk about the Book? It vaunts the prestige of Voice, whose unimpeded flow is mimicked and duplicated in the unfurling of the scroll around its post. The spoken word and creation constitute a single divine deed. 'In the beginning was the Word, and the Word was with God, and the Word was God. He was in the beginning with God. All things came into being through him, and without him not one thing came into being. What has come into being in him was life, and the life was the light of all people' (John 1: 1). The Word: life and *logos* form an over-arching block. 'The mouth of the Lord hath spoken' (Isaiah 40: 5). The written word is dead, the voice is alive. It is the very breath of creative Life. Hearing is connected directly to the Bouche d'Ombre, the Mouth of Shadow, as Hugo called it, which professes without revealing itself. Do the French not still say: *parole d'Évangile* (for our 'Gospel truth')? Jesus never wrote anything (except once, in the sand, like a Tuareg). Nor did Socrates and Buddha. What is God, after all, 'that vast shadowy word refulgent with light', said Hugo (to which Gide added: 'the depository of every ill-defined concept')? French *Dieu*: a diphthong. A phoneme. And Scripture, in the endless muttering of invocations, a kind of auditory spell?

Only living speech can restore a quality of mystery which cold writing, excessively conceptual, conceals or withers. It traverses the idea in order to lay hold on things themselves. Or – to put it in the poet Yves Bonnefoy's words – to traverse the botanical rose, and grasp this precise rose under my window, requires breath and vocal cords. Just as a text placed in a mouth and in space is suddenly endowed with a body which escapes its reader, and which the literary corpus had hidden from his sight. Myths are stored in written form, but they enter us by way of the ear, in the trembling or furious evocation of a speaker, a semi-literate bard equipped with lyre or tambourine. The divine is recited in cadence, erect, while rocking one's torso, tapping the beat with one's foot, a stick serving as orchestral baton. A saying, proverb or line of verse, 'writing that scans', says Julien Gracq, 'makes do without verification'. The Trojan War thus came down to us borne by 'singer-reproducers' called *rhapsodes*. But the fact that our speech-propelled God arises in us by way of the throat, following the pulsations of our blood, does not prevent our monotheism from being essentially *grapho-propelled*. The anteriority of the sonorous does not exclude the primacy of the sign.

Script has already been in pursuit of the various charismas of song for three thousand years – without attaining them. The supreme *frisson* is forbidden it. It is the bellows of the lungs, the vocal cords, that bring us into contact with the warm sources of our beliefs. As warm as the 'breath of life' breathed into Adam's nostrils to bring forth a 'living soul' (that is to say: a live animal). Yes, nothing separates the *nabi*, the prophet, from an inspired musician. Mohammed, it is said, was illiterate when a 'book descended into his heart'. He neither read nor wrote. He *recited*, transmitting under dictation words received from Gabriel in a state of auditory trance. Reverberated a (thunderous or murmuring) voice in our direction. But it is the scriptural retention of those whispers, on the basis of the memory traces of an individual psyche, that enables us to outline a collective personality. Departure from Egypt, Crucifixion of Jesus, Flight to Medina: each of those non-events, concerning which contemporaries knew nothing, was transmuted into a crucial historical event through the flabbergasting effect of a rhythmic transposition – 'at last raising a page to the power of the starfilled sky' (as Valéry said of Mallarmé).

The spiritual sphere that Teilhard de Chardin called the 'noosphere' is no steambath. It seems soft and shapeless, but it does have a skeletal structure: our entirely material manner of fabricating and ensuring the circulation of signs. Beyond its physical or mechanical elements, this *system* includes the institutional, economic, educational and juridical environment without which our contrivances would not be able to function (every machine functions within and through its surroundings, with which it forms a system). Such is our 'mediasphere'. The great revealed religions, which date from before the advent of illustrative procedures, go back to the mediasphere historically inaugurated by the manuscript and closed by typography – to which we give the name 'logosphere'. A long stretch of time in which a rare and sacralized written text – Bible, Gospel or Koran, in which the world is summed up – serves as a sea mark, a lighthouse for an ocean of recitations. It is impossible to bring the familiar refrain 'oral/written' into play in this case. The written word is present as a pendant, a facilitating device, a link in a chain descending from heaven to earth. Our writing, moreover, is called in Hebrew *Mikra*, which means 'reading'. 'Let us acclaim the Word of God,' says the Catholic priest, for his part, after the sermon, brandishing the Holy Book. He does not say 'let us acclaim the text of God'. In the logosphere, *speaking* and *reading* remained more or less synonymous. Westerners had all learned, as of the eighteenth century, to read in silence, but the authors of Antiquity had works read to them by a slave, as they most often dictated their literary texts. They were taken down in shorthand. They condescended only to sign their letters (authorial literary writing begins in Byzantium and, in our case, in the eleventh and twelfth centuries). Our cantors still allow that high era to reverberate down to us, in synagogue or church, with their tenor voices and ample tessitura. Does not the author of Maccabees conclude the last of the *Historical Books* by formulating the wish that the 'fine ordering of the narrative will *charm the ears* of those who *read* the work'? The Bible, then, as a fabulous opera in which all hearts open to each other? It behooves us, between the verses of the Psalms, to revive the bellowing of horns, the clang of the tambourine and sistrum. But without the traces on paper, who today would dream of reawakening the lost audiovisual and rhythmic components of our acts of grace?

'The true objective history of a people', Hegel notes, 'begins when it becomes a written history.' He maintained – not unreasonably – that the state, history and writing appeared together (and nothing tells us that they will not disappear together one day). In having the history of the Eternal begin at the moment it is objectified in writing, might we not be effecting a confusion between the time of illumination and the (later) time of its entry into an archive? By reabsorbing history-as-life into history-as-narrative? Was there no humanity before the hieroglyph? Hegel's vision has become a bit myopic. Who can deny that there were living legends before our mythological narratives? Abraham, had he existed, in conformity with his myth, would have lived between the eighteenth and sixteenth centuries before Christ, in the midst of Mesopotamians singularly prone to writing (as is shown in the half-million engraved slabs exhumed in various excavations). But Genesis does not indicate that he would have been able to read and write. When he buys a plot of land from the Hittites, in Makpela, in front of Mamre, the contract is oral. Apparently, no paper was signed. Are all those juicy rumours to be consigned to the dust-heap – for lack of documentation?

Undoubtedly, popular/oral traditions preceded expert/written composition. Fragments recited out loud, stemming from various schools, were kept in reserve, then reactivated in accordance with perceived necessities and through the addition of supplementary material. A classic (but contested) scheme involves four principal sources. The oldest, the Yahwist, dating from the tenth century, under Solomon, in Judah (source J). The Elohist, from Israel and the North, in the eighth century (source E). The Deuteronomic, collected after the fall of Samaria (source D). And the Post-Exilic, or Priestly (source P). Whatever the case, it remains that the result of these splicings and stitchings associates the revealed with the scriptural. The writing *digito Dei* of the Law constitutes the nub of the matter. The Bible, we will be told, retraces the childhood of Judaism that best conforms to its adult form (as is the case with the Gospels for Christians). But the inseparability of revelation from the first verbo-graphic episode of the Bible is not an anecdote. It dramatizes in an image the inherence of the 'letter' in the idea of God. Writing, moreover, produces its own signature, and Moses brandishes as a trophy the Eternal's own manuscript (since He used his index finger as a stylus). Exodus 32: 16: 'The tablets were the work of God, and the writing was the writing of God, engraved upon the tablets.' Our mother-religion, as we shall see, does not share the notorious contempt of linguists and philosophers for writing as a mere graphic derivative of language. Condillac was of the opinion that 'it will never have the slightest effect on the structure and the content of the ideas that it will be charged with conveying'. Rousseau, that it 'serves only as a supplement to speech'. And Ferdinand de Saussure: 'Language and writing are two distinct systems of signs; the sole justification for the latter is to represent the former.' Even today, the 'languages of paradise' or the question of knowing which language Adam spoke (and whether or not Hebrew was the primordial language of humanity) inspire more fantasy and semiological investigation than the no less thorny question of the origins of writing. God, it would appear, was less of an idealist than our universities. He understood very well that with inscription, He was wagering His entire fortune, which is our memory. To create the world through speech is one thing. But if no one retains any trace of it, to what avail? Here on earth, in order to preserve something or someone as living, it is strategically wise to fix it as dead. The letter killeth, perhaps, but it allows for endurance and revivals. Christ dead and resurrected 'according to the Scriptures'. Still.

The Long March of Signs

Where does the Letter come from? The graphic sign representing an acoustic phoneme?

Arduous and sinuous was the advance of what we summarily call writing – a term which is too vague, at this stage, to enlighten us. Recall the principal phases, in overly schematic form. First phase: *pictography*, when signs are quasi-images, outlines that recall or suggest the palpable appearance of things. This is a figurative shorthand. The second: *ideography*, which is a derivative and stylized form of the crude pictogram. The third, which is decisive: *phoneticism*, in which the sign no longer denotes things, but spoken words (cuneiform had already broken with all visual mimetics). In point of fact, the two last procedures, the ideo- and the pho-nogram, fused in a rather long transitional phase, illustrated by the Egyptian hieroglyph, which is an already recapitulatory (but as yet hybrid) rebus, combining visual and phonetic memory. It is this *coupling of a trace and an utterance*, a graphic notation and a phonic form, which crowns the slow movement of symbolization, issuing in writing in the proper sense. Specialists in search of origins debate the question of boundaries or triggering thresholds between the various stages; whether it is preferable to place, between picto- and ideogram, or between ideo- and pho-nogram, the decisive line separating an uncontrolled proliferation of unpredictable marks from an organized code (*code* being understood as a stabilized repertory of discrete, separable and reusable marks). Is pictography the infancy or the prehistory of written culture? At this juncture we will adopt the hypotheses of Jean-Jacques Glassner, showing that the Sumerians had already acceded to abstract thought with cuneiform. What is indisputable is the vector of the general trend, which goes in the direction of a growing compression by way of an economy of marks (more content for less container).

The first known system of notation, *cuneiform*, which slightly precedes the Egyptian hieroglyph and the Chinese ideogram, appeared in lower Mesopotamia towards the end of the fourth millennium, shortly after the formation of the first city-states. This is the name given to writing in the shape of a wedge or nail, an angular shape stemming from the direct imprint of a bevelled reed on raw clay. Sumero–Akkadian civilization flourished in the mud of the deltas in which civilizations are born, a region of silt and clay, with neither forests nor metals, but potentially rich by virtue of the proximity of great rivers, the Tigris and the Euphrates, allowing for artificial irrigation. The soil is alluvial, favourable to the raising of small livestock and the the growth of edible grains. The exit from a culture of survival everywhere obeys the familiar sequence of a positive feedback loop: accumulation of agricultural surplus, growth in population density, formation of a regulating centre of power, hierarchical distribution of the surplus. And thus a need for accounting instruments. A need to classify, arrange, retain, distribute spatially, label and predict. To note the swelling of rivers, eclipses, the cycle of the stars. The utilitarian and economic origin of writing, which initially served to compile catalogues, lists, schedules, almanacs, and so on, is in no way incompatible with its religious uses, since temples served as banks and administrators of economic life (the famous tablets of Uruk were found in a sanctuary).

Man does not go from the simple to the complicated but, rather, the other way round. This unburdening bears the name of 'technical progress', which appears to be promoted by the law of least effort (to do less and to have more). In matters of notation as elsewhere, man began with the pictographic or ideographic system, then the syllabic – thus with the more complicated – before arriving at the alphabet. The decomposition of a language into its simplest sounds, followed (or preceded) by the invention of a system of discrete marks, limited in number, representing those sounds or phonemes visually, required more than a millennium. From the borders of Egypt to northern Syria, there were numerous written alphabets, not counting those prior attempts constituted by proto-Semitic writing systems, which remain difficult to decipher. The most promising parsimony (thirty signs) made use of cuneiform – and is illustrated by Ugarit, today Ras Shamra, in Syria – around 1400 BCE, before disappearing suddenly in 1185, with the invasion of the 'peoples of the sea'. This was the system subsequently used by the Semitic languages – but not exclusively, since Hittite, an Indo-European language, was also written in cuneiform. Here we find an aptitude for crossing over that is absent from the spoken language. For a system of writing can be applied to set down a language other than the one for which it was composed. Phoenician, Greek, Latin, Turkish or Vietnamese. A literalized God becomes *translatable and exportable*. In a condition to travel. And potentially universal.

On the path of rectification, every code becomes the raw material of its still more formal successor. In order the better to deliver *what is*, one takes increasing distance each time from *what resembles*; and the incorporating instance of one period becomes the incorporated of the next. Alphabetical writing, an arbitrary segmentation of the spoken chain, is much further removed from living speech than the ideogram or the pictogram – which remain, in essence, a writing of things, not of sounds. Now it is in the degree of separation between a thing and its notation that the productivity of a code is measured. The more abstract it is, the more simple; and the more simple, the more encompassing (nothing resists the digital). What occurs here is a kind of turnabout, in which the inscriber gains, with every move, precisely what he renounces. Etymologically, the devil is he who separates (*dia-ballein*), and the symbol is what joins things and people (*sym-ballein*). Man advanced in the symbolization of things through an investment in the diabolical (or the diacritical). And he ended up discovering God by playing the devil; he made his way to the infinite via the paths of separation/decantation. Akkadian – an imperial language, but quite profuse and elaborate – was defeated by the Aramaic of small Syrian kingdoms, because the latter had fewer signs. The writing of Uruk IV consisted of 640 different signs. It was unable to withstand the twenty-two letters of Phoenician. Any more than the alphabet originating in Phoenician could withstand the binary code of today. He who reduces wins. To progress is always to abridge. If we take the Egyptian case, the *hieroglyph* engraved on stone gave way, in Egypt, to *hieratic* writing, which was already more economical and cursive, which would in turn yield to a *demotic* inked on to papyrus and simpler still (towards the seventh century BCE).

Since the genesis of fiduciary currency parallels that of writing, the same productive attenuation has been observed in the case of money. The first Sumerian tokens imprinted into clay regulated economic exchanges: counts of goats and sheep, contracts for house sales, fruit deliveries, builders' estimates. In the long transition from barter to electronic money, payment was made first in livestock (the *pecus* of *pecuniary*), then in thalers, lingots or metallic coins, then in paper money, cheques, credit cards, and finally figures typed on a machine. The heavy-indivisible was replaced by the manipulable-divisible. The tangible by the intelligible. The voluminous by the attenuated.

A Mystical Machine

An alphabet is an instrument for decomposing the continuous, the human voice, or submitting sonorous flows to the regimen of the discrete. Like God Himself, it goes towards *more* meaning by way of *fewer* signs. But those terms are quantitative, whereas what is at stake in the move from visual transposition to coded transcription is basically not a downsizing so much as an uncoupling. It is a radical dis-

connection. A grapheme is a *cosmic disenchanter*. A personal God, which is a
notion, not a given, requires a notional space, freed from the ballast of the natural
by *non-motivated* signs. At which point God attains His liftoff velocity in relation to
similarities, suggestions and correspondences. The 'YHWH' diagram cuts the cord
linking it to the laurel-bedecked Powers, trident and lightning-bolt in hand, dragon
head and lion paws. The arbitariness of a 'gratuitous' system of discontinuities cuts
the paths of analogy between the intelligible and the sensuous, words and stars,
voice and storm. The history of our God begins where the comic strip ends, when
the *graphein* bifurcates, with one branch for images and the other for symbols.
Earlier, we were in gestation. This time, it's childbirth.

Despite its phonetic values, the hieroglyph remains attached to the old enchantments of the image, and even in its popular, cursive form, demotic, it does not break
completely with representation. Only a purely conventional graphic can silence the
buzz of the world. In our alphabet, the letter A is no longer an inverted oxhead, with
its two horns as legs; it is what precedes B, full stop. Diacritical, its shape no longer
counts, but its place does. Egyptian writing is still a magical web cast over individuals and things. It dreams of capture at a distance, of amulets and mirrors. The
hieroglyph is to the alphabetical sign what magic is to religion; spell is to prayer; or
divination to prophecy. Is Thoth, the baboon who invented Egyptian script, not also
the god of magicians and medicine-men? Despite the retrospective homage one is
prepared to pay the god Aton, the sun god of the pharaoh Akhenaton, one wonders
how a non-figurative god, disengaged from the cosmos, could have emerged from a
writing system that had not totally broken with astrology.

To be sure, a God who knows how to make Himself understood by men, who
utters the Law and enters into a contract, cannot be a Martian. It remains a fact that
Yahweh, at the end of His itinerary, has lost His animal body, whereas Baal, that
other 'Lord of the Heavens', remains associated with the bull, and El with the lion.
The Great Seceder resides 'in the depth of the immobile, sleeping azure', even if He
may happen to 'descend' here or there, preferably on a mountain peak (there being
no comfortable junction between heaven and earth). He is no longer on easy terms
with the world as it is. The Graeco-Roman immortals, who are men more human
than the rest of us, still were. All the pleasures of our condition, without the flu and
without finitude. Those eminently sociable immortals eat and drink, ride on
horseback, stage ambushes, and copulate. They each have a sex – *theoi* and *theai*.
They don't preach morality to us, and for good reason, since they are as immoral as
we are. Between the *man, only better*, who is the ancestor, or genius, or hero of the
place, and the *man, only less*, who is the God of everywhere and nowhere, is the
distance that separates the alphabetical sign from the imitative simulacrum. Only a
machine for disfiguration like an abecedarium can engender something like a
Wholly-Other. And only a 'lettered' God can take off from His bases and leapfrog
over walls, like the Phoenician himself, exemplary in his agility, a man of commerce
and navigation. Who brought his linear script (the straight or curved line replacing

the angle) along with his merchandise. In the South, at Sinai, he encountered the hieroglyph, which issued in a hybrid *proto-Sinaiic* script, midway between Egyptian and Lebanese, but appears not to have had any progeny. To the East and the North, he encountered Mesopotamian cuneiform, another occasion for interbreeding, whose issue was *Ugaritic*, a refined cuneiform which, for its part, would have a descendant: Phoenician, which gives its notation, among others, to old Hebrew (modern Hebrew, with its square letters, would appear only in the second century). There is no more of a hiatus between the Canaanite El and the biblical *Elohim* than there is between the Ugaritic consonant and the Phoenician–Hebraic consonant. The break, the variable in terms of expansion, is the transition from Mesopotamian mud to Phoenician fibre, and the systematization of the scroll. Change bodies, and you will change minds.

Our alphabet has become *medio-adaptable*. Just as writing escaped the Book, the letter is currently becoming emancipated from its support. It leaps from paper to disk, wall and screen. Such was not the case formerly, when matter dictated graphic behaviour, by virtue of its instrument. A material to be engraved, like clay or marble, did not authorize either pencil or triviality. Bamboo excludes chisel or awl. Wax (from which Roman tablets, whence the *codex*, father of the book, would be made) calls for a stylus of ivory, bone or metal, but excludes reed or goose-quill (which is adapted to parchment). To each substrate, its kind of truth: one does not write one's private diary on birchbark or marble. The succession of traces demonstrates that a change of material reverberates in a change of notation. Our successive forms of writing stem from an evolving dialogue between formal structures and matter. In cuneiform, the symbol enters into dialogue with the earth, origin of life. With a bevel-edged reed to imprint 'angles' into the fresh clay tablet which the scribe keeps warm in the fold of his hand (whence the smallness and characteristic shape of the tablets, bulging in the back but flat in the front, where the signs are incised). It is an abundant material, inexpensive, kept moist in jars and allowing one to erase and rewrite immediately after. But once dry, it becomes friable and burdensome. As for steles, which receive official charters or votive formulae, they require a chisel, and thus stiff, solemn, right angles. It was in trading the qalamus reed for the chisel, and a soft material for a hard one, that habits of writing underwent elongation and contraction (long and short alphabets).[2]

The Hebrews betrayed the expectations of protocol. The rule had been: the heavier the support, the more solemn the message. The Mesopotamian gods tended to dictate on to stone imported at great expense from mountainous regions: kings on clay. As the Roman emperors issued promulgations by chisel on to marble or bronze. The nobility of materials ('engraved in marble') generally proceeded in tandem with the majesty of deeds. For a material is already a sign in itself, the index

---

[2] Émile Puech, 'Origine de l'alphabet', *Revue biblique*, April 1986.

of an intention, or the mark of a pre-eminence. The form of writing used in the period of the First Temple (from 850 to 586 BCE) appears on a variety of materials: stone, pottery and coin. It was in its characters, with their long descending bars – which, over the course of time, had become symbols of national resistance and rebirth – that the four letters of the divine name were written, including during the period of the Second Temple, once Aramaic cursive, the official language of the Persian Empire, replaced the older graphic convention. At the time, Aramaic was the common language of the Near East, employed in the chanceries of Egypt and Assyria (it would also be the language of Christ). That consonantal alphabet, itself issuing from Phoenician, served the Hebrews for the transmission of sacred texts (and not merely for their correspondence, ledgers and contracts). But the deposition of the tetragrammaton in sacred characters on a support with as little prestige as papyrus, as was discovered in Qumran with the Leviticus Scroll (100 BCE), reveals a certain broadmindedness, or practicality. The Qumran manuscripts, it is true, suggest a certain hierarchy of supports (silver leaf rather than papyrus, suggesting important revelations about the placement of treasure). That hierarchical disposition was habitual. Homer, for the Romans, was a parchment. But a simple sheet of papyrus was not deemed unworthy, even by sectarians, of receiving the Word of God. Every language borrows from its neighbours, and biblical Hebrew (as opposed to the Mishnaic Hebrew of the Talmud) may have owed a distant debt to Egypt, which exercised an influence over Phoenicia. In its writing habits, however, it was affiliated, by way of Aramaic, with Sumeria. What it owed to Egypt, where the plant was abundant, was essentially the support, which, unlike tablets, was easily transportable. Produced in thin strips, beaten with a mallet, glued together with its own sap, smoothed with pumice stone and cut into rectangles, papyrus allowed for writing in ink, following a lightweight ductus, with loops and downstrokes. It also allowed one to roll the sheets assembled edge to edge in a scroll. Although it was degradable by humidity and unsuited to being folded (which would be the specificity of parchment), in a dry climate the papyrus archive travelled successfully both in space (as far as Dura-Europos in Syria) and in time (the Egyptian funerary texts) far better than tablets of wood or wax. Papyrus reigned for nearly four thousand years, from the Egyptian Middle Empire to the European Middle Ages (the last document being an eleventh-century papal bull), by way of the Roman Empire (after the annexation of Egypt) and Islam. But it was in Hebraic culture that the papyrus scroll took on all its symbolic value. It could be unfurled endlessly, in a continuous movement: a symbol of incompletion, but also of perpetual repetition – whereas the Roman *codex*, by its very rigid, square form, ascribed value to limits and closure. The laconic Empire of the *limes*, contracting its thoughts into maxims and apophthegms, savoured its right angles. The loquacious people of the desert unfurled its land and its text as far as the eye could see, endlessly. The West and its straightnesses, the East and its volutes . . . .

Aftereffects of a Techno-Piracy

In retrospect, Egypt and Mesopotamia may be hailed as *the lands of the threshold*. They did not cross it. The Hebrews took that step. And therein lies, no doubt, the Jewish miracle, as one speaks of the Greek miracle: in the conjunction of the right code and the right substrate, effected midway in the buffer zone of Palestine. A culturally backward region, in a sense, one which acquired writing after its great neighbours, but a zone of exchange and commerce, in which people did not live closed in on themselves, where cross-breeding was possible. Voltaire believed that the idea of a Supreme Being could be born only in the heart of vast empires. This is too mechanical a perspective. The interstice proved more productive, because it was propitious for the 'cross-fertilization' that borrows the best from every rival: the support from the South, the notation from the East. *A closed religion, but an open culture*, Egypt exported its papyrus, not its hieroglyphs (which were not disseminated beyond its frontiers). And baby Moses, or Mosis, was rescued from the waters of the Nile by a cradle of papyrus. *An isolated culture, but an open religion*, Mesopotamia did the reverse. It disseminated its cuneiforms, not its support. In making use of its median position to short-circuit one by the other, the Hebrew people ingeniously joined the two halves of the symbol. The Egyptian influence allowed it to transcend clay, a factor of metaphysical blockage. And the Mesopotamian to transcend figurative facility.

In this the fertility of dual cultures, of which the mythical Abraham already offered a fine literary example, is verified. His name in Hebrew designates he who traverses, the essential shuttler (the *Uri*). He would have come from 'the land between two rivers'; he would have frequented sanctuaries, gardens and statues. His father, a manufacturer of idols. His wife Sarah and his servants, people of the soil. A halfbreed, in brief, like his heir Moses, and also like Theodor Herzl, the prophetic author of *The Jewish State* (Vienna, 1896), an Austrian Jew born in Hungary, travelling through Paris. Creative characters because they are double. Half stock, half flow. Sedentary and nomadic, plain and desert. One in the Other. Such was the feature highlighted by Freud in his *Moses and Monotheism*. A mad historical exercise, to be sure, a wholly imaginary speculation and which concludes, as of necessity, with the murder of Moses by his people in conformity with approved doctrine (the primordial murder of the father of the horde). But the Viennese doctor got to the heart of the matter by making Moses the stranger within. Even if he did have his mother, Josabeth, as a nursemaid, he was an adopted son raised in the Court by the daughter of Pharaoh as an Egyptian prince. Cultural bastardy is the surest gauge of intellectual innovation.

Such innovation consists in allowing writing to slip from one domain of competence to another. A disturbing contrast indeed. Eight Mesopotamian tablets out of ten are about economics, with mythology coming in a poor second. The first signs to be incised were numerical marks: cylinder-seals and envelope-bulls of clay were for the most part accounting documents. Writing was for merchants and accountants. Now the Hebrew writings that have been preserved reverse those proportions. No doubt the Persians reserved matters of accounting and taxes for themselves, leaving poetry to their satellite populations. As for the Temple before the Exile, it burned down, and its archives along with it. The temple was the national bank, and the leading holder of real estate, along with the King. Is that why we have so many myths and genealogies, and so few contracts? As though the first preoccupation were no longer the satisfaction of the needs of the economy and the administration. It is difficult not to see in all this a transference-pirouette of technology, which is used for ends other than those for which it was first fashioned. Monotheism as a superior form of poaching (in the sense given to the word by Michel de Certeau in his *Arts de faire*). Or a singular case of a general phenomenon destined for the best of futures, the *productive misuse of tools*. It reminds us that a tool has no preassigned function. The 'logic of usage' can cause the trajectory to deviate at any given moment, even turn it against its promoters. The aftereffects of this form of tinkering, the fecundity of this extravagance, moreover, give to the history of techniques, both material and intellectual (if it is possible to distinguish them), a baroque and poetic *cachet* that is not without affinities, for our greater profit and pleasure, with its opposite pole: an anthology of the fantastic. The first steam engine (Savery, 1698) was conceived not to propel a vehicle, but to draw water from the bottom of a well. The French Minitel was not made to arrange assignations. Nor was the Internet invented to link obliquely dissident civilians, but, rather, to protect the networks of the Pentagon from enemy interception. In order the better to make war, not money or science. In the Greek world, the theft of fire by Prometheus furnished the human adventure with its point of departure. The hero thus filched from the gods the secret of the fundamental arts, ceramics and metallurgy. The theft of the sign by the 'wandering Jew' might well be its counterpart in our culture. It derives its essential feature from the effrontery of the poor nomad who dared to steal from the rich man of the city what was not made for him. Better still: what had been invented against him.

In principle, a herdsman without livestock has no need for a means of accounting and registering juridical decisions, specifically those that bind individuals without family ties into a city. He has neither the material means of invention nor the political conditions of use. When kinship functions as the social bond, both economic and political, as it does in oral society, the casting of exchanges and contracts in black and white is not a necessity. Then, the milieu: writing has a shared interest with hydraulics. It trickles out of deltas and along rivers (the Nile, the Yang-Tse, the Euphrates). Regions where irrigation allows progress beyond day-by-day survival, on condition that floods be anticipated and stars observed. The birth of writing, the alluvial deposit of strong empires, with highly structured economies, in fertile plains, presupposed an abundant materiology: grass for papyrus, water for clay, fire for cooking. The wanderers of the desert did not have those natural resources. In addition, and above all, the nomad evaded the grasp of the central power, the point of convergence of the various forms of wealth, which made use of writing the better to draw surplus-value from the land. The need for writing was felt by those who had reserves to account for, tasks to assign for the maintenance of canals in good order, prisoners and booty to distribute: the masters of the surplus, administering waters and granaries. As Lévi-Strauss reminded us in an entirely different context: 'Writing appears to be associated, in permanent manner, solely with societies founded on the exploitation of man by man.' Its development presupposes and promotes the accentuation of internal divisions in the group.

A nomadic society has fewer such divisions. The matter of posture, first of all. A man who writes is not *viator*. The *viator* stands erect; the writer is seated. Let us observe *the scribe crouching* close to the earth. Painted limestone, eyes of quartz, a masterpiece of the ancient Egyptian Empire that can be contemplated in the Louvre. The first clerk charged with writing of whom we possess a living representation (around 2550 BCE) is seated, cross-legged. The artisan-bureaucrat, taking notes under dictation, raises his head. The scene is calm; he is protected, at ease. This is a man *at rest* and rather corpulent, not in a hurry, with a good position and no fear for the future. Writing is not made for wandering bands, the unstable bereft of possessions. Landholding in miniature, with its fieldwork transposed. The furrow of the lines, the *page* as a small field (*pagina* comes from *pagus*), the writing reed as the ploughshare's blade. Culture: what remains of agriculture when the harvest has been garnered. An empire's technology, a luxury of the rich. Developed in order to count steres of grain and heads of cattle, and to transmit the orders of the monarch.

This practical *misappropriation* was accompanied by a moral *reversal*. Like the invention of metallurgy, the invention of writing had repercussions which intensified the division of labour, the inequality of exchange, and class conflict. But the adepts of the Only God turned that evil into a good, by reversing an anti-egalitarian instrument of subjection (of peasants by administrators) into a tool of national liberation (of a people in relation to empires). What had augmented differences in status enabled, under a different dispensation, their diminution. A factor of segregation in an opulent society was revealed to be, after the reversal, a factor of cohesion for a band of 'Habiru', as the turbulent, disreputable bands from the Middle East were known. The history of mnemotechnics is a sequence of political and social subversions.

The Three Contributions of the Written

When we look at its cognitive function, as a producer of knowledge through the diagramming or listing of things, humans and dates, rendering the sequential simultaneous, there is a mystical function of writing that is generative of transcendence. And its most abstract form, the alphabet, produced the most abstract version of the divine. The enemies of God, who are in general aristocrats, empiricists and sportsmen, enamoured of physical exercise and good health, instead of squandering their energies in sermons against sermonizing, would do well to incriminate not only spelling, that 'repressive archaism', but writing itself. With adequate counsel, they would be able to lodge a complaint against the invention of the alphabet on three grounds: undue democratization, oppression of the instinctual by the conceptual, and obessional neurosis. This is not at all our intention, but the tenor of the proceedings might be imagined rather effectively.

First, the abecedarium vulgarizes mysteries by reconciling poles – the mystical and the accessible – that had hitherto been opposed. As a machine for countering figuration, it shatters the old magic of resemblances. As an instrument of distribution, it imposes a break with the ontology of secrecy and with initiatic cults that rely on the oral – and opaque – transmission of confidential formulae. The Levites constituted a separate tribe charged with the service of the cult, but not a caste beyond class, aggrandized by its secrets. Alphabetical simplification puts mysteries within reach, and places all observers on an equal footing. Thirty or twenty-two signs rather than four or five hundred is a quantity that an entire tribe can master, not merely an elite or the clergy. It has been calculated that one per cent of the Egyptian population were literate at the time of the pharaohs. And what did the alphabet change in the economy of the divine? It transformed an esoteric practice of the sacred into a public service. A secret social 'enclave' into an outdoor cult. The linearization and standardization of characters meant that the Hebrews did not have to polarize into clerics steeped in secrets and laymen with calloused hands; hence the priestly people. Every adult male can decipher the ancestral trust, provided that he has learned to read, and thus to pray. Which is to say that a letter-based (and non-figurative) God substantially augments the chances for collective understanding. Anyone who is unaware of Scripture is not so much ignorant as impious. As a result, after the advent of modern times, the Jews became the most intellectualized people on the planet. One can be a good Christian and illiterate (provided that one is neither deaf nor blind). But an illiterate Jew is a square circle. To worship, in this case, is to study, and to study is to participate. In Hebrew, the 'wisdom of Israel' and 'Jewish studies' are contiguous terms. Monotheism is in itself educational, bound to the school and to ascetic apprenticeships. It exercises the faculties of the mind, perhaps to the detriment of the eye and the sense of touch, but the eye is rather lazy, and the sense of touch is frequently deficient in any event. Deciphering and interpreting, more than contemplating and guessing, favour a gymnastics of the neurons, for it is more difficult to retain a sequence of signs than a drawn profile, a stone silhouette or a plumed totem. Such would be the first virtuous circle of the symbolic constraint.

Secondly, writing brings about the advent of 'the concept that no longer changes and remains eternally identical to itself' (Hegel). It permits the transition from the circumstantial to the unconditional, and from the particular to the universal. 'The material support of this eternal concept', Kojève continues, 'is no longer historical Man, nor even the sage, but the book that reveals through discourse (which it materializes in the form of printed words) its own content.'[3] Paradoxically, only a text can decontextualize and, by virtue of that fact, engender a belief emancipated from its spatio–temporal inscription. So long as there is no verbal exchange except 'in context', between contemporaries, an entity lacks the means to isolate itself from its native environment, or to be transmitted without alteration. Transcription, on the other hand, cuts short the words of the speaker and flushes them out of the water. Detached from their emitter, they are free to fly with their own wings. To become autonomous. And absolute. In oral society, the context hems in. No Law, but customs; no Absolute, but the relative. A view from above is impossible. One is either a participant or one isn't. To convert someone else to something that is not there is unthinkable. In order to share his 'religion', the Bororo, should he be so inclined, could only incite his neighbour to come and live in his tribe. In the first stages of oral culture, life is local, and the locals are glued to their myths, which do not become unglued from the group. Between the timeless archetype and the lived moment, there is no room for a space of becoming. Escape from the dual subjection of collective being to space and time presupposes an *essentialization* of what moors us to it.

Thus did the Hebrews draw the best possible advantage from the challenge of the desert, an environment whose stimulation was proportionate to its hostility. Problems of administration, nourishment and transport were more arduous there than anywhere else (and such was the case until the last century, including colonization). When logistical constraints are maximal – and movement is a question of life and death – locomotive inventiveness is optimal. In any event, to choose the written over the image was to cut short the traditional cult of the ancestors, which entailed a perpetual fabrication of effigies – portraits, busts, statues or simulacra. *Imago* in Latin first designated the wax mould of an ancestor, which a Roman of high lineage kept on a shelf or in a niche of his atrium. The *jus imaginum* was the right reserved by a noble to parade the effigies of his ancestors in the forum or the street. The image was the visible substitute for the invisible deceased. It was thus with the religious sense of the old regime that the tutelary function of alphabetical purification compelled a break. The ancestor was no longer a burden to be borne, but a mere genealogical initiator.

Thirdly, there is a strong link between writing and *idées fixes*. Without wanting to confuse piety with neurosis, we are none the less obliged to note that obsessive

---

[3] Alexandre Kojève, *Introduction à la lecture de Hegel* (Paris: Gallimard 1947), p. 413 / *Introduction to the Reading of Hegel*, ed. Alan Bloom (Ithaca, NY: Cornell University Press 1969).

temperaments have a tendency to scribble. 'A tradition', says Freud, ' founded solely on oral transmission, would not have the obsessive character specific to religious phenomena. It would be listened to, evaluated, and eventually rejected like every other bit of news from without.'[4] *A fortiori*, a religion of sin and debt has a greater need than another to *insist*, to inscribe in the psyche a materialized memory trace, a searing and tormenting refrain, ideal for the overly scrupulous. The fetishized text latches on to the fetishist, like a walking ghost. It fuels *idées fixes*, ruminations and litanies. The fact that the 'primal scene' can circle back on itself – not only in the magic of a ritual of expiation, but in the semiconscious muttering of a daily text – increases the hold of the past on the present. The graphic incises the superego in the pious ego, and an engraved charm is optimal for repetitious rumination and observance. Fundamentalism, in this respect, may be viewed as a pathological hypertrophy of the written trace. The cult of the book veers into sadomasochism when the God-mad begin their inner gyrations, like dervishes. Without going to that extreme, this stereotype fits the 'orthodox', the prisoner of Scripture, Memory's slave .... .

The Worm in the Fruit

The conditions of the birth of God would one day prove to be those of His death; but it would take twenty-five centuries to realize as much. Why that turnabout? Because a God who can be taken literally is a God who can be placed in contention and in contradiction with Himself. The transition from oral *mythos* to written *logos* introduces divinity into the infernal logic of argumentation, the principle of identity and non-contradiction. A God who is recited and hammered in is entrancing. A God who is transcribed but also visually examinable, thus an object of study and no longer a *closed matter*, is obsessive. Writing ultimately brings one from ontology to philosophy, and from psalms to the *sed contra* of scholasticism. A God who is read and no longer sung becomes accessible, and thus vulnerable to simple reason. The insertion into a system is the price to be paid for an entry into memory, and what has been gained in facility of transmission is lost in creativity and inventiveness. The little boys of Sumer – and above all of Jerusalem, more numerous – are required to visit their schoolmaster, and copy and recopy lists of figures and words under dictation. And the good pupil will return to what he has read and retains in full view – whereas one cannot revisit what one has heard. The auditory is pleasurable and flowing. But grammar is not as gratifying as a melody.

As soon as God was gripped by 'graphic reason' (Jack Goody), the emotive was expelled from its inner shelters and undone by exposure to rationalization and the

---

[4] Sigmund Freud, *Moses and Monotheism* (New York: Norton 1939), p. 137.

subsequent formalism. Just as the revolution of writing was potentially an episte-
mological revolution, a theo*graphy* was already pregnant with a theo*logy*, and,
consequently, with a *logomachy*. With the intrusion of enumerative and classifica-
tory reason into the domain of what had been received and intoned, the
communitarian God of tales, sagas and myths borrowed the paths not only of
dogmatics, censorship and medieval canon law, but of disputation and academic
conflict as well. By way of the confrontation of concepts, interpretations and
schools. The categories of true and false did not issue from oral communication.
And when the (universal) notions of truth and error encountered the (localized)
worlds of traditional belief, religions became violent and imbued with death. A God
couched in script is already on the defensive, and thus preventively bellicose.

In the short term, and well before the flourishing of the Greek notion of theology
– along with the unreasonable practices encouraged by a God who has to be
demonstrated (and no longer sung, scanned or danced), our sole God found only
advantages, both psychological and symbolic, in moving from the old mouth-to-ear
relation to the hand–eye system. First of all, He gained in authority. When the oral
predominates, until silent reading prevails, what is written has an air of the *pre-
scriptive*, a legislative value. A sacred text gains by remaining anonymous and not
reflecting upon itself as text; holy books do not talk about books (or scarcely ever).
God, the only acceptable author, expressed Himself through the voice of His prophets, apostles and evangelists, who, in the current context, would not be eligible to
collect royalties, since they do nothing but record and transcribe. Like that of man
in Revelation, the role of those who write in the Scriptures has been effaced. And it
is on this condition that the Scriptures can perform. 'The Spirit', says Athenagorus,
'makes use of the prophets as the flautist does the flute.' Instruments produce the
divine music, but they must be eclipsed if it is to be heard as intended: as a
supernatural uncreated melody.

The idea of God, in our various theologies, whether negative or dogmatic, has
retained the stigmata of character. A hidden God, *Deus absconditus*? And for good
reason. It is always a specific individual who speaks. A voice is transparent and signed
in the first person; timbre and intonation tell all: age, sex, mood, and even the ulterior
motives of the speaker. No need for handwriting analysis to unveil them: intuition
suffices. A God who chooses to hide His face is thus condemned to graffiti, which is
the *incognito of language*. Yahweh the evasive conceals Himself in it as in a cloud or,
rather, as in a lightning-bolt concerning which one wonders after the fact where
precisely it fell. Moses, through a special act of grace, was able to see Him from
behind. 'But my face shall not be seen' (Exodus 33: 23). Indeed: an individual will be
able only to read Him, and then spend his life wondering what He may in fact have
meant. To see God from behind is to see Him once He has passed, already elsewhere,
post festum (when you read this, I will already be far away). Such is the difference
between a writing God and a speaking God. One can catch up with the latter, but
with the former, one always arrives like the police on the scene of the crime.

God the Incomprehensible – as He was called by John Chrysostom, who denounced every effort at elucidation as sacrilegious – *God the impenetrable*? A grapheme is unjustified. Capricious. Just as the print-image is the justified image of someone or something, so the arbitrariness of the symbol (in relation to trace or icon) adds to its ascendancy. Not knowing the authors of the Bible – the Pentateuch being conventionally attributed to Moses – augments its sacral quality vertiginously. Such is the argument by authority of 'as it is written', and not 'as was written by so-and-so at such and such a place and such and such a time'. As a reader, I find myself at the foot of a semiotic precipice, a peak of signs which I can only attempt to ascend, with many a subtle interpretation, but which entails a disproportion. I will never overcome it, this enigma, and when I believe I have deciphered all the meanings, there will still be one that eludes me. *Inaccessible, inexorable, intransigent God*? We can reply to someone who challenges us *viva voce*, but a sealed document descends on us like a meteorite. Who can pretend to outwit a holographic will (written in the hand of the bequeather)? 'It is written.' Inflexible. One is obliged to execute it, or forfeit one's honour and risk damnation. Every speech act calls forth another with which to retort, negotiate, inflect. The spoken word is an outstretched hand; the written word, a pointed finger. Fateful. Fiery letters on the wall. *Mene Tekel Upharsin*.

Plato, in his celebrated condemnation in the *Phaedrus*, emphasizes the regrettable aspects of written culture (enfeeblement of individual memories, humiliation of the ancients, irresponsibility of authors, profanation of mysteries, etc.), but no one would pretend that all its aspects are good. And Rousseau's rancour against the written, which corrupts the voice, travesties the authentic, and ends up 'subjecting God's word to the rules of grammar' and the priesthood, offers an echo twenty-five centuries later. The slow decadence of illiteracy has gradually brought the divine from a savage to a domestic state. Inner faith has been reified; the sacred trust has been arrested and frozen into dogma. The hierarchies of bookish knowledge rigidify the free circulation of affect. With, at the end, the cult of the Book, battles among the erudite, scholastic repetition. But let us not anticipate the agenda.

The Invisible One with His eye on us is said by the Bible to be forebearing and all-merciful. The All-Furious deems Himself 'slow to anger', but bears a strange resemblance to the bastard who observes every failure with an eye to punishment – indeed, to the tendentially paranoid sufferer from psychic rigidity. It is fortunate (for Him and for us) that His followers have tempered what seems ineluctably sadistic in a God concealed beneath a web of enigmas by canticles and psalms . . . . The sign by itself, stripped of all timbre, creates a pleasure deficit that the fluencies of ritual strive to alleviate. Our religions of the Book make up for it with gesture and song. And our ceremonies are what a voice is to a score, or melody to the rudiments of music. Everything that restrains and contains the disincarnation of the letter compensates with its corporeal plenitudes. It is the function of liturgy and its vibrant inflections to unpack and redeploy, in acoustic space, the ellipses of graphic compression, which go so far as to compact the Infinite into four consonants – the Tetragrammaton (YHWH), all-time champion of the *abstract*.

We do not find the clergy, dogma, or the Inquisition in oral society. An offshoot of the normalizing effects of script, 'the tyranny of the letter' ultimately gives rise to that of interpretation, and the clerical monopolies on commentary. Such is the ransom of mediological 'progress': the vector surreptitiously substitutes its own interests for those it strives to serve. It is the customary reversal of meaning by its vehicle. Every technological generation (writing, the printing press, electronics, digitality) is confronted by just such a subversion from within, worse than a full-frontal attack because it is unexpected and comes from behind. Hence the compensatory sequence of antidotes. The Christian tendril will emerge in time to balance the letter with love. An outgrowth of the Judaic, that plant that grows on rocky terrain will cause things to lean in a direction opposite the Word, towards the Flesh. By bringing about a greening of the arid, a feminizing of the Law. Consider it a rectificatory footnote, a recourse against a written God who has become, with the Pharisees, a bit of a hack.

The Milieu/Medium Deflagration

Let us summarize the long eastern odyssey. Up until the point of emergence from the dilemma. From 3000 to 400 BCE, in the span separating bulls of clay or inked stones from papyrus scrolls, while speaking bipeds, leading a happy and settled life, gradually mastered a system of notation, they had no need to migrate. And when others were obliged to pack their belongings in order to save their skins, they had no mnemonic devices at hand. That bind cut short the road to transcendence rather abruptly. Until the moment (as yet impossible to fix in a chronology and on a map) of the *short-circuit between migration and the alphabet, which produced the spark*. This forbidding environment was a springboard for the leap into the purely mental. The necessary condition for the blossoming in myriad minds of a sovereign acosmic Subject – on a wholly different level from the solar disk Aton, an as yet cosmic entity but not endowed with speech, a presymbolic god who gave life to men but remained mute and did not subsequently throw himself into the mêlée – was a minuscule detonator: the consonantal notation of thought (Semitic languages do not notate vowels). It was the contact between the desert and the spelling-book which ignited the monotheistic rocket, and we are still deriving benefits from the capacity of its thrust.

A holy alliance. A coalition of factors. A combination of circumstances. Let us forget at this point the linear order of mechanical causality. The milieu, the desert, suggests but does not impose. The medium, the written, authorizes but does not command. The Greeks used the medium, the Phoenician alphabet, and satisfied themselves with a pantheon of voyeuristic gods. The Arabs, before Islam, were accustomed to the desert, and remained animistic. It was the conjoining of tool and society which initiated the break, an alliance whose conditions were to be found neither on the banks of the Nile nor on the shores of the Euphrates. We may wonder why Mesopotamia – which has its desert marches in the north and invented, in the south, writing in the strong sense – was not the midwife of monotheism. It contributed greatly, as is well known, to its narrative models, which the Hebrews brought back from their stay there. Old Sumerian sources haunt the entirety of biblical cosmogony. The Noah of the first flood, for example, is a retelling of the Akkadian poem known as the 'Supersage' (composed around 1700 BCE). The story of Moses saved from the water is a duplicate of the legend of King Sargon of Akkadia (2200 BCE); Babel is a contraction of Babylon, which means, precisely, 'God's Gate', and their Towers parallel each other. The ziggurat is not so very far from our spires and steeples . . . . But it is quite a distance from the heavenly King of Kings, to whom the ziggurat offered a landing-stage at the centre of the city, to the omnipotent Yahweh whom we know, Even if the Most-High appears in the oracles of Balaam, and is not unknown to the Aramaeans, the civilizations of the interfluvial region remained polytheistic. And their centralized pantheon, a magnified – and human, all too human – reflection of their political centralization (Babylon, around 1750, was the capital of a unified kingdom). Why then did the Only One not enter through the Babylonian 'gate' to which He seems almost attached? Let us risk an interpretation: an excess of prosperity and fertility. Too much water, too much grain. Marshes, palm-groves, gardens, dykes, gates, silos, fortifications. The superpowers of Assur, Nineveh and Babylon were the spiritual victims of their temporal success. But God's game is loser-wins. Strengthened by their harvests, granaries, canals, terraces and sanctuaries, those dominant civilizations were too sure of their reserves, too caught up in their own undertakings, too inhibited by their own military might to be distrustful – and to rid themselves – of the inertia of the senses. To look for an *ersatz*, or a concentrate of divinity. Unchallenged, they failed to respond. To be sure, they took their gods out for a breath of fresh air on occasion, promenading their effigies from sanctuary to sanctuary on chariot or boat (the Egyptian solar craft) to tour the perimeters of their territory. Those tillers of the soil and fishermen had the means to stage a breakthrough – the wheel and written letters – but not the vital need. There was little strain in the relations between the brick-makers of Babylon, the boatmen of the Euphrates, and their Masters On High. Sheltered by crenellated ramparts and enamelled postern-gates, the Babylonian world lay on a thick bed of clay, much like its supports, which were often incorporated into its walls. Relatively little wood, but a profusion of bricks. How was one to overcome the temptation to build, and the false assurances provided by real estate? Read Herodotus (who none the less saw only the ruins of Babylon, where Alexander died): 'On each side of the river, the outworks extend their arms to the shore . . . . The city itself is filled with houses of three or four storeys; the streets cutting through it are straight . . . . The postern-doors are equal in number to the roads; they too are in brass and lead to the very edge of the river ... .' *Ex Oriente lux*, to be sure, but not in a straight line. From the end of the fourth millennium, according to archaeologists, the wheel and writing were available. What remained was to make of their combination a system of life and thought. But what was required in addition was a sense of threat and urgency. Secure behind their river-ramparts, protected from the desert, blinded by their own hegemony, burdened by hundreds of temples, altars and chapels, what need would an innovative population, but one showered with blessings, have had to break the numbing comfort of sedentary life? They were not grabbed by the throat, commanded to clear out, and compelled to improvise – lest they lose everything – a small box for God. A chest glimmering with gold to be carried on one's shoulders with two poles, and even suitable for placing on an oxcart. That nomadic psycho-object, the unknown masterpiece of a nation's furniture, would mark the improbable encounter, to the benefit of a God more snobbish than His predecessors, of the custom-made and the ready-to-bear.

5 Portable Yet Homebound

If I forget you, O Jerusalem,
let my right hand wither!
Let my tongue cleave to the roof of my mouth
if I do not remember you,
if I do not set Jerusalem
above my highest joy . . . .
(Psalms 137: 5–6)

In expelling the voluminous, which impedes displacement, monotheistic writing invented something prodigious: a portable God. Yet His worshippers would in short order tether the Holy Word to a Holy Land. From inscription to circumscription: that reversal would appear to bring into relief an invariant of human communities, be they agnostic or believing – the necessity of surrounding walls, of an enclosure, with the concomitant imperative of separation issuing from it. Such would be the 'Jerusalem syndrome'. The Holy City pits the two compulsive tendencies affecting monotheism – one to deracination, the other to establishment – against each other. The Moses complex and the David complex. To be sure, the 'eternal capital of Israel' has no monopoly on that ageless conflict (any more than Oedipus of Thebes has on the complex bearing his name). De te fabula narratur.

The Eternal, as He rises, is centrifugal. Every time His Eccentricity appears, it is in order to whisper to his confidants: 'You think you have everything here at home. Wrong! Your true home is not here. I await you elsewhere.' Abraham is the emblematic figure of that taking to the road as a calling oneself into question. Prompted by the heavenly xenophile who regularly chooses somewhat bizarre individuals as his messiahs. Those who are distrusted by their family or tribe ('no man a prophet in his own country'), the foreigner who doesn't fit in with his surroundings. Yahweh or the call of elsewhere, the contempt for the proximate. Far from his worshippers, He demands of them a tele-cult, the better to outstrip the narcissism of the sedentary, to upset routine with an appeal to the road. The characteristic pronouncement of the prophet: 'You who have escaped the sword, it's time to leave! Don't stop. Invoke the Lord from afar . . .'. The command thus issued to the sedentary to move on gives the chosen soles of wind, favouring at every turn transit, traffic and trade. Islam, Braudel reminds us, 'is *par excellence* a civilization of movement, of transit'. 'It would be nothing', he adds, 'without the routes traversing its desert body, animating it and infusing it with life.' But the road is worth little without an incitement to take to it, a 'clear out! lose yourself the better to find me'. How better to give us a desire to leave than through a Promise? To Abraham: 'I have given you everything from the Nile to the Euphrates.' After the carrot, the kick in the rear: 'Walk before me, and be blameless' (Genesis 17: 2). Meaning will no longer dwell behind, but in the future – whether collective, with Yahweh, or personal, with Jesus. In both cases, He who would have us march begins by having us hope. By warning us to remember His utterances wherever we go. Without resolving the question of the chicken and the egg – of whether the media of mobility precipitated His coming, or His advent precipitated their emergence – we may note that this Will-o'-the-Wisp has no greater enemy than parochialism.

What technical innovations are intent on accomplishing, as we have seen with the Internet and mobile phones, conceals what one may be allowed, indirectly, to do with them, which is not immediately apparent. Thus writing is vaunted as a memory-bin without any awareness that it propels the wheel. And yet the two function in tandem. Once the founding myths have been fixed, a collective belief can stop being a writ of house arrest. Worship in its specific site is no longer obligatory. Diaspora is no longer dilution. And in point of fact, after the fall of the kingdoms, the Judaean diasporas of Mesopotamia, Palestine and Egypt did not by any means interrupt (on the contrary!) transmission. Under the oral regimen, mythologies had affixed changing schemes of recitation, each version with its potential variant, to immobile supports, steles and statues. And now we find ourselves, once the Book has been compiled, with a canon *ne varietur,* combined with a mobile support, a small cylinder of engraved skin, which may be transfigured as a 'tree of Life' and 'pillar of the world'. Which allows for a virtualization of territory – without diminishing the feeling of affiliation. Writing lowers the politico-symbolic cost of mobility.

'As numerous as your cities, O Judah, are your gods.' Jeremiah's imprecation could have been addressed to all of Antiquity, with its divinities *intra-muros* and the names of god and place being substitutable for each other. Athena is from Athens, but the God of Abraham is not called the God of Hebron. Amon-Ra, who was cosmic, resided in Heliopolis, near the tip of the delta. Osiris, the god of vital impulses, dwelled in the Nekheb, further to the south. Anyone who consecrated himself to one or the other of those figures with restricted mobility was obliged to settle down near them. Specifically: to pile up quarry-stones, hew blocks, erect an altar, and congregate around it. Now the physical city is a political community and, by virtue of that fact, perishable. The affiliated divinities did not survive the *polis,* but our a-topical God did not burn with Solomon's temple, for the simple reason that He did not inhabit a sanctuary, but a scroll. He is to be found wherever a Jew prays and observes the Torah. Nebuchadnezzar, Antiochus and Titus all pass, but the hide remains. A few lengths of skin sewn together and rolled around a pole. The permanence and ubiquitousness of a God *accessible* wherever a *yad* followed the lines, a *sofar* was unrolled from right to left, or the Name was muttered in the dark. Words in place of stones extend the duties of the officiant, giving a divine vernacular a *scope of action* without precedent.

The God-Wagon

A wanderer cannot materially offer an altar or a statue to his Protector. Turning necessity into a virtue and misfortune into a source of pride, the inventive shepherd decides that his heavenly counterpart, unlike the *vulgum pecus* of surrounding deities, regards altar and statues as sacrilegious. Much as the 'bohemian' artist of 1850 in Paris converted his exclusion from the academy into a deliberate refusal of honours, the vagabond of the City-States proclaims that household gods are not worthy of him. No pedestal, no figurines. He thus compounds the censure of the social milieu with that of the supreme Law. That decisive turn would have been impossible had it not been propelled by the graphic.

What could be more gripping in the Shrine of the Book, in Jerusalem, where the Qumran scrolls are displayed, than those miniature squares of papyrus, the *tefillin* of the period (first century BCE), which are viewed through a magnifying glass, because the characters are between 0.5 and 0.7 millimetres in height? What could be more *divine?* Hebraic micrography is the exact opposite of the neolithic megalith. Like the *Urim and Thummim*, letters studded with precious stones and worn as a breastplate by wandering priests, which would disappear at the time of David. It is the inverse of the great stone structures exhibited by Celtic Europe, its menhirs and dolmens, its oversized burial mounds on which skulls and bedecked skeletons were piled. The colossi of Easter Island and the great Mycenaean constructs. The *tefillin, Urim* and *Thummim*, and *mezuzah* (the small scroll of calligraphed parchment affixed to the doorframe) are so many taunts directed at the pyramid of the Egyptian neighbour, a primitive and outlandishly large form of symbolism. The handwritten scroll contains no body; it does not serve as the emblem of an idea; it is an act of defiance aimed at massiveness. Now God can be perched on the head of a pin, not on a tombstone. The *meta is to be found in the mini.* Such would be the irony of the Infinite. He prefers the diminutive, the lower-case. Our ancestors, Gauls or Celts, honoured their ancestors by reserving the use of stone for them and keeping wood and vegetal matter for themselves, the living. They allotted *them* the noble matter, slabs and blocks on a huge scale. Thirty-six-ton megaliths impede our view of the beyond; the encapsulations of Qumran, at three milligrams, keep it ever so slightly open.

Bereft of any written accompaniment, our Breton mausolea remain as mute as oysters. If we take leave now of the night of forms in order to browse through a 'history of art', a register that is still petrified, but decipherable (through texts, myths and legends), what precisely are we told by the marble of friezes, the sandstone of colossi, the bronze or alabaster of statuary, the black diorite of victory steles? First of all, that the divine *weighs*. Whether big of breast or profusely buttocked, deformed or adorable, mother-goddesses, like Egyptian sphinxes or the androcephalic bulls of Khorsabad, are imposing and can be seen from afar. Their command of the surface is broad. A father is burdensome, but one can still carry him on one's shoulders, as Aeneas did Anchises. But how is one to hoist a chryselephantine Zeus or Pallas Athena on to one's back? No detachable parts, no joints. The first advantage of the *read* God over the *seen* god is related to scale: an increase in space. Jehovah offered this comparative advantage over other modes of transport: the history of the cosmos packed into a half-metre cube. His faithful can settle in or take off with it ('They left Raphidim and camped in the desert'.) This first step does not appear impressive, yet .... . An abyss separates the pyramid, the ziggurat, the magnificent postern-gate from the fine vegetal sheet smoothed with pumice stone. It is the one that separates a weak but immobile divine, unsuited to caravan travel, from a divine that has been simultaneously enriched and slimmed down. Our future was played out in the threefold perilous leap from the *in situ* to the *in petto*, or from the constructed sublime to the notational sublime.

The circulation of a minimalist and self-propelled God is linked to an apparatus whose originality is a function of its very banality. *The Holy Ark*, which was able to 'follow the Hebrews in the desert', from encampment to encampment, until the crossing of the Jordan, *in fine* – what precisely was it? Not a throne, but a simple wooden box, with a gold lid, the *kapporet*, topped by two small sculpted angels, the cherubim. A wooden chest, a camp trunk that can be carried by two or by four with horizontal support-poles. Or mounted on wheels. The Ark prompted the Word to climb aboard, a prosaic equivalent of the flying chariot in which Ezekiel sees the glory of the Lord (Ezekiel 10: 18). The eleventh-century Talmudic master Rashi said of such vehicles 'that they had no solid framework underneath, just occasional planks, like those we use for transporting wood'.[1] The discovery of the Dura-Europos frescos has subsequently confirmed such comments, which are, to be sure, all hearsay.

That nomadic object was not about to become a cult object out of mere whimsy. Small cause, great effect. Representations of the wagon of God have varied (those who painted it did not actually see it). In theory, it served strictly for the transport of scrolls of hide – a pastoral material if ever there was one – protected by a casing, the substitute for the original tablets. With the passage of time, it ceased to be a focus of attention. The support was so suited to the message that the latter lost interest in it. Noah embarked all of Creation on his ark, but he forgot the seeds of the trees with which he built his ark. This is what we do with the Law. For three thousand years we have been glossing the Ten Commandments, while forgetting one detail: the fact that the 'two Tablets of witness, Tablets of stone written with the finger of God' were lugged by Moses while he descended to the camp at the foot of the mountain. And broken *motu proprio* as he confronted the golden calf erected by Aaron. He would make duplicates, we are assured, with his own hands. Magnified by legend, those tablets would in fact have been made of rather common clay, of the Sumerian sort. Had they been similar to the Hammurabi Stele, the Law of Babylon, which weighs four metric tons and is two and a fifth metres high, Moses would have climbed the mountain in vain. He would have been obliged to leave the Law up there.

Concern for detail appears with the Almighty's very first words on Sinai. He is not an intellectual, but an operations specialist. He has nothing in common with those inspired graphomaniacs who offer you, when you are on a trip, a long way from home, their complete works in twelve bound volumes, with no concern for how you

---

[1] 'L'écriture et le livre d'après les écrits de Rachi', in *Le Livre et l'historien* (Paris: Droz 1997), p. 45.

are going to drag the additional pounds. Yahweh, for His part, puts His letter in an envelope. He thinks postal. For composition is nothing if you can't deliver into the very hands of the addressee (and this is the most difficult thing to do). We have known all too many of those contents without containers, those values without vectors. In this respect, Exodus (the second book of the Pentateuch, which forms its core) leaves nothing unexplained. It can be divided into three more or less equal parts. The first tells how Yahweh managed to bring the Hebrews out of Egypt, and ascend to the desert (1–15); the second what Yahweh had to say to Moses atop Sinai, the list of commandments, interdictions and allowances, or the Tablets of the Law (15–23); the third, what to do with those stone Tablets, where to put them and how to transport them (24–40). Yahweh is a meticulous, almost obsessive logistician (God is a virgin). In his eyes, the portage is as important as the package. Thanks to which Moses was able to come back down to his people properly equipped. Yahweh, both commander and foreman, spoke to him as one would to a cabinet-maker, a weaver or a carriage-technician, 'ruler' in hand (as He did with Noah, before the Flood). He furnished him with a copious blueprint (acacia wood, two and a half cubits in length, height and width one and a half cubits, gold rings here, bars there, etc.); then instructions for the lid, called a 'mercy seat', in Hebrew, *kapporet* (from the Akkadian *kaparu*, to cover over); and finally, the tabernacle in which to lodge it all, namely ten curtains of fine twisted linen, twenty-eight cubits long, four wide, and so on. (Everything is there: decorative cords, clasps, hooks, motifs.) And then a recommended reinforcement, with wooden planks, plus the disposition of doors, curtains, candelabras, hour-lines and cardinal points. For every strap its hinge. Fifty pages (in the Pléiade edition). Ikea has never produced a more precise assembly manual (even a fool can do it). All the more so in that considerations of balance enhance mobility. The collapsible object even undergoes transformation *in fine* into a travel guide, a beacon light, depending on whether or not the Cloud, Yahweh's Splendour, crowns the Tent. The last verses of Exodus: 'Wherever the cloud was taken up from the tabernacle, the Israelites would set out on each stage of their journey; but if the cloud was not taken up, then they did not set out until the day that it was taken up. For the cloud of the Lord was on the tabernacle that day, and fire was in the cloud by night, before the eyes of all the house of Israel at each stage of their journey.'

All of a sudden, the divine changes hands: is passed from the architects to the archivists. From a monument, it becomes a document. The Absolute recto–verso economizes a dimension, two instead of three. The result: the flat sacral (as miraculous as a squared circle). One metre twenty by seventy centimetres high, more than the ingenious invention of a baggage-handler, it was a form of life insurance. With the north pole in one's backpack, one could wander without ever losing one's bearings, submit to exile without betraying – one's Fathers and one's people. Be deported from one's memory-sites, without forgetting. To appreciate the scale of the innovation, think of Greek Antiquity, the example of an urban civilization in which the ostracized citizen, such as Oedipus, became a non-person. To leave one's household gods, altars and funeral urns was to sever an umbilical cord and see one's soul confiscated along with one's identity card. With its hand-inscribed bodyguard and two poles on its shoulders, the priestly people carries its Patriarchs on its back – without breaking its Ariadne's thread. Exile might still be painful; it was no longer destructuring. Thus were water and fire reconciled: *mobility and loyalty, errancy and affiliation.* The crucial bit of furniture could even be erected into a protective totem: the geometric centre of the military camp, rallying standard on the battle-field, reassuring palladium, potentially a trophy for the enemy in the event of defeat. With the Absolute in safekeeping, God in a chest, the place one comes from counts less than the place one is going to, in keeping with a history endowed with meaning and direction. Without such logistics, would the flame of monotheism have been able to survive so many routs?

It is understandable that the ban on representation – 'Thou shalt not make graven images . . . . Thou shalt not have any image of beast, bird, four-legged animal or fish' – should be formulated in the middle of Exodus, on the brink of a forty-year trajectory. Abstention from petrifying the divine was, for one of the faithful in the open country, without any assured shelter at each stage of his journey, with decades of tribulation to anticipate, a rather welcome bit of advice. 'If you don't travel light, you'll stay there.' Why should the interests of the body be harmful to those of the mind? The fasts and bans on foods of those obsessed with purity, who observe *kashrut*, which are excellent for the stomach and the intestine in a hot climate, similarly address considerations of hygiene (and the removal of the foreskin pre-vents infections of the male organ). Iconoclasm is well suited to the interests of the refugee for whom priority given to material questions will improve the prospects of reaching his destination. Statuary, icons, altarpieces, temples and capitals would have been so many weights chained to his ankle. But this is no longer the case when the wanderer ceases to be one, if he relaxes at an oasis, at the self-important village with its cumbrous effigies. For there is no city without its temple, and consequently without a Golden Calf. Is it not significant that the relapse into idolatry overtakes the Hebrews with each halt in an inhabited centre, when the Eternal stops being their 'rock' because they have come upon wood to carve or clay to mould? Such is Moses' presentiment when he comes to the Jordan and the people see on the other bank 'a land with flowing streams, with springs and underground waters welling up in valleys and hills, a land of wheat and barley, of vines and fig-trees and pome-granates' (Deuteronomy 8: 7). He knows that easy water, the desert equivalent of the easy money of the city, will place his God in danger; and with a full stomach, the essential void will give way to a realm of simulacra. Hear, O Israel:

Take care that you do not forget the Lord your God, by failing to keep his
commandments, his ordinances, and his statutes, which I am commanding you
today. When you have eaten your fill and have built fine houses and live in
them, and when your herds and flocks have multiplied, and your silver and gold
is multiplied, and all that you have is multiplied, then do not exalt yourself,
forgetting the Lord your God, who brought you out of the land of Egypt, out of
the house of slavery, who led you through the great and terrible wilderness, an
arid wasteland with poisonous snakes and scorpions. He made water flow for
you from flint rock, and fed you in the wilderness with manna that your
ancestors did not know, to humble you and to test you, and in the end to do
you good. Do not say to yourself, 'My power and the might of my own hand
have gotten me this wealth.'

Thus the premonitory threat. 'If you do forget the Lord your God, and follow other
gods to serve and worship them, I solemnly warn you today that you shall surely
perish' (Deuteronomy 8: 19). Moses had a foreboding of the poignant fate of a
people for whom insecurity is a synonym for spiritual strength, and established
might a synonym for an inner weakening . . . .

In Praise of Baskets

Monotheism excels in the arts and crafts of compaction. Pierre Janet (*Les Débuts de
l'intelligence*, 1932) saw in *basket behaviour* the origin of human intelligence.
Noah, who managed just in time to insert all of Creation into a kind of basket,
would certainly not have objected. Such is the specificity of the species: chimpanzees
pluck fruits one by one, but without gathering them. Provision/prevision. Nor do
animists, who glean their spirits along with things, collect their pickings. They live
for the moment. No container, no future. He who gathers anticipates. No stock, no
civilization. Noah gathers in order to preserve the past work of God. What is a
basket – or a floating container? Something astonishing. An artefact (originally in
wicker) which serves to: (1) concentrate the scattered, creating unity out of the
multiple; (2) convey the whole from one point to another. That specifically human
genius for miniature assembly was opportunely imparted by the Creator to Noah.
And the Hebrew people placed it in the service of its Protector (and, through Him,
of its own security) by inventing ingenious phylacteries, *tefillin*, small quadrangular
boxes in leather containing passages from the Bible, written in miniature in black
ink, attached to straps which the pious wear on their forehead and left arm (originally for the whole day, now during the morning service). Every religion needs
receptacles of some sort, given that it exists through its social function of regularly
distributing its containers of nourishment for body and spirit. That is how it fed-
erates, satisfying the double vocation of the 'religious', in which may be read in

Latin the indissociable duality of the act of assembling. *Relegere* is to collect residues, gather traces, accumulate. *Religare* is to bind individuals to each other, weave bonds. Whether secular or revealed, religion is the art of holding individuals together by tying them to a common foundation. There is no tethering of the individual to the collective that does not presuppose a weaving of myths and events. The use and manipulation of the basket satisfy those two imperatives. The basket safeguards and forewarns. It combines scruples (proceeds so that the past is not totally lost) and forethought (places the accumulated heritage at the disposition of one's descendants). Pious men are men with baskets since piety consists in preserving and disseminating. But in order to carry, as we have seen, one must first gather, reduce, condense, and it is transcription that reduces freight and carrying costs to a minimum.

To go right to the heart of the matter, and say everything in a few words, will remain the performance *par excellence* of the God of the West. He cuts out the superfluous. It is His trademark, and will even precipitate the emergence of the physicomathematical sciences in the seventeenth century. In the government of nature, via the laws of physics and mathematics, God can claim to be the friend of scientists and rationalists, facilitating their labours, which consist in fitting many phenomena into several algebraic formulae of extreme brevity. He works with an eye to economy, and satisfies Himself with what is strictly necessary (*ex pauca, tam multa*, in Leibniz's words). Parsimony of explanation, consisting of deducing many concrete applications from a very limited number of abstract principles, was no offence to a Being as sparing as He was of His presence (to the extent that even His name was not to be pronounced). An economy of means which is the height of pride. And a good calculation. The less one gesticulates, the better one transmits. Too taken with Himself to condescend to indulge in figuration, God renounces the sensible in order to lay claim to it. The genius of the Hebrews, by forswearing the prestige of visibility, turned that handicap to its advantage, by practising an *augmentative diminution* (the symbol says more than the thing): to scoop out in order to firm up. Yahweh gains in energy what He loses in mass. He renounces the dedication of things that are heavy. No steles and little epigraphy (in which the edifice serves as a substrate). *Ostracas*, ceramic fragments, which are the poor man's tablets, serve as mementos and sketches. But above all papyrus, sewn sheets that can be stuffed into a jar. The advantage of a corpus that is simultaneously mobile and immutable; you can move it around without damaging anything. A fertile paradox: a God that is movable but stabilized, punctilious and prone to wander (in the open sky or in the depth of a cave). Writing alone allowed the Hebrew people to be totally dispersed without losing its skin, memory and faith in the process.

From the Centrifugal to the Centripetal

Let us recall: he who goes to the wilderness comes from elsewhere and is going elsewhere. He emerges from it all the better in that the amorphousness of the Infinite diminishes his dependence on specific places. But the crossing itself is not infinite. Moses took off from a populous delta and expired at the age of one hundred and twenty on the plains of Moab, within sight of Bet-Peor, on the other side of the river. It was Joshua, according to the legend, who would take Jericho. As for him, he looked on the city from afar, from this side of the Jordan. Moses is the man of movement, not establishment. He resists settlement like a temptation. Better not to arrive; the most important thing is to tear oneself loose. Call it *the Moses complex*. We still need to understand how one makes the transition from Moses to David: from an ambulatory non-place, the Ark, to an obsessive site, Jerusalem; from a mystique of wandering to a strategy of occupation; and why messianic man cannot live on time alone – without, ultimately, a residence to refer to. The Holy *Land* is an ambiguous term, which plays on native soil, agricultural land, and national terri-tory. No doubt because it partakes of all three. But why sanctify a land? Answering that question requires us to leave the land of tools. More precisely: to disentangle, in the monotheistic skein, what partakes of the technical from what partakes of the political.

   We began our journey with the mobile ark and we arrive at the immutable Holy of Holies – the third chamber, the most recessed in the Sanctuary, in which only the high priest enters, once a year for Yom Kippur. Through what concatenation does a God who is technically decentralized by the Letter become – and to such an extent – a source of centralization? First of all, through the appeal of the soft to the hard and the mobile to the fixed for the sake of its physical preservation. The commanding centre of the tribes in march formation was initially no more than a tabernacle, quite simply a tent (*tabernaculum* in Latin). The 'meeting tent' that sheltered the Ark of the Covenant (which has become, for Christians, the small cabinet, with a lockable door, in the middle of the altar, containing the ciborium with the con-secrated wafers). Then, the shelter was in need of a shelter, of boards to protect the hangings, and of cut stones to protect the boards. In other words, of a temple. Point zero. The safe. As though an epidemic content, the sacred sign, were transmitting to its container its own *aura*, in a cascade of virulent metonymies, but in reverse, the whole for the part: the Ark for the scroll, the tabernacle for the Ark, Solomon's Temple for the Tabernacle, and Eretz Yisrael, the land of Israel, for the second Temple (rebuilt lavishly by Herod, and set ablaze by Titus in 70). Thus did the Document, the anti-monument, turn into the Hyper-monument. At once sanctuary and capital. Once the portmanteau-words were in position, the outlines of con-centric circles of sanctity, like so many halos, could be detected around them. The scroll sacralizes the Temple, which sacralizes the City of the Temple, which sacralizes the entire land of Israel. Centrality is a metastasis: from the Temple to the

City, and soon to the country, promoted to the status of center of the world. Such would be the ricochets of the uniqueness of the divine, whose small change is the expansion to the environs of the interdictions and rules on cleanliness: one must not allow dogs to enter the holy city (any more than leopards, foxes and hares, or even their hides, the Graeco-Syrian king Antiochus III specified in a proclamation), because they are proscribed in the sanctum of the Sanctuary. The Qumran scroll, known as the Temple scroll, adds that anyone who has slept with his wife or has had an ejaculation will abstain from entering the city of the Temple for three days (same restriction if he has touched a corpse). Every blind man will be banned for life. But that also means, as noted by a second-century Talmudist (Abodah Zarah 4, 3–6) 'that to live in the land of Israel is equivalent to all the *mitzvoth* of the Torah, and he who is buried in Israel is as though he had been buried under the altar of the temple'.[2] Contagion does not have only negative sides.

The umbilicus in the middle of the sands produces a contrastive space, a hardened centre and blurred margins. It radiates from an untouchable nucleus, but one with elastic borders. The people of the desert are as ignorant of natural frontiers as of state boundaries. Even today, the State of Israel, like a people on the march, does not recognize any definitive boundary for itself (and it is true that the limits of the ancient kingdoms varied over the course of centuries). Contrary to Roman space – which was defined juridically in and by *fines*, legalized territorial limits, for which the notion of *limes* had a structural function, in which the centre, Rome, was defined by its periphery – monotheistic space is 'a circle with extendable and contingent limits, constructed from a necessary point', Jerusalem, in which the periphery is defined as a function of the centre. But there are different kinds of centres. Rome kept itself sedentary, as the centre of an identifiable zone of civilization that was *closed* (specifically to the *frisson* of the infinite), a centre that instinctively called for dogmatic and geographic systematization. Jerusalem, in the grips of the 'nomadic', radiated a variable and negotiable space from a non-negotiable centre, an anchorage open both to the infinite above and to the indefinite below.[3] There was a second Rome, Byzantium, and even a third, Moscow. For a pious Jew, there is not, nor could there be, a second earthly Jerusalem. Christians, Simon Mimouni has noted, were to spiritualize, shortly thereafter, the City of reference – and all the more easily in that the Romans had just destroyed it. For them – and that is what already distinguished the spirit of Christianity – it was not indispensable to rebuild it, as the Pharisees aspired to. But so deep was the rooting of the prophetic in the soil that

---

[2] Quotation from a lecture by Simon C. Mimouni at the colloquium 'Les Villes saintes, Jérusalem dans les consciences juives au Ier et IIème siècles de notre ère', Collège de France, May 2001.

[3] Umberto Eco, 'La ligne et le labyrinthe: les structures de la pensée latine' in *Civilisation latine. Des temps anciens au monde moderne*, ed. Georges Duby (Paris: Olivier Orban 1986).

when John, in his Apocalypse, sees the new Jerusalem descend from the heavens, he has it land on the site of the old one.

Founded in the Canaanite period at the beginning of the Bronze Age (around 3000 BCE), 'Rushalimum' appears for the first time in an Egyptian text of the Twelfth Dynasty, around 2000 BCE. The Pentateuch mentions the town of Salem, not far from Mount Moriah, the alleged site of the legendary sacrifice, assimilated to the Temple Mount. David expelled the former occupants, thus allowing his son Solomon to erect the Temple, or to rededicate the temple that was already there to his God. To what end? As a home for the Ark of the Covenant. The Tablets of the Law disappeared in the sacking of the city, and thus the second Temple, rebuilt on the site of the first, upon losing its first justification, discovered its essential vocation: as a compass. Structuring a space of affiliation around an anchoring point. Since the audacity to make a new ark was lacking, as a substitute, the *kapporet,* the 'mercy seat', was refabricated, a lid transformed into a pedestal and placed in the Holy of Holies as a support for the expiatory rites of Yom Kippur.[4] Wherever Jews might be, thereafter, they were to pray facing the City 'chosen by God so that His name be honoured there', whose axis was superimposed on the Aron, the niche carved into the wall of the Synagogue facing the City, in which the Torah was to be found. A religious space is not Euclidean but 'anisotropic', endowed with gradients, from the high pressures of the centre to the peripheries. This does not confer the same affective properties on all zones (the 860 square metres of the Temple Mount are more controversial and harrowing than the entire territory of Gaza). The polarity cosmos/chaos, habitat/uninhabited characterized the pagan *oekomenos*, which repressed the savage beyond the *limes*. But an aptitude for travel made the desolate less repulsive, and the populated less attractive, since, in the desert, a readable God might very well feel at home. Nevertheless, everything transpired as though agricultural enclosure plagued the herder like a debt. As though the return of the *local repressed* struck the dislocated more harshly than it did others. As though the monotheistic liftoff was to be paid for by a more severe landing than that experienced by autochthonous polytheism, which assumed from the outset the affability of things and the magic of places. Heavy would be the geopolitical cost of uniqueness. One God, one people, one land. A tabernacle, Zion. The One in His Onliness expels the rhizome; it craves roots. In the eyes of Joshua and Ezra, small sanctuaries, scattered as at Arad in the Negev or on the Elephantine Isle near Aswan, perhaps inherited from the neolithic, are a blot and a sign of disorder, offensive to God. Woe to the secondary or tertiary centre. From Babylon, where he seethed, Ezekiel had a vision of the future temple, and was intent on seeing only one – luminous, definitive and exemplary. Shame on the sanctuaries of Garizim, near Nablus, and Leontopolis, in Egypt. That plural was to be buried in the 'Valley of the Multitude' of Gog and

[4] See Jean-Michel de Tarragon, 'La Kapporet est-elle une fiction ou un élément du culte tardif?', *Revue biblique* (1981), pp. 5–12.

Magog. We know, through Flavius Josephus, the price paid by the Samaritans, bearers of pre-exilic traditions, for having wanted to worship God on their own: eradication.

The Monotheistic Paradox

It is always disconcerting to see religions refined and elevated to a measure of abstraction clinging tooth and nail to a rectangle measuring fifteen paroxystic hectares. Coming from the people who, more than any other, freed the realm of spirit from the petty chauvinisms of the land and its dead, such an obsession is unexpected. And all because David, three thousand years ago, tired of dragging his oxcart, abandoned at the frontier of the land of the Philistines after the disaster at Shilo, then negligently stored in a series of houses, decided one fine day to put a stop to his travels in Jerusalem (Samuel 2: 5), which was equidistant from the two tribes of the South and the ten of the North. He had, after all, to allow the people that had just consecrated him king to graze somewhere. And so it was Zion, from which he cavalierly expelled the Jebusites, settling into their fortress and 'building all around'. There did he erect his house, assisted by Hiram, King of Tyre, 'with cedarwood, carpenters, and stone-cutters for the walls'. Relaxation. 'See now,' he then said to the prophet Nathan, 'I am living in a house of cedar, but the ark of God stays in a tent' (2 Samuel 7: 2). The Lord then felt scorned, and asked Nathan to have a residence built for Him of hard materials. 'For I have not lived in a house since the day I brought up the people of Israel from Egypt, but I have been moving about in a tent and a tabernacle.' Thus David built him a temple in his turn. Then he made war, annexed other cities, consolidated his territory. Forty years of wandering for Moses, forty years of reign for David the sedentary, thirty-three of them in Jerusalem, the City of the Temple. Once one has unpacked, one doesn't move again. The camp was eliminated. *Pro aris et focis.* Or the opposite of the Moses complex: what counts is to stay put and make a show of force. Call it the *David complex.* The two are in perpetual counterpoint and combat. A contemporary translation: the party of movement and the party of order. (In contemporary Israel, Yeshayahu Leibowitz the Prophet, and Ariel Sharon the King.)

Just as the need to materialize catches up with the most committed spiritualist in the form of rosary, breastplate or amulet, so the need to localize imposes itself on the migrant or expatriate as soon as he is constrained to abolish his present in order to rediscover the past, binding them to each other through an epic. The most deracinated are the first to play up the question of roots (recently arrived immigrants, above all from America, constitute the lion's share of fundamentalist settlers). Yahweh was aware of humanity's collective unconscious when He threw up the distant mirage of possession *ad vitam aeternam* (although on condition that the contract be respected) of a land flowing with milk and honey. 'If you observe my commandments, I will bring you to the place I have chosen for my name to dwell there.' The centrifugal people of the *sukkah* – the temporary hut set up on a balcony or in a garden for eight days during the feast of 'booths', *Sukkoth*, commemorating the wandering in the desert – has curiously arrogated to itself a messianism more centripetal than the norm. While the adept of Saint Paul awaits the reign of God over all the earth, that of Samuel awaits it at home, surefootedly, in *Eretz Yisrael*. The first article of the declaration of independence proclaimed in the Knesset: 'The land of Israel was the birthplace of the Jewish people. Here their spiritual, religious, and political identity was shaped. Here they attained to statehood, created cultural values of national and universal significance, and gave to the world the eternal Book of Books' (Tel Aviv, 14 May 1948).

In a monotheism *stricto sensu*, with neither hearth nor home, there should in theory be no holy cities, no sacred stones, no taboo sites. No hilltops more inspired than others. For the Spirit listeth where it will. Holiness of heart and memory of the word ought to dispense with the dumb fixity of inert things. Thus should it be, but thus is it not. The theory does not apply in fact. And reason protests. What was the good of dislodging God from nature, through writing, if He simply returned to govern men with stones? If one is obliged once again to kill and to die, like a pagan, to safeguard an empty sepulchre here, a mosque there, or a wall, the *kotel*, dubbed by Christians 'the Wailing Wall' – and what indeed could be more surprising than a wall in the face of the Unlimited? Herod, whose temple-barracks was situated at the *limes* of the Empire, facing the threat from Persia (the great ally of the Jews), was not exactly a model of independence. But above all, did the Infinite not come among us in order to shatter the old law of land surveys and protective walls? And free us from the entrancing spells of the past? Why then kiss the wall with one's lips, as the orthodox, with their curls and black robes, do every day of God's creation?

Topographical superstitions have their reasons of which monotheistic reason ought to know nothing, but which impose themselves on it whether it likes it or not. Here we touch on an enigma, which some call a 'scandal'.[5] Protestants – who renounce pilgrimages and relics – also have a tendency to shield their eyes against the return of the geophagous repressed. The sixteenth-century European reformers could not have cared less about going off to liberate the Holy Sepulchre. The reading-places of the reformed were not *loca sancta*. Anyone who derives nourishment from the Word is a bit less inclined to fetishize this or that hill, vestige, or pile of rubble. Protestantism overestimates words and underestimates stones. That is both its strength and its weakness. It produces more philologists than archaeologists. More hermeneutical essays than exploratory digs. The fetishization of the sign (*sola Scriptura*) is normal – a reality to which intellectuals of the confession owe their specificity. Every system of beliefs sanctifies the circumstances of its birth. The evangelists were too attached to words to idolize woods, as though exegesis freed

[5] Rabbi David Meyer, 'Ni terre promise ni Terre sainte', *Le Monde*, 9 January 2001.

them from folklore. Thus, if one of the reformed travels to Jerusalem, whose recollection he admires, it is more as someone who is curious about (lapsed) 'memory-sites' than with the soul of someone who is flayed alive. He was not party to the Quarrel of the Holy Places. None the less, it remains the case that Lutherans, Calvinists and Anglicans also have in Jerusalem their churches, 'garden tombs', institutes and outposts.

The Jerusalem Syndrome

There are *places of truth*, like the moments of the same name. The former have over the latter the advantage or the disadvantage of remaining in place, if not in the same state. They petrify contingency. King David left only one address: the Old City. The place where all the dead at the end of history will be called on to be reborn remains fully visible, unforgettable, teeming with life. And the truth unveiled in that passionate and passion-provoking site – crowned by the Esplanade of the Temple and Mosques – deserves close inspection – not despite but because of the fact that it is neither beautiful to behold nor good to hear. And remarkably difficult to *think* (like every conundrum that obliges one to think against oneself).

The mount where God lives, predestined site of unity and *summum* of division, where five hundred video cameras, inserted under roofs, keep an eye on the children of Abraham? A message of universal love whose adepts are motivated by hatred of neighbour and cousin? Moralizing is not enough. There where the dark side of a God of light is revealed, we would do better to dispense with colour photos and sermonizing clichés, and confront reality – metal barriers, barbed wire and fortified terraces. Strange: the bounds of the Infinite. The residence of the Unlimited converted into a jailer's paradise, in which the struggle to occupy every square inch of terrain occupies every minute. Jerusalem: a city in which, from one neighbourhood to the next, people don't speak to each other, don't even see each other; where the concern for division, between the four sectors – Jewish, Christian, Armenian and Muslim – into which the city is split, is at its most obsessive. If the Eternal had remained upstream from His tribes, understanding would reign among those who pray to Him in churches, mosques, or at the Wailing Wall; and the pious celebrations of the brotherhood of Abraham would not ring so false. All believers would be able to pray in their own language, but side by side, and without spying on each other. If the place were in conformity with its concept, it would belong to no one in particular, but would float above the fray like an enclave of grace. And the supranational status of *corpus separatum* that the United Nations had conceived for the Holy City in 1948 (Resolution 181) would prevail. The site of the sanctuary, of which Elie Wiesel felt entitled to observe that it 'miraculously transforms every man into a pilgrim', would not be available for appropriation, unless by the UN. It would be neither divided in fact nor divisible in theory. All the elect of Revelation would bathe there in the sweet light of dawn. That miracle occurs solely in our edifying editorials and lay sermons.

Beyond the customary paradox (the monotheistic utterance contradicting its message), what troubles us in that theocratic enclosure – more akin to a battlefield than to a crypt, in which each religious order defends its national colours tooth and nail – is to see the emergence of the unthought ethnic presuppositions of religious adherence, as well as the strategic underpinnings of theology. The derision of doctrine by circumstance. The history of the Only God, in Jerusalem, goes nowhere; it has become a cartography, and a demography.

Between two alleys in the Christian quarter is lodged, without any particular ostentation, the Holy Sepulchre, an unattractive and complicated sanctuary constructed at the alleged site of Golgotha by Constantine, and destroyed and rebuilt ten times over since. It is a miniature holy city, a maximum of differences in a minimum of space, a labyrinth of latticework screens, a maze of contested borders, trespasses and acquired rights (rights of presence, celebration, procession, etc., which the briefest suspension can invalidate). Every square metre is a subject of contention. With its numerous chapels, oratories, reliquaries, stairways, balconies and terraces, the neurotically territorialized Holy Sepulchre is divided into common parts and restricted parts, affiliated with each of the seven Christian communities charged with custodial upkeep: Abyssinians, Armenians, Copts, Greeks, Latins and Syriacs. The prerogatives of each are established by the *status quo* of 1852, which is still in force, from a time when the Sublime Porte arbitrated conflicts between the Churches and the European powers. Candles of different widths and lengths are lit according to which community one belongs to. The principal cleavage opposes the Orthodox, who have been installed there without a break since Byzantium (and for whom this sanctuary is a bit like their own Jerusalem or Rome) and the Latins, installed since 1853, represented essentially by the fearsome Franciscans, who are solidly implanted in the holy sites. As for the dust-ups between brothers and sisters, brandishing crooks and crosses on the *Via Dolorosa*, the skirmishes and vexations that the co-tenants of the Sepulchre visit on each other, endlessly preoccupied with containing and spying on each other (the most impoverished, who are also the senior members of the Christian faith, Ethiopians and Copts, having been pushed back on to the roofs, into humble shacks surrounding the crypt of Saint Helen), a theologian may choose to see in them no more than a form of folklore for tourists and journalists. A shrug of the shoulders is akin to a denial. To avoid confronting the symptom of a compromising repetition compulsion in the psychopathological sense ('an uncontrollable process, of unconscious origin, through which the subject repeats painful archaic experiences without remembering their prototype and with the firm conviction that, on the contrary, such behaviour is fully and solely motivated by present circumstances'). Is not the archaic precisely that which is destined to return as soon as one looks elsewhere?

Beyond its picturesque aspect, the trapezoidal city, with its eight fortified gates and bossed stone wall, should pose a problem for postmoderns deluded by a romanticism of the nomadic. Shepherds want to go home too. No kinetics without a corresponding statics. One takes to the road only in order to stop somewhere, the promise of every land ought to be kept, and the alien is a native in sufferance (just as the healthy person is merely someone who is unaware of his illness). The arena of controversy, our theological corral, reveals the utopia of an a-topical God. In strict doctrine, the Infinite should remain extrinsic to the finite. The opposite is called idolatry. But what does the daily newspaper teach us if not that the supreme void also is in need – like any other Baal, Pargali or Mazda – of visible and tangible boundaries (enclaves, green line, checkpoints)?

We Are All Mammals

Why the confinement of the Infinite? Perhaps because it is not enough to believe in Heaven to cast off the trappings of an earthbound mammal. A religious animal, to be sure, but the adjective, in its glory, eclipses the noun, which takes a malign pleasure in reminding us of itself. Ethology (the science of the behaviour of animal species in their natural environment) informs us of the territorial habits of baboons and whales. Through what miracle would we be exempt? And yet revolts against animality (nationalism, chauvinism, ethnicism) are so repugnant to us that we deem pathological reflexes concerning which it would hurt our pride to admit just how banal they are, from the zoological perspective. We are beginning to penetrate the biological mechanisms that govern, in the individual, the maintenance and defence of the integrity of the self against the non-self (in tissue transplants, for example, or when confronting specific viruses or bacteria). As yet we do not know very much about the markers of collective personalities, antigens of the *we*, immune responses to the *non-we*. The only thing we can surmise is that they are linked to territoriality. Perhaps because the stability of a haven or shelter protects us from the evanescence of time, by consoling us for dying. Rocks relieve doubt. Like a dyke against entropy, against our own propensity to amnesia, against the geological erosion of our testimonial mounds. An antiquity visible to the naked eye – the hill of Zion and the valley of Josaphat, concerning which the Book informs us that one day the nations will be judged there – dispels our anxieties of loss. The Promise is uncertain, but its stakes can be seen, measured and touched. And that is what guarantees Jewish *continuity*, despite the diaspora and the Shoah. The Mount of Olives and the Holy Sepulchre guarantee Christians *de visu* the continuity and the solidity of their faith (since the fifth century), beyond the splintering of rival communities (Latins, Copts, Armenians, Syriacs, Greeks, Abyssinians). For Muslims, Al-Quds and the Dome of the Rock attest to the continuity and unchanged unity of Islam, despite the fratricidal conflicts between Shiites, Sunnis, Ishmaelites, and so on. Every localization diminishes us, to be sure, but it allows us to exist for others and for ourselves. Or rather, the dumb persistence of a site facilitates the *prolongation of perseverance* necessary for awaiting an accomplishment, be it 'millennium' or 'Second Coming', perennially postponed until the morrow. When the anticipated does not occur, a borderline, a demarcation palpable to eye and foot – we, here; them, there – renders the disappointment acceptable. Beautified by distance, by the deportation to Babylonia, the Mother City looms like an uncorrupted dream, recharging our batteries. The attachment reinvigorates, the harsh consoles for the soft, and our disorientation clings to such cardinal points. 'Here David stopped.' 'There, in that cave near Hebron, Abraham buried Sarah ... .' Fools who pretend to invalidate a religion because of its anachronisms mistake what is a good for an evil. It is the very function of myths to repair in us the damages of time. If a religion were not ana-chronistic, it would lose its most profound *raison d'être*, which is to dress the wounds of our finitude by giving yesterday a dimension akin to *always*.

More than anything else, God likes to gather. 'Enlarge the space of your tent, let the canvas of your homes be distended' (Isaiah 54: 2) The people must be gathered in Jerusalem 'like a single man. ... For my house will be called a house of prayer for all peoples' (Isaiah 56: 7). That pious wish is comforting, but it goes beyond the means of its end. An error of omission. It chooses to see – or, rather, write – only half the programme, not its application (which is implemented in silence through a combination of modesty and hypocrisy). For in practice, *it is impossible to bring together without dividing*. To galvanize some without bruising others. The God of Israel promises to ravage all the nations that do not obey Him. Judah will be restored against them all (Jeremiah 24: 5–7). If I consecrate, I separate. If I separate, I set apart as holy. A people apart needs a space apart. Religion binds, to be sure, such is its definition; but in order to do so, it antagonizes. And if it did not divide, it would not bind. As Odon Vallet has written:

> to agglomerate a crowd is to capture an audience, to empty one sanctuary for another, exhaust one clergy to the benefit of its rival. Every new follower of a church is unfaithful to another one. Every militant of a cause becomes the enemy of the adverse cause. Wars of religion are the bloodiest of all when they amalgamate ideas and men to constitute confessional factions. They can be broken only through beatified murder. 'Happy shall they be who take your little ones and dash them against the rock' (Psalms 137: 9).

Might the universal not be coextensive with the universe? For the members of a community of filiation, like the Jews – even more than in a community of vocation, such as the Christians – reference to the Holy Name, blessed be He, ought to be sufficient. Why not an address of 'general delivery' for Him who sees us from everywhere? When one dwells in the ubiquitous, what importance can a residence have? Alas, *Homo religiosus* apparently fails to break free of *Homo politicus*, duly surveyed, reticulate, and perpetually primed for conflict. The One for all, so called, is always the province of a few (like the meaning of a thing). Escape from that all-too-human mosaic is impossible, to the extent that no universal religion has ever been deduced from a universal God – except in the minds of a few illuminati. The Eastern churches, who choose their own patriarch, admit as much: in Greece, Serbia, Russia, Romania, etc., there is an overlap between ethnic and religious identity. Whether defensive or not, the Orthodox nationalisms play their game honestly. But do not the denominations of the West, which are more subtle or discreet, behave in exactly the same way? We begin to wonder whether *religion* is not a word which promises more than it delivers. Whether our great symbolic implementers of connection are not ways of casting in a positive light an endemic evil, which we seem intent on diminishing through a variety of devaluations (by way of idiosyncrasy, folklore, local colour). And what if, finally, *genius loci* were the poetic name for a rather unimpressive *fatum*, which is the difficulty of our beliefs (as opposed to our forms of knowledge) in making do without a habitat, in being valid for all? In that case, when it comes to universal religions, those beautiful lies, there would (and could) be only specific cultures with greater or lesser propensities to expansionism and annexation. By 'cultures' we should understand networks of correspondence conjoining myths, places, and jealous ethnic groups. Those networks, which lie side by side or interlock without perceiving each other, are neither interchangeable nor superimposable (and it is they that are unique, not the God on whom they confer their own uniqueness as a justification for their own). We may congratulate ourselves in that the 'international community' is able to promulgate a moral code of virtually universal applicability (the Universal Declaration of Human Rights), provided we bear in mind the fact that legal norms are weak in their capacity for unification. It is when a unifying bond is strong that we can talk about a specifically religious bond, but in that case there will be customs posts and front lines, be they ideal (defence of orthodoxy) or physical (defence of territory). Monotheism, like the others, yields to the manias of exclusion that it is, moreover, quick to condemn elsewhere (the intolerant one is always the other). Do not the geopolitics of faith signify, *in fine*, the submission of the flock to its pasture? No doubt it is a very good thing that a person from a particular culture is intent on maintaining his cultural identity, his eyes fixed firmly on his birthplace (or what he deems his birthplace), much as a debtor wishing to honour an ineradicable debt would never stop acquitting himself of it through pilgrimages, gifts and communitarian excesses (and this would be all the more emphatically the case when one decides to keep oneself at a distance from the fold). It is a very good thing that the Holy City, destroyed seventeen times over, has been rebuilt just as often by its children. But the God who has chosen His lodging there seems sarcastic indeed. When He opens up a corner of the planet, ever so slightly, to a bracing sea breeze, it is in order the better, on the morrow, to slam the door shut in the face of all those with no claim on his native land.

We would prefer to think that such fixations on land, demands of exclusivity, with their paranoid and persecutory aspects, bore witness to a bygone nightmare, a phase of humanization that had already become obsolete. And that with the Internet, the Airbus, the Dow Jones and the migratory flows, 'globalization' was smoothing away the unfortunate rough edges of identity neuroses and fundamentalist enclaves. This does not seem to be the case. It is enough to wander through the Old City to understand that cyberspace and the exploits of collective intelligence have done no harm to the instinct for demarcation. In fact, they awaken it, more tense, more grating than it was in the nineteenth century, the age of old-style nationalisms. In the 'territories', as they are called, with unintentional aptness, internauts, the children of Abraham or Ibrahim, pray to the same God, but one commemorates as a catastrophe (the Nakba) what the other celebrates as a benediction (a State). Truth on this side of the Jordan, error on the other, as Pascal might have put it. As though the Most-High needed an airport. As though He could attain true bliss only by preventing the bliss of the other. And the proof of this can be seen at the precise spot where all the elect were supposed to gather for the Second Coming, to celebrate, in love, the defeat of the Antichrist . . . . What a pity, Alphonse Allais once said, that cities were not built in the country. Or the heavenly Jerusalem was not brought down a peg or two . . . .

Why should we be surprised, then, that the unification of the peoples of the Book is the horizon that recedes along with the advance of the ecumenical marcher? And that between Judaism, Islam and Christianity there is so great a gulf separating official acts and 'goodwill gestures'? Or that the Roman Catholic Church continues to abstain from sitting majestically on the Ecumenical Council of Churches, which brings together Lutherans, Anglicans, Protestants and the Orthodox, in Geneva? Technologies of communication everywhere seem to whip up the ardours of slumbering antagonisms. Is the Only One our greatest hope for the reconciliation of all human lambs beneath the same shepherd's crook? But the abyss separating the heavenly Jerusalem from our own spans the hiatus between what we are intent on *thinking*, within the false light of doctrine, and what we cannot fail to *do*, in keeping with the chiaroscuro of our feelings. A complex (be it of Oedipus, Moses or David) is an 'organized set of representations and memories, with a high affective charge, and partially or totally unconscious'. It repels us, and it motivates us. Let us not forget to remind our adorable polymorphously perverse cherubim to love their mum and respect their dad. But let us not fail to realize that when the day comes, those dear little blond heads will not be averse to raping Mum and murdering Dad.

The Realpolitik of God

The so-called irrational elements of human behaviour should not be regarded as inexplicable (lest one fall into irrationalism oneself). A personal complex, Freud *dixit*, is constituted on the basis of the interpersonal relationships of one's infantile history. That history determines the way in which the person finds his place in the family, and appropriates it. The gesture of implantation, in which the sign is seized by the soil, partakes, for its part, of a political complex. It affects collectives, not individuals. It is clearly not specific to Hebraic culture (any more than the Oedipus complex is specific to Greeks), but it finds in a singularly long history of dis-possessions, ghettos and persecutions the wherewithal to nourish itself and amply affirm its value. A complex of this sort is constituted, in each community, on the basis of the intercollective relations of its protohistory. Although they are accidental at the outset, those relations determine its future, and specifically the imaginary place which that community arrogates to itself in its space of reference. The Bible is replete with such 'primal scenes', scenarios which are half-real, half-fantasized, and apt to generate anxiety (the failure of Moses) as well as joy (the reign of David), without it being possible to separate clearly, in episodes that have been constructed to traumatize or galvanize, what has been fantasized from what has been recorded.

The solidification of the wooden ark into a stone temple was no doubt inscribed in the formation of the Lord of Lords as a shield of identity. Now, if one is to have an identity, one is better off having a territory, and if one is to have a territory of one's own, one is better off treating one's neighbour as an adversary. The starry vault above is not enough. Aristotle's 'prime mover' alone is capable of remaining an abstract universal, but that mover moves only things, not people. A Christian professes that God is graspable only through the mediation of the community that has recognized itself historically in Him. Ought we not to reverse that proposition? The Judaean community came to grasp itself through the mediation of the biblical Eternal, whose impregnable transcendence permitted it to forge, in all immanence, its collective personality. This is why the need for a God who is One is revived in times of misfortune. It is the ultimate talisman of critical moments and places, imposing itself at frontiers and behind the lines in the wake of catastrophes. A threat of dispersion, through an immune reflex, provokes regrouping. Hence the openly polemical tone of this God of self-defence, to the extent that any *we* affirms itself by opposing itself to a *them*. To be a Jew is not to profess a doctrine, but to share a culture. 'To declare oneself a Jew', Blanchetière observes, 'is not to confess a personal faith, but to declare oneself solidary with a community.' And thus to practise the rites and repeat the gestures that tend to distinguish us from our neighbour, far more than our private thoughts or beliefs. 'More than beliefs, it is rites which weave the protective web of Jewish identity. These rites trace a dividing line (between Jews and Gentiles). They form a link among all the subgroups. By binding the generations to each other, they perpetuate group identity.'[6]

Victor Hugo: 'Every bird story ends with a cat.' A God flies off, and behold: an army, a state, or a church . . . . Does the victory of sign over soil end with its

[6] Francis Schmidt, *La Pensée du Temple* (Paris: Seuil 1994), pp. 14–15.

reversal? A Being whose essence is violent entry enclosed into and by his parish? The well-intentioned (one would like to be of their number) who want to 'free the holy places from the vicissitudes of the political and reciprocal exclusions' forget one detail: reciprocal exclusion is constitutive of the sanctity of such places. As stipulated by the etymology of the word: what is 'sanctified', 'holy', is what is set *apart, separated* from the profane and the impure. Might there not be, in the very notion of the sacral, a germ of apartheid? Western diplomats who work on the status of Jerusalem, who deplore the spectacle 'on both (Jewish and Muslim) sides of a religious appropriation of political questions', project the modern idea of secularism on to cultures which are quite at a loss to distinguish the religious from the political, for the very good reason that they *owe their existence to a mixing of genres*. In the Holy Land, a distinction of levels seems as necessary as it is impossible. God, a born extremist, is the diplomats' worst enemy. Quite apart from the fact that His decrees are irrevocable, the Absolute will not allow anyone to relativize matters.

The young Israeli recruit who has taken an oath to the flag upon entering Tzahal, the Israeli army, receives her Bible along with her gun. The Cross in the Russian army. *Gott mit uns.* During the Cold War, the American Senate incorporated 'one nation under God' into the Pledge of Allegiance, and shortly thereafter the Federal Bank began minting dollars with the inscription: 'In God we trust'. Polytheism relaxes ranks; mono- closes them. One is a matter of options; the other an obligatory ordeal. The former does not favour communitarian mystiques, but is more agreeable for individuals in daily life, whose civic solidarities it atomizes. A polytheist may, if it suits him, play one god off against another. Should a misfortune, hail or the plague, befall the city, the god responsible does not compromise the others in his eyes. Should he himself fall ill, he will assume that it is his own fault for not having done what was required for one protector or another. Monotheism, on the other hand, exacts a price for its undeniable advantages as political federator in the form of considerable perturbations of a moral order; for evil is necessarily on *its* account, without any possible alibi or evasion. If the only God allowed Auschwitz, what should we think of His justice … ? But let us not skip over centuries. In the short term, strategy is of cardinal importance. Thus the strategists of the Jewish people, and first of all the intelligentsia of scribes in charge of collective destinies, turned themselves into its heralds. Those soldiers of identity were trained by a hostile external milieu – Egypt, Babylonia or Palestine. The distress of exile has always made for the best patriots (Bolívar and Miranda realized they were Venezuelans in Paris, just as San Martín, later on, realized he was an Argentine), since the farther away one is, the more one idealizes the homeland. The best (and the purest) part of Judaism came from the Diasporas. On the banks of the rivers of Babylon, the elites did not content themselves with weeping. While waiting to rediscover the lost centre, they invented nothing less than the local synagogue (for lack of a central altar), obligatory circumcision, the weekly (and no longer monthly) Shabbat. It was not by chance that Isaiah, Amos and Hosea, champions of the only God, were also the torch-bearers of independence. They served their country by refusing to dissociate the temporal from the spiritual. Their entire claim to glory lay in managing to 'positivize' extreme distress (the collapse of Samaria, the Assyrian invasion, Egyptian hegemony) through an eschatological reading of various disasters that inverted their apparent meaning. Ephraim the prostitute, Samaria the impious, were punished as idolators. The enemy was thus the vengeful arm of the Lord. He who destroys Israel is the servant of Israel. In his proclamations against the nations, Ezekiel inserts not a single one against the king of Babylonia. 'He and his army have worked for me,' Yahweh tells him in confidence (Ezekiel 29: 20). Similarly, God will 'gain glory for [myself] over Pharaoh' (Exodus 14: 4–7). This is not a paradox, but a case of forethought. God was constructed in opposition. He is a cuckoo, if you like to think of Him like that, since He builds His nest in His neighbour's, but impious nations help to *establish the difference*. Or to rediscover it. It may be through scholarship, as with *Wissenschaft des Judentums*, the intellectual movement promoting Jewish studies in a scientific context, which emerged in Germany in the nineteenth century. It can also be through a way of life, by flaunting a style, a way of dressing, ostentatious signs of holiness, like the Hassidim of Central Europe. Contemporary Zionism was strengthened in the hollow of a Russian, German or French lap. And the Jew from Brooklyn or Sarcelles turns out to be more wilfully Judaic than the sabra of Tel Aviv (more narrow-minded as well, and more stubborn). The same can be said of Muslim fundamentalism, which is more virulent in London than in Riyadh, and in New Jersey than in Tunis. If it is true that one forges an ego by snatching it from an Other – in the case at hand, an Egyptian pharaoh, a Seleucid sovereign or an Assyrian despot – the Eternal was not wrong to congratulate *in petto* His enemies, and to make Cyrus of Persia, in passing, an anointed of the Lord, almost a second David. *Realpolitik* is often a *politique du pire*. Babylon made Zion through rejection – and without Nazism, would Israel have reappeared? In gouging out the eyes of their king, Zedekiah, the ignoble Nebuchadnezzar was to open up those of his subjects, the refugees of the city in ruins. Verdi, finally, might well have revised his libretto and ended his chorus of slaves with a '*grazie*, Nabucco!' Thank you, *agent provocateur* of God. Unpleasant, but political. Political, and consequently unpleasant.

BOOK II
Deployment

6 One For All

Go therefore and make disciples of all nations.
(Matthew 28: 19)

Around the first century of our era, Yahweh had a son, and it caused a scandal. The strange news was propagated by the disciples of a charismatic miracle-worker, a preacher who had strained relations with the national authorities, and died igno-miniously. This Jesus, a prophet of uncertain profile, was called Christ by the evangelists. A posthumous baptism, or a kerygma resulting in an anticonformist Pater noster, psychological and without borders, to be disseminated in all direc-tions. Translated into accessible language, accompanied by a plebeian support, the codex, the call to rally to the new messiah was spread by itinerant missionaries throughout the Roman Empire from before the advent of Constantine. 'An admirable propagation', and in fact quite astonishing, which would be perceived by his followers as the irresistible proof of a divine will. God the Father was thus to displace the God of our Fathers.

'How can the same become the other?' Such is the mystery of transformation which we call creation or revelation. With the Cross emerging from the star of David, the second birth of God poses the same question to the mediologist as the formation of a star to an astrophysicist or the appearance of a new form of writing to a palaeographer. Let us translate into our own idiom: through what practical mediations was a Jewish sect, one among many others, able to leave the orbit of Judaism and form its own galaxy? Or 'a new and dangerous superstition' (*dixit* Suetonius) to become, in a rather short space of time, the 'true Roman religion' (*dixit* Tertullian in the following century)?

The ascent to the status of a regime of the new required more than three centuries. The secession was submitted to as much as desired, experienced as a last recourse, not without hesitations and remorse. Simon Mimouni, an expert on Judaeo-Christianity, dates from about 150 CE the irrevocable separation from the parental formation. The Council of Jerusalem in the year 49, in which the ancients called on Jews and Gentiles to sit at the same table, with exemption from circumcision? The Jews, he observes, accepted that converted pagans need not be circumcised, at least not in the first generation. The anti-Jewish polemics of Saint Paul? A continuation of inter-Judaic polemics, which were a custom. For Judaism remained plural in the first century, just as nascent Christianity was. And frequently on the brink of civil war. The Roman authorities, according to the historian, did not actually distinguish between Jews and Christians until 135.[1] Protochristianity, he concludes, is a division of the study of ancient Judaism. Which is to say that the distinctive features that we will attend to here (the Marian cult, the institution of the clergy, the replacement of the scroll by the *codex*, etc.) – innovations which at the time appeared scandalous or incongruous – are traits of maturity, not of adolescence. Our ascendant God – iconographic, multinational and magisterial – would not be stabilized until the fifth century.

---

[1] Simon Mimouni, *Le Judéo-Christianisme ancien. Essais historiques* (Paris: Cerf 1998), p. 483.

Jesus Effaced by Christ

Let us return to the first century. In what did the novelty of the notorious *kerygma* consist? The word comes from the Greek verb *keryssein*, meaning to proclaim, announce, raise one's voice. As an auctioneer or town crier (the *keryx*) does to attract the public's attention when he has good news (*evangelos* in Greek). And what does he say, this deviant vociferator? Simply this: Jesus is Christ, who 'died for our sins and is still alive'. Jesus is a Hebrew name (*Yeshua*); Christ, a Greek word (*Christos*, meaning anointed, consecrated, a translation of the Hebrew *Mashiah*, from which comes our word *messiah*). He who designates Jesus as the messiah, who holds that he is the *Christ*, will be called a Christian. The core of the heresy lies in the equivalence posited between an individual and a category. One is not currently a Christian for venerating 'the Socrates of the Galilee', as Voltaire called him, or the 'gentle dreamer' so dear to Renan, one of the great sages of humanity along with Zoroaster, Pythagoras or Thales. Nor for awaiting the advent of the Messiah, a hope shared by all Jews. One becomes a Christian by virtue of a *hyphenation*. A banal refrain for us (Jesus-Christ-our-Lord), and in reality infinitely litigious. That fragile hyphen, which alone sustains Christianity, like a pyramid standing on its vertex, has been the object of attentions as vexed as they have been fastidious, and Christology has torn nations apart during the six or seven theologically unstable centuries during which to decide on a dogma was to adjudicate the fate of the world. If so many experts and martyrs were necessary to establish the plausibility of that association of two terms, it was because this matter, for a Jew, was in no way a matter of course. Otherwise, there would never have been the case of Jesus. Neither trial nor execution. No Christianity either.

If Christ predominates when Jesus is eclipsed, by virtue of a joint rereading of Scripture intent on showing that everything, finally, transpired as predicted, the crucial phase of Christianity is not 'the life of Jesus'. It is that of a 'return to' after his death. The messianic perception of the figure was a matter of bibliography, not biography. The Gospels say very little about the man Jesus. Or rather, they do so by way of his sublimation into the Resurrected. The resplendent figure is deduced from the Good News, not the other way round. And his personality, which is exceptional from our point of view, was probably less unprecedented in a world as traumatized as it was, in utter disarray, in which messiahs, prophets and consolers of every stripe abounded. If the extraordinary had made its impression on its own, simple reports would have been sufficient. What triggered everything was the moment at which the whole of biblical memory was mobilized by the evangelists, at which witnesses of witnesses began circulating in the Jewish communities of the Empire, and their retellings turned into rumour. And, above all, the moment at which they were ratified, invested with public and legitimate authority by a canon, like the one called Muratori (from the name of its discoverer in 1740), which has been dated back to the end of the second century (there would be others). At which the twenty-seven books of the New Testament were dissociated from those of the Apocrypha (such as the Gospel According to Saint Thomas, and numerous Apocalypses and Epistles) and deemed valid for liturgical service. Apostolic and patristic time thus commands the time of the Gospels, even if we tend to see it as a mere supplement, as though the profane history following sacred history concerned it in only the most distant manner. We yield to narrative illusion, which projects the deferred as though it were immediate, and forget that without that second degree of the legend, the initial event would not exist. 'Crucified' would be written without capital or definite article. And Joshua would have joined the common grave in which tens of thousands of anonymous souls were left to rot, slaves and rebels tortured in conformity with the customs of an age in which gallows were a common sight. It was the intellectual labour of the Monday that rendered the Friday holy or 'good'. The Cross as a sign of recognition (adopted in the fourth century), then the sculpted image of Christ on the Cross, the crucifix (which appeared in the Middle Ages), have led us to see the Crucifixion as our principal focus. But the crown of thorns, the spear, the dice, the hammer, the sponge, and the sign INRI, all the paraphernalia of the primal scene, were deposited by tradition. Not before the second or third generation. Not one of his disciples wrote about Jesus during his lifetime. With the exception of Matthew, the apostles did not do very much for their master. Too close, no doubt. One never discerns the genius of one's contemporaries, even less so of one's associates. Any more than one witnesses the death of one's next-door neighbour.

A prodigious working-through: to convert a fiasco into an apotheosis, humiliating torture into a claim to glory, and a calamitous counterproof (what kind of God is this who allows Himself to be spat upon?) into a proof of excellence. The subject had – dare we say – facilitated his posthumous rescue by cultivating a certain vagueness about his person and his mission: doctor, master, holy man, servant, saviour, king, son of man, son of God? There is no clear answer. 'But who do you say that I am?' (Matthew 16: 15). The disciples were to fill in the blanks. Title to be determined, according to desires and affinities. Centuries of controversy and Christology itself, the discipline that formalizes the ontologically uncertain nature of Jesus (man of God chosen by Him, no, divine man, no, Son of God …), were to issue from that deficient *curriculum vitae*. From that 'failed to present his documents at the proper time'. The evangelists, and then the Church Fathers, did so in his place. Without them, the Galilean would no doubt have drowned in the fog of the mystery cults of the East. And we would now be debating, with due gravity, the – double, simple or triple – nature of Isis, Mithras or Serapis.

A functioning god induces a fever, and it is when the cardiogram of a population reads flat that his death certificate can be drawn up. Those that are surreptitiously wrapped in purple shrouds – Mazda, Apollo, Augustus, Mao or Lenin – are then consigned to archives or sarcophagi. Dead memories. Cultural pilgrimages. Visits to mausolea. The fact that Jesus has caused millions of hearts to beat in thousands of places over twenty centuries cannot leave even the most unimpassioned historian cold. Let us wonder, rather, what that vitality owes to this curious detail: Christian emotion was never personally aroused by Jesus himself, a pathetic figure if ever there was one. The man–god who lived and died virtually incognito, a subject more of indifference than of censure, was not a contemporary of (nor was he instrumental in) the affective storm associated with his name. One is almost prepared to believe that the misfortune of Jesus was the good fortune of Christ. It is well known that misprision is the rule when it comes to individual celebrity (both deserved and usurped). Since the reputation of men – and even more so of their ideas – is a sequence of misunderstandings, the only interesting point is to know whether or not they are productive. With the disciples of Jesus, symbolic productivity attained a zenith which has not been surpassed since. The fertility of this *unhinging* of word from fact is clear in the Pauline venture. The most effective practitioner of trans-figuration, the one who made the Crucifixion legible and intelligible in the mental categories of his *milieu,* the Jewish diaspora of the Roman Empire, who bore witness to it all around the Mediterranean, was not himself witness to anything at all. It was Paul the polyglot (Greek, Aramaic, Hebrew, Latin), the overtalented Pharisee, the forger of concepts, 'who did everything for Jesus', not although but because he did not know him. It is not a matter of seeing and hearing but of causing to see and listen which makes the difference. A proof that in matters of transmission (in time) and contrary to communication (in space), directness is not recommended. It is the 'repetition' which is decisive. In this case, 'real time' remains sterile.

Is it far from *hysteresis* (deferment of excitement) to hysteria? Conversion hysteria, says the Freudian. *Nachträglich.* Symbolic efficacy is at its most potent after the fact. Tradition repels us like an abusive grip of the past on the present. All those hands of the dead clinging to the living . . . . Marx adopted that commonplace observation in a frequently quoted sentence: 'The tradition of all the dead generations weighs with inordinate heaviness on the brain of the living.' He complained about it, even though he himself owed his influence to the ability of our dear departed to proliferate as so many ghosts (and that of Marx, which weighed so heavily on the brain of Marxists and anti-Marxists, has by no means performed the last of his capers). 'Thus it is', he added, 'that Luther put on the mask of Saint Paul.' He missed the essential point, which is the two-way traffic in plastic surgery, through which the living are no less busy recarving the face of the dead. Luther resculpted Paul's profile before turning it into a mask. Just as Paul of Tarsus remodelled Jesus to his personal use and appearance. And when, today, we look at the face of the Saviour, who knows whether we are not staring at the erudite Pharisee become a Christian?

'The Wolf Man understood intercourse only at the time of the dream, at age four, and not during the period when he observed it, and the dream confers on the observation of intercourse its efficacy after the fact.' Just as memories, in order to make sense, must be spoken, and reorganized through their articulation, the memory traces left behind by Jesus could be transmitted only by being remobilized, reinserted into the collective psychodrama, and shaped into confirmations. Everything here was a matter of intelligence. The advent of Christ was played out in people's heads, 'mentally'. One takes up the same materials – Isaiah, Melchizedek, Hosea, Passover – but they are 'framed' as so many announcements or preparations for an event which had just taken place without its first beneficiaries being aware of it. The Resurrection was undoubtedly an act of psychic and intellectual reparation, an *interpretative coup de théâtre* that 'absorbed' an incomprehensible affective cataclysm by reintegrating it into the echo chamber of Scripture, by way of the crucial category of the Messiah, which was familiar to all. The accusation of abjuration voiced by the high priests was thus turned into the proclaimed resolution, the one that Israel had always awaited. The outlaw heretic was converted into the refounder of the Law. And that acrobatic feat was effected under emergency conditions, amid the panic fever of the 'last days', occurring at a time of catastrophes (the Maccabees, Massada, Titus, the Roman occupation). If the night is long, it is because the Great Day has arrived. 'The time is fulfilled and the Kingdom of God is near. Convert and believe in the Good Tidings' (Maccabees 1: 14–15). Disciples and first witnesses, numbed by the imminence of the end of the world, would then have fled the traumas reality had just visited on their dreams into an imaginary (because rearranged, rephrased) past. The Gospels, Epistles and Acts are not their dreams. But we may be authorized to read in them a series of *abreactions,* affective discharges of writing through which they freed themselves from the memory of unbearable events (the rout, the rejection, the accusation of charlatanism). They 'positivized' the immediate failure of a decision to speak that had been delayed too long, by way of a traditionalizing reinscription of the misunderstood pariah, subsequently relegitimized by the national archives. They thus neutralized its devastating effect on the minds of those in the first circle. There is always a more or less long interval between the trauma and the abreaction (it is in and through language that this type of therapy is effected). In this case the delays were considerably shorter than in the Jewish odyssey. The unsigned narrative became first-person testimony. The transition was from four centuries to a few decades of separation. The three Synoptic Gospels were definitively established between forty and seventy years after the death of Jesus, in 30. The writings of Paul, which are the earliest, stretch from 50 to 63. We do not possess any autographed manuscript, to be sure, only copies of the originals. The oldest known manuscript is the torn fragment of a papyrus (remains of verses of the Gospel According to Saint John), around 120 or 130. But the interval between the autographed manuscript and the copy is significantly shorter than in the Old Testament. We should recall that four centuries separate Virgil from the oldest known manuscripts of his work, thirteen for Plato, and nineteen for Euripides. Such is the advantage of religious scrupulousness, which takes great pains to collect its traces (*relegere*), over academic culture, which is more nonchalant.

The Tradition Effect

To browse through the Acts of the Apostles, the oldest document on the origins of the Christian movement, plausibly composed or collected by Luke – a physician by profession born in Antioch and a companion of Paul – is to have the impression of travelling a royal road. It follows a straight line, without dead ends or bifurcations, that begins with Jesus' farewells at the end of his life (which is significantly abbreviated, like a short day's lesson) and ends with the arrrival of Paul in Rome, a pope *in partibus*. The little family of the beginning expands before our very eyes into the people of God, much as a seed stuck into rich soil sprouts and flourishes. 'To what may the kingdom of God be compared? It is like a mustard seed; when it is sown, it is the smallest of all seeds, but once it has been sown, it rises and becomes bigger than vegetables; it grows branches, and the birds of the sky can nest in its shade' (Mark 4: 30–32). As a child grows, unworried and self-assured throughout all his ordeals. The Messiah blooms into his message, lives again through his disciples.[2] Such is the *refoundational* miracle of a well-managed transmission: simplifying the complex, and dispelling hesitations. The image of the Cross growing as straight as a tree effaces the violent conflicts among communities, between 'Hellenizers' and 'Judaizers', Peter and Paul, those of Antioch and those of Jerusalem. Having the Symbol of the Apostles fall into their mouths, synchronized, all twelve at once, dove or roast lark, one fine summer's day, avoids questions about polemical zigzags, or compromises prerequisite to the subsequently endorsed profession of faith. Such is the price of co-operation: bringing dissidents back into the fold, binding up wounds, diminishing the apparently random, smoothing away rough edges. Make way for the triumphal smile of a highly political Providence, more aware than we were of what had to be done to achieve the most direct result: acknowledgement by the various Jewish communities of the Diaspora that the Torah was both abolished and fulfilled in the person of the Messiah.

'The Good Word spread,' we say. And we imagine the sweet dissemination of a point of light first seen in Judaea and spreading to the surrounding areas. We fantasize a truth (in the singular), self-enclosed, which subsequently radiated out into the more or less heterodox local Christianities, dismembered fragments of a lost totality. There would thus be a point zero in space and time – say: Jerusalem, the morning of Sunday 9 April of the year 30, the Easter of Resurrection – from which,

[2] On this subject, see Simon Mimouni, 'Les représentations historiographiques du christianisme au 1er siècle', *Théologie historique*, vol. 114; *L'Historiographie de l'Église des premiers siècles* (Paris: Beauchesne 2001).

like the rays of a light bulb, there would be deployed several divergent branches of interpretation (Aryanism, Nestorianism, Monophysism, etc.), later to be dubbed heresies or deviations from the norm (of a monolithic bloc of faith). Everything indicates that it was the other way round. Viewed in time, the Christian phenomenon presents a circular base, an archipelago of contradictory sects and movements, which was concentrated into a single focal point over the course of centuries, under the iron hand of emperors and Church Fathers, synod by synod. The plurality of communities preceded the unity of the Church, just as heresies preceded (and allowed for) the fixing of dogma. The staff became straight (*ortho*-dox) through a give-and-take of distortions in the opposite direction, under a tireless strong arm mediating between secessionist factions (Alexandria, Antioch, Carthage, etc.).[3] We are obliged to abandon as a delusion what appeared to be obvious: that 'at the origin of Christianity was the Christ'. Its obviousness disguises a creed as an observation, but by reversing terms, since had there not been the later movement, the root itself would not exist. *The after made the before* – just as the destruction of Jerusalem gave rise to Moses and Abraham, in order to inspire the demoralized denizens of the Diaspora, and with considerable success (as revealed by Judaism's exceptional resistance to Hellenistic and Roman claims). The notion that 'it was Christianity that invented Christ, not the other way round' will seem a paradox or pirouette, but common sense is never anything other than *a cultural relation of forces sublimated into a consensual commonplace.* Those who impose their mental framework on others have the ability to *rewrite what preceded as a function of what followed.* Such is the rule of the game of transmission. It functions by imperceptible recontextualizations, touch-ups and displacements. And also by master-strokes – bold translations or self-fulfilling prophecies. We find such questionable techniques every time a commanding idea takes hold of a crowd. Maurice Sachot, for instance, has underscored the ingenious manoeuvre of the Carthaginian Tertullian (the first theologian in the Latin language). At the end of the second century, he upset the chessboard, without any commotion, by effecting a permutation of *religio* and *superstitio* on the squares reserved for key-words.[4] Magisterial. Baptizing the Christian dissidence 'religio' meant nothing less than supplanting the official imperial dispensation, since *religio* in the Roman world was inseparable from state power. And at the same stroke delegitimizing the *status quo*, since the imperial cult, founded on a pseudo-*religio*, was basically only one more superstition among others. A vertiginous inversion of the signs of legitimacy, by which a totally marginal and seditious sect posited nothing less than its candidacy for the direction of the centre of the world. That is what we call a 'daring move'.

---

[3] Manuel de Dieguez provides a good description of this historico-theological process in *Et l'homme créa son Dieu* (Paris: Fayard 1984).
[4] Maurice Sachot, 'Histoire d'un retournement et d'une subversion', *Revue des religions*, no. 208 (1991).

Fact and Faith: To Each Its Law

Verifying theology by history is a reflex reaction when we suspect that a discordance between the two may place the former in danger. We may be justified in thinking, however, that the distinction between the two orders restores each to its vigorous and substantial autonomy. The confrontation of epigraphy and archaeology, on the one hand, with catachesis and dogma, on the other, is an exercise that is as disappointing as it is futile. The Bible has its dictionary of internal concordances, but the search for internal/external concordances between the 'truths of faith' and documentary data, with the aim of confronting a verifiable fact with this or that verse of Scripture, comes to an abrupt end. When it comes to the birth and adolescence of the theological Christ, we can reconstitute an itinerary, mark out the stages. When it comes to the birth and adolescence of the historical Jesus, we are and will remain in the dark. What is symbolically the most celebrated trial in the history of humanity is still not over, and the Passion of Christ, despite – or because of – its narratives, remains a matter of controversy. Were we to find, some day, sources that are more impartial and direct than the Synoptic Gospels (were we to discover, for example, the tombs of Herod the Great or Agrippa, with their dynastic archives, or the records of the recording scribe of the Sanhedrin), they still might not resolve the question raised in any way. A sum of *indices* is in principle incapable of making or unmaking a *symbol*, since those two categories of sign are not of the same nature. Why be shocked that historical investigation and exegesis, archaeology and theology, should have nothing to teach each other (that might be a source of reciprocal concern)? Within the unsinkable hull of the ships of faith, information and interpretation form two watertight compartments. A circumstance that has for two centuries sustained a dialogue of the deaf which has had the advantage of captivating Greeks and Trojans without troubling the confidence of one party or the defiance of the other. Agnostics and the convinced – since Renan, if not since Voltaire – have kept an eye on each other. The latter in order to validate sources, rectify datings, excuse contradictions between Gospels – in sum, to authenticate 'the message of fire and love'; the former in order to establish the falsity of the aforementioned hypotheses, demonstrate that miracles are impossible, dates faulty, and place indications incoherent – in sum, to denounce an imposture. Sceptics (whom no report or testimony will move), like apologists (who put their trust in doctrinal authority when it comes to separating the wheat from the chaff), are ultimately indifferent to each other, and that is all to the good.

The question of faith is played out in the deltas, not the sources. And the logical principle of non-contradiction is of minimal use to the extent that there exist not several truths, but several 'realities' (virtual reality being only the most recent, which does not annul the preceding cases, but gives us an additional reality). The reality of belief has its own realism, just as critical positivism does. Each one has free run of its domain. A Christian has no reason to be bothered by reading in Saint Mark, at a few pages' distance, a thing and its opposite. Observing that the Synoptic Gospels are not in agreement on the number of apostles – sometimes fourteen, sometimes eight – does not in any way change the fact – which is highly symbolic, and in harmony with the twelve tribes of Israel – that, by tradition, there are twelve apostles, and twelve there will always be.

The Resurrection is life emerging from death. Entropy vanquished. The slope in reverse. A promise that empowering, that encouraging, biologically irresistible, discourages material proofs and counterproofs. On what objective scale, on what Rosetta Stone, might we rely in distinguishing true from false? On our historical sources? They are themselves already interpretations. As are our commentaries, interpretations squared. We know the Jesus of his ten thousand biographies solely through the attestations of those who held him to be the Messiah, with all their heart and soul, and who were, above all, talking to themselves when they called Jesus 'Christ'. Such 'bearing witness' attests above all to the faith of its authors, and to expect it to yield the wherewithal for determining 'what actually happened' is to reach a dead end. The evangelists are too convinced of their cause, too much party to the deification of their master, to be able to be heard as witnesses in the judicial sense of the word. Luke saw nothing, but he knows from Paul, who himself has heard it said . . . . Mark knows from Peter, who was part of it all, but where did he go? Matthew recopied into Greek, it appears, his old notes in Aramaic. John didn't pick up his pen until he was approaching old age. They all write for our edification, not – or not only – for our information. *In order to make us believe* in certain signs, more convincing than others; as painstaking apologists, and not as false witnesses. 'Now Jesus did many other signs in the presence of his disciples, which are not written in this book. But these are written so that you may come to believe that Jesus is the Messiah, the Son of God, and that through believing you may have life in his name' (John 20: 30). 'I have transmitted to you what I had myself received' (Paul to the Corinthians). There is no cheating. Each one bounces off the other. It is a triumph of suggestion (which they 'pull off' among themselves). As for external witnesses, principally the Romans, they suffer from the opposite shortcoming: hostile prejudice, with the dumb incomprehension of the conservative (save the *status quo*). At the turn of the first and second centuries, they are disdainful and vague. Two lines of Suetonius, ten of Tacitus, a page of Pliny, his letter to Trajan, which was more circumspect.[5] Which completes our circle. Amid the small groups of the convinced, on the scene, too much empathy. And when it comes to the imperial bureaucracy, too much antipathy. An affair involving wretched paupers, provincials to boot. The Roman intelligentsia did not take care of its poor (who would, in short order, figure out how to take care of *it*). In brief, the elements of the

---

[5] See Tacitus, *Annals* 15. 44. 3; Suetonius, *The Life of Claudius*, 25. 4; and Pliny the Younger to Trajan, *Letters*, 10. 96.

case take us from an excess to a deficiency of complicity. Between the inspired bumpkin of the outskirts and the contemptuous official from the prefecture, nothing, or just about. Flavius Josephus, with his *Judaic Antiquities*, represents a more trustworthy go-between, but his allusions to Jesus are taken to be dubious interpolations. A single instance does not a habit make; the *juste milieu*, the vital centre, is lacking. No 'white book' is possible.

The Gospels do not hide the fact that they were personalized addresses or efforts at indoctrination, not objective reports. *Incipit* from Luke: 'Since many have undertaken to set down an orderly account of the events that have been fulfilled among us, just as they were handed on to us by those who from the beginning were eyewitnesses and servants of the word, I too decided, after investigating everything carefully from the very first, to write an orderly account, most excellent Theophilus, so that you may know the truth concerning the things about which you have been instructed.' That instruction was a vast narrative composed of a thousand smaller ones, reworkings of reworkings, a metalegend. The inflationary traffic of mouth-to-ear established, link by link, a long chain of hearsay – a successful transmission. When one is aware that 'to transmit is not only to communicate and reproduce, but to invent and produce', the *ex post ante* seems only natural. What manuscript can traverse centuries of annotation and interpretation without becoming a palimpsest? Without taking on mass, being shaped by surroundings which alternately absorb it and are absorbed by it? The author of *The Invention of Christ, Genesis of a Religion* summarized the trajectory in three principal phases, one for each century. The Jewish milieu of the first century constructed the figure of the Messiah in Aramaic, with all the more fervour in that the destruction of the Temple in 70 deprived it of its territorial anchorage. After which, the Hellenic milieu (that is, above all, the Hellenized Jews of Antioch and Alexandria) made of him, in the following century, the master of a philosophical school capable of competing with the others. Subsequently – and this is the third cycle – the Roman milieu made of that wisdom to be taught a religion to be instituted, on the juridico-political model of the *civitas*. *Jerusalem*: this Jesus is indeed the Christ. *Athens*: this Christ is indeed a master of truth. *Rome*: this head of a school is indeed our Dominus, Emperor of heaven and earth. The issue of each transformative sequence serving as preamble to the next.

The creed is received as a *primary* form of evidence. Occasionally, a sudden flash in the small interpretative events that we call personal conversions, lightning-bolts of the soul. The new convert proclaims his faith in Christ, but his exclamation reverberates through thousands of others. 'Truth has become.' A new God appears to be calling us. Unless He is responding to our summons. Little Jesus was turned into a 'divine child' posthumously. And provided with a duly drawn up birth certificate after five centuries of study of the texts and doctrinal disputes. When Denys the Small – a theologian of Byzantine origin, who died in 530 – fixed the birth of the infant-God in the year 752 of the Roman calendar. On Christmas Day, because it was the winter solstice, a date on which there was consensus. Luke and Matthew

had already selected the place, Bethlehem, the city of which the Messiah could not
but be a native, since it was the city of David, *according to the Scriptures.*

Render unto the Apostle What is the Apostle's

Might the Church have done itself wrong while pretending to do itself good (with a
genius for self-abasement worthy of the Jesuits at their best)? The various successes
it attributes to Providence are merits accruing to the Church itself, or merits it has
declined out of humility. The apostles-and-disciples of the first generation number
about thirty individuals. The historic champions of propaganda. The contents of the
New Testament, if words have a meaning, cannot be qualified as evidence of genius.
Nothing that was not already said in the Old. 'Thou shalt love the Lord thy God' is
to be found in Deuteronomy (6: 4–5). 'Love thy neighbour as thyself' is in Leviticus
(19: 15–20). 'The Son of Man', as Jesus is called, is in the Book of Daniel (7: 13), to
describe a saviour come down from Heaven. The dragon of the Apocalypse is the
seven-headed Leviathan of Canaanite mythology. The Beatitudes? A classic of
wisdom literature. The Messiah? A Jewish concept (which can be found even in
Iran!). Like the Incarnation. The Christian text is not a hotchpotch, but an echo
chamber, in which a change of emphasis within Judaic tradition (of which it fur-
nishes a radicalized and simplified *compendium*) may be detected. The innovation –
which, despite appearances, is not only one of form – lies in the globalization of the
project, its opening of the message to the Gentiles: more than an addition, it was a
shift in the foundations.

   Forget the preconception. Vulgarization is the least vulgar of activities. For a
doctrine, whatever it be, and *a fortiori* one of salvation, it is the ordeal by fire, the
via crucis. The Essenes or the Gnostics would no doubt have shuddered at the
thought of exposing themselves to the *vulgum* through a *Vulgate,* or 'common
version'. The word designates specifically the translation of the Bible into Latin by
Saint Jerome (342–420), on which he is said to have worked for twenty-two years,
and Christianity emerged from the abasement of that act of abnegation. Any
obsessive in his corner can fabricate a small system for interpreting the world,
replete with jargon and subtle refinements. So much skull juice. A wheel spinning in
one's head. It is getting it to spin in the heads of others that is the trick. The greatest
of arts. The gold medal. To disseminate, propagate, make shared. *De propaganda
fide.* Under the entry 'Propagation', the *Dictionnaire de théologie catholique* contains ten dense pages. The *Dictionnaire encyclopédique du judaïsme* contains none.
A minuscule sign of an essential – and generational – difference.

Ad augusta per angusta, towards august realities through strait gates: the motto
invented by Victor Hugo for the Company of Jesus could serve as the moral of the
deployment of Christianity. A lesson in strategy. Or how to make a strength of one's
weaknesses.

First, *doctrine*. All the traditions of the various rival Israels are at work, on and against the movement that seeks to define itself. And they tear it asunder, just as they had already fragmented the face of Jesus, who turns out to have more than one, when seen close up. There is, in Mark, a Pharisee who, 'as soon as the Shabbat arrives, goes to teach in the synagogue'; for John, a zealot who expels the merchants from the temple; then, the Essene, in Matthew, who delivers his sermon on the mount; and let us not forget the baptist, who had himself initiated in fresh water by John the Baptist, just prior to the end of the world. And all this made for an excellent Messiah whom the adepts of rival tendencies, within the Diaspora, would be able to divide up, each one inflecting the message to its own ends. That kaleidoscopic profile, with its splicings and interferences, might have resulted in a faulty reception. Yet the movement was able to draw from its own incoherences a capacity for proliferation, turning each version of the Christ into the grappling-hook that moored it to a different tendency. What was thus being sketched, *in nuce*, was an exceptional aptitude for the far-flung dissemination of a culture. The universality of the transethnic God initially stemmed from an adding together of various particularisms, without sectarian exclusions. Rich and poor, an anti-Roman resister and a collaborator, a Hellenizer and a Judaizer, can all find a shoe that fits. And a way of turning things to their advantage. The stubborn and the supple; prudes and spouses; subversives and conformists. For every excluding or recommending formula – 'touch nothing unclean; then I will welcome you' (2 Corinthians 6: 17) – we can find another that contradicts it: 'Let marriage be held in honour by all' (Hebrews 13: 4). If I don't want my sister, a young widow, to remarry, I'll quote Saint Paul (1 Corinthians 7) at her again; but if that prospect suits me, I'll quote some more Saint Paul (ibidem). Everyone has his share of the new truth, and we all have it in its entirety. Wondrous is the agenda of Saint Paul: 'There is no longer Jew or Greek, there is no longer slave or free, there is no longer male and female, for all of you are one in Jesus Christ' (Galatians 3: 28). Out of pragmatism, the abolition of discrimination in Christ, prior to the authoritarian unification of practices and dogmas by the Christian Empire (in the fourth century), began with a grand welcome to all, without a priori or interdiction.

Next, the *teaching*. Just as the kaleidoscopic variation of faces of the Lord, transformed into a spirit of openness, permitted a receptiveness to contradictory imaginary aspirations, the philosophical modesty of the message, such as it was, was turned into 'evangelical simplicity'. Genius, in this arena, consisted of *daring to be simple*. And even expedient, in order the better to expedite things (anyone who wants to disseminate broadly begins by sifting out). We are not dealing with a scribe. He dispenses a teaching of the streets to ordinary people, orally and without embellishment. He speaks, through parables and proverbs, of everyday life. What sneers that candour (and what derision such foolishness, like the resurrection of bodies) would provoke among the aged scholars of late Antiquity (Porphyry, Celsus), who were accustomed to more consistency! No physics. No logic. No cosmology. In relation to the other wisdom doctrines then on the market, here was a rather feeble product, bordering on the nugatory. Hence the efforts of Paul and the apologists, as early as the second century, to inject some discursive and scholarly panache – and not to lose face with their peers. Dogmatic theology would succeed quite well in this, but for a long time, as far as the dialecticians of the agora were concerned, the first formulation, a masterpiece of naivety, had the status of a comic strip presented to a thesis jury (in the old style). The Athenian experts harangued by Paul on the Areopagus asked him politely, in the end, to go his way: 'You can talk to us about this matter some other time.' Even Luke, in Acts, the unconditional follower of Paul, cannot conceal the fiasco. That 'theoretical weakness' gave him his magnetic power over the general public. The one that buys biographies, not treatises, exposés, not essays; and prefers the 'true story of' to 'discourses on the origin of'. Or noble sentiments (love, charity, hope) to logical arguments. The evangelist (a bit like our current media figures on radio and television, and in interviews) bets on the low against the high, the street against the academies, the marginals – immigrants, artisans, women – against the centre. And compounds the Holy Spirit with the spirit of childhood. Little Jesus confronting the Doctors of the Law? The proposition was irresistible. And thus it was that that mad logic took hold of an Empire desiccated by an excess of rationality, in which speculation and erudition isolated the intellectual elites from the heart of the population. If you want to captivate, don't write philosophy books; tell a beautiful story.

Mega biblion, mega kakon: a great book is a great evil. The Christian opuscule encapsulates life and death in a hundred pages (the seed contains the whole of the tree). Evangelical telegraphy. A series of recitatives, short and dense, easy to memorize. The resonance of the minimal. A language that is both fluent and striking. 'Rise up.' 'If the seed not die.' 'Let your yes be yes.' Phrases like that spread like an epidemic, which was their aim. An acoustical facilitation of memory (hearing being the principal sense, before the liturgy was made visible, around the twelfth century, with the death of Saint Bernard). Parables are also a mnemonic technique. Producing an image conveys a supplement of meaning in fewer words. The Good Samaritan, killing the fatted calf, casting pearl before swine, the worker of the eleventh hour, foolish virgins and wise: they ricochet like a good story flitting from mouth to mouth, because it's easy to remember and casts the teller in a good light. Less is more. Epitomization marked a break with the profuseness of traditions. 'Thou shalt teach these commandments to thy children and thy children's children.' Two hundred and forty-eight commandments and three hundred and sixty-five prohibitions, in the Jewish version, are transmitted less easily than seven capital sins, and three theological virtues.

Brevity is rarely tender. Evangelical ellipsis also marks a break with Rome's gemlike clarity, the laconic attractions of Latin *sententiae*, the chiselled concision of the aphorism. Christian style brings a touch of tenderness to the dryness of that wit. With a propensity to intimacy that is both fluent and childlike: completely different from the stilted posturing of Cato, the affected style of Caesar. Here, the parsimonious remains fluid and good-humoured. Is it the passion for contact and impact that explains the communicative instinct of abridgement, which can be extended to the treatment of relics (*pars pro toto*: the saint's little finger for his whole body)? To translate, for a learned doctor, is to pad; for an apostle, it is to contract. The proselyte, who needs to circulate and recruit beyond the circle of initiates, is driven, by profession, to make less out of more. The liturgical transmutation of a wafer into a *host*, the tent into a *tabernacle*, painted panels into a *portable triptych,* a cross into a *crucifix*, the circle of a necklace into a rosary (*chapelet*, in French, meaning little hat), a profession into a *symbol* of faith (the short formulation of the creed common to all Christians), the road to Jerusalem into a *labyrinth*, a whole name into a *monogram (the chrism,* consisting of X and P superimposed) or into IHS (Iesus Hominum Salvator, Jesus Saviour of Men). Of a complete title into a rebus (*ichtus*, fish, an acronym for Jesus Christ Son of God the Saviour), of a bulky prayer book into a *breviary*, of the missal (which had itself replaced, in the thirteenth century, the medieval sacramentary) into the *parishioner* (the Mass book, which was a further abridgement). He who transmits will always go for the more easily manipulable. *Vade-mecum*, memento, index, syllabus. Guideposts and catalogues. The vastness of cathedrals, and of Saint Peter's in Rome, should not conceal from our eyes and ears the deeper genius that consists in transforming, in every domain, a magisterium (from *magis*, plus) into a ministry (from *minus*).

In this sense, this emporium of everything-for-a-farthing was *modern* long before its time. Poetic and practical, one because of the other. Apollinaire's 'Zone': 'Religion alone has remained completely new religion / has remained simple like the hangars of Port-Aviation / Alone in Europe you are not antique, O Christianity / The most modern European is you, Pope Pius X.' It was the Christians who invented or enthroned the prospectus, the advertisement, graffiti, the abstract, the jingle. And, above all, the logo, a formidable vector of identification and communitarian transmission, which can be imprinted on all sorts of supports, and of which the fish on the walls of the catacombs remains the perfect emblem. When it comes to imagery, staging, and the fabrication of plots, the faith in the new Saviour of the world (a man and no longer a nation) would have nothing to learn from our communications experts. What they do, amply financed, for presidents, the new faith did for an Absent, and without charge. The heady freshness of their short cuts fuses with an entirely classical taste for the brio of percussive brevity. They are captions, 'eye-catchers', much as the New Testament is an abstract of the Old, the vector of a divine *lite*, unburdened by legalistic rituals, made lighter so that it goes further (a bottle in the sea is more likely to travel if it is a flask, not a jug). A Christian has always been (and still is) a ballistics expert. Profile the message, make it aerodynamic so that it cuts through the surrounding inertia and atmospheric noise. The abbreviation of matter by form enables both the poverty of the Cistercians and the spread of the missionaries. Everything tapered, in order to simplify and thus electrify – Radio Vatican, Catholic TV on KTO. In order to concretize the abstract, and jolt the mind. 'I am the way,' in the last analysis, is a touch of charismatic presumptuousness, which might be expected from a fanatic prone to exorcism ... . Making it viable and practicable by all and sundry is more unexpected, and altogether more convincing.

Letter-Men

With the Galilean retrieved for the good cause by his followers, pious and loyal Jews, how is one to win the old world over to this new God, whose way is no longer fear and trembling, but smile and allusion? The first transition, from Jesus to 'Christ', was played out in a confrontation with the Old Testament, through a series of Scriptural manoeuvres. The second, from Jesus Christ to the Christian Empire, required, in addition, a good pair of legs. Since the Master's mission had failed in real time, what was needed were liege-men to take up the task after the fact. The new Spirit, born of a labour on the Letter, produced new letters to be posted, and thousands of miles to cover.

The Apostle was simultaneously the letter and the road. In the literal sense. In Greek, the language spoken by Paul and the Hellophone Jewish communities of the Mediterranean basin, *Apostolès* and *Epistolè* have the same root. The Apostle is good for an epistle; he already *is* one in flesh and bone. He is a letter from the Christ, 'written not with ink, but with the spirit of the living God'. The Messiah's missive to the future addressed – tatooed, as it were, on the body of his escort. While washing the feet of his disciples before dying, the Son prepared his correspondence with humility and forethought, and a sense of detail worthy of his Father dictating instructions for the assemblage of the holy ark. In those days, we should recall, a message circulated at the same pace as the messenger (on horseback, by boat, most often on foot), and anyone who wanted to travel a long way had to look after his harness. Since the Hebraic or Judaeo-Christian communities were dispersed, one was obliged to make visits, use trustworthy envoys, or the imperial postal system. The best way was to make the connection oneself. This was what our circulating letters did before the written deposition of a memory which was already collegial, and would soon be collective. Like their itinerant master, our travellers talked as they walked, stopping beneath a tree or under the awning of a house. Like Jesus himself. With Word and itinerancy travelling at the same speed, they went off to found or refound communities. Paul laid claim to those of Galatia, Philippi, Thessalonica and Corinth. Following Paul's four journeys through the Mediteranean (between 43 and his death) is still a challenge to our contemporary tour-guides. The roads of the Empire will have proved their usefulness. One for all and all for One – when your homeland is neither the city where you were born nor a specific people, but the whole of the civilized world, you end up with a lot of corns.

They go in twos, like our nuns and policemen; and when they separate, they continue on their way, each with his deacon. To the four cardinal points of the *oekomen*: towards Nineveh, India and the East (Thomas and Bartholomew). Towards Anatolia (Andrew and Philip). Towards Babylonia (Jude and Simon). Towards Antioch (Matthew). Towards the Ionian cities, to Ephesus (John, brother of James). Faith helps to build the chain, and the chain in turn instils faith (the addressee of the letter spontaneously becoming its new sender). The missionaries adjust themselves orally to link up with Jesus, as he had done with the Torah. 'It is not only through the cities, but also through villages and the countryside that the contagion of this superstition has spread,' Pliny would observe in the year 112. But until the second century the Empire was tolerant on matters of religion, even if there was movement in the provinces, uncontrollable and worrisome zigzags. The first great hunt for subversives would take place much later, in 250, under the Emperor Decius.

Their displacements were quite well documented, notably in Acts (Luke himself being a great traveller). They follow the paths taken by legions and traders, which linked the numerous Judaean settlements to each other. The apostolic undertaking may be regarded as a centralized office for the redirection of correspondence intended to win acknowledgement – as much among the old believers as among the 'God-fearing', those pagans who were sympathetic to the Jewish cause – of the messiahdom of Jesus. In an age in which signs detached themselves from bodies only with difficulty (the disalignment of the two velocities dating only from the optical telegraph), delivery was personal. The *apostolos*, God's envoy, was also the *apostoleus*, he whom a community sends afar, as head of a naval expedition or the maritime functionary charged with supplying armaments for ships. There is, in the word, a curious combination of fleet admiral and commercial traveller. One takes to the sea as well as to the road in order to haul along one's Church, 'the boat of Saint Peter'. Barnabas took Mark and embarked for Cyprus ...'. The shipwreck of Paul and his centurion in the shallows of Malta, as they sailed for Italy, is described quite precisely at the end of Acts.

The Angelic Codex

An easy relation with the audience, a lightness of the propagating surface. The high-tech of the day or the *codex*, the ancestor of the rectangular parallelepipeds we call *books*, was almost immediately put to use and profit. It was through that tradesman's entrance, between the second and fourth centuries, that Christian truth made its entry into society. On wings of doves, as was appropriate, and behind the

backs of the great and the good. Indeed, there was not a single intellectual authority
in the Roman world who saw the *heimatlos* God coming, and then, all of a sudden,
He was there. Too late to send Him back to His encampment.

How had He managed to slip through? Through homilies, harangues at crossroads,
meetings in homes. And, as of the second century, through writings. There had long
been, in the Empire, rectangular wooden tablets, hollowed out on one side and
smeared with wax, on which notations were made with a stylus (and erased with a
simple spatula). Those tablets could be joined together by cords or leather laces,
inserted through holes in the tablets. The result was a *polyptych*. It was used for
little things: sketches, note-taking, short texts (Martial consigned his epigrams to
one). Copies for display continued to be made on scrolls, as in the Greek world. The
genealogy of the Good News has its origins in this accessory. From it comes our cult
of the Book. From that rectangle, our page, of which the very notion was unknown
until then. From that wooden frame, our back cover. From those cords, our binding.
Palaeographers have compiled statistics from which it emerges that in the third
century, 'the manuscripts of Christian authors comprise four times more codices
than scrolls, whereas those of Latin authors comprise fifteen times more scrolls than
codices'.[6] Copies of the Septuagint, for Christian use, have the form of a codex,
while Judaism was affirmed in a '*volumen conserved*'. Yahweh continued to be
unscrolled on a ribbon of vegetable matter from the right, and to be rolled up from
the left (linear movement and continuous reading).The Gnostic manuscripts of Nag
Hammadi, written in Coptic and dateable to the second and fourth centuries, discovered in Upper Egypt in 1945, are codices bound flat, like our contemporary
books; whereas the Essene manuscripts from Qumran, discovered two years later
but dated from the first centuries after Jesus, are in scroll format. Every confession
has its materio-symbolic fidelities. The Church remains faithful to the folded sheet,
notebooks bound together; the Synagogue to the antediluvian scroll. It came to us
from the Egypt of the pharaohs and disappeared from our libraries around the
fourth century (until its rebirth as the scrolling fax).

It was under Constantine, then Theodosius, the first Christian emperors, that the use
of the (more easily accessible) codex was generalized. In view of the synchronization
between the takeoff of the faith and the abandonment of the *rotulus* (from which
our theatrical 'role' comes), the advocates of Providence would have had good
reason to locate God in His proper format: had the principle of the book been
discovered after the computer screen, claims of a miracle, at least a technical one,
would still have been made .... The effects of a medium are so consistently foreign
to the intentions of its inventors that one is inclined to detect an invisible hand

[6] Yvonne Johannot, *Tourner la page, Livre, rites et symboles* (Paris: Jérôme Millon 1998),
p. 29.

behind it all. Did not the prehistorian Leroi-Gourhan, a materialist and a believer, discern an almost biological tendency at work in the lineage of artefacts that impels them towards their perfection? Just as there is no large-scale regression of the living (genetic combinations going from simple to complex), no long-term regression can be discerned in the history of our objects. Cultures exchange them with each other, but always in the direction of the future. One group may borrow a less simple language from another, or a less refined religion, but we know of none that exchanged a plough for a hoe. Or a colour television for a black-and-white set. Or a parchment book for a papyrus scroll (even if our current screens do in fact 'scroll').

Sheets of papyrus cannot be folded (too brittle). Only one side can be written on. The reader has to hold it with both hands. It is difficult to handle (while unrolling one side, one has to roll up the other). One sees only a small portion of text at a time. A scroll cannot be leafed through – which has its advantages: the codex requires one to turn the pages with one's hand, whereas one can advance one's 'yad' (the small stem ending in a hand with pointed index finger) over the volume at one remove. This avoids profaning the Torah by touching it with an impure hand. But the scroll has neither index nor synopsis. *To leaf through* with one's finger. *To locate* through pagination and table of contents. *To number* pages. Or *annotate*, writing in the margin oneself: such gestures, which seem timeless to us, have a history. But above all, the old format did not allow the same economy of raw materials. Twenty-eight metres of scroll (which is the transcription surface of Numbers and Deuteronomy) is only 216 pages in the codex. Which gives us the entire Bible in 1,500 pages. To be sure, the absence of punctuation and of separation of words facilitated the process of reduction so dear to Mnemosyne. At this stage God is not only transportable, but manipulable. The scroll–Ark apparatus had allowed an elite people to circulate in its region with its national God. The Book–sermon apparatus will allow an elite to have a multinational God circulate over continents. It is the same *mobilization*, but ratcheted up a notch and with diminishing formats. The in-quarto (the sheet folded in four) allows the officiant to chant before his lectern, *coram populo*, voice and gestures sustained by reading. After the in-octavo (its sheet folded in eight), which will be, later on, the humanist format, not to mention the in-12 and the in-16, familiarity will be pressed to the point of fabricating a pocket God – a mini-Bible to be concealed in one's socks or the swirls of long hair.

Harmony of ends and means. A God poor in spirit speaks to the poor in money, and makes contact through the most economical means. He has the mind of a child, and makes use of a toy. He is close to the gynaecea, and something of a gynophile. He takes to the notebooks which the women of Rome used to note down in shorthand, with stylus of bone or ivory, in minuscule characters, errands to be run and the week's expenses. Pagan Rome made use of scrolls for public life, and for more intimate occasions there were those little wax tablets, easily erasable (like our 'magic slates'), with protruding edges, no bigger than a hand. No grandiose dialectic? Not to worry – we'll use the servants' staircase. Yahweh was a *He* addressing an *us*. His successor (and rival) will be an *I* addressing a *me*. I answer in person to a personal voice. He speaks to me familiarly, I to him more formally, but in our private encounters it is no longer the survival of a people but *my* life that is at stake. Hence the need for asides, for short intimate conversations, which were not permitted by the magnificent *sofer*. The inner voice has found its channel. And when, starting in the seventh century, the words of the text will be separated by Irish monks (until then *scriptura continua* reigned, requiring reading aloud), murmured – and then finally silent – reading will become possible. God, said Saint Paul (1 Corinthians 1: 21), decided to save mankind through *kerygma*, not *didache*, which is argued instruction. No need to compete with those wells of science. I will make my basilica from your notepad.

The new Law triumphing over the old? This was depicted in bas-reliefs on the tympanum of cathedrals, as in the Porch of Glory in Santiago de Compostela. On opposite sides of a majestic Christ, the central column of truth, we see, confronting each other, the prophets on the left, hugging their *volumen*, and the Apostles on the right, *in-quarto* in hand. As in a hundred medieval wood engravings, altarpieces or paintings, in which the Apostle, the Saint, the Church Father at the foot of the Cross, holds the Book to his chest, the symbol that dispenses with all speech (the first representations of the codex date from the fifth and sixth centuries), facing the empty-handed Virgin. The rectangle reassures; the *volumen* upsets. It attests, in the eyes of the medieval Christian, to a sinuous, insinuating and ungraspable mind, gliding and slinking like a fox (*volpes*). Undulation yields to angularity; the straight and straightforward triumph over the sinister circumvolutions of the scroll. Now the wanderer can attach the Gospel to his belt or his wrist. The mere sight of it is a comfort for the lost pilgrim, 'the stranger sighing on his treeless plain'. His own private Jerusalem.

Let us not forget the material, the flesh of that angel bearing and transmitting the Holy Spirit. The appearance of the codex followed almost immediately that of parchment – the 'hide of Pergamum' that was said to have been invented in the second century before Jesus in order to deal with the lack of papyrus in that city, whose library was intent on rivalling that of Alexandria. Codices of papyrus have been found (Nag Hammadi, for example), and *volumen* in parchment, but over time the two fused. The animal skin (sheep, goat or calf) offered a support that was at once more solid and more supple. It is thick, but it can be thinned down from both sides, and its smooth surface, amenable to the use of a quill, can be easily erased with a scraper (whence our palimpsests). One inconvenience: the raw material is expensive. One more reason why books were scarce in the Middle Ages.

Proof by Ratings

From the perspective of 'mass psychology', in terms of effectiveness, the Church was right to diminish itself by attributing to God's intervention rather than to its own genius what is called in its lexicon the 'admirable propagation' of the faith. The divine summons effaces the propitious circumstances, the spiritual exhaustion of an Empire undergoing dislocation, the devotion and talent of its propagandists. Christian apologetics delights in emphasizing the 'absolute disproportion' between the insufficiency of the means at its disposal and the obstacles it encountered, from which the supernatural and predestined character of the faith's expansion is concluded. Such were the fruits of the missionary apostolate that they surpassed human capacities. 'A propagation so admirable constitutes a veritable miracle of a moral order, marking a positive intervention of God in favour of Catholicism.'[7] That the ubiquitous reception of a belief is the proof of its credibility is an argument already put forward by Irenaeus and Origen, and one that Saint Augustine was happy to turn to advantage. How might one have arrived at this point: the Empire officially converted, caught 'only in the nets of faith' cast by an infinitesimal number of unknown, feeble and unskilled men? 'Would the Crucified have ever been capable of such a labour had he not been God made man?' (*Faith in things one cannot see.*) *Consensus omnium* is an argument of prestige, not of truth. The eternal banner of the *fait accompli*. 'What is believed always and by all has every chance of being false', Valéry would observe one day. It is the thought of a man given to solitude, not a militant. To make the validity of a belief depend on the number of its believers is the logic of the political, of publicity, of popularity. It imposes itself on us currently as a habit – better still, as something that is self-evident, the culmination of all our public (intellectual and contingent) debates. Saint Augustine, more scrupulous than we are, is not so easily satisfied by democracy's own argument from authority, opinion polls, whose inherently shocking character he is prepared to admit. It is the sinful nature of man, he says, which is responsible for the clouding of his judgement, barring him from the paths of simple reason, necessitating his recourse to authority. That principle constitutes the expansive force of truth for anyone who does not have instinctive access to it. God alone can make do without authority, since He is pure reason. We, for our part, need external guarantees, like those offered by the Church and the faith of the multitudes. *Crede ut intelligas.* Believe, poor sinner, so that you may understand, since you are too weak to understand by yourself, without external assistance . . . .

The apologetic argument of *quod semper et ab omnibus* – what is believed always and by all cannot fail to be true – is double-edged, since by that standard, Allah is more 'true' than our Good Lord, and Mohammed more credible than Jesus. Epi-

---

[7] *Dictionnaire de théologie catholique*, XII, 1, p. 694.

demic for epidemic, the propagation of Islam was to be still more impressive, in terms of both its coverage and its speed. A hundred years after the death of the Prophet (632), his doctrine covered a span that stretched from the Indus to Spain (by way of Poitiers). In the footsteps of Omar, the Omayyads transported it west from the East. And the time between the death of Mohammed and the Hegira was a third of that between the death of Jesus and the beginning of the Christian era. The transport of Christ took place at the speed of boats and pedestrians, not of Arabian horses. It was slower, but also (or therefore) more peaceful. The last imperial persecutions, at the very beginning of the fourth century, could do nothing against a faith that was already established in Asia Minor, in Thrace, Thessaly, Spain, Germania, Gaul and Armenia. Mithras was stuck, confined to the camps and their men. Jesus Christ won over even the Court, through wives like those of Diocletian and Commodus. He even infiltrated the legions, despite the theoretical incompatibility between the military condition and the Christian. One thousand eight hundred bishops in the West and the East at the time of Constantine. The evangelizing division of territory had no need of a state in order to make its dominion felt. Because the Word was already allied with a Power, the Church.

Streamlining of the vade-mecum, reinforcement of the organization. Less written material, more administrative personnel. Such would be the specific difference between the latticework *Deus* in relation to the more sombre *Elohim*. In mediological terms: the codex in place of the scroll, a reduction in OM (organized matter); and the new Israel in place of the old, a consolidated MO (materialized organization). Perhaps the two engines, one technical, the other living, of a long-term transmission are in constant and inverse relation (when one decreases, the other swells), a conjecture yet to be tested. What remains certain is that the success of Christianity was to owe more to its personnel than to its instruments.

7 The Mediating Body

Outside of the Church, no salvation.
(Saint Cyprian)

In the long term, propagation would not have been possible without the help of the Hierarchy. Whether Papist or, later on, Presbytero-synodal, it has been the unloved member of the Christian Movement, which periodically accuses it, not without reason, of being unfaithful to evangelical values. But to oppose the Word to the Institution as good to evil is to forget that the message itself (the Gospel) would not exist without its vehicle (the Church), which has shaped it and carried it unto us. How was one to give a substitute homeland to the followers of a god without a country and with anarchic propensities unless they were integrated into an organism that was spiritual, to be sure, but endowed with a skeletal organization? The resiliency of Christianity ought thus to be sought less in its values, which were for the most part borrowed from ancient traditions, than in an unprecedented vector, the archetypal institution of the West, the Roman Catholic Church. An 'imperilled monument', but one under whose shelter a deracinated God came to be implanted and to flourish for centuries.

Jesus: God is coming. He's due this evening. Don't waste any more time.

The apostles: Christ is coming back. He'll be here tomorrow morning. Hurry up.

There was no decent soul at the time with the audacity to come up with the right prognosis: neither God nor Christ was on the horizon. Neither this evening nor tomorrow morning. Be satisfied with His Church. And accept that partial good with patience.

The impasse was forgivable. Better to bring men good tidings than bad, if you want a good reception. The announcement-effect aroused enthusiasm, and for good reason. Given all that failed to transpire afterwards, the Good Tidings may, alas, be entered under the copiously represented category of 'information plausible but unconfirmed as of this day'.

The Prey for its Shadow?

There are two Churches: one visible, the other invisible. Like the Christ whose bride it is, the Church has a dual nature. Human and divine. The faithful *know* that the eternal and invisible Church is the mystical body of Christ. But they *see* only the real one, God's people in flesh and bone, charged not with incarnating but with *preparing* the return of Christ and the Last Judgement. Their hope is with the *societas perfecta*, but they live in an awkward compromise which enables, somewhat haltingly, access to the perfect community of the end of time. The old-regime prophet reminded us that we had to *await* the kingdom of God. His successor went a step further: he *announced* it. A Christian can be compared to a moviegoer who has paid for his ticket and is still waiting for the beginning of the film. For twenty centuries, history has been projecting a coming attraction, and he does not protest. Faith is a disappointment overcome, and the Church an efficient administration of a mortifying setback.

In the long term, one learns resignation (just as one grows accustomed without problem to minimalist art). But the fanatics of the Millennium and the Second

Coming, the readers of Isaiah and Saint John, invariably balk at taking the preparations for the feast for the feast itself. Impatient people who are listening out for
the Last Trumpet or the arrival of the Antichrist take their impatience for an anticlerical argument. But the visible Church is there to make the disappointing slowness of things acceptable. In the sixteenth century, other men in a hurry would seek
to cut short such difference/deferral [*différance*], mouldy adornments and corrupt
purple, such perpetual postponement of deadlines, in order to return to the living
heart of things, the lost Message, a candid Jesus not yet diverted from his course or
damaged by the impediment of a Church. They advocated a universal ministry (the
priesthood of every Christian); the right of any assembly of men and women
gathered together anywhere to listen to the Word of God to constitute themselves as
a Church, with no other constitution than the Bible; the opportunity to choose their
spiritual leaders freely, without any delegation of power, but only in so far and for
as long as God bestows on them the requisite charisma. They called themselves
evangelists or *congregationalists*. And their wishes were not satisfied. Either their
communities fell under the sway of princes, becoming once again alienated to the
temporal sphere. That was what happened to the Lutherans and Anglicans (the
Queen is head of the Church of England). Or they generated their own internal
hierarchy, through a different feat of organization. That was what happened to the
Calvinists. Despite their pious vows, such was the situation of the reformed
Churches, with their provincial and general synods, their consistories, their
assemblies invested with authority in matters of faith and discipline ... . Luther
sought to discard the organization. And Calvin founded a different one. No
apparent way out.

But might there not in fact be a reason inherent in such irrationality? And why
would the toothing stone of the primitive Church still be awaiting completion,
without anything allowing us to predict the advent of the Reign of God, which
would render every Church useless and without purpose?

That the New Covenant was intent on being present to all – not only in Judah and
Samaria, but 'unto the ends of the earth' (Acts 1: 8) – is something we can all
understand. But why, then, through *specialized personnel*? The search for an answer
compels us to enter a shadowy zone where we have been toiling for the last two
thousand years, and which does not culminate in the cloisters, mitres and croziers of
a specific clergy. The metamorphosis of a *movement* into an *establishment* has
recurred a sufficient number of times, since the emergence of Christianity, for the
subject to supersede the clerical/anticlerical reflex. Mass ideologies have shown us
since then that the transmutation of gold into lead is not a prerogative reserved
solely for divine bureaucracies. Alfred Loisy's famous line ('we were waiting for
Christ, but it was the Church that came') can be transposed to more than one
register. The Communist: we were waiting for the proletariat, but it was the Party
that came. The republican: we were waiting for cosmopolitan Reason, but it was the

nation-state that came. The liberal: we were waiting for the free market, but it was the trust that came. And so forth. In place of the message, the medium (which accomplishes it while contradicting it). Is that how mankind manages to live on?

In the beginning, a freely accessible God, free to be used as we wish. At the point of arrival (three centuries later) a corps of professionals, with security nets, badges, regulations and travel passes. An open fraternity awakens as a closed system. The greatest interiority (the deciding soul) has engendered the greatest exteriority (the episcopal hierarchy). The 'all equal before the faith', free men and slaves, circumcised and Gentiles, becomes 'ecclesiastic immunity' and 'privilege of conscience' (which removes the cleric from ordinary jurisdictions). Disconcerting and bitter would be the 'black box' whose entry is the Sermon on the Mount, and whose exit is the Roman Curia. What, then, transpired between input and output? The duties and constraints of the inscription of a Word in time. Messianic expectation did not give itself a remunerated ministerial corps for the sadomasochistic pleasure of interrupting the great *agape* of equals (the first Christian communities held their property in common) but because it could not be revived without giving itself stature and statutes. The proof *a contrario* is the fate of comparable messages of salvation which, for lack of institutional tutors, evaporated over the course of centuries. This is what happened to the Gnostic tendencies contemporary with the earliest Christianity, which remained, when all is said and done, marginal or minority schools of thought. Those mini-unanimities did not grow into Churches; they failed in their quest for a 'common touch'. They remained philosophies. The Jewish people, strong in its memory and biological fecundity, succeeded in 'conquering the power of death' (Jesus to Peter, Matthew 16: 18). The dissident of the catacombs did not even have that hope, the excess of births over deaths. He was an asocial being living on the loose, whose identity would have to be constructed in its entirety once the break between the Sages of Israel and the disciples of Jesus had been consummated. 'Induration' and 'durability' share a common root. The Church's congealing of the will-o'-the-wisp was the price to be paid for being freed from the land and its dead. It is the flip side of a king without a kingdom, a Messiah without a people, a master without a (captive) audience.

A Deterritorialized God

Promised Land, Holy Land, Holy City – the New Testament knows nothing of such expressions. The Pauline epistles make no reference to the Land. The Word became Flesh and 'dwelt among us'. Where was it? A mere anecdote. No fleshly attachment to the soil, no supernatural pegging to a plot of land. It is the body of Christ that is the territory and true Temple of the Christian. There are at present many Jews who do not separate their fate from that of Israel. How many Catholics bind their faith to the Holy See as a state? The imaginary space of the former is a radiance surrounding a heart. The space of the latter is centrifugal, dynamic, afocal, the sum of its vanishing points. The Host can be shared anywhere, 'in spirit and in truth'. Yahweh remains politically competent in a given space (however imprecise it may be, the auspicious 'between the Nile and the Euphrates', the maximal option, being subject to many a squeeze of the accordion). The peregrinatory character of Christian existence also makes of the Church a people on the march, like Abraham. The Christian is a man 'towards', not a man 'in'. Yet his march is not orientated towards a magnetic centre (despite the folkloric all-roads-lead-to-Rome). The dispersal of the apostles after Pentecost was without melancholy. For Jesus had left the Temple for good. When Peter, Paul, James, and the others packed their bags to 'go teach unto all the nations', in keeping with Jesus' plan, it was without the slightest need to see Jerusalem again, for it was a point of departure, not of return. The penitential achievement of the pilgrim lies in the pilgrimage itself. 'Strangers and travellers on the earth,' says Saint Paul. Even if a calvary is required at the end of forgiveness, and the stations along the Way of the Cross and the spires of Chartres are visible from the main highway, the road of the convert resembles those paths that lead nowhere. The political price of the Only One remains high, but the second Israel reduced it considerably by pursuing the movement of deterritorialization, the disenchantment with places begun by Judaism, before swerving off course. The question of sovereignty over the holy places, which is crucifying and central for the Jew and the Muslim, is not, for the Holy See, a strategic or crucial question (and, for the Protestants, not a question at all). It is in the order of the negotiable. At the cry 'The al-Aqsa mosque is in danger', tens of thousands of Muslims rally to the esplanade of the Mosques and declare themselves ready to die. Beneath the Dome of the Rock, the footprint of Mohammed is venerated; Jesus' footprint in the place of the Ascension does not galvanize Christians to a comparable degree. As the Melchite priest of Nazareth recently observed: 'for the Christian, it is always possible to go pray a little further on than the spot where he is accustomed to doing so; in Islam, it is unimaginable.'[1]

'The fact that I don't live in Jerusalem is secondary. Jerusalem lives in me,' writes Elie Wiesel. 'Forever inseparable from my Jewishness, it remains at the centre of my commitments and my dreams.'[2] Rome does not haunt the dreams of the Catholic in this way, and even less so those of the Christian. It retains, to be sure, a bond of filial memory with the capital of the Caesars, become the city of the popes. Saint Peter's Square will be for the Catholic a place of inspiration and replenishment to which one comes to perform one's devotions, as a sign of faith and unity. Catholicity is in communion with the See of Rome, but it is not the See but the Pontiff that is holy.

[1] Émile Shoufani, *Le Monde*, 21 November 2000.
[2] Elie Wiesel, 'Jérusalem: il est urgent d'attendre', *Le Monde*, 18 January 2000.

The primacy of the apostolic see (*Roma locuta est, causa finita est*) does not stem from the divine will, and when the tradition evokes the rock on which Jesus will found his Church, it designates Peter's faith, and not the site of Saint Peter's (it was only at the end of the fourth century that the bishop of Rome, Damasus, would invent the pun in order to ground his power). Papal supremacy is a function of the contingency of the various powers (it has in fact existed only since the fifth century; previously every bishop was a pope, and the Pope was simply a bishop among others), as well as of a written forgery, Constantine's celebrated donation (composed in the eighth century by the Curia and antedated, the document would invent the donation of the city of Rome to the Pope by the Emperor Constantine, in 330). The sacral quality of the Vatican State is currently no more than the effect of a ricochet. That absolute monarchy by divine right governs the smallest state in the world, but it is a state like any other, without particular privilege, except in the realm of protocol (the nuncio, dean of the diplomatic corps). Christian faith, which is not acephalic, is acentric. It is the drop of quicksilver, running in all directions, which exasperated the powers that be. Celsus saw no better sign of the dangerousness of those 'fanatical Galileans' (Epictetus) than their refusal to tie themselves to a country, a sanctuary, like everyone else. For the Roman mentality, an a-national and anarchizing God, who could invoke no *mos majorum*, no ancestral custom, bordered on atheism. Unthinkable or barbaric.

Certainly, solidly built sanctuaries would arise following legalization (the first basilicas date from 313). Through a brutal inversion of foundations, the escapees of Judaism were obliged to huddle around their Torah at the very time when the homeless of the new faith were laying the bases of a ground plan of long duration. The smooth, open and uniform space freed up by Saint Paul managed to turn to profit its lack of inscription in existing geopolitical reality through a deliberate reutilization of the grid of the imperial habitat. This was going to change the face of the lands of the West. The whirlwind ideal of the pentecostal, the free intensity of the God-mad, would never have permitted the grounding of Christianity in the substructure of the Empire. Since no one has access to the Most-High on his own, the question is whose step-ladder one will borrow: tradition or decision. The Christian relation to transcendence is by way of a voluntary assembly (the *ekklesia*), within an agreed-on enclosure (the diocese). The faithful are 'convoked as a people by the Word of God', and the people does not pre-exist that Word. No cleric without an attachment (the 'gyrovague' or wandering monk being the exception), no bishop without a see or *cathedra* (while awaiting the cathedral). There is, in fact, a cartography of perimeters of the divine, and not a series of free-floating epiphanies. But here the implantation is not first, but second. It is a means, not an end.

Deterritorialization exalts the men of the breakthrough, not those who are obsessed with the difficult burden of endurance. The apostles arrogated to themselves the mission not of interpreting but of changing the world. They had at their disposal neither logic nor physics, as did the academics of the day. They had nothing but an ethic and their feet. From that internalization of faith, there might have resulted an ethereal and abstract *Primum movens*, an intelligible and unconditioned Demiurge of the Platonic sort, a Mind without heart, projected into the air by his ubiquitousness. Incarnation, with the weight of its ballast, brought subtlety back down to earth. In our day, it is not easy to gauge the scandal provoked by that inversion of signs. 'God chose what is foolish in the world to shame the wise' (1 Corinthians 1: 27). Things were upside-down. A transmutation of all values. The body as a grave? It was the lever of salvation. The cross of infamy? It was the badge of glory. The outlaw? He was your Lord. Place what is low on high, and everything will go well, or better. 'We proclaim Christ crucified, a stumbling block to Jews and foolishness to Gentiles' (1 Corinthians 1: 23). In the wisdom of the Greeks, matter is evil and the aim of philosophical *askesis* is to extricate the soul from the prison of the body. Nor does the Eternal compromise Himself in the world of the Jews (let alone with the first passer-by, to make a demigod). Whereupon a man of audacity and insolence arrives and consecrates the shameful, declaring: I deliver through the body, and through it I enter into communication with the beyond. And as a recompense, I promise you that you will be able to discover it anew, your body, on the day of the Resurrection of the chosen. Saint Paul, in view of the Last Judgement, exhorts his brothers to 'offer their bodies as a living host, holy and agreeable to God'. He makes of the Church 'the body of Christ', of which the converts are the members (and the bishops the head). And whose consistency will provide consolation for a certain isolation in relation to one's community of origin. Christianity, the inventor of the *ego*, individualized the relation to the divine, but if it had remained an individualism of salvation, it would already have entered the museum of anthropology.

Homo viator casts his anchor somewhere on the globe at random. And, in truths of faith, by necessity. The latter compensates for the former. Unlike his elders. Open the newspaper. A surge of Jewish fundamentalism issues in a *territorial inflammation* (hold on to Hebron, keep Mount Moriah). A surge of Catholic fundamentalism issues in a *doctrinal inflammation* (hold fast to transubstantiation and infallibility). To the *nostalgic furor* of the elder brothers corresponds, among their juniors, a *dogmatic furor*. One cardinal point for another. For lack of a geographical fixation (no salvation outside Jerusalem), a clerical fixation (no salvation outside the Church).

The Wisdom of Danton

'One destroys only what one replaces,' sighed Danton one day in 1793, as the desacralization of the body of the king sacralized, by displacement, the body of the

French nation. That all-too-lucid revolutionary was indicating what all revolutions forget, and what the years take on the burden of reminding them of, to their surprise. The Christian revolution would not have succeeded in trampling on the ethnographic had it not swiftly replaced it – one for one – with the organic (sublimated into a 'mystical body'). The consolidated assembly of the Lord (the *ekklesia*) assumed the functions which had until then devolved to the *qahal Yahweh*, the people of God. An *ersatz* anchorage, the price paid for the call to 'cut loose your moorings'. Did the revolution consist in privatizing the Eternal, substituting a first-person creed for the 'do as our ancestors do'? It had as a counter-feature the formation of a *trans-ethnic ethnic community*, a *new Israel* endowed with sees, circumscriptions, patriarchates, dioceses and parishes. And gradually provided with distinctive insignia. Until Vatican II, there was *Latin*, planetary vehicle and adornment; a ceremonial *gestuary*, signs of the cross and genuflection, an intercontinental language of gestures; and a multinational *liturgy*, as if 'raising a standard for the nations' (Esdras 11: 12). One holy ark was needed to replace another.

Whether in Ancient Greece or in contemporary India, religious observances have no need of dogma or a channel of faith as 'pillar and bulwark of the truth' (I Timothy 3: 15). One is, by right, of a specific religion when one is from a specific city or caste. Orthodoxy is pointless. In an autochthonous tradition, the soil of a lineage and the bedrock of citizenship replace a written canon – to considerable advantage. When habit no longer inspires, it falls to a decision to do so. The category of truth introduced by Christianity into the religious universe undoubtedly had, among other functions, that of providing ballast, roots for free-floating belief, which asks of the abstract space of dogma (the decision of truth, voted in an assembly after debate) the *definition* and *circumscription* refused it by a God whose limits are indiscernible. Whence the need, which would be grotesque for a Greek or a Hindu, to label and certify levels of truth (as in philosophy, the science of the true, but here for purposes of internal organization). For there are hierarchies within the articles of faith, which descend from the true to the probable. On high: *revealed* truth, the Gospels. Then, *authorized* truth, the Church Fathers. *Authenticated* truths, the lives of saints. Finally, *alleged* truths, the hearsay of tradition. Such scales of truth were fully deployed in the Middle Ages, but the conciliar decisions of the first centuries prepared the way. We should perceive in them the perverse effect, in the objective utterances of faith, of a subversive subjectivization of the acts of faith. Perverse, because unintended and reversing the alleged intentions of the utterer. 'You are Peter, and on this rock ...'? But Jesus said nothing even distantly resembling the 'no one can have God as a father if he does not have the Church as a mother' of Cyprian, Bishop of Carthage, even less so, his famous 'outside the Church, no salvation'. 'Hierarchy' is a term unknown to the Gospels. Like those of heresy, dogma, bishop, and even (sacerdotal) priesthood. That lack was not even a lack – at the time. With God being awaited on the morrow, what need for a Mother of the Faithful, sole authorized interpreter of Scripture, sole dispenser of sacraments, sole channel of grace? The prophet of the familyless neither anticipated nor wanted the *Una Sancta* (any more than Marx anticipated or wanted the Party). It was unpredictable, *for lack of a precedent.* An *extraterritorial divine* had never been seen. Now, less mother turned out, in the end, to be more catechism. An effacement of the natural bounds of loyalty was sooner or later to be balanced out by a series of inequalities of rank and status within the effacing institution.

There is no Hebraic – or Greek or Roman – ecclesiology. Nor are there articles of faith. Nor any Congregation for the Doctrine of the Faith (the former Holy Office). For the Greeks, for whom gods and men share a common essence, for whom 'religious' and 'civic' are synonymous, the clergy is a magistrature elected or chosen at random (anyone can be a 'priest'). Not a sacerdotal caste. For the Hebrews, a 'kingdom of priests and a holy nation', the administrative service of the Temple, a minor clergy, devolved to the tribe of Levi, which was awarded maintenance of the cult because it was the only tribe to be excluded from possessing land. They were a tribe of paupers, virtual pariahs, whom the others were expected to support, and who did not have jurisdiction over the realm. The king was not permitted to enter the Holy of Holies, which could be entered only by the high priest. But the Eternal was not the property of the Levites. He might, if He so pleased, outflank His servants and address His people directly through the mouth of the prophets; and anyone might interrogate the Torah, the supreme instance, directly. Let us go a step further. The City of Antiquity, like the Hebrews, had no clergy for the simple reason that *it had no religion.* It was Christianity that invented religion as something apart – a separation that had no meaning for a Greek (who did not even know the word, since he did not separate the human and the divine, matters civic and those pertaining to worship), nor for a Jew, because in Judaism, nation and religion are one. In Jerusalem, Athens and Rome, civic ritual was religious, and religious ritual civic. For our three mother-cultures, the extra-religious would lie outside the city or outside the people. Which made it unthinkable. Thus those cultures could not reflect the inner/outer relation, or problematize the opposition between belief and non-belief (they are within). The convert, on the other hand, is called on intellectually to ground a decision of thought. If the gods of the city or the nation can make do without an organ of selection, such an organ is a vital need for the God of Jesus. For He was by no means a matter of course. He was to be found neither in the cradle nor in the forum. For which reason He needed a bureaucracy.

Every rabbi is free to read as he likes. And every reader is free to choose his rabbi. In such cases, there is no institution decreeing the truth. Among the Pharisees, everything could be said. The holy text remained *open.* Why? Because the family *encloses* on its own, through mother, foreskin and *kashrut.* The unity of the Jewish people is granted materially and ancestrally (kitchen, circumcision and baths); the Christian people, in its formative stages, did not have that foundation; hence the extreme fragility of its future. The pluralism of tendencies within Judaism (Christianity having been one of them), the more or less accepted separatisms, were a luxury that Christianity in its early stages could not indulge in without risking dismemberment. Here it was by way of the corpus that one could form a corps, and anyone who meddled with the corpus attacked the corps. The freedom to be part of (or not) gives rise to other constraints. Because one is born a Jew (and adapts to customs), one has no need to prove one's Jewishness by latching on to one or another interpretation of the revealed word. Because one is born French or Belgian, one has no need to prove one's Frenchness or Belgianness by elaborating on the exact meaning of the national colours. There can be a hundred ways of being Jewish or French; none has the value of a principle. To the individual who voluntarily submits to baptism, the social bond is not extended in the same way. This is why Roman Christianity is not, strictly speaking, a religion of the Book (like Judaism, Islam or Protestantism), and that for two reasons – ceremonial and doctrinal. The ritual of the synagogue refers the believer to a text; Holy Communion refers him to an event, which is the Last Supper. In Jewish homiletics, one listens to – or reads – the word of God. In the Mass, one eats and drinks it. One swallows not words, but consecrated bread and wine. The gustatory (and masticatory) culmination of the union of souls with God. Thereafter, and above all, it is the institution, as a last instance, which decides what should be read, and how, and at what time. This decision is both for the worse and for the better. For the worse: the alienation of free inquiry and the spirit of obedience. For the better: the need to argue over revelation and to structure one's understanding of the text, which is no longer sufficient unto itself. Ecclesiastical mediation, which charges the expert with rendering God's word explicit, bore within its flanks a discursive – and ultimately rationalist – mediation (rationality also being a structure of mediation). It relativizes the absoluteness of the sacred text (Christianity is not a fundamentalism of the written). This is where Abelard, Saint Thomas Aquinas, and our universities stem from. And our *lycée* classes in philosophy, a reverse scholasticism.

Those who incriminate the institution in the name of free will should be careful of the perverse effects of their good intentions (the reversal of the result, the only historic law of which one can be sure). Protestant self-service has also had its unexpected effects, transferring from the multinational papacy to local powers the charge of administering the instituted (*cuius regio, eius religio*). Did not Lutheran secularization give freedom and the last word to kings, presidents and, when the time came, to a Führer, allowing politics itself to become religious, that is, worthy of organizing the souls of men in its own interests? And beyond the totalitarian, we have seen how the idea of a self-instituting society can issue in the very Anglo-Saxon cult of the majesty of free enterprise and the temple of Wall Street. Evangelical individualism also comes at a price – which is its opposite, social conformity.

Let us summarize. When a Creator is not pledged to a land or a people, He needs a corresponding institution. 'Nothing is as depressing as a shapeless belief,' Hugo used to say. Such a belief will not take long to remedy the situation, the angel playing the beast, with rather dubious results. Whence we may derive a precautionary principle for our princes and pastors: if you free a man from his religion, give him a homeland. If you free him from his homeland, give him a religion. If you have neither doctrine nor hearth in reserve, at least insert him into a network. Give him a familial affiliation. A solidarity that will augment him. But don't leave him on his own, without beacon or buoy; the drift will devastate him, and you will regret it.

The Costs of Succession

The first thought that comes to us is that the Church was wrong and Jesus right, he who put all men on equal footing, on the same level. And what if it were the other way round? What if the Church did not proceed as stipulated in the Gospel? And what if the tradition were better informed than Jesus about a mystery that he, for good reason, could do no more than intuit: the paths and means enabling the traversal of long periods of time. He told his disciples at his last Passover: 'Do this in remembrance of me.' But how could he have intuited all that was implied by sticking to that come hell or high water? Implementing a successful succession has never occurred without much gnashing of teeth. In the life of any collective – family, empire, sect, regime, school of art or thought – it is the moment of truth. The test and the magnifying glass – fissures made visible. The succession to the throne or to the position of general secretary. The assignment of shares to co-heirs. Percentages of distribution rights. Distribution of the silverware. Civilization might be defined as a slow effort destined to reduce the costs of succession wherever possible, and the state of barbarism as one in which the passing of the torch is effected amid bloodshed or through a simple relation of forces. By war (of succession or devolution), murder (of the dauphin or the tsarevich), usurpation, *coup d'état*. Which is precisely why the trustworthiness of a new regime, or its future prospects, can be appreciated only after the death of its founder. Can it survive him, or not? The rule also holds (and to what an extent!) in the realm of the mind. How is an inspiration to be perpetuated after the disappearance of the inspired one? Some adherents to the doctrine prepare for the supreme ordeal well in advance; in general, they are the ones who don't make it. Like Auguste Comte, they write up their last will with the greatest care, designate their successors, foresee competent organs. Others, like Marx, improvise, and their wake is traced through good years and bad. Jesus, however, belonged to the ranks of the unconcerned. Neither programme, nor contract. No clear orders. Jesus committed suicide *intestate*. His heirs presumptive could have subscribed to René Char's dictum: 'Our heritage is not preceded by any testament.' They laid claim to the inheritance, and made up the testament afterwards. Through recourse to a slightly abusive term. *Testament* is in fact an incorrect Latin translation of the Hebrew *b'rit*, meaning covenant.

There are at present three known forms of testament: *holographic*, under private seal, written, dated, and signed by the hand *de cuius*; *authentic*, dictated to a notary in the presence of two witnesses; and *mystical* (in a sealed and registered envelope). The New Testament does not correspond to any of these three cases. Moreover, Jesus did not clearly designate an executor (the proof being that the Eastern Churches, guardians of the initial orthodoxy, do not admit the primacy of Peter). His apostles did not write under his dictation. If it were examined today by a notary, the New Covenant could no longer be called a Testament. The injured parties, should there be any, would have grounds for talking about a forgery. It is the patina of the *fait accompli* which endowed the substitute with its authenticity.

What does it matter? The important thing is that there should not be escheat, a default of heirs. That the preaching should be taken up anew, ministers should follow each other, an episcopal body should be constituted. And that in the twenty-first century, the biretta of the princes of the Church, the emblem of a cardinal's eminence, can be said, without too broad a smile, to be red *like* the blood of the first martyrs. That exploit, the maintaining of the same, is all the more commendable in that the disciples were obliged to invent everything, since succession by birth (by right of seniority, the son) was excluded (the prophet having remained celibate). Succession by relationship as well (Jesus had brothers, but from a different marriage, if we may put it that way). Thus it was the Holy Spirit who came to fill the familial void and the juridical absence. And teleguided the appointments, elections and laying on of hands. The 'passing' to the Germanic 'barbarians', the sacking of Rome, the various schisms, should have clouded the issue. Not at all. The apostolic succession ('in a straight line') aligns the current Pope with the shadow of Peter. What blood dynasty could compete with that . . . .

The Last Supper, however, does not look like the foundation of an organization. The Church is properly said to be a 'fact of tradition' – from *traditio*, the act of transmitting (from the verb *tradere*, consigning to another, passing on the message). The term encompasses 'all things concerning religion and which are not in Holy Scripture' (Littré). It is rigour itself. There is nothing in Scripture concerning the transmission of Scripture. Jesus does not seem to have been particularly preoccupied with his bodily future. His posthumous bride was discovered gropingly, through a gradual and instinctive empiricism. In honour of her deepest being. The Church is essentially concerned with time. It is *a surmounting of death and an out-manoeuvering of time*. Its birth, according to doctrine, at the foot of the Cross, on the day of Resurrection, illustrates its function to perfection: assuring the durability of the perishable. The fact that its formation partakes of mystery, that it was ascribed by its agents to the supernatural, is entirely to be expected. Just as a choral chant joining different individuals transcends in beauty the mere sum of their diverse voices, the capacity for elevation of fleeting humans successively mounted on each others' shoulders outdoes their individual talents in fertility. The layering produces an exponential result, which is properly superhuman, and surpasses our derisory resources. When one does not attend to the practical means involved, transcended as they are by the sublime end that conceals them from view, one can only 'deify' the outcome. To climb, not to descend, is our first movement: man looks more willingly up in the air than down at his feet. As it happens, the apostolic age confused the spirit of organization with the Holy Spirit. Perhaps because there is a measure of the sacred in every living body, be it collective or individual.

And what if our celebrated 'soulful supplements' were first of all *bodily complements*? We expect from our beliefs a surplus of oxygen, but they manage to achieve it only by lending us the succour of a supplementary body – to us who have so little. An additional bit of porterage, if only an entourage – of mutual assistance, attentiveness, conversation – such as one sees on the signs at church entrances for 'life's wounded', the handicapped and the isolated. And who can claim that he is so well entrenched in his social setting, so satisfied and so great, that he does not need this? Under the auspices of a transcendence that watches over us, we thus find ourselves connected to an immense hearth, with our own place at the fireside. What greater favour could there be than this: to feel ourselves existing for and through others, the appendix of an organism a thousand times less biodegradable than our own? To become a member is a rather narcissistic and all-consuming social project. Pascal had observed as much: 'To be a member is to have life, being, and movement only through the spirit of the body and for the body.' And he added: 'One loves oneself because one is a member of Jesus Christ. One loves Jesus Christ, because he is the body, the *corps* – of which one is a member. All is one, one is the other, as with the three Persons.' To believe is to join the ensemble, to attune oneself, symbiotically (to believe in History, also, was to participate in a vanguard on the march, in the communicative warmth of the 'working class'). Whether secular or revealed, a religion offers succor in that it incorporates us into a reality that is larger and more durable than ourselves. And religious, in the Latin sense, is the proper qualification for all those forms of adhesion that allow us to live together without excessive violence, the 'alia quibus cohaerent homines', as Cicero put it in his *De Legibus*. Spiritual performance can be evaluated in terms of the growth of our coefficiencies, and one can almost gauge the degree of success of the various utopian or mythical propositions that serve as landmarks through the centuries in terms of their capacity of reintegration, re- (as opposed to dis-) memberment. Of the assurances of co-operation, and thus of increased efficiency, that such collective prostheses are able to furnish to individuals. 'Come.' Join us. Join yourself. Give a people to those who no longer have any – or do not yet have one .... Adding on a body, a *corps*, entails two extremely necessary and precarious things: *mapping* the environment, or endowing a surface of circulation with a measure of viability, according to certain thresholds, holy places, and recommended itineraries. And ordering the days according to an organizing thread, by fitting the multiple temporalities of becoming into a common *calendar*. In sum, making of every life a voyage through the liturgical year and the procession of sacraments, from baptism to extreme unction. Giving a meaning to the adventure? A series of landmarks and appointments. A compass and a datebook, with which everything begins. Places to go to and dates to celebrate. Jerusalem, Rome, Mecca, Lent, Ramadan, Hanukah. An inch-by-inch combat against the indefiniteness of unconnected things, disorientation, is won via *rhythm* in time and *landmarks* in space. To the roadmen of God, the gratitude of the errant. For having kept to the slope, eschewing the panic of a space and time bereft of marks and stations.

A Hierarchy to Make the Chain

In order to transmit, one has to get organized. And to organize, alas, means to hierarchize. One did not know this at the beginning. One became a member as soon as people began to assemble in a basement to pray together. The Spirit flourishes where people gather together (Irenaeus and Hippolytus hold that a believer can no longer participate in the Holy Spirit if he deserts the *ekklesia*). The *ekklesia* was the thing that belonged to everyone. *Koinônia*, in the first century, meant sharing and openness. But a hierarchical organization had already begun to take shape during the time of the apostles, in the various local communities, with the 'presbytes' (the elders, the directors) and the *diakonoi* (the servants). The first witnesses of the Word, and that includes Jesus himself, had no words to grasp a phenomenon that was as shocking as it was unpredictable. Necessity appears to have laid down the law.

The notion of an episcopate or an 'overseer' (the bishop) is not in tune, to say the least, with the spirit of the Gospels. No *primus inter pares*, no formal and closed College. At the very most, one can say that Jesus conferred on his disciples the title of 'fishers of men', with the 'power to bind and unbind'. After the death of the Master, the Apostles recruited younger seconds, the *synergoi*, itinerant associates like Titus and Timothy, Barnabas and Priscilla. So we already have an organizational chart. With a duplication of functions characteristic of any group *in statu nascendi* (political party, ministerial cabinet, enterprise or sect): every collaborator (or *synergos*) will choose another to work at his side, to relieve him and eventually replace him, once he has been moved up a notch. 'What you have heard from me through many witnesses entrust to faithful people who will be able to teach others as well' (2 Timothy 2: 2). The advantage: an assistant who takes on another is no longer one himself; he becomes an elder, a senior, a master. The social division of religious labour is no more capricious than the division of labour *tout court*. What is in fact needed is (1) to divide up the zones of intervention and competence (in order to avoid a duplication of tasks); and (2) to indicate, to the outside world, precisely who is qualified for which service. In order to know and make known who is doing what, and who is who. How, otherwise, can one ensure the validity of sacramental acts and ministries? Daily life has its obligations. One needs a service personnel (but one that can be trusted) to oversee the offices of charity. A minister is a servant. One begins with minor ministries charged with *agapae* (meals offered to the poor); caring for widows and deacons; aid to the poor; mutual aid; hospitality (a traveller carrying a letter of recommendation is received as a brother); burials. And one ends up with the major ones. The community meal: who is seated at the table, and who serves (it is difficult to do both)? Public homilies: who reads the Scriptures out loud, and who listens? Processions to receive the relics of saints: who marches at the head, and what order for the cortege – adults before children, but virgins before or after widows?

A liturgical service, for example, is a spectacle. Profane or sacred, it rests on a division between stage and pit, altar and nave, pulpit and public. How are people to be distributed? Where should the dais be put? The measures taken by authority negotiate such trifling irritations and embarrassments, which make for the triviality of any collective – at ground level. Such questions are raised (or, rather, resolved before being raised, with a measure of urgency and as mere expedients, thought of as provisional and secondary, that is, not thought of at all) as soon as it is a matter of *following up* on an act of witness, an instant of grace, an exceptional encounter. They have the effect of an annulment as soon as the charismatic effervescence subsides. Such effervescence *never provides the solution to the questions it raises*. A seer, prophet or 'guide' is by definition an *energumen*. The Latin of the Church understood by that term one possessed by a demon (from the Greek *energein*, to breathe life into, put into action). But the man of God was also a fanatic, possessed by the Holy Spirit, demanding trust without being particularly trustworthy himself. The features of spiritual perturbation as intermittences or deviations from the norm are inherent in its exercise. A virtuoso at upsetting balances may ignite the flame; he does not pass on the torch. Revolution or Revelation, Spartacus or Jesus, are all uncontrollables, free electrons provoking the spark. Only the professionals of a return to order will make of it a persistent glimmer. In the libertarian Barcelona of 1936, Malraux evoked in depth the 'organization of the Apocalypse'. Or the failure overcoming the insurrection by virtue of its very victory (when the Communist snuffer descends on the anarchist flame). Giving the floor to this person rather than that, a position of command to one rather than the other, is already to quash a certain spontaneity. Dousing the flame (or lowering the voltage) in order to be able to pass it on is the bitter contradiction that haunts every act of transmission.

Gifts of the spirit cannot be programmed, and are non-hereditary. Different ones are called for if information is to survive its emitter, or the flash its genius. Charismatics are not particularly cautious when it comes to these matters (if they were, the charisma would evaporate). They have the merit of breaking up a *status quo* and the inconvenience of not instituting another. Now if no arrangement has been made, with due discernment, to move from the unpredictable to the repeatable, the breakthrough will have been in vain. The Holy Spirit cannot be commanded. Yet it must be. I, an already ordained bishop, ordain you a priest. The ordained is an individual inspired on command. Investiture initially affects the liturgy, and secondarily the teaching. Categories emerge, some entitled to transmit, others not. A hierarchy exists as soon as the holders of certain functions can be substituted for others *without the reciprocal being possible*. The bishop can be a 'lector'; the 'lector' cannot replace the bishop. Such is the *relation of order*. One can choose one's form of community, but how can one escape the inegalitarian relation which alone gives body to a communitarian entity? The ministers of the Legitimate (or the authorized commentators) repress the others; if they did not, they would not be ministers. A neophyte is not ordained into the episcopate; a filtering process is called for. This is already, in essence, the duality of the clergy and the laity, or *docentes* (teachers) and *discentes* (learners). The pure remove or demote the less pure. Or they purify them according to certain initiation rituals, entitling the profane to enter into contact with the divine, touch sacred vases or the scroll of Scripture, in successive degrees (the *cursus honorum*), up to the final sacred communions (forbidden to cantors and sacristans, second-class ministers).

The most expensive part of posterity is the transition from adjective to noun. Initially (in Clement's epistle to Rome), *laïkos* was a mere epithet designating 'one who has no sacred ministry to fulfil'. At the same time, and in tandem, *kleros* still designated only a function, not a state. Until the day on which the occasional use was transformed into a personal status. Divine election was bureaucratized. One had started out with the notion of *service*, and a bishop elected by his faithful; and one arrived at the notion of *dignity,* by which only a bishop can enthrone a bishop. Even if this led to a comparison between the Church and God's ship, with its pilot, sailors and passengers – bishop, deacons and friars. Each function would be linked to its remuneration, the tithe (the people were obliged to provide for the needs of the clergy). After two generations, the *itinerant* apostle was replaced by the *sedentary* bishop. *Hierarchies of function* became *hierarchies of perfection*. And supernatural graces (the gifts of healing, tongues, or science) became the decrees of attribution or prerogatives of rank, linked to careers. It was with the Emperor Theodosius, who generalized, standardized and officialized the system (395), that the 'obscure commutative relation between modes of knowledge and power' (Émile Poulat) would emerge in broad daylight. It would take effect, at each level, via a *territorial switch*: the diocese for the bishop, and, as of the fourth century, the parish for the priest. At the head of his territorialized cell, the pastor held powers that were at once political, administrative and spiritual. In Hippo, currently Bône, in the year 420,

Saint Augustine commanded, judged and levied taxes. The bishop was the local monarch. And consequently, in the community, also garrison commander and police commissioner.

God was at the end of His tether. The bureaucratization of grace was a *second- and third-generation need* (on which the fate of the first was dependent). Jesus the charismatic began by personalizing the bond between man and God, but the organization issuing from the Nicene Creed (325) ended up depersonalizing charisma by way of a priesthood or ministries that did not take into account the character of individuals, for whom only the decision of authority and the proper form of ordination according to the rules counted. That chilling rechannelling became the province of the great-nephews – the successors, not the initial conveyors, of turbulence. The connective tubing became of prime importance as soon as the experiment was intent not on breaking, but on establishing a *chain*. Jesus baptized/ baptizer. Paul/Timothy. Who, once Paul disappeared, would lay hands on one younger than himself. The ambassadors of the Word pass it on *from hand to hand*.

This duty they must, all the same, be duly accredited to perform. Chronologically, the tracing of lines of sacerdotal demarcation (no body without membrane or filter), with rites of installation (laying on of hands or simple benediction) distinguishing the chosen cleric from the lay mass, took place at the same time as the tracing of lines of division among the clerics themselves, with the hierarchy bishops/priests/ deacons. Only bishops and priests [*presbytes*] can confer baptism and ordain deacons (from the Greek *diakonein*, to serve at table). The synchronism attests to the two elements required to constitute a body: closure (in relation to the outside) and hierarchization (within). A limit and degrees. Or classic pyramidal inequality – of which it is not certain that our current implementation of information and knowledge networks will be able to rid us.

Christian identity was affirmed through successive retrenchments from the milieu, enclosing itself in increasingly more exclusive circles. Plunged into the baptist movement, itself close to the Essenes (five hours on foot between the Jordan, where John the Baptist pardoned the sins of anyone who asked him to, and the secessionist monastery of Qumran), Jesus would soon turn his back on it, going into the cities and mixing with commoners. A first boundary. With the prophet dead, the apostolic movement would again close ranks: no ritual sacrifices, since purity dwelt in the heart. No chosen nation; there would be no participation in the war of liberation (68–70). A second enclosure within the first. Which was positive to the extent that such reductions of audience do not produce *in fine* a *residue*, a retractile and threatened islet, a sect, but a totalizing core, present to all and ready to swell into a great circle, the circle of circles. That expansive growth, as we can reconstitute it today following the canonico-liturgical texts of the early Church, occurred for the most part between the period of the *Didascalia* (as the stage directions of the dramatic poet to his interpreters were called in Greek) and that of the *Apostolic Constitutions*, attributed to Hippolytus, priest of the Church of Rome, probably written in Greek around the year 200 and translated into Latin towards 380–400. The first document is still unaware of the clerical separation of functions (it does not know the term *kleros*), and considers it normal that the bishop should recruit his assistants directly from the people on a volunteer basis. The second theorizes the break and elaborates the grades, recommending the existence of remunerated *permanent* positions. From this it may be seen that the Church did not wait for Constantine and marriage with the Empire to normalize and formalize its situation by modelling itself on political officialdom. It institutionalized itself *motu proprio(f)*. The Roman model of the *cursus honorum*, and papal decretals (letters regulating questions of discipline and administration), intervened to complete a process that was already well under way in the fourth century. It is true that when it came to questions of organization, the best builders of pyramids had been the Latin-language theologians, frequently of African origin (Africa being the cradle of the Latin Church), like Tertullian and Cyprian, Bishop of Carthage, who preceded the imperial officialization by a full century.[3]

Thus Operation 'Posterity' is far from a clean slate. It has its fixed costs, which can be reduced only with difficulty. The opening to the future demanded the adoption of ranks, grades and barriers. This also applied to the House of God, where there are spaces that are authorized, reserved and forbidden. Separated from each other. One does not enter a church as one does a common mill. And once inside, there is a regulated progression, from narthex to choir. The latter will be separated from the nave by a *chancel*, a balustrade or railing, often preceded by a *kneeling-stool*. Or if not, by a *glory-beam*, supporting a crucifix or a calvary. The space reserved for clerics is separated from the laity by a rood-screen, a wooden or stone partition.

Christianity is reputed to be the first religious system in the West to have taken into account *the weight of things*, sheltering our minor administrative crises from the supreme meaning. That disqualifying of the Eternal in fact completed a retreat to heaven which the Hebrews had already initiated. In Egypt (as, for other reasons, in the city-states of Mesopotamia), the divine and royal bureaucracies were conflated, with pharaoh placing himself at the intersection of cosmic forces and earthly realities. In Jerusalem, their divorce began: the king was not a god, and God, the only, the absent One, may be opposed to him at any minute. But the Temple remained the centre of Jewish life, and it was not by chance that Spinoza saw in Moses' state the model (and foil) of theocracy (*Tractatus theologo-politicus*). The people of God, Israel, was a social given. The City of God, of Saint Augustine, was a mystical entity. A point of perfection situated ahead and above, 'exiled in the course of the

---

[3] Alexandre Faivre, *Fonctions et premières étapes du cursus clérical*, Doctoral Thesis, Université de Strasbourg II, 1974 (Thesis 8258).

ages', awaiting the day when 'justice be turned into judgement'. What is produced at this juncture is a dehiscence, a divergence between above and below. Gratian ascribes to Saint Jerome, around the fourth century, the ecclesiastic separation of levels of responsibility. The cleric is initially he who enters the ecclesiastical state with the intent to render a service. Major and minor orders were distinguished, in the seventh century, by the tonsure, which was recently abolished.

And the marriage ban will come only with the Lateran Council, in 1123. What remains at the inception is that liberating demarcation of two levels denied by theocracy, and from which our modern secularity would emerge. We are relieved. This is the positive side of the matter. But it is precisely because the clergy is not everything [*tout*] that it was necessary to make it a *whole* [*un tout*] unto itself. In order to be able, like Saint Augustine, to subordinate the order of the flesh to the order of the spirit, or the earthly City to the City of God, one must begin by dissociating them. Cleric comes from *kleros*, the part, the separate lot. 'The Lord's share', the *sorte electi*, those chosen by God. The self-enclosure of an integral and integrated divine body is the flip side of the coin on which may be read the promising theoretical separation of priesthood and empire (Middle Ages), altar and throne (monarchy), Church and State (republic).

Deserters of the zoological as we political animals are, we would do well to scrutinize closely how a durable centre of belonging comes to be engendered. In that respect, the birth of a Church is a lesson in the way of things, to be examined as an archetype in the clinical understanding of groups. Advocates of hermeticism and the esoteric have a tendency to relegate organizational charts to the margins of thought. It is a way, among others, of escaping the reality of human syntaxes and the sad divisions imposed by the constitution of a collective identity, whether profane or sacred . . . .

On Ecclesiology as a Political Science

Saul of Tarsus shared two virtues with Marx's Saint Paul, Lenin: personal ignorance of the master, and a sense of organization. The latter is, basically, a successfully implemented paradox, which consists of setting up walls between men, and immediately consoling them for it thereafter with a series of gangways. Walls, in order to construct a *world for oneself*. And passages, in order to remain *in the world*. Sectarians retrench, but they forget the connective channels. The door without the threshold is half the programme. In order to have a world of their own, they no longer inhabit the world as it is. Opportunists, on the contrary, open up doors on all sides, forgetting the walls. To make the transition from sect to church, doors have to be open *and* closed. The invention of purgatory, in the twelfth century, is testimony to that constraint: Paradise *and/or* Hell. Don't give up, nothing is closed, you'll get there. In Christendom, there is always room, between the extremes of damnation and beatitude, for pedagogical apprenticeships, which function as a waiting-room: the state of the 'blessed', between 'venerable' and 'canonized' (average sainthood); the status of the 'catechumen', between sinner and baptized; of the 'penitent', between faithful and excommunicated; of 'godfather' or 'godmother', between father and mother and anyone else. In the church as a building, there is also the narthex (where catechumens and penitents have to stop), between the nave and the parvis. And in heaven, purgatory, between hell and paradise. Wherever one discovers an inequality, one will find a step. Wherewith to escape despair (it's inaccessible) without lapsing into facility (no tollbooths).

The refusal to sacrifice to all-too-human Caesars, in the name of the transcendence of the divine, can be interpreted as a first limit-position. 'We are different from you.' That intransigence allows for a recharging of the sacral batteries, which had lost too much of their charge through the deifying laxisms of late Roman culture. The Christians thus revalorized the notion of the divine, devalued through a surfeit of apotheoses, the serial deification of the emperors having effaced the barrier between the transcendent and the immanent. By rediscovering a structural verticality amid the proliferation of gods, demigods and heroes, the Christian, as Constantine immediately understood, had given himself a formidable capacity for political *restructuring*. This was ideal for an Empire undergoing decomposition. The first of the bishops, a new Moses, the convert emperor could lay claim, in the name of the One, to the government of all. At the cost of a characteristically Roman confusion between magisterium and magistrature. Forcibly channelled into the Single Party in Communist societies, divergences in doctrine become crimes against History and the People. In the One True Church, divergences in doctrine immediately turn into crimes against God and the Pope.

The fantasy, however hopeless, is irresistible: to attend *de visu* the 'birth of a society'. Grasping the crucial, imperceptible moment in which a random *mass* crystallizes, congeals into a distinct *whole*. That *experimentum crucis* betokens, to be sure, a thoroughly naive nostalgia, and the social sciences were born on the day when the question of 'the origin of society' was consigned to a desk drawer – to the file labelled 'fantasies'. A linguist can be recognized by the fact that he never talks about the origin of languages, just as an anthropologist never talks about the first social contract. 'Let us begin by dismissing all the facts,' Rousseau himself said, while inventing the man of the state of nature. But for us, the origins of Christianity would be what comes closest to the impossible return to the source. With its constitutions, its law, its administrative departments, its language, its schools, its feast-days and days of mourning, its tribunals, its economy, its elected leader and its functionaries, the specific characteristic of the visible society of the invisible God is that we know where and when it was born. That characteristic gives ecclesiology, our first science of organization, 'the awe of beginnings'. Whereas the first mutterings of the others are buried in a poorly documented night, the birth of God's organizational chart is far better attested.[4] Beyond the Acts of the Apostles, which are more theological than historical, we can consult, in particular, the *Ecclesiastical History* of Eusebius (Bishop of Caesarea, in Palestine, 255–340), one of the first to reconstitute in chronological order 'the successions of the holy apostles, as well as the time elapsed from our Saviour until us', the decretals of the pontiffs, the conciliar canons, the monastic rules and the testimony of the Fathers. The amplification through legend and the apologetic perspective do not, it is true, make for works of history in the modern sense of the word. Just as there are no biographies of saints, only hagiographies, for this crucial period we know of no history of theology which is not a theology of that history (as in the case of Saint Augustine). We had to wait for the Maurists, in the sixteenth century (the Benedictines of the Congregation of Saint-Maur), and the great figure of Mabillon (1632–1707) for critical history to make its entry into the precincts of the sacrosanct.

Just as the support is concealed in the message that it makes possible, so the organization is hidden away in the final organ, so that to make one's way into Christian reality through its texts is to confuse an effect with its cause, or the end with the beginning. What we regard as a source and foundation is already in itself an effect of organization, since the collection of normative texts (decisions of authoritative councils or books assumed to be inspired by God) resulted from an ecclesiastical (or administrative) decision. To read Christian institutionality in the light of doctrine is a bit like trying to swim upstream. We can see this from the impossibility we face in disentangling, in doctrinal debate, conflicts of interpretation from factional battles. The Arianist extreme left (Christ was only a man) expresses a southern separatism; Nestorianism (Christ duplicated himself), an eastern dissidence. Various *isms* translate or encode dynastic and national struggles (each province wanting to be sure of its theology and its church). It should not be forgotten that the first seven Councils were *convoked at the behest of the Emperor*, and held in the imperial palace. Political decisions often entailed the creation of a new structure of authority (synod, council, assembly) above the previous one, deemed to be insufficiently docile. Our (revealed) *dogmas* were at the time (arbitrary) *decrees*. Tradition has erased the signature or the decider's *coup de force*; and a deposition of faith was constituted, a sum of ecclesiastic submissions transcended as theological mysteries, advancing in the direction of a reinforcement of imperial unity and authority (g). The Pauline metaphor of the body recommended that one attend first of all to the head. The organizational chart of authorities and that of truths were thus in a position to reinforce each other.

There were, in the beginning, for catechesis, the *didascalia*, free schools preparing catechumens for the baptismal symbol. They were gradually transformed, around the fourth century, into authorized schools or *catachetics*, in which bishops, the

[4] Jean Gaudemont, *Les Sources du droit de l'Église en Occident du IIe au VIIe siècle* (Paris: Cerf 1985).

possessors of revealed truth, were alone entitled to inculcate the creed. The heretical or deviant scholarch was also forbidden to teach (such as Origen, in Alexandria, by his bishop, in 231). Thus proceeded the doctrinal consolidation of the succession from Christ to the Apostles, from the Apostles to the bishops, and from bishops to bishops, until the Lord's boat was stabilized. The aim was to produce what was repeatable (*ut cum dicas nove non dicas nova*: say things in a new way, but do not say anything new). Power detests the unpredictable. The struggle ended, for the most part, with the promulgation of the dissidence as a state religion (the Edict of Theodosius, 380).

For whom the Angelus tolls

We should not pretend that 'hierarchs' exist only in consecrated positions. The postal or ministerial employee who sends his requests, rung by rung, up the hierarchical ladder is still behaving like a cleric of the Church, even like a veritable angel. For the society of functionaries has the same pyramidal structure as that of the angels (the least democratic and most highly militarized collective in existence). The odious word 'hierarchy' was forged not by a cunning despot, but by a most saintly Doctor of neo-Platonic descent, Denys the Areopagite, to designate the order and subordination of the different choirs of angels, distributed in three plateaus. The lowest: the principalities, archangels and angels. The middle: the virtues, dominations and powers. The highest: the seraphim, cherubim and thrones. In heaven as in the army. The struggle against the demons does not allow for any imprecision. The *milicia cœlesti* are as disciplined and closely ordered as shock troops, where everyone is in his place. That functional hierarchy projected to heaven, while magnifying them, the ranks of the ecclesiastic state – *minor orders* (lectors, exorcists, acolytes, subdeacons) and *major orders* (deacons, priests, bishops) – a state which it in turn guaranteed. We find it hard today to confront the harsh truth of the angels, whose greeting-card sweetness masks their martial aspect. Note that in the Church, it was the founders of orders or the generals, like Gregory the Great and Loyola, or even Saint Bernard, who took the angels seriously. Hawks, not doves. Men of action, not rhetoricians. The suppression of the fundamental truths of Christianity by with-it Christians currently finds expression in familiar sentences of the following sort: 'There is something angelic in pretending that a community of the faithful can exist bereft of a hierarchy.' It is precisely the opposite that should be said, and a reader of the Pseudo-Denys, the founder of angelology and the first anthropologist of the bureaucratic phenomenon, would himself have offered a rectification: 'There would be something demonic in pretending that a stable community can be deprived of a hierarchy.'[5] It is worrying to see, so bad is the press

5 *De cœlesti hierarchia*, sixth century.

Emmanuel Tranes, 'Synaxis of Angels', Byzantine and Christian Museum, Athens

received by all that is instituted, to what extent our dubious discourse manages to invert the fundamentals of doctrine. If the formation of a group identity obeys constants imposed on all, believers or not, and before which we are not completely free, our bad faith will be understood. We congratulate ourselves because democratic societies have emerged from religion to devote themselves to the free production of their future. But would they, for all that, be unscathed by the prerequisites of collective existence (which, in our would-be scientific jargon, we call noise reduction, information filtering, organized redundancy), whose set would constitute what we have called elsewhere the 'political unconscious' of humanity? If we resist that flattering illusion, we will not hesitate to say: *clerical truth and religious lie*, on the model of the title 'novelistic truth and romantic lie' (René Girard).

We all dream of *spiritual co-operatives*, or, to put it more modestly, circles of affinities in which cohesion does not come at the price of subordination, and the authority of their inspirers would at last be able to do without an organizational chart (tenure, echelon, rank, dignity, etc.). What can be observed from our modern movements of ideas, in the very heart of atheism, does not respond very satisfactorily to that pious (albeit agnostic) wish. Had it done so, the Christian incorporation would possess little more than a curiosity interest, restricted to ancient history, for us. Would it not be, rather, a kind of anticipatory revelation? Without making it into a standard – and, even less, an unsurpassable – model, it helps to elucidate the obscure birth of those profane circles of collective utterance called schools, disciplines, and at times even 'human sciences'. The latter have in common with the ecclesiastical corps the production of 'doctrinable' statements, intended to *assume authority* in a scholarly circle. That domain of statements can be recognized by its suffixes in *ism* (and not in *ics*). They currently result not in creeds, articles or confessions of faith, but in charts, methods, programmes and manifestos, and are the (permanent) theatre of (parochial) quarrels, struggles (for succession), splits and schisms. What new doctrine is not intent on 'having its family', and what family is not intent on 'producing doctrine'? Christian orthodoxy went through procedures which were those of Freudian or Marxist orthodoxy, with their 'psychoanalytic societies' and 'proletarian parties'. Beyond the intellectually committed, the palaeo-Christian is in a position to explain their own actions to contemporary militants who – whether white, red or black, in the name of a strong conviction, a reason for living, or a position of principle – 'rally' or 'subscribe' to this or to that. In this circumstance we may find reasons for melancholy or joy, according to the mood of the moment; every breakthrough effected by an inventor in its time and place, in language or in thought, is not doomed to go up in smoke the day after (joy); but its prolongation will result in yet another agglutination, or straitjacket of rules (melancholy). As though what the exceptional innnovator, managed to snatch every so often, through his work or his existence, from the various conformities of the group, came back to him like a boomerang, after his death, in the terroristic or fastidious administration of the various sparks of his genius.

We begin, despite ourselves, to regret that Christians don't take more advice from Nietzsche, their best enemy. 'What you are reproached for you should cultivate: it's your best part.' Their Churches, with their foibles and turpitudes, are no doubt what they will have done best. Their success in the longest experience of transmission known to our history deserves at the very least a bit of consideration from the anticlericals (that we all are). To be sure, we should always appeal from the Church to the Gospel. The institution, that permanent counter-testimony, is appalling. But the absence of the institution, which would see testimony itself disappear, is depressing. Of two evils, insufficiency or nothingness, collectives in good health prefer the lesser. Only individuals can outwit the instinct of preservation and opt for suicide through intransigence. And even then, those martyrs will be brandished as an example, a classic case of misappropriating a corpse, by their Church or Party, International or State, who make use of the dead revolutionary on their followers in order to legitimate the order they have established.

The critique of the spirit of orthodoxy is an endless task, to be taken up every morning, so inclined are the divine powers to regiment bodies, and the secular powers to regiment minds. The Tridentine, triumphalist, crushing and intrusive Church. An earthly Power. The medium (of faith, science, the people's will, etc.) conveys the message, and grows fat in the process. In the face of the drive to domination and the atheistic, lawless and faithless clericalisms that have come in their wake, the efforts of irony to preserve the incoherence of the world will always be on the agenda. Secularity is too precious, and too precarious.[6] Hence the theoretically calming notion, that of liberal deism, of taking the icing without the cake: the Supreme Being without the 'Infamous One', community without closedness, the spirit without the body. Voltaire: 'I die worshipping God, loving my friends, not hating my enemies, and detesting superstition.' The mainspring of the spirit of the Enlightenment is the refusal of the Incarnation and of History. A 'formative, remunerative and vengeful God', Chief Architect charged with the portfolio of natural weights and measures, taking care not to politicize relations or to entrust his interests to a petty sect, would give us the good Lord without his negative aspects. *Religion within the limits of reason alone* (no Calas Affair, nor Galileo, no *auto-da-fé*, no *fatwa* ...). Ideal. But the actual history of the last two centuries, and that of the civil cults of revolutionary France in particular, has not responded favourably to the Kantian hope. We have a choice, in point of fact, between two possibilities. Either such a 'natural' religion, in its opposition to the 'established' ones, leaves the circles of initiates, whereupon it will be embodied in an establishment, which will be nationalized (Orthodox, Lutheran, Anglican) or consigned to a group of notables

[6] See Henri Peña-Ruiz, *Dieu et Marianne* (Paris: PUF 1999).

(Freemasonry). And one relapses into arbitrariness, inspired egotism, or the cult of business. Or such a religion declines the risk of existing, and its paper God will remain a topic of polite conversation. Voltaire's minimalist religion was in itself excellent (*h*). It did not harm anyone, but it excited only Monsieur Homais (mobilizing street protests is not a goal for pharmacists, but there are always fanatics who haven't read *Candide,* alas, to excite the crowds). One-armed or tainted. The bitter alternative of either an 'imbecilic' principle, bereft of mobilizing force, or, on the other hand, an emotional force all too lacking in principles. We are perpetually in search of the middle ground. Our domesticated democracies explore it warily. It may be doubted that the West of the twentieth century, with its torture and mass killings, managed, in the final reckoning, to embody in its behaviour the Enlightenment reason that it invoked from its lecterns. The protest of individualists, who take pleasure in mocking fables and religious myths, is careful, on the whole, not to get involved with anything that smacks of the collective, and we can understand that reserve on the part of lovers of humanity. As for the misanthropes, their eyesight is too good to imagine that there is a panacea, a great message abandoned somewhere, which we have only to pick up and offer to future generations, like a key to happiness at last regained. Should people miraculously attempt to govern themselves according to the Sermon on the Mount, then, yes, there would be an end to the law of idiosyncrasies and oppositional positions. We would all speak Esperanto. Which does not appear to be in the offing.

8 Salve Regina

The ascension of the God of love found precious support in femininity. And necessarily so, since God, in making Himself man, was obliged to pass through a sullied womb. Hence the necessity of creating for Mary, Mother of God, an exception to the Jewish rule regarding impurity. This in turn freed up the endless play of physical attractions. The cascading logic of the Incarnation would make of Christianity the least misogynistic of the monotheisms. It acculturated the desert to a certain urbanity. Specifically, it enthroned the Marian cult, feminized the angels, authorized images, and encouraged the female saints. A God of proximity, a rejuvenated father, discovered in this outgoing and tender deployment of flesh and its nuances not only an expanded network of support, but an effective means of conquering hearts and imaginations. In order to reign, no longer over a chosen people, but over the whole earth.

If what was needed, whatever the cost, was a founding act of carnage, a union through murder, Freud, it would appear, confused genders: the cement of monotheism, the Law of the Father, was made with the blood of the mother goddesses. The scapegoat, strictly speaking, should have been a she-goat. Sand and sign restricted divinity to a regimen of dryness. Until the great turning point, however, divinity had been vitalistic and matrilinear: oral, visual, awash with rain, piss and milk, a source of nourishment. Woman irrigated the earth and caused life to sprout. Through vulva, breast and mouth passed seed, children's tales, and recipes. Ishtar in Sumer, Kali in India, Artemis in Ephesus, Cybele elsewhere. Demeter in the Greek countryside, Ceres in Rome. And even earlier, the swollen Venuses of the palaeolithic. In separating Yahweh from His spouse Asherah, orthodox Judaism shattered those horns of plenty. The mother goddesses were as ancient as baked clay. The Matricide occurred later, with the age of metals: iron pot against clay. And the regulations imposed on the Christian Empire would mark the revenge of the pure against the impure: there would be a ban on nakedness, and a closing of baths, gymnasia, brothels and stadiums (where dress tended towards the skimpy). The Olympic Games would be ended. *Agape*, charity, would win out over *Eros*, sexuality. In Ephesus, the Virgin would supplant Artemis, with her breast shaped like a bull's testicles. Origen castrated himself. Asceticism, mortification, penitence, and a new darkness. Libidos in mourning, sex at half-mast . . . .

None of this is false, but the story can be told differently. The Son of Man worked himself free of the male chauvinist rut. Let us begin again. Elevating Himself to the universal through a leap into the abstract, but falling shortly thereafter into an Eastern province, the rigid Almighty, whom Pompey was stunned not to find in the empty Holy of Holies, might well have stewed in His egocentrism. A messianism of merely local interest. With the strange *rabbi* who spoke of love and chose the scene of a marriage, Cana, for his first miracle, there occurred a second leap, via the flesh, which would give God wings that allowed Him access to the whole earth. The leap of an angel, his arms in the form of a cross. Where did he get that insane boldness from? From His descent into flesh. A nuclear incarnation (something that was not at all central in the Jewish world), transmuted into an inexhaustible conflagration. How could the Eternal have a Son of flesh and bone without losing His transcendence in the process? That provocative wager, instead of condemning the undertaking, would give it the lyrical means to effect its planetary end. And first of all to win over the more disobedient half of the species: the daughters of Eve.

Virile Rome had long lampooned the 'housewives' religion'. Such was Saint Augustine's sneer – before his conversion. Such ridicule would count for a good deal in its ultimate success. If it succeeded in defeating Mithras, the great competing cult of the first two centuries, it was because the macho bullfighter had only the soldiers of the legions in his camp. Even today, women are in the majority in convents and monasteries as well as among the observant. It is true that the Church prefers, to that end, aged, chaste and celibate women; and outside the liturgy, Madame Everyman, submissive and prolific. Flesh will have as its specific property the bearing of shame – and of children. Virgin or mother, saint or matron, with no middle ground. Excluded from the priesthood, for Catholics, and unsuited for the confessional. Yet it is none the less the case that whereas a woman does not 'rise' to the Torah, she has access to the Holy Table. In the house of God the Father, she is to touch nothing; in that of the son-God, she says the catechism, administers communion, and can even, in the absence of a priest, officiate at funerals. From one transmission to another, we have moved from the dorsal port to the ventral.

A problematic transition, to be sure, and one that remains incomplete. A great distance had been traversed, starting from a theoretical dissymmetry. 'Woman is for man, man is for God'. The ancestral relation of order seemed to be nature itself. Hence the interdictions that seemed easier to get round than to do away with openly. One cannot deny that the New Covenant had the merit of at least restoring the balance within the immemorial duo desire–repulsion, inspired by Eve, Pandora or Kali, who were always both harmful and nourishing. As ambiguous as the soil, which nourishes the living *and* receives the dead. The emerging faith cut the apple in two. Animal and Dionysiac, entangled with the serpent, riding a goat, sorceress and agent of Satan. But also, later on, conduit of grace, smile of pardon, the 'mother with faithful breasts' – Mother of God. The beginnings were orthodox. Saint Paul, from the first, is unsparing in his anti-feminism (he orders women to remain silent at meetings and forbids them to teach). With the result that twenty centuries later, the women of Christian Europe reply in kind to the organizer. They are sullen. In acceding to equality, many desert the Mass (just as their sisters contest the synagogue). From exclusion from the priesthood to the ban on abortion, the anthology of humiliation could fill an entire volume. Tertullian, Saint Ambrose, Saint Jerome. Without forgetting Gratian's decree (1140) stipulating that woman was not made in God's image. Why such relentlessness? Why do the children of Abraham prefer to meet in paradise in the bosom of the Father, rather than the Mother? Why does God so have it in for girls, whereas Zeus and his friends regaled them with honours and feasts? With them, the fair sex was part of the action. It dwelled on high, in the Pantheon, where it had a voice to be reckoned with. Down below, the cults were mixed: there was Pythia; there were the Vestal virgins, sacred prostitution and high priestesses. The Book made short shrift of all that.

Reparation and Repentance

Since the evolution of customs (among the faithful themselves) has produced an increasingly inconvenient tension between the legal and the acceptable, men of God have deployed prodigious feats of exegesis to smooth away the rough edges – which are enormities for us – of the *Tanach* (the Hebrew acrostic for Torah, Prophets and Writings), not to mention the edicts of Saint Paul. The liberal (and liberated) believer invokes the chronological excuse. Let us grant that the Eternal, too, is unable to leap beyond His era, and that one cannot ask more of the heavenly Patriarch than of the patriarchal society that sustained Him. Like children, like Father. Thus, what one society has done another will be able to undo, and if what were at stake were no more than the 'situation of women in the ages of Abraham, Paul and Mohammed', every hope might be entertained (modernize and reform!). It is true that the housewife may be traceable back to the woman-in-her-tent of the lineal societies of the desert – a tent she was responsible for weaving, mending and setting up on her own. The same applied to milking cows and gathering wood. Such was the way of the Bedouin world. Fed after the boys but before the dogs, girls were there for the 'Be fruitful and multiply' of the Lord (monotheism is instinctively populationist). Offspring, in addition to survival, ensured the future of social relations (shepherds possessing, as a political demarcation, relations of con-sanguinity and cousinship). Nomadic societies were harsh. Unstable, quarrelsome, with a surplus of males. Virile warrior societies, highly competitive for survival as a result of the scarcity of available resources. Shepherds by trade have never had a taste for the bucolic or the pastoral – these are fantasies of the leisured city-dweller. For them, to live is to move on. A breeding female offers assurance, but slows things down. Impedimenta. Great with child, she is obliged to restrict and economize her movements. The traditional sexual division of roles: couvade and chase. Cooking and hunting. For her, storage, enclosure and warmth. The depository of various modes of nourishing slowness, gestation and germination watches the fire, the kitchen, the grain and the children, while the predator of the natural milieu runs his risks outside, with his weapons and tools, hunting and grazing. Continuity versus Innovation. To women protective cover; to men, discovery.

From that ancestral division of economic and imaginative roles would issue com-mandments, customs and rituals. 'Blessed art thou, Eternal, Lord of the universe, who did not make me a woman,' runs the blessing of pious Jews in their morning prayers, as enjoined by the Talmud. A number of modernist rabbis, masters of benevolence, have suggested that with that contemptuous formula, man thanks God for subjecting him to observances which were not incumbent on women. He thanks Him for having to do more than his sisters. This is ingenious, but not entirely convincing. It is true that there has been progress, on the margins and obliquely, in liberal Judaism (where one finds women rabbis – hundreds in America, and about ten in Israel), and still earlier in reformed Churches. None the less a latency remains, a resistance to modernizing efforts for which the historical-geographical explanation cannot completely account. The Father's misogyny is not contingently cultural, but foundational. Victor Hugo summed up the impasse: 'Man alone on earth is of the sex of God / Man is the fallen being, woman the impure being / Life, which is exile for man, is prison for her / Created out of flesh and not with soul / Satan whispered his lugubrious epithalamium.'[1] Eve is accursed, responsible for all the ills of the sons of Adam, whom she deceived by telling him nothing of what God had whispered to her just before about the dangers of the tree. Original sin is thus her doing. She, the seducer, lies? 'The devil's gate,' Tertullian would affirm. The proper ordering of Creation, which subordinates the part to the whole and the rib to the skeleton? We are assured, in a generous rereading, that *rib* [*côte*] should be translated as *side* [*côté*], and that God was intent on making woman not 'the product of a superfluous bone', as Bossuet would have erroneously understood it, but the other side – or half – of man. It remains a fact that the two were not created at the same time, but the one following – and in the service of – the other. That woman exists for the sake of man, and man for the sake of God, is explicitly *inscribed* in the prehistory of salvation. At least in the first version of the myth, since Genesis gives us two (but isn't the ambivalence on this subject our own?). The first (I: 27): 'So God created humankind in his image, in the image of God He created them; male and female He created them, and said to them: "Be fruitful and multiply." ' The initial Adam is masculine/feminine, and that asexual being takes life, animal engendering, and reproduction in hand. Except for the symbolic order of names and laws devolving to Adam alone, who 'gave names to all the animals, the birds of the sky, and the wild beasts'. The second Adam (II: 18) is a solitary male, concerning whom Elohim says that it is not good for him to remain alone. 'I will make him a helper as his partner.' Whereupon, 'He took one of his ribs and closed up its place with flesh' – a bit more than a double; a bit less than an encounter. The animals were not sufficient company. Optimists interpret: it is woman who will allow man to make the transition from nature to thought. Without Eve, we would not have any history, since we would have remained in paradise, like the beasts: stifled with happiness. She who triggered perdition would also have triggered salvation. Such sympathetic efforts to redeem matters may provoke a smile. As Saint Ambrose would say in the fourth century: 'It is woman who was for man the origin of sin, not man for

---

[1] Victor Hugo, *Œuvres complètes*, ed. Jean Massin, vol. X, 1.

woman.' With the anteriority of Adam, and the badness of Eve, biblical andro-
centrism is originary. Of Adam and Eve, we know only male children: Cain, Abel,
Seth (with whom they reproduced remains an enigma). Noah and Abraham had
only sons, and Joseph had only brothers. In the primordial genealogies, the girls are
forgotten.

The Written, a Sexist Medium

On those poorly healed wounds, we may cast a grain of salt *ex officio*: the masculine
underpinnings of the symbol. Beyond its contents, it is writing itself that would have
had to be erased in order to do away with the contempt of the great Phallocrat, or
the benign neglect of His servants. Words, with history, changed gender. Today,
when bookishness has been feminized – since it is women who, as of now, buy,
write, publish and criticize printed works (as is demonstrated by statistics on
reading, publishing houses, and the literary supplements of our newspapers) – we
forget that for a period of three thousand years, books and women were strangers –
indeed, enemies. Cunning and tenacious. Since what is written is no longer, in the
West, a lever of social power, any more than elective office, males are at liberty at
present to abandon writing and Parliament to the 'other party' and to support,
without fear, electoral parity. They have more serious matters to attend to elsewhere. In the industry of images and the circulation of money, precincts whose
import is far from negligible, they retain the lion's share for themselves. Thus it is
that we have lost sight of everything in the technological unconscious that removed
Word from Flesh. The dry exploit of the producer of signs from the moist womb of
the agents of reproduction. The Written-Father, in His tenuous and controlled
stiffness, is repelled by the lascivious and dissolute creatures who do not sufficiently
dominate a body that is subject to the phases of the moon to abstract themselves,
gravely, into a book, a cerebral activity. *Tota mulier in utero. Totus vir in libro.* Not
a single woman among the seventy translators of the Septuagint ... .[2]

The letter is purity, since it is a dispatch from the supernatural. Woman is sullied,
because she is stuck in nature. A short circuit is forbidden, or counterindicated.
Mater is matter. The written is the Spirit: *Écrit est Esprit.* Ever since the bottomless
night of signs. The Egyptians called their hieroglyphics 'sacred words', and we know
of no (painted or sculpted) Egyptian scribe. The Greeks attributed to Zeus the
importation – by way of Cadmos, King of Thebes – of 'Phoenician letters' into their
country. And for the Hebrews, 'Scripture is from God.' And thus the prerogative of
the men of God. The *sofer* (the handwritten scroll of the Torah), moreover, can be
borne only by a parchment drawn from the hide of a ritually pure species (and

[2] The Greek translation of the Hebrew Bible, compiled in Alexandria between the third and
fourth centuries BCE.

inscribed with a pen made of a reed dipped in black ink). Similarly, the table on which the sacred object is placed must be covered with a cloth or fabric. How can the hands of a woman ... ? Phylacteries are rolled exclusively around the arms and foreheads of men. 'Better to burn the Torah than to entrust it to a woman,' according to the adage. An orthodox rabbi will make sure that he does not shake the hand of an unknown woman (lest she be menstruating). Women pray in a space reserved for them; and when the physical setup does not permit a clear separation, a *mehitsah* – a wooden or cloth partition – is introduced; in Sephardic synagogues this was drawn like a curtain when the scrolls were removed from the Ark and read. The Temple, which is the house of Scripture, must preserve its sanctity, even from unwanted eyes .... . And Leviticus (12: 1–8) stipulates that a woman who has just given birth is to keep her distance from the temple for forty days if she has had a boy, but sixty if she has had a girl. A handicap with its specific tariff. In synagogues we find neither wimples nor winged coifs. Nor any sisters or women of erudition (such as Teresa of Avila and Catherine of Siena, 'doctors of the Church' by title). To which may be added the social role of writing as man's instrument of domination over man and over things. The mastery of such a tool of magical control, through the substantial identity between things and their marks, must be the object of a guarantee for the user. What is written is a gift of the gods which relates its user to the donors. The tradition was sustained in the Christian Middle Ages, when the prerogatives of writing devolved to tonsured clerics. It may be suspected that the values of femininity were not transmitted through them. The cult of Mary, 'blessed among women', arose to its great heights in the Church from below – belatedly and laterally.

Such is the custom: where and when the written is valorized, woman is devalued. When the place of worship is a study hall, when prayer and reading are one and the same, the place accorded to woman, the 'lesser' version of man, appears exiguous. Unsuited for the sacrificial rites, physiologically unfit for circumcision (the sign of affiliation is male), juridically for divorce. Excluded from Bar-Mitzvah, first communion, and Yeshivoth, the institutions of Talmudic learning (unless a waiver be arranged). Such is the sexual inconvenience of the *God that is read in relation to the God that is seen*, and which Christianity has not entirely eluded. Medieval iconography ritually places man-with-book facing woman-with-child. The Virgin holds Jesus; the Apostle holds Scripture. For one, Maternity; for the other, Authority (or authorship) To each his labour. Women engender amid suffering, and men as well. For the one, babies; for the other, books, which are the children of the celibate. Labours of writing by hand fall to monks, in the *scriptoria*, not to nuns, or extremely rarely (the monasteries of Sainte-Croix and Sainte-Cécile). Despite the requisite qualities of attentiveness and patience, they were in general not deemed worthy of a mission as sacred as that of copying. And had to ask their Mother Superior for authorization to open the Bible. A remark by Richard de Bury, Bishop of Durham and Grand Chancellor of England, is quite eloquent as to the separation between those two universes. 'Barely does that beast, so endlessly deleterious to our studies, discover the corner in which we are hidden than, with a brow lined with wrinkles, she tears us away from it, demonstrating that we occupy the furniture of the house to no useful end, and we are useless for domestic economy.'[3] In the twelfth century, the rise of orality characteristic of courtly culture – epics, *fabliaux*, love courts – favoured the second sex. The art of conversation suits women well, because they are sociable and frivolous. Study and exegesis remain the province of the Fathers and Brothers. A tropism and prejudice that de-Christianization did not immediately remove. The Workers of the Book, in the nineteenth century, refused to hire females, and not only for fear of a plunge in salaries. 'Morality as well as the proper confection of our work oppose the notion that women be employed as compositors,' we read in the statutes of the French typographical society in 1849.[4] 'Love of women and of books are not sung in the same choir,' runs the refrain. For a long time, bibliophile circles retained the masculinity of English clubs. And the *liber libro* (free by virtue of the book) resonates like a gender slogan.

How might one expect those 'conservatories of writing' (Odon Vallet) that our religions are to take the initiative? Quite the contrary. The Talmud is more macho than the Torah, the rabbis than the patriarchs, the mullahs than Mohammed, and the bishops than the Gospels. Such is the reverse side of the backdrop of faithfulness, which kept alive languages that had died – Latin, Hebrew and classical Arabic – and even permitted the secular renascence of holy languages, as we saw with Hebrew in the twentieth century. Museums of signs become indecipherable, repositories of obsolete languages, abandoned by civil society – Gheez, Slavonic, Coptic and Latin: such exclusions are a mandate to persevere for many a clergy. The inertia of the heirs no doubt exceeds the will of the testators. And the general atmosphere of desacralization renders the sense of being out of phase all the more striking. Feminists (for whom the Pope is public enemy number one) are to some extent correct in seeing in church and synagogue the principal 'reproduction apparatuses of patriarchy' in a secularized West emerging from it, but with its eyes focused on the past. Such animosity is an act of homage to the long memory of the men of God. Is it Scripture that makes use of various clergies to extend into the videosphere sacral values on the brink of ruin? Or, rather, our eminences who take His Late Majesty the Book hostage in order to hold on to their vanished powers? Whatever the case for such *reasons of clergy* (as one says *reasons of state*), 'symbolic' man, committed to the sacred, tends, within the monotheist orbit, to relegate 'indicial' woman to the secular margins. Branded by the Devil, the daughters of Eve, above all in the Latin world, continue to pay an exorbitant price for that victory of the Symbolic over the

---

[3] Albert de Neuville, *La Femme et le Livre* (Liège: M. Thone 1918), p. 20.
[4] Paul Chauvet, *Histoire des ouvriers du Livre de 1789 à 1881* (Paris: Rivière 1964), p. 213.

Imaginary that is incarnated by the Book, and which broke with thirty thousand years of the bisexual divine.

The First Temptations of Christ

Let us not avoid the issue. The Word became man, not woman. And the Son himself transmitted his sacerdotal ministry only to males. The Twelve know nothing of parity. Having recalled as much, we should none the less note that Jesus is by no means the most 'macho' of prophets. He is friendly to women (especially if they are not part of the family). He allows himself to be approached by one of the impure – without any concern for the old precepts ('Speak not with women'), to the point of provoking gossip and making his disciples ill at ease (John 4: 27). He accepts their company, and his attitude will be reciprocated. His disciples had already fled him, when holy women assisted him in his agony and burial. He enters the home of Martha and Mary (Luke 10: 38–42). He approaches the Samaritan woman, who is overwhelmed (John 4: 9). He forgives where stoning is called for (the adulteress). He allows the fair sex to accompany him as a cohort on the roads of Galilee – without going so far as to open the inner circle to it (which is why the Roman Church still does not ordain women today). He assigns lowly women responsibilities, to the point of making them witnesses, before the fact, of his Resurrection (a malicious medieval commentator would explain that priority as the calculation of a shrewd communicator: since women are more garrulous than men, the news would travel faster). Neither contempt nor repulsion. Jesus, with female sinners, acts not as a severe father, but as a big brother. Shall we say an elder sister? A feminine side has been discerned in Him. His refusal to take up arms, in an occupied country, is not particularly virile. He can be wildly angry, but does not sow the plague or death in his wake. He evokes neither original sin nor its curses. He preaches virtues reputed to be feminine: love, gentleness, meekness, charity. A lamb addressing sheep. Tenderness, devotion, abnegation. No shame in that. The Eternal was never a child. Jesus was a babe and an adolescent. And as an adult, he does not forget the young of both sexes. Yahweh scolds; Jesus smiles. No ritual, he says, exempts us from loving, and there is no love without proof, deeds and gestures. The Incarnate allows himself what had been forbidden to the Immaterial. Touching, for example. In the literal sense. He cures the leper with his hand, and the blind by touching their eyes. He alleviates bleeding. He cures death by touching the casket of a widow's only son. 'When the Lord saw her, he had compassion for her and said to her, "Do not weep." Then he came forward and touched the bier, and the bearers stood still. And he said, "Young man, I say to you, rise!" The dead man sat up and began to speak, and Jesus gave him to his mother' (Luke 7: 13–15). Such physical contact, which was far from customary, openly pursued during the Sabbath, did harm to his reputation among the masters of ritual observance. Jesus is touching and touched, moved by distress, mourning, handicaps. Some have even detected a slightly unbridled charm or perturbation in our sacred history, an *odor a femina*, vials of perfume. Grace, kisses, incense and myrrh waft around this deviant rabbi of ill repute, with his limited concern for ritual bans, who has himself anointed, and his feet wiped, as he lies prone on a bed, by the long hair of a sinning female. No purifying gestures. That freedom of manner announces a shift in inflection. The New Covenant rounds off the angles; after the stiff nape, the swan's neck. The harsh God of Hosts, who avenges and punishes ('Thy right hand, O Eternal, has crushed the enemy'), is followed by a gentler version, who forgives and disarms. And flowers, not little stones, adorn graves. Conviviality comes to the desert. Jugs of wine and bread on the table. The Mediterranean in Arabia. Or rather, an oscillation between the arid and the verdant, as a result of the geographic providence which caused Jesus to be born and to preach on the rim of the desert plane east of the Jordan. There slipped into the geological collapse of the Dead Sea a verdant strip a hundred and fifty kilometres long and fifteen wide, a cultivated region, hospitable to settlers, one where it was possible to grow wheat. Jesus submits to the ordeal of the desert, but without becoming a hermit. He quickly comes back to the orchards, fruits and palms. He slips into that intermediate corridor between the peoples of the sea and the fanatics of the pebble, between harsh consonants and the vocalic warbling of the washhouse. Contrary to his predecessors, Jesus does not have the mind of a notary. He tells stories, digresses, thinks out loud. A parable is less inclined to rigour than the Law. The Protestants, who would be the first to adopt the principle of a universal priesthood and feminine pastors (in France as of the 1930s), are also the advocates of the spoken word against written Scripture. Jesus *speaks* between the lines, they insist, following Luther ('Christ is the Lord of Scripture, which is his servant').

Perhaps every God has the traits of the traces he leaves. From His square characters, Yahweh retains an angular, rough, stony aspect. The Eternal of Jesus speaks Aramaic and subsequently espoused the Greek alphabet – minus vowels. We should also note that the first-century Judaeo-Christian milieu was highly Hellenized, through either ancient acculturation (Alexandria) or proximity (Samaria). The Gospels were written directly in Greek. The entire theo- and Christological elaboration of the first three centuries can be read as a long and subtle mental sifting, consisting of pouring a certain Hebraic verticality into the folds of Greek culture, which *re-encoded* it in terms of suppleness. Émile Poulat observes, quite accurately: 'To believe is also to formulate one's faith, thinking it in a specific phase of culture and civilization: the believable is transmitted through the thinkable.' And the thinkable is transmitted through the sayable. *Christos, Ev-angellos* (Gospel), *Ekklesia* (Church), *Hairesis* (heresy), *Angellos* (messenger), *Eu-charistia* (communion) ... : all the key terms of the new faith emerge from the Hellenic mould. A framework for living, and thus for thinking. At least until the moment when the gentleness of the Aegean smile would give way beneath harsh juridical Latin. The Greek alphabet is round, not square. Its less emphatic notation flexes its lines, features curves and above all vowels. The diction of kerygma in the language of Plato – a language of translation for the Hebrews, but a mother tongue for Christians – brings to a guttural divine bristling with consonants the feminine flection of (more flowing) open vowels. Vowels voyage. They undulate. They belong to the coast, to ports and markets. Phoenician. Mercantile. Mellow. Hospitable. Meant for agoras, gynaecea, wharves and landing-stages.

Becoming Androgynous: The Christian Angel

The feminization of the ranks included the higher spheres. The heavenly function-aries, in the Old Testament, are rather fierce and masculine in temperament. The ambassadors of the Most-High (*malak* in Hebrew, *angellos* in Greek, the messenger, the forerunner), the divine wings, are not far from the warrior angels of Zoroaster, arrayed in battle order, weapon in fist, swordbelt, standard. 'The Lord will send against you His armies.' Those fierce soldiers are quite different from the fluttering blond curly-haired creatures who do the Lord's errands in our paintings. They are called by their first names, whereas their distant airborne ancestors were cloaked in anonymity. Nor do the cherubim of Eden and of propitiatory rites have a right to their own names – nor does the Angel of the Lord who appears to Moses. It was after the return from Babylon that Michael, Raphael and Gabriel would appear, the only higher angels to frequent ordinary mortals (note that in Genesis, the tempting serpent does not have a name of his own either. Abbadon, Asmodeus and Satan were also latecomers). The Only One – and this is understandable – was reluctant in His early years to personify his entourage. The Talmud would be more generous. The Yahweh of the beginning subcontracted His messenger services surreptitiously, with the residues of a surviving polytheism, and a bit of shame. A reutilization of minor figures from a prior life – perhaps the seventy children of the God El, whom the tradition would, in a way, have reassigned as escorts (where they retain the suffix *el*). Those incongruous and slightly out-of-place flying creatures have a bad reputation among serious people, the purists of the letter: 'motifs borrowed from paganism', residues of the East, djinns or genies. A Babylonian superfluity useful, at best, to decorate the Ark, but nothing more. That suspect entourage would be taken up shamelessly by Christian iconography. With it, the angels would take on indi-viduality and fly with their own wings. The cherub was a bird of prey, a sentinel destined to frighten. His Christian counterpart reveals himself to be more affable and prepossessing. He begins gyrating at the beginning of the fifth century, bor-rowing from the pagan Victories, the *Nike*, their svelte appearance, and their slightly flirtatious gait from the Cupids and plump, winged genies of Graeco-Roman mosaics. In pastoral texts, the Angel eroticizes the message. He changes sex,

From top to bottom:

Winged Genius,
Assyrian bas-relief,
880 BCE

Cherub, ivory,
Syrian, 800 BCE

Seraphim, mosaic,
Basilica of San
Marco, Venice,
twelfth century

Frangos Katelanos,
The Archangel
Michael, Icon,
sixteenth century

Fra Angelico, The
Annunciation,
Florentine fresco,
around 1442

Leonardo da Vinci,
'The Virgin at the
Rock', oil on wood,
1490

Poster for the
Applied Electrical
Arts Exhibition,
Italy, 1896

Raffaello, Madonna,
oil on wood, 1514

becomes transsexual. It was the *sons* of Elohim who perceived, in Genesis 6, that 'the daughters of men were beautiful'. The bow-bearing angel of the stained-glass window, with viola da gamba and slender fingers, whose music brings heaven down to earth, on the other hand, has a girl's smile. Such is the languid, effeminate side of mannerist Annunciations and Pre-Raphaelite dreams. Those handsome birds of paradise traditionally earned the disfavour of the Church Fathers (which had already been the case, in the world of the Jews, for the Sadducees, conservatives of the Mosaic Law). Female saints and women in general were naturally sympathetic to them. Same wavelength, flowing from source and sex.

Tell me how many angels you have in your entourage and I'll tell you what kind of a God you are – if you are one of omnipotence, mercy, anger or tenderness. A good God is never alone in Heaven. A merciful God cannot contemplate Himself eternally in the mirror of His perfection – the impassive cause of Himself, an indifferent mechanician. As soon as He is obliged to intervene here on earth – making His announcement to Mary, bringing Jesus back to Heaven – He needs intermediaries, and women excel in this role (as is revealed by every clandestine struggle). A nice reversal. In order to redeem us from Eve's sin, God needs men, to be sure, but He also needs the daughters of Eve. The God of the metaphysicians, whom one might expect to be more broadminded, has no truck with holy women and with our foibles. Useless intercessors. An absolutely infinite being, the circle of circles, is self-sufficient. And His indifference is reciprocated: the *Ens perfectissimum*, Robespierre's Supreme Being, the eye in the triangle of speculative Freemasonries, hardly affects women, and says nothing to children. Neither parables nor Christmas tales, neither mangers nor colour prints. He is a great eminence without either legend or fantasy, intended for the solemn and the privileged – of the male sex. And producing only masculine clubs: lodges, the studios of the venerable, spiritual Rotary Clubs. Such cerebral coldness never gave rise to an endearing contagion, or ignited a fire in the hearth of the have-nots. But that, perhaps, is its function: to serve as a firescreen against feminine unreasonableness.

Every Christian infant has a right, in the West, to an attendant guardian, as soon as he is born (in the East, one must await baptism). That private protector is a Catholic invention – rejected by Protestants (who are too concerned with spirit to admit that flesh, too, is capable of conveying grace). The celestial bodyguard is the hope of orphans, prisoners, travellers lost in the night. Of cities as well, which, in their misfortune, can entrust themselves to their 'archon'. Saint Michael the arch-angel, the most solicited, was that of France (the Nazis, moreover, capitulated on his feast-day, one 8 May). And we have the right to address our prayers and wishes directly to them in church – something that is impossible in a synagogue. Thus the liturgical ornament becomes a purveyor of salvation. Its prettiness is operational, gracefulness serving as a mainspring. Man (*homo* and still more *vir*) does not manage very well on his own; he needs his 'angels' (and one doesn't say 'angel' to a mere friend). The hostesses of Paradise bear witness to a concern to add a few more rungs to the ladder rising from the mud to Heaven. For we find it hard to climb it all alone. This knowledge is more familiar to the humble than to the powerful. And thus it was that the feminine repressed of the Word, agreeable and indulgent, made its return in Christendom via the people – pious images and children's tales, vignettes and stories for the pure in heart and the 'simple of spirit'. A singular religion of the Book, one in which colour-prints come closer to the essential than exegeses . . . . A theology without words, our religious painting exudes many a confession of humility (one always needs someone smaller than oneself). Lift! The Ascension of the Son, like the Assumption of the Mother (about which Scripture has nothing to say), is effectuated by an aspiration upwards, but this is plain to see: there, too, the heavenly conveyors have to lend a hand. With considerable straining of backs, arms and thighs. The Holy Family itself cannot retire to its heavenly quarters through its own efforts, without an obliging cushion of pink and perfumed flesh. The economy of salvation knows nothing of self-administration, the self-service of the customer in a rush.

The most rigorous theologians (from Saint Paul to Saint Thomas) have always betrayed a certain disdain for such equivocal psychopomps – and the worship they might turn to their advantage. Charming, but ambiguous and not really part of the team. Theologically incorrect. If there is but one God, he ought to be alone in Heaven. What need of assistants? An only God having recourse to intermediaries would no longer quite be one. The impure polytheistic survival would thus smack of the adventitious and the folkloric. On the other hand, we may wonder whether 'diluting' the only God, as one dilutes a wine that is too strong, does not make Him more easily consumable by the unaccustomed. Catholicism, in this respect, is like a (wily) monotheism intimidated by its task, which would have been injected, as an aide, with small doses of polytheism. From above (the Trinity), below (the saints), and the sides (the Virgin and the angels). Such cross-breeding ensured for it an optimal transmissibility.

Acculturation to the milieu in which one lives allows one the better to penetrate it, to turn the adversary's weapons against him. Thus the Church managed to conflate the Pure and the Gentiles, by selecting from within those two rivals (hence its conviction that it was forming a *Tertium Genus*, a third race, neither Jewish nor pagan). At the risk of disqualifying itself in the eyes of the other two. That moral and political discomfort was the lot, for a period of three centuries, of a heresy couched between two orthodoxies. Blasphemous in the view of the Temple, which saw in such dissidents overly Hellenized Jews, more or less apostate cosmopolites. And troubling in the view of Rome, who, like Pliny the Younger, perceived in such fanatics a contagious Jewish extravagance (whereas the mother-religion enjoyed a recognized status).

Without seeing in the Christian summation the mark of a premeditated strategy, we may note that it assuredly reveals an immense political talent, which is never without a side prepared to receive all comers and affirm that 'one leaves ambiguity behind only to one's own detriment'. The point of origin of our era, being the point of arrival of several others, enabled a synthesis (which is 'always governmental', noted Proudhon) with the necessary regenerative aspect of that type of assimilation. All the tributaries of mythology converged to lift the boat of Christ, to which many a lost legend, many a figurative and symbolic motif, came to do service. The mysteries of Isis, Orphism, Mithraism, the hermetic Gnosis, Mazdan astrology (the magi) and a hundred other modules of meaning. More or less purged, reinserted and reinscribed residues – such as the ansate cross, the symbol of life for ancient Egyptians, fused into the monogram of Christ. Or the paschal candle, which takes up the flame of Mazda, the Iranian god of light. In the tide of religions of salvation, each one made use of whatever came its way. The nascent Church would not have succeeded in cannibalizing the Empire – so formidably polyphonic, so admirably composite – without prolonging its most salient tendencies. The very banality of its stock of fables (the classic union of a god and a mortal woman becoming the Incarnation, the prophecy of the Pythoness becoming the Annunciation, the cycle of Osiris becoming the Resurrection, etc.) secretly facilitated a metabolism of the folklore of the masses. Where some see a proof of eclecticism and inauthenticity, we may detect the homage of a newcomer to the continuity of the species. Every era has in relation to its predecessor a right of prolongation as well as one of inventory, and that gratitude is our humanity. Christian legend made headway, fortunately for it and for ourselves. It would certainly be depressing if tens of millions of intelligent beings, who built in turn Nineveh, Sumer, Babylon, Thebes, Athens, Alexandria and Rome, had imagined, anticipated or reflected for nothing, and if amnesiac successors had dreamed of ejecting them from the debate because a saviour, who was genuine, had been born unto us on a bed of straw, yesterday morning, in a manger, in Bethlehem.

And the Logos Became Eros

A culture that honours images does honour to women. An old constant of civilizations, which traverses ages and latitudes. The oppression of one's sisters goes hand in hand with the destruction of icons – witness Kabul, Karachi, Algiers. He who bombards statues also stones adulteresses. He who closes museums will eventually confine his women. The reverse is also true: wherever images have a right to exist, women have a right to participate.

What transpired with Christian imagery is akin to what happened with the protective mantle of Mary: endorsement came slowly, and not without problems. Acts remains rather reticent on the Mother of the Lord. The Gospels have almost nothing to say about Mary. The centuries and popular piety subsequently gave her parents (Anne and Joachim), a death (in Ephesus), theological status (the immaculate mother), armorial bearings (twelve gold stars on a blue background), and numerous titles: Misericordia, the Good Haven, Deliverance, and so on. So sacrilegious was the irruption of the body into the supernatural that more than one council was needed to acknowledge the legitimate daughter of the incarnation: the Icon. Four centuries of controversy, to be precise, from the first Nicene Council (315) to the second Nicene Council (787), which recognized the legitimacy of the image. As for devotional images (of male and female saints), they would not appear until the thirteenth century, in convents. We have retraced elsewhere the various detours and penalties through which the ban on representation was lifted.[5] And how the plastic expression of the 'true faith', timid and initially derivative from the mythological clichés of Roman culture, would manage to catch up with and overtake its written expression. In Byzantium, sacred art would become an art directed, controlled by the Letter (an icon was venerable and authentic only if it bore the 'ecclesial attestation' of a citation from Scripture). And the icon, presentative rather than representational (of the Lord, of the Virgin, of the saints and the angels), would remain, until the Italian Renaissance, assigned to liturgical functions. Slow and different as its birthing may have been, the creature was there. It is called Christian art, an unprecedented violence to the most formal injunctions of the Creator. Our privilege as citizens of the West. The fact that the spectator of a painted icon was for a long time merely a believer, and its author was not a painter but a monk, through whom (and not by whom) the image was elaborated, can do nothing to counter that overwhelming fact. For an aesthete, there are great Jewish and Muslim artists; there is neither Jewish nor Muslim art. Were it to include only anonymous artisans, with unsigned frescos and sculptures, there would still be, in the full sense of the word, a Christian art. The art of Judaism cannot be detached from its religious history.[6] It is an aesthetics of reading, 'destined to exalt the beauty of the Torah' (Anne-Hélène Hoog). The *menorahs*, the elaborately crafted reading hands, the fabrics and *tikkim* (the cylindrical containers of the scrolls) add glory to God, not meaning. They are not detachable from the cult. Christian sacred art is.

For the 'anti-formal' elder, the image of a creature cheats the Law. For the figurative junior, manipulating brush and chisel, it confirms it. Once the man-god is defined as 'truly god and truly man' (in the Council of Chalcedon in 451), nothing remains in law to forbid the celebration, through images, of the marriage of sense and the sensuous. There were indeed, among Jewish iconoclasts, violations of the second commandment of the Decalogue – on the sides of sarcophagi, in certain necropolises,

[5] See Régis Debray, *Vie et mort de l'image. Une histoire du regard en Occident* (Paris: Gallimard 1992).
[6] An eloquent demonstration of this is to be found in the quite beautiful Museum of the Art and History of Judaism in Paris.

in the synagogue of Dura Europos,[7] a magnificent illusionist surprise. Ambiguous concessions to pagan taste, from the Hellenistic era, tolerated on the margins. At the time of the Roman wars, the Jews, having returned to decorative motifs (tracery on capitals, fleur-de-lys, allusive serpents), did not 'suffer', according to Tacitus, 'any effigy in their cities, even less in their temples' (*Histories*, V, 5). In the cult of the Son, on the other hand, the image is neither extraneous nor transgressive. Anyone who can do more can do less, and anyone who can make Himself flesh can make Himself line, form and colour. Incarnadine tones follow incarnation. The fact that blood had to be spilled in Byzantium between iconophiles and iconoclasts (between 730 and 742) to surmount the desert taboo and translate the double nature of Christ into a theology of the Image (as an emanation to be *traversed*) shows how deeply the interdictions were entrenched. It did not occur without zigzags and jolts, between excesses of trust and defiance, until a median path was found which would claim that the image is not a model but a tension that elevates to the divine model. The Church finally concluded a marriage contract balanced between feminine and masculine, a fascination for and a rejection of images. We shall not return here to that protracted theological and emotive experiment, with all its trials and errors. It is framed on high by the derisive donkey of the Palatine Hill, *Alexamenos worships his God*, and down below by *Man is the mouth of God* by Paul Klee. Between a graffiti and a sketch, between catacombs and museums, two thousand years of visual approaches to the the Invisible.

The icon was no mere vicissitude. The Only One was born of a shattered golden calf and a curse without appeal on the idols of the East. Joshua's reform purged Jerusalem of its Canaanite and Assyrian deities. In placing in the Temple, four centuries later, a statue of Olympian Zeus, the Hellenistic king Antiochus IV incarnated 'the abomination of desolation'. We should understand that the heirs of those uncompromising Judaeans felt nauseous at the sight of such a relapse into idolatry. Maimonides would clearly state that Christianity was an idolatry, and Jesus a false prophet to be eliminated. But that would be said as a matter of course, in passing. Just as the Christian junior felt obliged to clarify matters with his ancestor, like an unfaithful son with his father, so did Judaism pursue its path as though nothing had changed. There is not a word about Jesus in the Talmud (except under cover of 'Balaam the impious'). As Yeshayahu Leibowitz put it: 'If Jesus had not existed, the Yom Kippur prayer book would be exactly the same, without a single letter changed.'[8] In this we may discern what appears to be disdain for a success-orientated heresy which plays both ends, Idol and Law, against the middle. The Christian shamelessly joins the worldly and the repellent. A double strike –

[7] A locality situated on the banks of the Euphrates, in Syria, on the caravan route between Aleppo and Baghdad, where a synagogue of the Hellenistic era, with extremely rich mural decorations illustrating the principal scenes of the Bible, was excavated in 1928.
[8] Yeshayahu Leibowitz, *Israël et judaïsme* (Paris: Desclée de Brouwer 1993), p. 95.

adding, to the Saint Johns who don't need to see to believe, the Saint Thomases, who believe only their eyes. And the propagation of the faith (like the authorities charged with the task) went one better than Scripture by combining the masculine prestige of writing with the properly feminine charm of the image. The complete menu. Salt *and* sugar – at the risk of a sickening sweetness, the kitsch meringue of Saint-Sulpice (terminal drift).

Indeed, it is impossible to promote the Marian cult without conceding the retina its due. Let us reinsert things in their temporal succession. Who made use of images in Roman Antiquity? Women, the friends of sorceresses and talismans. Those who are most familiar with a stubborn underground prone to the archaic, with its spells and ecstasies, intended to capture shades or conjure away illness, death, loss of love, and fear. Such is the secret femininity of the entrancements of the image. The devilries of women, since the High Middle Ages, are episodes involving reflections and mirrors. Eros on the lookout. 'The idea of making idols was at the origin of fornication,' was literally the substance of a first-century Jewish belief. Eve both fascinates and allows herself to be fascinated by her eyes. Erotic turbulence and libidinal power of the gaze. In Greek, all words orbiting around seeing and icons are feminine in gender (*mimesis, eikon,* etc.). Symptomatically, the culture accorded more words than images to its gods, and more images than words to its goddesses. Greek goddesses are represented; Greek gods are recounted: artisans of the image, sculptors and painters, prefer the former; poets and philosophers, the latter. In the Latin myth reported by Pliny the Elder, drawn images were the invention, in Corinth, of a girl in love. With the Church Fathers, who, like Tertullian the Carthaginian, were reticent about the figurative compromise, idolatry and coquetry were both lambasted: the pleasures of the eye and the indecencies of women. Pope Gregory the Great, when he wanted to convince the hermit Secundinus to resign himself to pious images, compared 'the desire the hermit has of contemplating certain religious images with the desire of the lover to behold the woman he loves'. Calvin would take up this leitmotiv in his *Institution chrétienne*: 'Never is man moved to adore images without having conceived some carnal and perverse fantasy.'

Does not the mute complicity between the feminine and the figurative already surface in prehistoric times? There are, in the 'art' of 30,000 years ago, many more female bodies sketched than male ones. 'Palaeolithic vulvas' win out over penises. Ornamented caves attach more importance to the representation of the female body – breasts, belly and womb. Not to mention cult objects linked to fertility: pendants, amulets, figurines, statuettes. The Venuses of Willendorf, of Lespugue, of Grimaldi ... . Might it be the simple effect of a physical division of labour (the cutting of bone or wood requiring the strength of male muscles)? No. Those violin-women, the women on shields are small in format (like the art work of the Cyclades, less than twenty centimetres). Figuration revolves around desire; Eros evades the censor through images. That tradition dominated the iconography that was to come. It was a woman, Veronica (whose name means True Image), not an apostle, who received on a cloth, the *mandylion*, the imprint of the perspiring face of Jesus. Thereby becoming the world's first photographer, transcribing [*graph*] light [*photo*] on to a photosensitive surface. The entire history of Byzantium reveals a meshing in time between the promotion of the *Theotokos*, the mother of God and female medium of creation (Council of Ephesus, 431), and the entry of holy icons into the liturgy. In the sects of Christianity, the Virgin and images appear and disappear together. Byzantine iconoclasm was against the idolizing of Mary, and no doubt antifeminist as well. The iconoclast emperors were men, and it was the empresses, vengeful widows, who on each occasion, after the death of their husbands, restored the cult of icons (Irene, widow of Leo IV in 780; Theodora, widow of Theophilus, in 843). And the first image solemnly reintroduced to Saint-Sophia in 867 was an icon of the Virgin. The same applied in the West, around the year one thousand, with the *Majesties* (frontal Virgins holding the Son on their laps). The authorized transition from *signum* to *imago* accompanied the cult of the Madonnas. The Virgin appeared to the blessed more easily than her Son. Joan of Arc heard voices that probably would have made Saint Thomas laugh. Supernatural appearances have remained Mary- (rather than Christ-) based. As, throughout the Europe of the nineteenth and twentieth centuries, did the miraculous images with their sanctuaries erected around grottos and sites of apparition – from Lourdes and Fatima to Catherine Labouré and the chapel on the rue du Bac. Visionaries in spirituality, like clairvoyants in spiritism, form an almost exclusively female – or children's – club. Such is the sexual revenge of images on words. The image is *anima*; the written, *animus*. With a single glance and the naive grace

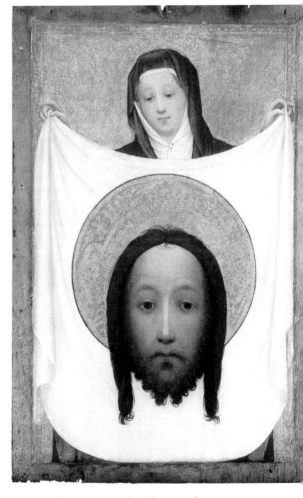

The first photograph: Veronica's Shroud or Mandylion, Vorderasiatische Museum, Staatliche Museum, Berlin

of her smile, the Madonna, innocence become woman, short-circuited a thousand complicated arguments. The Marian cult, a rhetorical short cut, constituted, for the propagation of Catholicism, an economizing of discourse (as we say, referring to energy). The fairy-tale maternal enchantment surrounding Our Lady of Perpetual Succour, and the Mother of Sorrows, awakens our childhood, nostalgia for a time before words, and fills to overflowing the simple and their humble faith. The Holy

Virgin, that image-filled corridor between heaven and earth, effects a leap beyond reading. Fewer impositions, more pain. By slipping not *into* but *behind* such manifestations of churchiness – under the two categories of *cult images*, objects of liturgical veneration, and *devotional images*, sources of individual piety – the Almighty enlarged His social base (what the tele-evangelist would call His ratings) considerably. He could now make contact with the illiterate – touch and mobilize outside the world of study.

So it was entirely predictable that the return to the Bible of the sixteenth-century reformers, should be relentless in both shattering the statues and *hauts-reliefs* of the cathedrals, and banishing the Ave Maria and the female saints from worship. And retrieving the dominance of the sacred text and the masculinity of the Temple. A diet of dryness once again, both for the eye and for the palate. No more transubstantiation in the wafer on the tongue; no more hyperdulia for the Virgin Mary; no more aesthetic debauchery. The return to the text never augurs anything good for the arts and the ladies. The prophetess Anne, who wore out her eyes reading, should not make us forget the statistical truth. To be sure, one cannot reduce the role of the feminine figures of the Bible to a numerical inventory. Sarah, Judith, Bathsheba, the Queen of Sheba and Susanna have a singular way of reigniting the future, opening Israel to alterity, catalysing unexpected dynamics. It is none the less the case that three books out of forty-five in the Old Testament bear the names of women: Esther, Judith and Ruth. And that four-fifths of the 3,500 characters in the Bible are men. The matriarchs Sarah, Rebecca or Rachel, wives or mothers of the patriarchs, have a sure place in the hearts of believers, a less sure one in their minds, and an even more limited one in their rites.

The Engine of Art

While other denominations tend towards the univocal, Catholic fantasy has as its mainspring a divided vision of the feminine, torn between angel and whore, saint and sorceress. That ambiguity ended up producing an aesthetic. And thus unleashing a dynamic. Fervour comes through the eyes, Bonaventura suggests – a happy supplement for faith, which comes through the ears (*ex auditu fides*). To the *Logos*, the lover of the Virgin with child adds *mimesis* (ornament, portraits, theatre, illuminations), which opens it up to feasts and indulgences forbidden to both Yahweh and Allah. The evangelical opening, having become an officially endorsed breach, ultimately entailed the appearance, after a *unimedia* (and unilaterally gendered) God, of a *multimedia* (and virtually unisex) God, capable of speaking to all our five senses, including the olfactory. Sacred art did not deprive itself of any of the entrancements of the senses, with the result that it ended up effacing the boundaries with secular art, little by little annexing portraiture and landscape painting, piano and organ, the domain of nature and that of grace. A vast gamut running from

Gregorian chant to oratorios, and from mysteries to be performed on the church parvis to theatre in the Italian style. The Jew is an expert reader; the Catholic is an expert in the arts of spectacle. He can remain in Christ while entering the Beaux-Arts, or the École du Louvre, or the Conservatory, or the Actors' Studio. Weakened by the rise of the Son, and the omnipresence of the Mother (the Church, an authoritarian and protective maternity), we can talk about a weakening of God the Father, but without forgetting that we are dealing with a total God, in the sense of a 'total art work', *Gesamtkunstwerk*. The grey is now expanded into colour. Becoming to its predecessor in the Temple what chanted music is to music on the page, or the movies are to the blackboard. By thus multiplying its emotive power tenfold, it will touch and mobilize far beyond its customary audience. Christian beauty is never gratuitous. And so much the better for it. We all know how boring art for art's sake can become.

It is by no means the Roman Church's most negligible achievement to have managed to rule over societies of men through women. With the pious image, it infiltrated the domestic hearth, and by dint of a kind of spiralling movement took over the throne room through the gynaeceum, princes through their mothers, spouse and daughters. And minds by way of hearts. 'To govern is to cause to believe,' said Hobbes, whom Churchill cited on the subject. Divine government made very effective use of that resource, and its long hegemony was also forged out of memories of first communion and death announcements. To make Himself even more captivating, God took on all the colours of the rainbow: white for the holidays, red for the martyrs, black for Lent, green for the innocents, blue for the Virgin, violet for penitence. He blasted forth sounds. And burned incense. All in all, He 'sensitized (and sensualized) his message'. Just as a good director should. John has Jesus say: 'My kingdom is not of this world' (18: 36). The first kingdoms to have laid claim to Christ did not understand him very well.

In Constantinople, Caesaro-Papism conflated the prestige of the imaginary with that of the symbolic. Had the prophet of Nazareth relativized the absolutism of the Caesars? The Christian Caesars made use of him to absolutize the relative. The pagan Caesars had succeeded in occupying all the recesses of the Empire without travelling, through the televisual delegation, *in situ*, of statues and medals in their effigy. A politically advantageous cloning by effigy that allowed one to test loyalty on the cheap, each foreign subject being called on to make public sacrifice before the image of the Emperor. Such was the *iconic tax*, which the Jews considered as problematic, as the monetary tax. '*Reddere Caesari . . .*'. According to Matthew the publican (or tax collector), this famous dictum occurred to Jesus while he was playing with a coin, a silver medal engraved with the Emperor's likeness. 'Render unto Caesar that which is Caesar's, and unto God that which is God's' is the reflection of a perplexed coin-collecting taxpayer. But by having himself represented on a gold *solidus* – heads, the crown and cross; tails, a frontal Christ – Justinian II (end of the seventh century) would in turn claim obedience and collect a tax as Jesus' representative on earth. In Byzantium, God and Caesar made common cause. Render unto Caesar, and render unto God? The theocrat evaded the difficulty by playing both sides: tails, his profile; heads, the triumphant Cross. As on Constantinian coins and Palestinian phials. And that Caesar–Pope was no longer local or provincial, since the first official Christian iconography had the advantage of being ubiquitous. It circulated like money, became the universal equivalent of the empire's values. Immediately comprehensible, this visual Esperanto had no need of translation. The image federated less deeply but more easily than the word, and the immense but composite Christian Confederation latched on to the *passe-partout*. A polychromatic and polyphonic God, conveyed through the interposition of frescos, mosaics and motets, went wherever He liked, passing easily through Customs. The psychomotivating sound–image came to the rescue of the Christian at a time when the *Ioudaios,* as Saint John called him, the Judaean deprived of land, had nothing left to console him but an unillustrated text (*i*). Not that he cared, to be sure. The Law was not written for the goyim. Yahweh was endogamous. Espousing humanity, on the other hand, is a project that can be fulfilled only through a policy of beauty. One does not govern the heirs of the Graeco-Roman world, which goes from Byzantium to Hollywood, without filling their retinas and their reveries, without satisfying the insatiable libido of eye and ear. In Scripture's tank, Christianity had placed a tiger: tenderness.

The Family in a Different Light

The magic of images and the captivation of eyes: such, for a God situated in an open economy, were the new levers of power. Ways of making war without waging it. He was the Lord, no longer of the Book, but of sensations. He was thus no longer the slave of grammar. Figures – Cross, Nativity, Glory – could travel without a dictionary, bring to the illiterate the light of hope, acclimatize in all parts the presence of love. What was the novelty? Was not the Almighty destined to conquer and dominate? Was He not always engaged in politics? Yes, but in overturning the relations of kinship, this God, who was no longer *ethnic* but *elective*, was no longer the administrator of a heritage but a pioneer of the unknown. We are all eligible – 'without consideration of race, gender or income'. The Only God of the chosen people (with a plurality in its internal life) excluded. This one allowed for inclusion. That reversal was perhaps, in the itinerary of our civilization, the *baptism of the world as will and representation*. The moment from which the West would be able to think of the social bond as something to be decided, not preserved. From which the institution of communal life would no longer be a matter of tribe – city, clan or family – but of choice, in the privacy of one's own conscience (and, one day, the voting booth). The moment when, for each individual, the future ceased to be deduced from the past. When history became something to be invented *ex nihilo*. Thereafter, *nature would no longer dictate the law*. Joseph did not choose the baptismal name of Jesus. One is a Jew by one's mother, but a Christian by baptism. One does not choose one's mother, but one can be converted at any age, and without asking for the family's advice. And the second birth, baptism, is superior to the first. As spirit is to flesh. With this God freed from His enclave, being-together was no longer founded on bonds of blood, since kinship by flesh was replaced by spiritual affiliation. 'Whosoever loves father or mother more than me is not worthy of me' (Matthew 10: 37). A reversal of 'natural' hierarchies: family bonds, those of the law, unworthy of an individual, are to disappear in favour of the community of faith. Chains to be broken. We didn't realize it, but Gide's 'Families-I-hate-you' and Breton's 'Let-it-all-go' are signed Jesus Christ: 'Whosoever comes to me and does not hate father and mother, wife and children ... cannot be my disciple' (Luke 14: 26). The true fraternity will be the voluntary one, the *ekklesia*. One does not inherit; one is co-opted. 'Here are my mother and my brothers!' says Jesus, pointing to his disciples. 'For whoever does the will of my Father in heaven is my brother and sister and mother' (Matthew 12: 46–50). And Tertullian could affirm, quite justifiably, that Christians were the most free of men, since they alone could choose their Father – maybe against their human mother. Did not Jesus affect not to recognize his mother and brothers when they came to meet him? The defenders of the sacred bonds of family would do well to take a second look before calling themselves 'Christians'. Neither Jesus nor John the Baptist founded a home of his own. And the Son of Man showed no particular respect for his mother: 'Woman, what is there between you and me?' (John 2: 3) My 'beloved mother', an ideal that would actually be imposed only in the Middle Ages (along with the colour blue), was not his style – he who would form a family only with those who followed the will of God, voluntarily. For God's design is accomplished through human action. Christianity 'disconnected' the family from the great sacred circuits by plugging every believer directly into a source of grace independent of his progenitors and compatriots. Your race and ancestors matter little to me provided that you believe in Christ. If you become a monk, you will forget your family name. If you become a priest, it will be forgotten for you. There are lineages of rabbis; there are no priestly lineages. That is the good news within the Good News: no more heredity.

Joseph, a rather colourless father; and Mary, in no way imaginable as a great lady. A home that commonplace does not incite one to an exaltation of roots. It signifies, rather, a farewell to the prestige of origins (so tenacious among nomads). And implicitly allegorizes the slippage from the received God to the desired God. We have lost sight of the intolerable subversive charge which that *chosen paternity* represented wherever a paternal power reigned (and, in Rome, it extended to a right of life and death over one's children). What an insult to the *patria potestas* and the law of the brothers! To become a Christian, in the Roman Empire, meant to choose to break with obligatory loyalties. With the juridical principle of the *gens*, with the bonds of blood. There had indeed been a Roman right to adoption – but it was centred on the family to which the newly adopted child was attached. And there is no legal adoption in an orthodox Jewish family, just as there are no monastic communities within the chosen people. Christian voluntarism brings us from a world in which parents acknowledge and declare their child to one in which children themselves lay claim to and declare their filial bond. Place of residence is free, or fluctuates. This is troublesome for 'household peace' and the neighbourhood police register. And the population rolls. 'You are Simon, son of John. You are to be called Cephas' (John 1: 42). Is there a more subversive and ambitious motto than this one: '*You must be born from above*' (John 3: 7). Which means: it is up to you to decide what to transmit. We are all in need of a destined community, it is true. A man without a destiny is a man who is lost – disorientated. But destiny, in this case, is a project: it is for each individual to take him- or herself in hand. Beneath the Cross, within his own conscience, the Roman centurion ripped up his birth certificate, transgressed his social status. 'Glorifying God, he said that the man was just.' Which was as much as to say that all nations would be admitted to the Holy Table. To artificial insemination 'by operation of the Holy Spirit'. And that every man could be born again. 'All of you are one in Christ Jesus' (Galatians 3: 28). For the first time, on a popular scale, outside the cosmopolitan elites (for affiliation with schools of philosophy was also a matter of deliberation), the super-natural would deserve its name.

A messianic leader is supposed to wage war. 'The war of the children of light against the children of darkness,' as the Essene hymns of Qumran recommended. Jesus was a messiah – or his disciples saw him as one. But he did not take up arms. He threatened no one. He was without zealotry. He did not connive, nor did he respond to expectations: his disciples (and others beyond them) expected that he would drive out the Romans, restore the monarchy, deliver Israel. Like a good Jewish patriot. Like others before or after him, false or true messiahs. And yet he was said to be the 'son of David'. A leader was being sought, the spark that would inflame the people. The Insurrection at the end of the street, on one's own lips. He would decline the crown. 'Are you the king of the Jews? – You're the one who say's so …'. Abstention. You'll find out. There is serious business elsewhere. They would accuse him of abandoning the struggle for independence. A shirker? Defeatist? Totally discredited? It was all said. Let us, rather, admire the finesse of the diversion, the performance by inversion. The Judaic revelation was addressed to a collective. It was ratified by an assembly, when the ancients gave their endorsement to Moses, returning from Sinai. The Jewish people were promised resurrection, not the individual. Prayer, too, was communitarian. At least ten men are required to officiate, the obligatory quorum of the *minyan*.[9] The Christian people begins with two individuals: one to give, the other to receive the sacrament. Jesus depoliticized God.

[9] In Hebrew, 'number', a prayer group, with or without a rabbi.

Herod Antipas, however much of a collaborator he may have been, did not obscure him. Nor the power of Rome. But he denationalized him, rendering him multi-national. For in forsaking solidarity with his own, he replaced petty solidarities with a great one. By closing his ears to the voice of blood, he broke the chains of consanguinity. *My* intimate God subverted *our* ancestral God, and globalized him from within. Less sail, and more wind. In that retreat to innerness lay an unlimited capacity for recruitment, since the Eternal Father could henceforth have foreign sons, who were not registered with the local authorities, all by virtue of an adoption ritual called baptism, which was valid anywhere. That is what enlarged the family circle to the planet Earth. The children of hope are by nature more numerous than those of memory (in the year 2000, a billion Christians, thirteen million Jews). In terms of proselytism: a goy is irremediable; a miscreant, redeemable. Thus a Christian always has something and someone to busy himself with – outside. The apostolic vitality of the Redeemer stems from his faculties of adaptation (to almost every environment: barbarian, Germanic, Celtic, Slavic, Saxon, etc.) and adoption (anyone can enter Christianity). Only one culture has subsequently surpassed it (*jeunesse oblige*) in plasticity: the American way of life, our new *lumen gentium*, which distributes images as the other distributes wafers. Elastic America (rubber is American) has that admirable suppleness of adaptation that Europe has lost (*j*). It can espouse, any foreigner at home; be espoused, at a distance, by any other. Not through indoctrination and lengthy catechesis. The holy communion is effected via film, advertisements, video clips and brand names. They too are rituals of adoption, streamlined sacraments that are all the more charismatic in that they have no dogmatic apparatus at all. The two traditions, of the Old and New Worlds, have fused in Pentecostalism or Anglo-Saxon evangelism, whose doctrinal and liturgical elasticity makes it adaptable and adoptable at all latitudes and longitudes (and particularly those of Latin America and Asia).

The swan's-neck is still a more effective conqueror than the stiff nape . . . .

9 The Last Flame

*The printing press is God's latest and greatest gift.
Through it, God is intent on making true religion
known through the entire earth, spreading it to all
languages. It is the last flame to be lit before the
world is extinguished.*
(Martin Luther, *Table Talk*)

*Upon His emergence from the typographical 'cradle', in 1500, our God, speaking
Latin, formerly polychromatic and couched in calligraphy, cloistered and chained to
His shelf, would soon be sprinting through the city in the vernacular. The printing
press made the Word 'practical and useful to all'. That new ease caused the Church
to lose its monopoly on reproduction and circulation. It would soon oblige it, after
the Council of Trent, to unsettle its certitudes and reinvigorate its sources of allure.
There was thus propagated, in the wake of the Reformation, an Eternal in black and
white, difficult to control, patriotic and erudite, polyglot, and with a certain wanderlust. With the possibility of home delivery. Bad news for the princes of the
Church, but excellent for educated fathers of their families. And when the Pilgrim
Fathers, in 1620, took it upon themselves to cross the Ocean with the Scriptures in
English under their arms, the result was a second Promised Land, North America,
an auspicious transplanting of the God of Gutenberg to the Far West.*

When the arts of memory undergo transformation, it is the soul of God that is transformed. In this sense the political history of the great Ordainer cannot be detached from His literary history, in so far as He was the first publisher in the West. If monotheism was born of the Letter, and its Christian variant was intent on appealing to the masses, we may infer that a change in the artisanry of the sign and the practices of publication would affect it to the core.

For a God who was essentially read, Gutenberg's invention proved a divine surprise. It was consequently baptized almost immediately a 'divine art' by Nicholas of Cusa, a cardinal, and the fifteenth-century Roman Catholic Church. The diabolical side of things would occur to it only later. The powers that be have always welcomed, somewhat absent-mindedly, the medium that would result in their decline. As for the theologians, unaware of the fact that 'extrinsic' vectors of distribution end up trumping the schemata of 'intrinsic' imposition, their minds were quite simply elsewhere. Unconcerned with such details. Even less so than men of letters, in their academies, would be by the industrialization of culture in the twentieth century. The disdain of the staunch practitioner of literature for the distribution services charged with disseminating his masterpiece to the humble masses. The ingratitude of clerics and wielders of the pen towards the workers who support their efforts is legendary. The Mind has little affection for the Hand that nourishes it – indeed, it seems almost ashamed of it.

But first, how did the sacred heritage of the Christian Empire manage to traverse the barbarian invasions of the Dark Ages? On the page, and by hand. Pagan schools were closed, and monasteries opened. The world of letters went into decline, as monks learned to write. In the sixth century, Cassiodorus, the Christian senator who served the Ostrogoth king, prepared catalogues, gathered up all the books in Greek he could find, and reconstituted a library. The monks made the *codex* their own. It spread through travel, group readings, the solitary practice of copying – always with the same protagonist, the ascetic of the monastic letter, whom Saint Benedict enjoined to combat idleness and observe Lent by taking a book from the *armarium* and 'reading it in its entirety and in order'. Books were rare and costly, and often, in Monte Cassino or in Rome, Roman manuscripts were scratched away so that the Gospels might be copied over them. Every centre of prayer became a storage centre, a warehouse of print. *Scriptoria*. A religious order was above all a community of writing-listeners, in which reading out loud accompanied every meal. From the High Middle Ages comes our Caroline script (from Carolingian), our lower-case typography. And the practice of reading in silence, a late monastic invention which dates from those times of intensive reading (few works, but regularly rehashed). Books were the sustenance of God. And His munitions. *Claustrum sine bibliotheca quasi castrum sine armamentaria*, wrote Godefroy de Sainte-Barbe in the twelfth century. A cloister without a library is a citadel without an arsenal.

The whole of existence revolved around the volume of Truth, a support for extremely complex arts of memory. The dwelling-place of God encapsulated and figured the order of the world in a rectangular parallelepiped which resembled, when fully opened, the Tablets of the Law. The insurance contract for this world came with a ticket to the beyond affixed. The finest materials were required for the *in-quarto*, which was edifying because it was itself an edifice, with its vaults, inner pages ordered on the model of a basilica, columns of words like pillars. With its clasp, its hard back, its ribbing and corners in metal, it was the foundation stone. Such is the image of the illuminated Breviary of Belleville (fourteenth century): the prophet Zacharias removes a brick from the synagogue in ruins and hands it, under a veil, to the apostle Matthew, who removes the veil and discovers a *codex*. Thou art Peter, and on this rock .... The Earth at the time was a square or a rectangle, not a ball, so that the miniature served as a microcosm, with the central fold as a median axis and the corners as cardinal points. And the World itself could become the great Book in which God had written His thoughts. '*Scritto in lingua matematica*,' Galileo would specify. *The Great Book of the World*: that cliché is testamentary in origin, the product of a book-based religion which could not get over the unprecedented convenience of having the memory of God and of men joined in a single *in-folio*, and the *Codex Dei* at home in the cupboard. Saint Augustine was in raptures about it. 'The new house of God', he wrote, "is more glorious than the old, which was made of precious stones, beams, and metals.' Coherence and firmness. A bulwark against the errant and the amorphous. Illuminated psalters, calligraphed books of hours, multicoloured breviaries. The monastic monopoly would wane with the appearance in the vicinity of the universities, in the twelfth and thirteenth centuries, of lay 'stationers', like the photocopying centres of our day. There work was done by the piece, the *pecia*, or the individual stitched section of a book in preparation, which was entrusted to a professional copyist. There were also seigneurial and royal bookshops. But beyond the world of merchants and the chancelleries, the Church remained the workshop and principal market for matters textual, whose rituals and censorship it administered (books of heretics had been burned since the Arian dissidence of the fourth century). To enter the School of the Lord was to begin to read. Believing in God and believing in the Book were virtually synonymous.

So much so that the material object, during the Renaissance, would serve as a safe-conduct for secular truths. The *codex* form, functioning as a blank cheque, would provide, from the beginning, authorized clearance for the sciences of nature, which were lodged in the same constructs of paper and leather as the sacred Word. The verifiable was to find its niche in the receptacles of the Revealed, which provided excellent cover for a change of function (more often it's the other way round) – a state of affairs that built a bridge between the revered object, the prayer book, and the object to be revered, the book of knowledge. Even if it was not yet science, it was already Christian policy that fifteenth- and sixteenth-century publishers were formulating. The great dates of that ambiguous transition are bibliographical events. The inaugural fanfare of modern times. A raising of the editorial and biblical curtain. A somewhat obstinate Augustinian monk, who taught Holy Scripture at the University of Wittenberg, saw, one fine day in 1517, to his utter astonishment, that a formidable stir was beginning to spread through the region. Why? Because his students had gone out and ordered a printing of the sheet he had nailed to the door of his church. He had thought of himself as a theologian. He discovered that he was a public-relations man. Like every other master of theology at the time, he put forward theses in order to launch a *disputatio*. Now he found that he was a gunner on a battlefield. Once the shot had been fired, momentarily disorientated by the impact and the noise, he ultimately decided to follow it. Which is what leaders do: catch up.

The Truth of a Commonplace

'Luther and Gutenberg': an old pair. The tandem has issued in so many simplistic formulae that historians delight in explaining that Hugo's *This* [the Nuremberg Bible]-*will-kill-that* [the Gothic cathedral] (see below) is a crude simplification, and that the causes of the Reformation are in fact numerous (the ascent of the bourgeoisie, the rise of national languages, the decline of scholasticism, the urbanization of Europe, etc.). Lead would be too base a metal to metamorphose into the gold of a new theology. All honour to the Lord. It is to the reformers, and to them alone, that the merits of the Reformation should be attributed, not to an obscure and marginally avaricious goldsmith. Where would we end up if … ? What role would remain for the Most-Holy, for grace, for the humanists? Only a naive materialism, it is true, would assume that a mechanical medium had, on its own, the ability to invent a culture independently of a global dynamic that it translated and reorientated in its own direction, like a railroad switch. The same causal feedback loop can be applied to typography as to writing itself – which authorizes, but does not command. *This* neither kills nor engenders *that*, but without *that*, there would be no *this*. Remove Gutenberg from the scene, and Luther becomes a prophet laid off for technical reasons.

There had been numerous heresies before 1517. Wycliffe and Jan Hus were the most notable. Miserable failures. Preaching by way of mouth and a few scattered texts. Neither unity nor cohesion. No ability to mould. Nothing precise and stabilized, nothing that could be spread. Pope Leo X's bull granting, in exchange for appropriate financial compensation, an indulgence to the provinces of Mainz and Magdeburg, because the construction of Saint Peter's in Rome was proving too costly, provoked a good deal of muttering. But the 95 Theses of the adversary Luther were reproduced and distributed throughout the state. And it was as though, in the words of a witness, 'the angels themselves had been their messengers and had borne them before the eyes of the people in its entirety'. And Luther himself, in all good faith, communicated his discomfiture shortly thereafter in a letter ... to the Pope himself. 'By virtue of a mystery that has astonished me before anyone else, fate has decreed that all the theses (among all those that I or other doctors have drawn up) have been disseminated to virtually the entire world. I had published them strictly for the use of our University and drawn them up in such wise that it strikes me as unbelievable that they can be understood by all.'

In 1517, movable metallic type was already seventy years old. The technology was emerging from its infancy. Or, more accurately, from its cradle, since books printed before 1500 are called 'incunabula' (from *cuna*, the cradle). Thus the Reformers' efforts came up against the 'admirable art', the *ars artificialiter scribendi*, which had just reached maturity. Now we may be inclined to see this as but one more achievement, after the invention of minuscule written characters (in the eighth and ninth centuries), the domestication of silence (thirteenth and fourteenth centuries) and the arrival of paper in the West (fourteenth century). Neither handwritten copies nor epistolary exchanges would disappear instantaneously. Manuscripts would retain their adepts among the aristocrats and freelance practitioners of thought. The printing press reproduced the familiar forms of the copyist – the disposition of the page, the indices and ornaments. The characters remained the same, with their ornate Gothic ligatures. And the most popular authors remained those of the waning Middle Ages. There was even a resurgence of the most traditional works of scholasticism and devotion (the *Vita Christi*, *Artes moriendi*, *Sententiae* of Peter Lombard). Amounting, shall we say, to nothing of consequence? Prudence is in order at this juncture. The new invariably seeks sustenance, in an initial phase, in what is old, in order to secure its letters of patent. The *Zeitgeist* starts out by hiding under the table, whence the 'stagecoach effect' (Jacques Perriault). The first railroad cars were stagecoaches propped on rails – which lacked nothing but their horses. Figure and ground: seventy-seven per cent of the *incuna-*

bula were in Latin, and half were religious texts.[1] Rome had no reason to be alarmed, and in fact the papacy offered many a hosanna to the new procedure, which proved useful in the crusade against the Turks. Whether lay or religious, authorities have a particular gift for mediological slumber. They are always convinced that they can transfer yesterday's ends to the new day's medium (television to sermonize and instruct the masses). Hence their disorientation when the genius of the misperceived dispensation hits them in the face. It is said to be the doing of 'barbarians' who, alien to the mould of the previous medium, rewrite the rules of the game before anyone notices.

'From before the end of the fifteenth century,' writes Henri-Jean Martin, 'approximately 27,000 printings have come down to us, representing undoubtedly more than ten million copies, distributed over less than two generations to a Europe counting fewer than a hundred million inhabitants.' As was the case, in the long run, with demographic pressures exercised on weaponry, the pressure of typography would win out over the forces of habit and the Holy See. It would relegate the *imprimatur* (permission to publish) to the past, outpacing customary forms of censorship. 'Greater familiarity with the Bible was the principal cause of the religious Reformation of the sixteenth century.'[2] There were 438 editions in Latin. And from 1517 to 1520, the publications of Luther have been estimated at 300,000 copies. Until then, commoners knew the Word of God solely through stained-glass windows and sermons by friars. But now several hundreds of thousands of the literate – clerics, academics, townsfolk – were able to poke their noses into the fundamental charter. This grasp of so-called revealed truths in Latin coincided with a new veneration accorded to ancient languages, both Greek and Hebrew. A Hebraist, Reuchlin, pointed out contradictions between the Latin and Hebrew texts. Stupefaction at the discovery that it was not the Good Lord that one had been reading. A scandal in the Church itself, which had forgotten that Saint Jerome's Bible, its vade-mecum from time immemorial, was finally just a translation – or a well-intentioned betrayal, as the best translations are.

Let us now consider the *context*.

With the Discoveries – Magellan, Vasco da Gama, Christopher Columbus – Christendom opened its windows wide, but the message of salvation that it was intent on disseminating abroad had become encrusted and befouled in its ecclesiastical cells. Benumbed in its houses of religion, an overprotected (and

[1] Lucien Febvre and Henri-Jean Martin, *L'Apparition du Livre* (Paris: Albin Michel 1958), p. 378 / *The Coming of the Book*, trans. David Gerard (London and New York: Verso 1997).
[2] Victor Baroni, *La Contre-Réforme devant la Bible. La question biblique* (Lausanne: La Concorde, 1943).

protectionist) market. A calcified deposit. Buried beneath layers of glosses, marginal notes, introductions and summaries encumbering the pages of old treatises. Through which the Truth could no longer be perceived. The act of recopying, to be sure, had already worked its way free of a liturgical context (for the Jews, the act of copying was still sacred, and implied a liturgy of prayer), but always within the limits of a faculty of theology. Several months to copy a work. And fifteen animals for an average format. One could get as many as sixteen sheets of small format out of one sheepskin, but the manufacture of parchment and the copying process were long and tedious (the monks complained). The Church seemed to be afflicted with gout. Like an old and obsessive antiques dealer, tottering under the burden of polychrome statues, jewelled treasures, altarpieces, pilgrimages, saints' relics, garishly painted Virgins, Ways of the Cross, pious imagery (which had proliferated severalfold, since the fourteenth century, through wood engravings). Encumbered by its works, the convoy of grace got bogged down. *En route*, it acquired 'mummeries and heathenries' without ever casting off any ballast. Such excess baggage proved a disqualification when clerics found themselves obliged to check three times before giving copy to printers, for whom the slightest error in recopying had consequences. What the Judaean had imposed on the idolators, with consonants on papyrus, the Reformer imposed on the Sorbonne pedants with print on paper: cutting down to the bone.

Which begins with a removal of corruptions. The imperative was to cleanse the body of the text, to separate the detritus from the precious ore. The accumulation had become such that various traditions could no longer be distinguished from their originals. In material terms, the hand press obliged one to cleanse the crust of sedimentary *lectiones*. For when a printshop makes an error, it is not one but thousands of copies that are infected. Thus Barker's *Perverse Bible*, in 1631, with its seventh commandment set as a Satanic verse: 'Thou shalt commit adultery' (the *not* having been omitted). To prevent a standardization of the error and the corruption threatening multiple copies, to nip the contagion of the false in the bud, one is obliged to *establish* the text. Such was the crucial role – to limit ourselves to France – of printer humanism, Lefebvre d'Étaples and Robert Estienne: to do away with commentaries and sponge up variants. 'The time will soon come', said Lefebvre, 'in which Christ will be preached purely and without contamination by human traditions.' And this will be all the more emphatically the case in that we will be able to go directly to the Hebrew and Greek, leapfrogging the four scholastic senses (literal, historical, typological and symbolic) of interpretation in Latin, thus reconnecting the spiritual with the certified. Logically, this return to sources could not fail to come up against old-style theologians practised in the oral and codified exercises of *lectio* and *disputatio*. Preaching, as far as the Reformer was concerned, was necessary in order to illuminate the letter by the Spirit. But his *Soli Deo Gloria*, Glory to God and to Him alone, is an implicit *no* addressed to the additions implemented by the Church. The founders, Luther and Calvin, would insist above all on pastoral guidance for personal reading. But the universal priesthood was above all the open book, revealed to all those who had eyes to see.

Between the Eternal and all that was new, something on the order of an exchange of courtesies was established. In the wake of recent procedures for engraving on copper (and not on wood), engineers bequeathed to the theologians the qualities of certain metals (antimony, lead, steel, copper), dyes, and rollers. The latter saw their audience grow. God, for His part, gave something of an endorsement to the commercial expansion; the Bible of forty-two lines conferred on it a *nihil obstat*. Typographers rose up to take Heaven by storm, but far from putting up a resistance, the titled owner of the premises welcomed them with outstretched arms. 'Do as you wish. Consider yourselves at home.' That initial climate of trust blinded both parties to what was ultimately at stake. To wit: the birth of a God emancipated from his official proxies. The pious producers of *incunabula* did not realize that they were opening the way to a break with the system of authority, nor that they were exposing the dominant theology to the heresy already constituted by the intrusion of the vernacular into the sacred tongue. After the expropriation of the authorized commentators came the destabilization of the authorities, who functioned, it was discovered, more as a screen than as a source of illumination. If God can give me a personal appointment in His book – which can, moreover, be proliferated at will – what need would I have of intercessors or chaperones? 'Every Protestant was Pope, a Bible in his hand': Boileau may not have realized how on the mark he was. The technology of reproduction disrupted the technology of control. Paper gave chase to the papacy, and *ceci tuera cela*, 'this will kill that', as Hugo summarized it in a long chapter of *Notre-Dame de Paris* (this, the Nuremberg Bible; that, the Gothic cathedral). The formulation was a bit forced, but the intuition was inspired.[3]

Mass and Power

The Reformation did not play the (spoken) Word off against the Book. It adjusted them to each other in a new complementarity. But where might the principal motto – *Sola fide, sola gratia*; by the grace of God, and only through the faith I have in Him – stem from if not from a 'reading for all'? 'I am not ashamed of the Gospel; it is the power of God', said Luther. I am not ashamed to publish in the vernacular, for it augments that power. Perhaps in an exaggerated and unconsidered manner, he would end up fearing, and Calvin along with him. There were too many books, they

---

[3] It would be developed and nuanced by Elizabeth Eisenstein in *La Révolution de l'imprimé à l'aube de l'Europe moderne* (Paris: La Découverte 1991) without the slightest reference to Hugo (who was neither a historian nor an accredited sociologist).

lamented, and the useless ones, those written by others, were overshadowing the indispensable ones – their own. There was a need to reduce the number, sort them out, censor. 'As for good books,' Friar Martin wrote, 'there have never been enough of them, and there aren't even now' (which is a line currently applied to television channels). Everyone, Catholics and Protestants alike, was worried by the prospect of a chaotic misreading of the Holy Word. Pearls before swine – or fools, boors or women. A precipitous and dangerous democratization. To be channelled and supervised. But if the papacy was quick to change its tune concerning the virtues of the admirable art, Reformers of all countries continued, despite their reservations, to adorn it with garlands of their making. Thus the Englishman John Foxe, in his *Book of Martyrs*: 'The Lord has begun to labour for His Church, not with sword and buckler to subdue His signal enemy, but by means of the printing press, by writing and reading. As many presses as there are in the world are so many fortifications against the great Castel Sant' Angelo, so that either the Pope will be obliged to abolish learning and print or, in the long run, print will exterminate him.'

Moreover, the preacher could now seek support in a trustworthy and understandable text, which was no longer a luxury item. The use of rag paper instead of parchment lowered the cost of manufacture tenfold, and broke through the physical ceiling for the reproduction of the divine Word, which had until then been hostage to the slow reproductive cycles of livestock. Of the one hundred and thirty copies of the Gutenberg Bible, thirty were drawn on vellum (the skin of a newborn calf). Three hundred and forty sheets measuring forty-two by sixty-two centimetres means a hundred and seventy animals slaughtered for a *single* copy (according to Aloÿs Ruppel). The pursuit of the Good News in the 'peopled world' of Europe would have required the utter decimation of livestock, and the choice would ultimately have had to be faced between nourishing souls and nourishing bodies. Starvation or Hell (a Sophie's choice of sorts). Paper support, easily stored and allowing a variety of formats, arrived on the scene in time to save both beef on the platter and the theological virtue of Hope.

But there was a hitch: the dynamic, once unleashed, eluded its sponsors. It generated in broad daylight a high-powered explosive: popular theology. In his lifetime (before 1546), Luther saw 354 complete or partial printings in *Hochdeutsch*, in addition to ninety-one in Low German. The sacred text was again becoming the book of a nation (as in the time of ancient Judaea). International Latin was no longer an obligatory intermediary. Populations lifted their heads, each one brandishing its totemic version of the common text. To each kingdom its Bible. The servants of the One-for-All woke up as nationalists. Luther dedicated the New Testament, translated into his own language, to the German people (1528). The theologian was German to his fingertips, and the formula would be pregnant with future developments.

For the cradle of mechanical printing, Germany, was also the cradle of the

Reformation. An urban phenomenon, like the new industry, which made its home in the free cities and towns, where money, customers and qualified craftsmen were to be found. Wittenberg, Luther's base, was a well-known typographical centre, and the Frankfurt fair, at the intersection of land and water routes, was a forum for biblical and bibliographical exchange. Calvin, for his part, timed his dates of publication for Frankfurt. He supervised accounts, frequented workshops person-ally, collaborated with master-printers, and was perfectly familiar with printing techniques – calibration, choice of typeface, page-setting.[4] In our own day, it is in circles linked with communication and new technologies that various modes of New Age mysticism are elaborated. It was the same in the Renaissance: evangelical faith flows from a milieu of printers, publishers, pressmen and companion-typographers. The spiritual and industrial maps can be superimposed. Mainz, Strasbourg, Zurich, Paris, Antwerp, Basel, Cologne, Augsburg. Northern Europe. The typographically retarded South remained apart. Milan, Naples, Seville, Córdoba, Genoa, Florence. Venice, a city of the North, with its numerous vanguard presses, proved a temporary exception in Italy, but the Vatican was careful to block the contagion. It is true that *printed* is not synonymous with *read*, and even less so with *understood*. And if there are statistics for production, we have none for audiences, or even literacy rates. All that can be ascertained is that where the printing press – that 'art given by God to Humanity', as Melanchthon called it – had not yet penetrated, the Pope could still sleep soundly. His enemy: intensive reading. As long as received tradition was winning out over the read page, Catholicism retained the advantage. For that was precisely the problem: the conflict in authority between the Church and Scripture. In which direction would the verdict finally tilt? Where was one to find one's Solomon? In the printshop or the diocese? The great Reformers, all of them saints and martyrs of the Book, would opt, in the last analysis, like Leibniz later on in his pathetic correspondence with Bossuet, for the party of the symbolic Father against that of the imaginary Mother (the Roman she-wolf). Attempting to effect an ecumenical reconciliation between estranged brothers, Leibniz, at the end of the eighteenth century, took on the defence, unsuccessfully, of the Oratorian Richard Simon, the French churchman who had prepared a critical edition of the Bible whose pub-lication was banned by Bossuet. The Church of France would eventually be punished for this by Voltaire's *La Bible enfin expliquée* (k). Anyone who rejects reform will be struck by a Revolution. Yet if the Protestants had the right exegesis, the Catholics had the right genealogy. The former believed they could return to a pure origin, convinced that the Church had succeeded in altering the sacred anthology. The Catholics were not wrong when they replied that the Word of God was to be found 'in texts as much as in the traditions of the apostles and their successors'. The Dominican who debated with Calvin in 1536 retorted that the Church existed before the Gospels. Even if he was exploiting them apologetically to

[4] Jean-François Gilmont, *Jean Calvin et le livre imprimé* (Geneva: Droz 1997).

rather dubious ends, the chronologies argued in his favour. 'It is *through* the Church that we have Scripture, and Scripture would have no authority without the Church.' *Ecclesia est prior scriptura et potior*, the Church is prior to and more powerful than Scripture. This is a bit cynical, but it is rigorously mediological.

With the arrival of lead characters, the One began to scatter into fragments. Through the proliferation of sects – which were soon legitimized – and the disintegration of unifying Latin. But also through new relations of proximity between the Word and its translators. They provided an echo more resonant than that of the preachers. The apostolate of the pen became more profitable, in terms of influence, than the other. Success was no longer mediated by contact with the crowds. Erasmus had already mocked the poor deliverers of sermons who shouted themselves breathless from their pulpits, while he was read 'in all the countries of the world …'. Defoe would later observe that 'delivering a sermon meant addressing a small number of humans, whereas printing a book meant speaking to the entire world'. And first of all to one's compatriots, in their own language. The nationalization of God, in addition to the charisma of intellectuals and the commerce of printed materials, is the formula for modernity's version of the inexpiable: the war of values.

A Theological Heatwave

A flame, said Luther. The word was well chosen. The printing press caused an abrupt rise in temperature in streets, palaces and chapels. Fervour, and many a blaze. What was sowed was zeal, and what was harvested was fire. Among flare-ups of this sort, from enthusiasm (the sentiment of who-has-God-in-himself) to fanaticism (which does not tolerate remaining outside the temple), the transition is minimal (in Rabelais, 'phanatique' was still the designation for an inspired poet). The sixteenth century of inspired languages was also that of the liberation of violence. The Apocalypse descended on the masses *unmediated*, without the shock-absorbers provided by the wiles of the Church, and the result was a holy impatience. With a desire to apply the orders of the Most-High *literally,* and without delay. It was that rage for immediacy which gripped the Anabaptists (I've got God on the line; don't interrupt; I'm old enough to understand). Thomas Münzer wanted to seize the city of Münster, and build the New Jerusalem without delay. The Church is a protracted exercise in patience. He who strikes out against the 'whore of Babylon' arouses in the people the revolutionary need for equality. On the heels of the humanists, plumply cosseted in their furs, come the emaciated visionaries. The illuminati and the deranged. The ruffians, the resentful, the generous, the geniuses and the insane. The Sartrean cast of *The Devil and the Good Lord.* With the end of the clerical monopoly on the production of texts and commentaries, on to the stage comes the new star of theological controversy, the motor of our ideological wars

Wood engraving illllustrating the title of the pamphlet, 'Description of the Divine Mill', commissioned by Zwingli in 1521

once God had left the set: *Herr Omnes,* Sir Everyman. In the propaganda print commissioned by the Zurich reformer Zwingli, 'Description of the Divine Mill', which is a staging of God's new bakery, we see in the middle, to the left of God (who is in the upper-left-hand corner), Karsthaus, an ordinary man brandishing his scourge above the mitred heads. Christ pours the Gospels into a grain-funnel, Erasmus collects the flour, Luther makes loaves of bread in the form of books, which Zwingli then offers to the princes of the Church, who reject them with visible annoyance. And above this select company stands the humble peasant, prepared to riot. A fine illustration of Christ as a subversive journeyman, allied with the people. The powers that be, both political and religious, sense that they are being over-whelmed by 'civil society', which is already giving an indication of what motivates it. As in Zurich, where private pews in the churches, a sign of aristocratic distinc-tion, would be pillaged. Bonfires of books would be lit everywhere. Decapitations, burnings, drownings, deforestation – especially by the rebel peasants of Germany.

Luther, attacked by his own extremists, made a sharp turn to the right, and took direct aim at them in his brochure 'Against the Murderous and Pillaging Bands of Peasants'. Such was the German war of polemical pamphlets, to which Thomas

Münzer and his millenarian beggars, fully armed, would succumb. That was when the Reformers began to grow anxious. Revolutionary circles had taken their tracts and sermons literally, and the stakes were being raised. Unintentionally they had opened the floodgates of anger. After Gutenberg, the naive had encountered knowledge. It was no longer possible to conceal from them that the Last Judgement had been scheduled by Scripture for the day after tomorrow. And that Jesus was particularly hard on the rich and the lukewarm. Luther sounded the retreat (better to do less, but better) and published his 'Sincere Admonition to All Christians that They Refrain from all Rioting and Rebellion' (1521). It was too late. The print-prone monk taking a stand against the the papist right was outflanked on his left. The scholar had become an agitator, and the fairly moderate leader of a school had, in short order, turned into a warrior chieftain in spite of himself. By conferring on thought 'an incomparable power of penetration', the screw-press (and *what* would be in the offing with steam?) no longer produced doctrines so much as epileptic fits. It inaugurated the era of press campaigns and manhunts. In which one wielded one's pen like one's lord wielded his axe, and the peasant his scourge.

Mediological transitions are like Russian dolls. Generations emerge from inside each other, every twenty or thirty years, and the young are quick to mock their elders (in relation to new technologies, cultural attitudes depend on their date of birth). The first generation to know the printing press does not have the reflexes of the second. 'Erasmus laid the eggs,' it was said in Rome, 'Luther allowed them to hatch.' But Erasmus renounced Luther; and Guillaume Budé renounced Calvin. The fathers disinherit the sons; the sons denounce the fathers (*Du bist nicht fromm!*). They reproach them for going fishing in the Rubicon, not leaving their studies, not making their knowledge more accessible. It was on that crucial point that the Reformers and humanists parted company. Calvin was intent on seeing his *Institution of the Christian Religion* (1536), written in Latin, appear in French (1560). The care they took to respond to the challenge of popularization dis-tinguished the soldiers of God from the moderates or 'Nicodemites' (Nicodemus visited Jesus by night). Portable pulpits, collapsible goblets, braided Bibles. The persecuted evangelists would rediscover the Jewish wiles of miniaturization in order to squeeze through the mesh. It was a frequently sacrificial struggle. A fount of erudition like Erasmus refused all militancy. He preferred Greek to local dialect, and his bookshop to the street. Unlike the doctor of theology, whose preferred genres were the sermon and the lecture, the new scholar devoted himself solely to his written works, which were not sufficient for community organizers, who felt the imperative need to mount the pulpit (as others, later on, felt compelled to stand on a barrel at the factory gates). To the passion for understanding they added one for convincing. A slave to writing like Calvin (250,000 words per year, after 1550) never forgot to preach to the simple, even as he gave oral lessons in exegesis to the erudite. Publication was no more than a springboard for him, and it was up to the spoken Word in its altruism, inhabited by the Spirit, to show the community the correct letter.

'When the Creator made birds,' Bachelard has written, 'He made a bird of prey and a nightingale. When man made aviators, he made soldiers and messengers.' When he made the automobile, he made tanks and ambulances. And when he made print, bookstores and massacres. Scholars and ideologues – often combined in the same individual. The printing press made reason cosmopolitan, and national passions took root more or less everywhere. It extended the personality cult (to authors and artists, our future great men), and inaugurated the knowledge of nature (botany, astronomy, physics). When Luther died, he was still astonished by what he had unleashed. His doctrine, in the space of a generation, had been outstripped by his method. When Jan Hus preached to a thousand of the faithful in his chapel, he failed to stir Bohemia. When the 'doctor of Holy Scripture' allowed himself to be convinced by his students in Wittenberg to have his ninety-five theses translated and published, his printed words galvanized followers who were prepared to do battle throughout the country. And eventually against Master Martin himself. The 'spiritual battle' immediately became a battle of men in which people killed and died for real. 'I cannot know God through my reason,' says the Protestant, 'He eludes my intelligence.' Granted, but the interrogation of a verse of the Bible out loud before an audience of the illiterate does call on one's understanding, and nothing is more conducive to tolerance and mental suppleness than a trilingual edition of the Bible (Hebrew, Latin and Greek), such as the Antwerp Polyglot published by Plantin. One has only to follow a mystical (allegorical and symbolical) reading of the Bible with a more historical and literary examination, and all of a sudden one finds oneself reading and analysing Moses and Matthew as one does Cicero and Plato. That deviation prolongs the reflexivity already inherent in writing. To translate, annotate and edit is to verify, confront, sort out the authentic from the dubious. To prepare copy, to compose, is to decompose, separate letters, words and columns. It is to align one's critical capacity with one's faith. Whence biblical scholarship. And subsequently, in the seventeenth and eighteenth centuries, textual criticism would be pursued quite openly. The emergence of scholarly editing at the very heart of belief. A printed God bearing science ... . But also iconoclastic hatreds, with crucifixes broken, books burned, families bloodied, Saint Bartholomew and Michel Servet at the stake – an augmentation of barbarism. It is always difficult, with our successive Aesopian idioms – print, audiovisual, Internet – to find the right gauge and measure.

When God Prefers Black

'Reading dog', Père Sorel lashes out at Julien in *The Red and the Black*. The old Catholic distrust of 'damned books' can still be read in the statistics: in terms of funds assigned for public reading and university and school libraries, Northern

Europe is considerably ahead of the South. As is the case with the Anglo-American paperback in relation to the French *livre de poche*. Northern Europe achieved literacy earlier than the rest, in the seventeenth and eighteenth centuries. But that head start entailed a certain price to be paid in penitence among the devout, who were so attached to the 'black art' (such as engraving) that they were for a time 'chromoclasts'. Dressed in black, brooding [*broyant du noir*], and driving black cars (Ford, the puritanical industrialist: 'You can order a car of any colour from me, so long as it's black'). The Protestant world – think of Bergman, Grosz, Klee – excels in black and white, a regime of Bibles without illuminations. It displays a predilection for sanctimony, abstract painting, formality, potatoes and boiled meat without spices. The Counter-Reformation of the South wanted to protect God from His own Letter, deemed to be dangerous (Rome placed Bibles in the vernacular on the Index), but as a compensation it gave us the privileges of colour, plunging necklines, the volutes of rococo, the carnivals and dances of the (true) Spectacle-State, that of Louis XIV; but also, more usefully, pasta, yeast and old wines. Vector Word, in its frigidity (even today more newspapers and books are bought by Lutherans than by ex-Papists); Vector Flesh, in its warmth. It is not surprising that hygienic regions (good bathrooms) with troublesome climates (long winters) are repelled by mould – while forgetting that penicillin itself is a mould.[5] The Reformation was of as little use to the arts of the table as to those of colour, banning the picking of wild mushrooms because their shape was too phallic. Need it be recalled that corruption, rot, the 'laboratory of life' judiciously hailed by Karl Marx, has given us, in addition to bribes and a host of social abuses, the most succulent cheeses, and minds more supple than are apt to be found among the Impeccable? In moderate doses, it has never frightened the gluttons of 'real presence' known as Catholics. Those for whom words do not suffice, who would savour the flesh and blood of the Lord beneath their tongue. A reversal in the distribution of weaknesses and strengths. A weaning of the eye in the North; a deferment of exegesis in the South. North of the Alps, bereft of stained-glass windows and sun, one distances oneself from an array of enchantments in order to read, by oneself, at home. In the South – with the exception of Camisard Languedoc – one idles in the piazza, ogling the girls, and before going to the brothel one stops in a church to breathe in the incense between iridescent frescos and polychrome statues. The diverse ways in which our ancestors worshipped a God in whom we barely still believe continue to govern our manners of eating, seeing and loving.

The history of the Eternal in the West has something pendular about it which is a bit depressing. When He becomes fully legible, He forgets the visible on which He was

---

[5] As we are reminded by Jean Clair in his sly *De l'invention de la pénicilline et de l'action painting* (Paris: L'Échoppe 1990).

so promisingly embarked. 'Cheese *and* dessert' would appear to be forbidden to our consumption of the divine. When the Word is advanced, the Image is inhibited, and vice versa. Our only God goes from one to the other and back, as a man who is ill at night tosses and turns in his bed but cannot find the right position. The Hebrew shatters idols, and soon thereafter takes to idolizing what has been written. Mesmerized by images hallucinatory in their realism, the medieval Christian makes the reverse journey: he places the Word under double lock and key, and gives himself over to the spectacular. The Puritan then makes the trip back, launching a second quarrel over images that perturbs the whole of Europe. Erasmus, prudently, ridiculed futile luxuries and privately censured the excessively white and costly marble of the charterhouse of Pavia. Images distract us from the inner life, he claimed; they insult the poor as well as evangelical simplicity. This may well be so, but the second generation of print added action to speech. What had appeared to be merely futile had now become odious. That generation attacked the spandrels of churches with pickaxes, tore up painted canvases, overturned statues (fifty in Lyon in a single day, in the square in front of the cathedral). 'Where the Huguenot is master, he ruins all images.' A Flemish chronicler, Van Mander, drawing up an inventory of altarpieces that had been destroyed, noted that the *Crucifixion* in Saint James of Bruges had been saved because, after it had been smeared over with black, the Huguenots had inscribed on it, in letters of gold, the Decalogue. The image blackened and profaned, the letters in gold on top: a perfect allegory. The images of saints were replaced, with Théodore de Bèze and his 'true portraits', by those of famous Reformers. Immaterial and edifying, only chorales were licit pleasures, and that was because they were egalitarian, without rich or poor, and took Scripture as their basis. For it should not be forgotten that iconoclasm was not directed solely against sacred images, but also against the mighty and privileged who paid for and enjoyed them, both donors and collectors. The breaking of images, more or less everywhere, was redolent of peasant Jacqueries or the Commune. It was the poor man's revolution.

Unlike Calvin, Friar Martin, an intimate friend of Cranach, his colleague at Wittenberg, held that the reproduction of profane (but not sacred) things was legitimate. He criticized an abuse (not a use), and his own pamphlets were illustrated. Dürer served him well, as did Holbein and Hans-Baldung Grien. He requested only that no image be placed 'in lieu of God'. With letters as agile as hares, the figurative crutch was no longer indispensable; the accessories of devotion need no longer be imposed where it was possible to read. Gregory the Great's former concessions to a prevalent illiteracy (admitting images as the Bible of those who could not read) were compromise solutions for a period in which texts were scarce; the printing press made them pointless. Because the important things could now be learned at school, or in one's family. Without the steel rod prolonged by a type mould of perforated copper, such belated iconoclasm would have been regressive or suicidal. Would pilgrimages (with Virgins held aloft at their head) have been halted had each of the faithful not had the possibility of carrying the Bible with him under his arm, or hearing it read at home by the appropriate authority?

The Family, both Vehicle and Sanctuary

A repetitive phenomenon: each new mode of circulation of the document-object-of-faith provokes in the faithful a new way of forming a community. Just as the digital promotes the small screen to the status of mini-altar, print, in times past, enthroned the *vehicular family* in its status as mini-church, guardian and conveyor of its treasure. Along with books of devotion and splendid collections of the Psalms of David, melodies still sung today, the Bible protected the Protestant family which protected the Bible. It was the guardian angel, in cotton paper, gilded and on display, read each evening by a Father to his wife and children. And transmitted from father to son. The least precarious of safeguards. For lack of a protective institution, transmission sought out a protected site, the most sheltered possible from the gallows and slave-ships. The household would be the channel for the administration of identity. The Holy Spirit fused with the family spirit, a union sealed *ex-libris*. The Eternal was admitted into privacy, which in turn domesticated His savage moods. And just as the Bible was good only if an established pastor – or, in his absence, a preacher – guided one's reading, the desacralization of the Pope was valid only if the hearth was consecrated, as the swing of the pendulum dictated. A change of mediating body. The paterfamilias as a protection against the tendencies of every man for himself and God for all. What his parish is for the Catholic, his family is for the Protestant: his university, haven and shield. And his fortress and catacomb when his temple is prohibited. Protestant morality might well be summarized as follows: 'Reading is good, and not reading is bad. But it is better to read in the living-room rather than in bed, sitting down rather than lying down, and in the appropriate company.' Family discipline, above all for the Huguenot and Waldensian hunted by the King's dragoons and the bishop of the diocese, manages to combine freedom and authority. This has nothing to do with the Vichyite slogan: 'Work, Family, Homeland'. The protective shield is, rather, an anti-consensus prophylaxis which has the advantage of not causing a stir outside, where the Papists control the street, with their processions and sacraments. Not a damper, but a form of self-defence.[6]

Is not the place of worship, in all its discreet banality, a kind of expanded family home, whose place of celebration would be the main room (with a harmonium in the corner, like the piano in a bourgeois salon), a dining-room table for the Holy

---

[6] Such is the anti-conformist role assumed in France, 'the family against the powers that be', by the National Union of Family Associations (UNAF), led with talent and pugnacity by P.-P. Kaltenbach.

Supper (at home too a benediction and grace are said), single-coloured panes of glass for bay windows, rustic benches allowing one to listen to one's uncle, the pastor, with due calm? The preaching is colloquial, familiar. The dialogue between sermon and psalms is a kind of expanded before-dinner conversation. 'Brothers and sisters ... ,' begins the pastor, in his black robe, or today in shirtsleeves. No liturgical colours, no mosaics or wall-paintings, no stained-glass windows to distract from the inner time of speech, the eschatological time of redemption. For the Protestant (as for the Jew, but in a more separatist manner), primacy lies with inner meaning. With history, not geography. With what one hears or says, not with what one sees. The Hebrews of Christianity (the white band of the pastoral robe has the shape of the Tablets of the Law) also prefer the memory of the invisible to the visual of the moment. They stripped their temple bare in order the better to espouse and retrieve the time of the Promise. To the institution, which displays and offers its organs and pomp to the first-comer (with its reliquaries, stained-glass windows and Pietà) they oppose the inner resonance of a moment of communion, the discreet grace of a chorale, a circle, a small organ. The simplicity of the announcements, of the portion of bread, of the goblets that do the rounds. It is not surprising that Mass is effective on television and Protestant worship on radio. The advantage of the Catholic television channel KTO over Télé-Réforme. Radio, the evangelical medium, protects one's privacy. It is less imposing, and allows its receivers greater freedom of interpretation and movement, with time to hesitate and mature. For 'truth without the quest for truth is only half the truth', as an excellent Reformist adage has it. A less stressful medium, more intimate, which reverberates better because it shines less resplendently. The Protestant microphone favours Gides; the Catholic stage-sets favour Claudels. In the recording studio, the various modes of critical authenticity; on the boards, the operas of dogma.

God Bless America

Guided by new maps and printed atlases, the Eternal, following the Reformation, prolonged his journey from East to West (his support, paper, also followed the sun, from China to Europe). With the 'black art', He propelled Himself across the Atlantic, a leap of 5,000 kilometres. There He was at the zenith of His trajectory – at the very moment, the Industrial Revolution, when, in the Old World, faith began to decline (the divine timepieces are well synchronized). Its chrome and nickel exterior cannot make us forget that North America owes its fabulous destiny to the encounter between God and lead. New England is the legitimate offspring of the Bible cult in Roman characters, just as that of the same cult in Latin and in Gothic letters is New Spain. Nothing reveals the contrast between two virtually contiguous states of God, that of the scribes and that of the printers, better than the mental abyss separating, from the beginning, Hispano- and Anglo-America. The regions of the *marvellous real* and those of the *amended real*. New England, where everything is done according to the Law, derives its juridical bias from a formalist Lawgiver, carefully cut off and freed from the censures of Rome. New Spain, in which the sermon rules and discourse mesmerizes, stems from an oral and clerical God, subject to the Index, to a control of ports and borders, whose metropolis proscribed the printing of the works of miscreants. Four centuries later, it still makes for two dreams in a single bed.

Although he was as old as the *incunabula*, Columbus, the veteran, was a man of the Middle Ages on whom the Bible bestowed the audacity to sail off to nowhere. But it was a copyist's Bible, not a printer's, without errata, not yet freed of its detritus of apocrypha, digressions and dubious legends, such as the notorious priest John, whose trace the Marrano of Genoa was intent on finding, whatever the cost, off the coast of the Indies. This priest John, king of a realm worthy of Nestor, thought to be intact and vaguely Ethiopian, fascinated medieval Christianity. He never existed. He was an error in translation. (In the Gheez language, *Zan* means *king*, not John.) A fertile error, an encouraging bit of gossip. In the reveries and journal of Columbus, there is much that is redolent of a Marco Polo *manqué*, Cipango, deliverance of the Holy Sepulchre, and an alliance with the Great Khan, an aspect that gives the West Indies their aroma of magic, reminiscent of the old chivalrous romances. 'That fragrance fusing blood and roses' that is specific to the waning Middle Ages. The Portuguese and Spanish explorers were guided by the oracles of Joachim of Fiore and the prophecies of Isaiah, intent on restoring the Ark of Zion from the West, and preparing the way for the Lord's return among us. Erasmus and the Reformation had not yet made their mark. And the Book whose inquisitive vanguard those compulsive bookworms were intent on being was still the chaotic book of spells of Rabelais's Sorbonne fiends, almanacs and jumbles of useless trivia.

Entirely different was the revised and corrected God of the new order, whose instructions the scrupulous readers of Elizabethan England, those obsessives of the Old Testament in flight from the Stuarts, were intent on following, line by line, by taking to the sea to 'repel and deny all acquaintance with impiety and evil', and *rediscover* the Promised Land described in Deuteronomy 8: 7. 'For the Lord your God is bringing you into a good land, a land with flowing streams, with springs and underground waters welling up in valleys and hills, a land of wheat and barley, of vines and fig trees and pomegranates, a land where you may eat bread without scarcity, where you will lack nothing . . . .You shall bless the Lord your God for the good land He has given you.' What work was ever more infused with energy, with vitality, than the Bible, whose archaisms carried modernity to the baptismal font?

The madness of the Explorers stemmed from a series of bookish reminiscences, and the *terra incognita*, from the very first moment the Christians stepped on to the sand, as their letters and journals testify, were realms saturated with memory. The divine scenario, in spreading throughout the lettered imagination, had given the Europe of the booksellers a will to bring its deeds into conformity with its words. Hence the launching of the *Niña*, of the *Mayflower*. The most literal reading possible, the rigorist one, was thus projected on to the North Atlantic by exacting traditionalists, for whom nothing was authorized that did not have its basis in this or that verse. In search of redemption, because they were better-educated than the average yeoman, the English small property-owners, but restricting themselves to a bare minimum (three religious holidays per year, and two sacraments, baptism and the eucharist). New Ancients, and leapfrogging centuries to the forgotten days in the desert, the Puritans disembarking at Plymouth knew how to read and write and their descendants, in the eighteenth century, would have proportionately double the number of individuals capable of signing their name as native-born Englishmen. As a return to the source demanded (a year after independence, Congress voted to import twenty thousand Bibles). But when they celebrated, those rugged individuals, churchmen without cassocks, dressed in black. The great migration to the land 'designated by Providence to be the site where man would attain his true stature' was to be credited to Abraham, Isaac and Jacob. For the Old Testament, more than the New, gave the Anglophones the scenario of the play they would revive: not escaping an England of nooses and burnings at the stake, but crossing the Red Sea anew. Confronting the wilderness like one's elders at Sinai. Falling to one's knees upon reaching Cape Cod. And upon arrival in Connecticut, withdraw into Canaan and thank Heaven for a first harvest.

To flee Egypt or Europe was to take leave of history and its ruses, and rediscover a temporality that was secure and immobile, virginal and Virginian, safe from the corruption of things and individuals. Between eclogue and paradise. 'All, all are free! Here God and nature reign / Their works unsullied by the hands of men,' wrote the poet of the new nation, Philip Freneau, in 1795. The thinkers of American independence, Franklin, Thomas Paine and Jefferson (who was convinced of the democratic potential of print, which safeguarded laws from oblivion and placed them where everyone could see them), espoused as a conclusive piece of evidence their vision of the new chosen people that had placed the Red Sea between itself and Evil. Between the old and the new temporal order. The United States dreamed an end of history as they began their own – the *novus ordo seclorum* inscribed on the great seal. They believed that with God they had exorcized the old, which has since then caught up with them. The land chosen by Providence for the New Jerusalem would be like the first of that name: Edenic, innocent and virginal; the Indians would be as superfluous and out of place there as the Jebusites were in pre-Davidic Jerusalem. A land which owed nothing to anyone, and on which no one would be able to do anything. All that remained was to extend it, pushing back the frontier to the Pacific, always driven by the same mytho-metaphorical impulse, transmuted into a 'gold rush' by the stagecoach and the steam engine. The petty theocracies of exiles on the east coast were mentally prepared for that spatial expansion – all the more so in that the threat of Evil loitering on the outskirts was unending, specifically in the form of the savage of the plains (who was soon to be vanquished by a pious genocide). Herdsmen and settlers reconceived in their mind the Desert State, whose borders are essentially provisional and expandable, in keeping with the interventions of God. Is not the 'shining city upon a hill' indebted to Zion atop its dune? Thus it was that what had been compacted on the Euphrates culminated on the Potomac, by way of Wittenberg, Amsterdam and London. The prophetic doctrine of a chosen people returned as 'manifest destiny'. The Book of Daniel and the Apocalypse of Saint John have known, in the United States, their ultimate issue, imbuing the expectation of the Millennium with colours of flame. And not merely with Mormons (Church of Jesus Christ of Latter-Day Saints), Seventh-Day Adventists and Jehovah's Witnesses. But as a national stimulant, in the Oval Office, where millenarianism has made its official entry. The final battle between the forces of Satan and Christ, just prior to the Last Judgement, does not result solely in Hollywood superproductions full of special effects. The fantasy of Armageddon, become a reality in a Manhattan in flames, is also capable of mobilizing energies. In the eighteenth century, the letter of the Bible had had positive effects on civil liberties. And effects that were less good in the nineteenth, when millenarianism justified and sustained slavery in the South, in the name of an old tradition of literal interpretation of the Bible. The Bible Belt of the South, timeless and idyllic, in which masters paternally looked after the well-being of the sons of Ham, their black slaves . . . .[7]

The French Declaration of the Rights of Man and of the Citizen (1789) was proffered 'in the presence and under the auspices of the Supreme Being'. That authorizing (as opposed to granting) entity (since whoever gives can also take back) is indeed transcendent in relation to history, but is a somewhat starched deity, an altogether unbiblical mix of Nature and Minerva. Deuteronomy, on the other hand, was the direct inspiration of the American Declaration of Independence (1776), which attributes the fundamental rights of citizens to their Creator, who has made a sovereign gift to His offspring of their freedoms (which are 'the gift of God', according to Jefferson). The Frenchman's goddess Reason harks back to Cicero, by way of Rousseau and the Jesuit colleges. The Americans' Providence-God issues from a Moses illuminated by the fires of his camp and democratized by the technology of mechanical reproduction. Such imprints cannot be effaced by a random decision of the Supreme Court, which, moreover, inaugurates its sessions with the formula: 'God save the United States and this Honorable Court'. Travelling clergymen in the West (Burt Lancaster as Elmer Gantry). Prayer breakfasts and national

---

[7] See Nathalie Hind, 'Sudisme et Millénarisme aux États-Unis au XIXᵉ siècle', *Anglophonia*, 3/1998, *French Journal of English Studies* (Toulouse: Presses universitaires du Mirail, 1998).

days of prayer. The President's oath on the Bible, at every inauguration, in the presence of a rabbi, pastor or bishop ('So help me God'). Family celebrations of Thanksgiving with turkey and stuffing. Witch-hunts. Revival meetings. Billy Graham and the tele-evangelists. Negro spirituals. Camp meetings. Moral majority. The Reverend Martin Luther King. Presidential prayers for the victims. Anyone who does not keep Habakkuk by his bedside has no hope of understanding anything of the land of high-tech, the only one in the West in which monotheism is at the control panel. Go west, old God.

And it is God Himself who forbids any state religion. He appears in the Constitution of every state of the Union except one. And His coat of arms constitutes the Great Seal of the federal government. *Annuit coeptis*: 'God favoured the beginnings.' The incomplete pyramid rises towards heaven, to meet the eye of divine providence. Since the 'Nation with a Church's soul' had placed itself at the outset, without a Roman intermediary, under the protection of the Eternal, it became possible, in Jefferson's words, to erect a wall separating Church and State. Articulating belief and dissidence, religious spirit and the spirit of freedom. (Tocqueville could not get over it, and for good reason.) It would be sacrilegious to recognize one form of worship in particular, and thus interfere with the 220 denominations into which the country is at present divided (94 per cent of the population affirm belief in God, and 63 per cent claim church affiliation). Political institutions – such was Calvin's creed – are too human and fragile to be accorded the right to fix any truth at all, a privilege reserved for the Omniscient God. But the wall set up by the First Amendment to the Constitution is not intended, as it is in a French-style Republic, to shield the State from impingements by the various churches but, rather, the reverse. Thus the legislator in Washington is there in order to allow Him on High to shower His grace over all the earth, until the fulfilment of time. In the materialist and mystical holy land, which is futuristic and archaic (and the one because of the other), a patriotic theocracy tempered by political democracy (in which 'secular', as we shall see, does not mean 'lay'), the God of the born-again Baptists does not have strained relations (quite the contrary!) with business. For the nation, as for the self-made man, economic success constitutes the visible sign of election. Deterritorialization (or the free disposition of oneself), inspired by the immensity of distances and sustained by pick-up trucks, motels and drive-ins, finds its natural counterpoint in the newcomer's attachment to his parish. And for the large proportion of the population subjugated by the sonorous image, church serves as the ultimate shelter of the written artefact, even if it be sung or danced (just as the universities do for classical culture among the elites).

Moses to the north and the *Virgen* to the south of the Rio Grande – Noah's Ark is still effective. As the Old World takes its distance, the Only One, quite consciously, exercises, in the New, His talents for unification, above all in times of war and catastrophe. The great unifying void is no doubt more necessary where centrifugal pressures are most pronounced and the risks of world leadership greatest. For better and for worse, for energy and empire, generosity and brutality, courage and arrogance, dynamism and simplemindedness, the United States has concluded from its time of birth a pact with the Most-High, a circumstance that exposes it to exemplary felicities and misfortunes. Despite the subsiding of conviction into public opinion and fervour into sheepishness, it seems quite intent on not cutting the umbilical cord. Europe the re-exporter could not predict, at the time of its centrality, what that switch would cost it: a displacement of the axis of the world. In the matter of God & Co., there can be no discussion: the cowboy leads. In the name of what else might it exercise its *dominium mundi*, dictate the law to the antipodes, manifest its indifference to the entire matter if need be, and gather the Christian West under its crook in times of peril? America is no longer the unpolluted sanctuary it once dreamed of, but the fact of being, by birth and intimate conviction, the confidant of Providence means that it can stand up for itself. The God of the Americans and Allah are evenly matched. In a holy war, morally, America is almost an equal. Different methods, a common postulate: Good against Evil.

BOOK III

Effacement

10 Parricidal Christ

The dead shouted: 'Oh Christ! Is there no God?'
He answered: 'There is none.'
All the shades began trembling violently.
(Jean-Paul Richter, 1796)

The Tarpeian Rock was near the Capitol. The Father had so successfully 'emptied' Himself into His Son, so dramatically involved Himself in the history of sinners, that as a result He finally lost His pre-eminence within the Holy Trinity, and with us as well. Thereafter we preferred to consider ourselves brothers in Jesus rather than children of the Good Lord. With a pre-eminent Christ at the head of its churches, the Christian West concentrated its preferences on the sole Mediator of salvation. The recent collapse of the paternal figure (and, indeed, function) further compromised the position of Abraham, 'the father of all believers'. The retreat of the Ancestor, deposed by the Son, reflects in the supernatural order a mechanism with which we are familiar in another context: the supremacy of the mediator, which vassalizes everything it mediates. Whereby the New Covenant fulfilled its promises: the plan of the Lord our God was indeed 'finished'. But it was finished in both senses of the word.

The modesty of the Only One, the delicacy of the Father. The discretion of the All-Merciful is well known. Nothing in common with thunderous Zeus. He does not come ashore with great tumult. He advances in the Garden of Eden as silently as a wolf – so much so that Adam and Eve can barely distinguish his presence. A trembling, a quivering of leaves in the distance. The Olympians were seen among Titans and colossi, but the Creator of Heaven and Earth preferred the tenuous. A burning bush to indicate His presence is not a forest fire or a tornado. One needs a trained eye. A rustling, almost nothing. So discreet, Yahweh, that He seems almost distracted. He has to be alerted, with shouts, as to what is happening in His Kingdom. 'Incline your ear, O Lord, and hear; open your eyes, O Lord, and see; hear the words of Sennacherib, which he has sent to mock the living God' (2 Kings 19: 16). It is the Devil who is the exhibitionist. And the megalomaniac. Lucifer has a body, and girth. He works with a flame-thrower, not a flickering light. He rolls out machinery, enjoys scandalizing his little audience. The Other prefers subtlety and the *je-ne-sais-quoi*. He doesn't strut; He 'passes'. When the prophet Elijah is summoned by Yahweh to the mountaintop, he goes to await Him in the wind, but finds Him neither there nor in the fire. He finally arrives, but in the 'sound of a mild breeze'. That mildness is a sign of respect. God does not seek to impose Himself. He allows us the freedom to choose Him. It is up to us to see and hear.

That proverbial restraint does not explain what has become, over time, out-and-out absenteeism (and to regard it as innate diverts us from raising the question of what is disquieting about it). Despite His ethic of evanescence, the Eternal was the essential contemporary of the Hebrews. Omnipotent and omnipresent. Jesus is that of the Christians. The Almighty, under their influence, slipped from politeness to renunciation. Churches currently flee theology (which relates to God) for morality (which relates to man). Stealthily, to be sure, but let us face the facts. God has, for quite a while now, been retired from active duty and assigned to the reserves. Where He was welcomed – who knows? – by the bantering, do-nothing gods of Olympus, with their seats in the dress circle, from which they looked on, in hilarity, as little men devoured each other.

A more advanced phase, or an eviction?
More like a silent but inexorable *deposition*.
Let us go back to the primal scene: Golgotha.

The Father Dies in the Son

'Son, my Son, why hast thou abandoned me ... ?' The All-Knowing opted to abstain from that particular 'return to sender' upon receiving the '*Eli, Eli, lama sabachtani?*', with its poignant echo of the Psalms. Did He veil His eyes rather than add sarcasm to distress? A dyed-in-the-wool Pharisee, although a native of Galilee, a peripheral province, and perhaps a bit too much of a miracle worker in the eyes of the Temple, loyal to the point of self-sacrifice, the victim, in his agony, personally did not deserve that ignominious suspicion. Had he not affirmed: 'My Father is greater than I'? Resisted Satan, who was pressurizing him in the wilderness to renounce his filiation? Staked his own life on God's loving generosity towards humanity, without which He would neither have created us nor delegated to us His most precious possession? Taught his disciples the *Pater noster*? And even substituted – in an unprecedented act of boldness – the spiritual Father for the fleshly father of each one of us? A doctrinal master cannot be held responsible for the posthumous visits to which he may fall victim. People took to invoking Jesus, who himself invoked only God; he even refused the role of master, presenting himself as no more than an elder brother. He would have cried blasphemy if he had been accused of being a 'Christian'. A Christian is someone who gives thanks to Christ before doing so to the divine principle. It was, moreover, from their adversaries, in Antioch, that his heirs presumptive received the sardonic name *christiani*, a derisory nickname of the sort that 'Huguenot' and even 'Marxist' would later be. And what would the pacifist have said about our soldiers of Christ the King, he who accepted only a crown of thorns? That model of filial piety played no role in the theological jolts provoked by the fixation of his sectarians on the 'image of the Father'.

The Passion fascinates the West. To the point of forgetting (so intense was the focus on the emaciated victim) that given the indivisibility of the Divine Trinity, it was God Himself who sweated blood, and then died in the body of the Crucified. He 'lowered' Himself into the Son in order to elevate us to Him; He 'emptied' Himself in him, through a transference of substance baptized 'kenosis', from the Greek word *kenos*, meaning *empty*. An unprecedented result: God was dead. For three days, He was not there. The birth of Christ was the *first death* of God. He reappeared on Easter Sunday. But for us, the only one to be resurrected was Jesus Christ. And it is to the Saviour (subsequently promoted to Father) that we feel ourselves indebted unto death. Not without ingratitude towards the actual initiator of the salvage mission. Yet what Christian would dare call himself a deist? And what atheist among us is not a Christian in spite of himself? Would he have the right to consume alcohol if Jesus had not had the excellent idea of transforming water into wine? To go to his local cinema if Veronica had not wiped the Holy Face? Of enjoying long weekends? We take off to bake in the sun, chew our turkey, ski, work hard or yawn in rhythm with the auspicious or inauspicious days of the Nazarene. Christmas, Easter and Pentecost, the Assumption, All Saints' Day. Our landscapes and calendars continue to inscribe us, whether we like it or not, in the 'society of Jesus'. Paul's theology was theocentric, but the practices which ensued were rather Christomaniacal. In slipping into the visible body of His son, the Invisible became *depolarized*. He is no longer a conductor of mental light. Or affect. What place other than an honorary place could a religion of intimate love and the senses assign to an Absent One beyond taste, an Incorporeal One without face, when the Incarnation grants me His *alter ego* to contemplate and the Holy Species, in communion, to *savour*?

Let us enter, in Paris, into an alleged 'temple of God'. At random. Saint-Sulpice. A Bossuet sermon carved in stone. The credo of France's Great Century become a huge nave. What form, what volume, will speak to us of the Father? Here everything rises and converges towards the Son. Let us consult the parish brochure. The description of the edifice says it all.

> *It was for Jesus alone, not for their own glory,*
> *that the builders of this church wanted to make it noble and beautiful.*
> *Everything here converges towards Christ.*
> *At the portal, it was he whom Faith beheld before the revolution.*
> *In the Chapel of the Virgin, Mary introduces Jesus to humanity.*
> *The great crucifix of the altar recalls his death on the cross.*
> *His resurrection and his ascension to heaven*
> *are the subject of the stained-glass window dominating the choir.*
> *After his departure, as he promised,*
> *Jesus remains with us through his untiring love,*
> *illustrated by the image of the Sacred Heart in the window to the right*
> *and by his eucharist, glorified in the monstrance of the window to the left,*
> *evoked as well, in various places, by the touching legend*
> *of the pelican nourishing her offspring with her flesh and blood.*
> *Jesus is present through his words,*
> *contained in the holy books to which places*
> *of honour are reserved in the choir.*
> *The biblical image of the sacrificed lamb, couched in the book*
> *of Revelation, whose seals he alone is worthy of breaking,*
> *refers to Christ, as does the wedding at Cana,*
> *at the altar of the Virgin, when Mary, certain that he will answer her prayer,*
> *says to the servants: 'Do as he tells you.'*
> *It is through Jesus alone that this immense*

'The Resurrection', Central Window of the Choir of Saint-Sulpice, Paris

> *construction in stone speaks to the heart.*
> *It sings in its manner, solemnly:*
> *'Christ has come, Christ is born, Christ has suffered,*
> *Christ has died, Christ has risen, Christ is alive,*
> *Christ will return, Christ is here!'*

Eloquent. The chorale of the people of God transformed into the chorus of little brothers and sisters of Jesus. From the adored Father to the Father in retreat, and not even named .... 'He who has Jesus has everything!,' one of the first priests of the parish, Father Olier, warned us in the seventeenth century. The implication: you can make do without the Great Other. How did we come to this pass? Through a procession that has lasted for centuries, and was begun by the first Councils. The degradation was already articulated with utter candour in the movement's first logo, engraved in stone, chiselled into sarcophagi, painted on to walls, moulded on to oil-lamps: the chrism, brandished as an insignia by Constantine. In the branches of the X (chi) superimposed on a P (rho), the two first letters of Christ, we find the alpha and omega. The sign that Christ is at the beginning and the end of everything (the first and the last stage of life).

Three Heads for a Single God

First of all, there was a new arithmetic of the divine. Hebrew had its All in One. Soon, the One would count for no more than a third. A considerable display of wit, since the dogma of the Trinity speaks not of subtracting but of deploying and completing. Perhaps, but only three centuries after Golgotha, our One and Only of times past split into three persons: the Father, the Son and the Holy Spirit. Tertullian (the inventor of the '*Vera religio romanaque*'): 'God is alone, yet He is not alone.' He found Himself obliged to make room for two fellow entities, of the same substance as Himself (the Son being *consubstantial* with the Father). We shall not go into the labyrinth of successive conciliar 'symbols', the extraordinary conceptual labour of processions, of the single nature in three Persons, and the 'communication of *idioms*' (what is specific to each – divine or human – nature). From which there emerged, in the sixth century, the intellectual conundrum of a God threefold in His unity. And in the eleventh century, a break with Eastern orthodoxy, for which the Spirit proceeds solely from the Father, not from the Son as well, as for the Latins. The Trinity, in its logomachy, is like a poisoned gift of the Greek language to the West, which no longer speaks it. Its lexicon and syntax are more commanding here than elsewhere. The Roman Empire had the immense merit of being bilingual (unlike its contemporary counterpart, for which English is the only *lingua franca*), and it is amusing to consider that our God owes His strange internal pluralism to the plurality of languages in the Empire (in which Greek, it should be recalled, was the koine, well before the shift to Constantinople).

Thus, with the advent of the Son, proclaimed, at the first Nicene Council (325), to be 'of one nature with the Father' (*ek tès ousias tou patros*), consubstantial, coeternal, begotten, not made, the Eternal found His prerogatives reined in. At the temporal level, the Son became *the Father's equal*. There was no longer even a generation gap between them! In place of a natural subordination, a supernatural co-ordination! And as a result, the baptized was to be immersed in the lustral pool, not once but three times. One makes the sign of the cross 'in the name of the Father, and of the Son, and of the Holy Spirit'. The elders had pondered, with utter rigour, on the single *substance* – and in the case of Spinoza, to the point of logical intoxication. Their successors (above all of the Greek Orthodox tradition, which is the oldest and most faithful to the sources) meditated on *persons*, pressing to the infinite (if the word is allowed) what separated and joined them. The theology of appropriations, after the Council of Constantinople (381), would subtly distinguish between the *creative* Father, the *redeeming* Son, and the *sanctifying* Holy Spirit. Each Person thereby had enough to keep it busy. And we are in need, for our salvation, of the complete triad, in its tricephalic plenitude. This headache of a dogma continues to receive tribute from us in the form of our tripartite organizations, our theses-antitheses-and-syntheses. But even in the heyday of Christendom, it remained a matter for clerics, as Jacques Le Goff has emphasized concerning the Middle Ages: 'The trinitarian scheme appears to have exercised its attraction above all in erudite theological

'The Trinity', Anonymous Flemish painting, around 1500, Shickman Gallery, New York

circles and to have had only limited resonance among the masses.'[1] Despite the icon of three angels visiting Abraham, the Trinity is visually askew. The first and third persons have been received more hospitably by doctrine than by the realms of ritual and the imagination. Although the Father is given precedence in sacramental formulae, just as He had previously occupied the upper portion of altarpieces and frescos, it is the person of the Crucified that is crucial for us. Of the three faces of the trifocal God, only one remains illuminated – at least in the Roman world, since the

[1] Jacques Le Goff, *La Civilisation de l'Occident médiéval* (Paris: Arthaud 1982), p. 128.

Orthodox East, more faithful to the Spirit, is more respectful of the rules of protocol, as the rigid visual hierarchy of iconostases reveals to all the faithful.

Catapulted to honorific status through the promotion of His Son, the Father, in
the West, was in effect kicked upstairs. The plot of Redemption relieved Him of all
current business. A *historical economy of salvation* brings logically to the fore an
uncertainty about the repercussions here below once the goodwill of the Most-High
is assumed not to be in doubt. All of a sudden, the great enigma of His Wisdom is
forgotten, like a deposit paid at a hotel. With the first Author of the lineage intervening *by way of* the second, the visible face of the invisible, it was to the Image
that could be touched, appealed to, and stirred to tenderness, not to the first principle, that candidates for salvation would direct their assiduousness. And all the
more so in that there was a direct link between the Virgin and the Son, as with the
Church, his spouse – which short-circuited the Father. For the latter, then, the
'oblique genuflection of the hurried worshipper'. For the Son, a moving recognition
and the desire to live up to the model. Therein lay the break. The Law came from
the Father; Grace comes from Christ. Does not the new dogma proclaim the
superior effectiveness of Grace over the Law? God was the figure in the monotheistic picture; He now became the ground. Spotlights and stars' names reversed
positions. From that permutation, the art and eye of the West were to derive considerable pleasure, with Byzantium banking on divine dignity, faithful to its abstract
meditation on the Unchanging. Our pictorial Renaissance was a celebration of that
fall of the Absolute into the relative (what could be more pagan than the efferves-
cent and aroused flesh of the Sistine Chapel?).

We were the ones who charged the Father with His *diminutio capitis*. But was that
not what He wanted? He took the initiative, having decided that we had fallen very
low indeed, to put Himself on our level – in order to raise the general level. A
glissando out of love and an exhaustion of self. In successive stages. The various
liturgies of the first millennium still respected the decision of the Council of Hippo:
'When one is standing before the altar, prayer is to be addressed to God the Father.'
Christocentrism surfaced only afterwards (under Frankish influence in particular),
with increasing emphasis placed on the divinity of the *Dominus*.

Jesus as Rebellion

Modern humanism completed the loss of status by reversing terms: from the
theological to the 'theandrical'. The 'unique person in two natures' watched His
human nature absorb the other like a blotter – to the extent that the civilizing
project began to wonder, in all logic, once sufficient time had gone by, whether it
might not be possible to reverse matters by making of humanity a divinity in the
process of evolving. Such was Auguste Comte's idea: a secular communion of saints.

It was more than an idea for the movement known as *Searchers for God*, at the end of the nineteenth century, which was constituted around the Orthodox philosopher Vladimir Soloviev and taken up by Berdyayev, Bulgakov and the Theosophists. A deification of humanity that would recur after the revolution of 1905, with the *Constructors of God*, Gorky and Lunacharsky. Their version of *Our Father* stipulated: 'Our proletariat, who art on earth, hallowed be thy name; thy will be done, thy power come.' And that power did come with ecclesiastical communism and the secular form of theocracy represented by that red logocracy. The Party as Church. The Second Coming at the barrel of a gun or at the bottom of a ballot box. Stalin the former seminary student. Humbert-Droz, founder of the Swiss Communist Party, a pastor. Garaudy, president of Étudiants chrétiens. The Heavenly Father, in wanting to incarnate Himself a bit too much, ended up as the Father of peoples, a living god, and the workers' paradise: a counter-utopia. The Word made Flesh become victim of its own wiles.

The Revolution as antechamber of the Kingdom of Justice had already done a disservice to the Creator and played to the advantage of Jesus the Just. The men of 1793, in France, were intent on cutting themselves off from the Father by cutting off the head of the Monarch by divine right, His incarnation on earth, but a considerable number did so in the name of 'the *sans-culotte* Jesus'. As revenge on behalf of the Sacrificial Victim against his Sacrificer. Literary and political Romanticism, throughout the nineteenth century, accelerated the family feud. God was the Power that was; Jesus, the Rebel. God was vengeance, arrogance and indifference: a right-wing Father. Jesus was love, fraternity and suffering: a left-wing Son. Joseph de Maistre against George Sand; theocracy against democracy. Old believers against young believers. The red heels of Versailles against the red bonnets of the Revolution. A veritable generational – and class – struggle. The Law, distant and harsh, against widows and orphans.

Democratization worked to Jesus' advantage because, unlike God, he enjoyed a double status. He was assimilated to the Father, and we are to be his extremely obedient subordinates. But he was also an elder brother, having defined himself as 'firstborn within a large family' (Romans 8: 29). He suffered, like us, from persecution. And he continues to be 'in agony until the end of the world'. All the humiliated can identify with him, be they unemployed workers, pariah poets, Jean Valjean, or the Count of Monte Cristo. Socialism, which was originally Christian before becoming Marxist, invoked him as a source. The revolution of 1848, which elevated fraternity as the ultimate goal, put itself under his auspices; and he was a direct inspiration for the universal, democratic and social Republic, to which he accords his blessings, accompanied by his angels, in the lithographs of the period. The Son has a range that the Father lacks: an immense political advantage. He can be simultaneously and alternately at the oven and at the mill, in the orchestra and in the gods. 'My favourite thinker,' President Bush calls him. But also that of the Zapatistas. On both sides of the divide. With Martin Luther King and with his murderer. Perpetually turning a weakness into a strength. Just as in the first century, the unstable identity of the Messiah allowed him to be simultaneously the Master of the Law for the rabbis, the Master of Wisdom for the Gnostics, and the Lord of the World for the Romans, his Father/Son ambivalence allows him to serve as portmanteau for both landless peasants and Brazilian estate-owners. A must-have for orphans in search of identificatory myths.

Tell me who your friends are and I'll tell you who you are. Now the Father and the Son, once the Jacobin revolution had taken place, no longer moved in the same social circles. Monarchs have their *Te Deum*, and theologians their quarrels: closed, and rather boring, circles. Jesus was the friend of the people and of the brilliant: poets, novelists and historians. A large audience. Victor Hugo was the exception; he did not forget the prior mystery, but he was as much a philosopher as a poet. In a word, deism in the Christian world became a philosophical position; and Jesus a literary figure, to be modulated by poem, serial, novel, song and musical comedy. The consecration of the writer would be that of the 'only anarchist to have succeeded'. It was no longer Bossuet or Malebranche who was calling the tune, but Alexandre Dumas. The arbiter of elegance had changed; the Eternal was no longer in fashion. We should not be surprised that it was a poet, in 'The Dream of Jean-Paul', who was the first to publish the announcement of His death, putting it in the mouth – a remarkable intuition – of Jesus himself.

> The church was soon deserted; but suddenly, a frightful spectacle!, dead children, who had in turn awakened in the cemetery, came running and prostrated themselves before the majestic figure on the altar, saying: 'Jesus, have we no father?' And he replied in a torrent of tears: 'We are all orphans; you and I, we have no father.' At those words, the temple and the children were engulfed, and the entire edifice of the world collapsed before me in its immensity.[2]

Out of Sight, Out of Mind

The aura of the Supreme has dimmed all the more in that the recent era, the twentieth century, was to be more dependent on the retina than its predecessors. The Holy Family is 'photosensitive', whereas the Patriarch discouraged paint and film. The Father, the Son and the Holy Spirit are to be worshipped and glorified conjointly (since Constantinople, 381), but they cannot be visualized to an identical

---

[2] Jean-Paul Richter, 1796. Quoted in Madame de Staël, *De l'Allemagne* (1810).

degree. That optical differential within the Trinity was already pronounced in the Latin Middle Ages. Both in the text, with engravings and woodcuts, and in churches, with frescos and stained-glass windows. Up until the Reformation, the contrast in potential continued to increase, between what was given to be believed and what was offered to be seen – the Good Shepherd, the Virgin, the Apostles and Saints. One could still see, at a distance, on the spandrel of cathedrals, the Father holding the Son to His bosom (unless it was Abraham). But the head of the line, initially the point of focus, had become visually blurred. Advancing towards us flanked by His increasingly picturesque escort, the ancestor, immobile, began to withdraw into the shadows.

As far as the chronology of the Patriarch is concerned, two dates might be marked in bold print. The year 787, the Second Nicene Council, the defeat of the iconoclasts. Which was excellent news, but for whom? For the Son, the immediate and corporeal model of our imitation. For the Virgin, the *theotokos*, 'Mother of divine Jesus'. For the saints and martyrs. For the Point of Origin, the gain was meagre: the ban on mosaics continued to take its toll, and the rare colour representations of God are the exception that proves the rule of what was iconographically permitted. The second *annus mirabilis*: 1839, the academic consecration by a man of science, Arago, of the photochemical trace. Two thousand years of images painted by man's hand opened on to the machine-made image. The *frisson nouveau* was transferred from the icon, the prayer, as it were, of the hand, inspired by the Spirit, to the imprint of things seen. That pagan naturalism, denounced as such by Baudelaire, relegated religious painting to the domain of the aesthetic, as a kind of genre painting (and no longer the area where things were happening). The new perceptual faith withdrew from the pious icon. And – unfortunately for them – angels can be painted, but not photographed. With the birth of the recorded image, it was a good thousand years of trust that disintegrated with nary a protest. An image fabricated by hand is a prolongation of a belief in words. It gives an illusion of reality, without passing itself off as reality. An image directly peeled from things by the lens has to be *believable*, that is, to have a counterpart in the reality available to the senses. In one case, one remains in the symbolic and unverifiable realm of signs. In the other, one swings into the practical (and verifiable) realm of information.

And that was not all. Filmed theatre, then motion pictures, brought a new disequilibrium into the conciliar trio. The Father was the most damaged, the least scenic. The Holy Spirit was even less filmable, always with the same face (once you've seen the tongue of fire, you've seen it all). On the other hand, every figure of little Jesus, from manger to cross, found its place in the repertory. His stage and costume in the medieval mystery before the cathedral portal. The magisterium rejected the theatre, but not the movies, which were immediately adopted. A comparative filmography of Father and Son reveals rather blatantly that the match was uneven. The Second wins by a considerable distance in that he has had the good grace of possessing a face, a life and a death, whereas the First was by definition static, unbegotten, and without beginning. The first celluloid fiction made in France brought the Passion to the screen, and several hundred films have emerged, in the course of a century, from the New Testament. From the Old, on the other hand, they can be counted on the fingers of one hand, albeit with larger budgets and in Cinemascope (Cecil B. DeMille and John Huston). These totally irrelevant costume dramas (with the exception of *Ben Hur*) provoke a smile, whereas the Son's films bring us directly to the heart of the subject. Dreyer's *Ordet*, Pasolini's *The Gospel According to Saint Matthew*, Rossellini's *Messiah*, Godard's *Hail Mary*, Scorsese's *The Last Temptation of Christ*. 'I am with you always,' said Jesus, 'even unto the end of the world.' In your rose windows, on your ogees, in your frescos, your oils, your movies, and even your flashbulbs. In all times, and in every medium, we would add, however much the devout might shudder at the thought. As in the last of the photo reports to date on the Son of God, the most recent chic after-effect of the Council of Nicaea, entitled INRI. Garish colour shots for gay magazines? Priests and the faithful protested. Forgetting, no doubt, that one preserves only by violating, and that sacrilege *à la* Buñuel is the ultimate tribute of the profane to the sacred. Keep me; violate me. No doubt sacred art, when it is intended for a place of worship and sacrament, is obliged to respect, quite legitimately, the observances of the magisterium and the expectations of the faithful (even though Matisse and certain crucifixes by Germaine Richier, in the middle of the house of the Lord, did once appear sacrilegious to a few prudes). But a sacred art, to the extent that it remains alive, remains a rhapsody of outrages and scandals. And what an immobile gaze assumes, in the domain of the figurative, to be an orthodoxy or the product of an academic canon – say, for us, Raphael or Fra Angelico – is finally but a freeze-frame in the sociological stream. It affixes on the collective retina the transitory (and abusively eternalized) state of an endless series of more or less heretical reuses, which once themselves provoked, in their day, analogous outcries. What continuity is there between our successive versions of Jesus: the dark moustachioed individual with the Pierrot eyes of the sixth-century Egyptian monasteries, the twig of a man bristling with pain in the Grünewald altarpiece, the plump, androgynous, ephebe of Caravaggio, and the Pre-Raphaelites' effeminate creature in a tunic? Nor were the troubling Mannerist virgins of the Renaissance all that comforting for an eye attuned to the Gothic. Faith travels, and so does the eye. 'Unless the seed dies,' there can be no regrowth. It is not easy, when God is reputed to be dead, to implement His resurrections. Which is what the Church of France persists courageously in doing by inviting atheists – Matisse, Lurçat, Braque, and not merely the believers Rouault and Manessier – to intervene in places of worship. Unity of place, with its concomitant genius, can occasionally replace unity of doctrine. As in the abbey-church of Sainte-Foy de Conques, the granular and changing stained-glass windows of Soulages.

In the face of revolutions in perception, Catholic theology proved better equipped than its sisters to confront the pre-eminence of the visual. The mechanical trace (of an image, not of sound) sat uncomfortably with the transfiguration. But television was welcomed (as the printing press had been) with open arms by the hierarchy. Far from being an aggravated case of photography, it appeared to the authorities that the audio component sublimated and redeemed the visual. It had been to little avail that photochemical imprinting had fuelled, towards the end of the nineteenth century, a few far-fetched reveries involving the Holy Shroud (the imprint of the Resurrected Son flashed on to a linen support); photography, in its muteness and brutality, was wounding to the supernatural. The medium of the cathode tube applied balm to that wound by miraculously joining the spoken word to the image. At least in the already 'corrupted' sector of Christianity, since, under the sway of the sanctifying fixity of the icon, the animated image was regarded as a bit too 'mobile' and profane for the hieratic tastes of the Orthodox. The age of mechanical reproducibility continues to irritate the Christian East, and we can understand why, if no one can climb Mount Tabor with a camera and return satisfied. The cherished transfiguration of the Eastern churches is effected by way of 'the living icon of love', produced by the hand of a man who prays as he paints and makes of the Icon a prolongation of Scripture. The small screen was thus in fact fated to be *Catholic*, right from the start (the first televised Mass in France: Christmas 1948). Does television favour the body? So does the Incarnation. Does it zoom in on faces? The human face is the mirror of God, His light, His icon. Is it beamed into the family home? So much the better. Each person reads the newspaper in his or her corner, but the family frames the screen in the middle of the living-room. Is the televised image without sound worthless? That is the sum of its superiority over the photograph. Cardinal Suhard in 1948:

> It can be said without exaggeration that this ingenious discovery comes at the proper time in the plan of the world's salvation. Woe unto us had we allowed it passively to slip into the hands of the sowers of discord and discouragement! What joy, on the other hand, if we succeed in using it as a providential extension of the Church and the Reign of God ... . The ways of God are inscrutable! All ye who search in secrecy, unknown, and without ever having known the light, it comes to you through this new and mysterious path, for the first time.

The same note is sounded by Pope Pius XII on Easter Sunday, 1949: 'We await from television consequences of the utmost import for the ever more striking revelation of the truth to the intelligence of the faithful.' Which is what helped to make *Jour du Seigneur* France's oldest television programme. The Protestant, more radiophonic, sees the added image as a diminution of the spoken word, a deprivation of truth. He denounces technological idolatry. 'The image', writes Jacques Ellul, of the

Reformed Church, 'partakes of the realm of reality. It is absolutely incapable of transmitting anything partaking of the realm of truth. It never seizes anything but an appearance, an external mode of behaviour.'[3] More open to the celebration of an audible and visualizable Son than of a Father ordinarily bereft of epiphany, the spontaneously audiovisual theology of Catholicism, for its part, has no hesitation in celebrating the fusion of Word and Image.

Insatiable Mediators

What appears to us more crucial for the decline of the Father than the incomparable figurative and dramatic potential ascribed to the Son is the logic of the Medium. It does not involve Jesus as a moral model, but Christ as a theological figure, He who causes incommunicables – the Eternal and the Temporal – to communicate. *Dominus. Kyrios. Our Lord.* Glorification through an accumulation of credentials, due to the transfer to the Crucified Son of titles formerly attributed to the Almighty, is not what is at stake. After all, he was in the 'shape of God' before being born, and 'in the likeness of man' thereafter. What is at stake is the ontological status of the Eternal incarnated in time as the 'unsurpassable, universal, and normative mediator' of salvation. He through whom one cannot not pass in order to approach God. 'No one can go to the Father except through me .... ' Why was it that the obligatory transit gradually became *intransitive*? What is needed is a return to the first post-humous reversal, the originary subversion. Jesus the homilist, who had proclaimed the Word, became, haloed with absence, He who was to be proclaimed. The 'Hear me, the Torah is to be fulfilled' was re-elaborated, after his death, into: 'I am the fulfilment, the suffering Messiah you were awaiting, the bearer of the sins of men.' Jesus would no longer be one more prophet in a long line (as the Muslims, with good reason, see him); he would be the Messiah whose advent had been prepared, *nolens volens*, by all the prophets. The announcer of the Last Judgement himself became the supreme Judge; the transmitter of the good news of God's kingdom became the very object of the good news.[4] The medium turned into the message. To the detriment of the Father, who had been so amply realized in the work of the Son that we felt free, without any major inconvenience, to consign Him to oblivion.

Ivan Karamazov: 'Who does not wish for the death of his father? ... What? ... Liars. All men want the death of their father.' Such is the simple law of life. Every living being wants to reproduce his genes, and once his infraction has been accomplished, his progeny dispatches him *ad padres* (to each his turn). Granted: every child announces the death of his father. A banality. Which in this case is

---

[3] Jacques Ellul, *La Parole humiliée* (Paris: Seuil 1981), p. 34.
[4] Maurice Sachot, *L'Invention du Christ, Genèse d'une religion* (Paris: Odile Jacob 1987).

insufficient. The son of man *intervened*. Now we know of no free mediation which does not exact its tithe in the course of its action. There is no such thing as a free lunch. The American dictum applies to the eucharistic meal. The Incarnation brought God closer to men (women and children included). Which is all to the good. But in humanizing Him, it humiliated Him, *nolens volens*. 'The most human of all the gods' becoming the the least divine of the three Gods of the Book. Jesus Christ, '*sole mediator* of salvation'? Let us not be deceived. We should not confuse him with a 'facilitator'. Is a 'mediator' not someone who intervenes in order to facilitate an arrangement, agreement or negotiation? And disappears once the affair is concluded? A huge error. Mediators are invasive creatures. Not by character, but by destination.

God supplanted by His very media .... One is never betrayed except by one's own, as the proverb goes, and in this case by what is best about them: the will of intermediaries to bring succour. The in-between was the strong point of the Christian formula. As we saw in the case of angels, at the level of transport. The angel is of great help to the Absolute, whose problem is not to furnish but, rather, to traverse the infinite space that extends between Him and men. How is one to move the message along? By recruiting envoys and go-betweens? Note that *teleportation*, or the ability to move about physically via waves (to travel by telephone), would resolve the practical problem, but appears to be as unrealizable for God as for us. Hence the embarrassment that the adepts of the Crucified resolved with a courrier endowed with wings, allowing him to move about rapidly (wings having the advantage of espousing the wind, the first vehicle of the biblical Eternal). Who, to be sure, cannot deliver the mail in person, get his shirt wet, or knock on doors. Majesty is never agitated. Solemn slowness is what befits eminence (senators, popes, presidents and monarchs). You go to the Lord; the Lord does not come to you. If He does not take the first step, someone has to be there to run His errands. An interface or go-between – to expel from the Garden of Eden, inform Hagar that she will give birth to Ishmael, Abraham that he will have a son by Sarah, and so on.

The New Covenant thus devoted its ingenuity to proliferating the shuttlers of grace or the elevators of salvation. Those who cause to rise (grandchildren to Paradise) and redescend (benedictions and tongues of fire). In order to reinforce, in both senses, the notoriously insufficient ladders joining Heaven and Earth in the Old Covenant. And it was this abundance of *middle terms* that made Christianity at once popular and operational, by transcending a sterile and paralysing face-off between High and Low, Good and Evil. That glacial separation of principles is what deprived the Gnostics of any political future. Those all-too-rigid dualists pitted a good God against an evil Creation, sacrificed feeling to knowledge, and placed beyond the reach of the average civilian a Supreme Being on whom he could gain no purchase. In such Neo-Platonic esotericism, the concern was only with rising, climbing to the divine, never with coming back down again. Since such ascents were to take place by way of the mind, there was no need for the fantastic, stained-glass windows, angels, or holy women. The Chosen are alleged to reach heaven without feet or hands, priests or sacraments, and without Jacob's ladder. As a result, no *Weltanschauung* emerged from that abstruse exercise in an elitism bereft of ergonomics. For lack of virgin mothers, saints and *putti*, clawed dragons and pudgy cherubim, Gnosticism failed to 'grip the masses and become a material force'. Too much software and not enough interface.

The success of Christianity, on the other hand, owed much to a rule of procedure that became paradigmatic: no eminence is inaccessible, but none is *directly* accessible. We can accede to the Father only by way of the Son; to the Son only by way of his bride, the Church; to the mystical Church only by way of a specific confessor. It was thanks to the superimposition of such pontoons and pontiffs that the most wretched could cross the sea of sin and gain the opposite shore. No separation that is not accompanied by an articulation between levels. The image is not the model, but we accede to the model *through* the image. The Father is not the Son, but 'he who has seen me has seen the Father'. That exceedingly obliging quest for redemption functions through its mechanisms and its endearments. The intercessor is not a spare tyre, an aid for feeble souls. He is not there to look pretty, but is an activator of inertia, the pivot of a system of *spiritual triangulation*. Faith, like desire, is aroused by a mediating third party. It is by *imitating Jesus Christ* that I obey God, by imitating the saint that I obey Jesus, by imitating the prior that I model myself on the saint, and so forth. That classical triangle is recounted splendidly in the third-person testament of the author of *Spiritual Exercises*, Ignatius of Loyola.

> When he read the life of Our Lord and the saints, he began to think and to say to himself: 'And what would happen if I did what Saint Francis did and what Saint Dominic did?' He took to imagining a variety of things that seemed good to him, and he always thought of things that were difficult and painful; and as a result of imagining them, he seemed to find within himself a facility for executing them. At the conclusion of all his reasoning, nevertheless, he always ended up telling himself: 'Saint Dominic did this, and I too must do it; Saint Francis did that, and I too shall do it.'[5]

It is by reading the biography of Ignatius that I will become a Jesuit, just as Madame Bovary falls in love by reading serialized fiction, or Don Quixote becomes a knight by plunging into chivalric romances.

Be careful not to underestimate the provider of services, the illustrator or recorder of sound. However middling it may be, the middle term has a propensity to devour the

[5] Ignatius of Loyola, *Le Testament* (Paris: Arléa 1991), p. 27.

others. The bishop should watch out for his vicar: his substitute may indeed replace him. The intermediary is fate itself, and ours in particular. Just as honour was the principle of feudalism and virtue that of the Republic, is not the medium the principle of our 'access society'? Its true champions, it should be noted, are our *mediators*. Has Jesus Christ superstar stolen the show from its Creator? Naturally. Everywhere, the second becomes the first. The network announcer who sees and presents himself as a modest employee ends up as the anchorman. The interviewer in a literary exchange spontaneously turns into its star, the fixed point exalted by his round of guests. The theatre director – in times past a mere intermediary between actors and audience – now receives the attention accorded only yesterday to the author. The actor, for his part, through whom the text comes to us, is now for us its soul and substance: he who places it in his mouth gives us the impression of placing it in the world. As is the case for the demiurge interpreter of classical music ('Gould by Bach'). In the forum, the spokesperson is promoted to the chairmanship. The deputy mayor takes over. Why should we be astonished by the fact that in the Catholic Church the vicar (who is theoretically charged with 'acting as a bridge') should supplant in symbolic value and ability to draw an audience all clerics combined – black, red or violet? The people of God, for everyone, is the Sovereign Pontiff, a phenomenon parallel to the current practice of 'rephrasing'. In the beginning: 'The comments of X gathered by Y'. Eight days later: 'As Y so rightly said while speaking with X.' Three months later (having brought out his collection of interviews): 'If we follow Y when he tells us that ... .' The century of interviewers, interfaces and interceptions has shown us the uncertainty lurking in every signature ... .

The Rout of the Fathers

Auteur [Author]: 'Said *par excellence* of the first cause that is God', we read under 'Auteur' in Furetière's *Dictionnaire universel*. The Creator of the universe and author of our days enjoyed maximal authority in times past. Now the quality of Eternal Father has become a disqualification. With the general crisis of genealogy, whose first casualty has been the fleshly progenitor, it has even become a glaring chink in the divine armour. How might the Author *par excellence* retain His status, if we no longer live in an authorial regime? How could the Father remain at the summit, if the paternal function has begun to leak in every direction?

The father–son relationship continues to pass itself off in theology as originary and originating. A supernature anchored in the most stable of patrons, that of both nature and our *mores*. The *pater* is the patron, the template; he administers the patrimony. The *genitor* procreates; he inseminates the mother. And the *parens* raises, educates in the law. Under those three fundamental senses, the Father once governed. He could give orders to Abraham, as the latter, the father of Israel, did to the children of Israel. He was the Law. He had the first and last word. He established what was forbidden. Without having borne him in his flesh, the father is alleged to recognize the child in spirit, through a speech act (the symbolic, a spiritual principle), while the mother devotes herself to forming his body (the imaginary, a carnal principle). A golden circumstance, with genes guaranteed. Now not only is the human experience of paternity not a historical invariant, but with biotechnology, the biological progenitor has recently been transnatured (not denatured, since there is no natural standard). Currently legalized, childbirth in conditions of anonymity prevents the father from recognizing the child. And beyond questions of legality, the new eugenics or 'progenics' allows the species to dream the solitary pleasures of duplication: *in vitro* fertilization, frozen embryos, test-tube babies, *post-mortem* insemination, lateral birth without parents, and so on. An engineering of the living which calls into question even sexual and generational difference is defilializing us. And making the human a bit 'diabolical'. Satan had whispered to Eve that we could become the equals of God by becoming the origin of our own lives, masters of good and evil. Which is more or less what awaits us in the near future, when we will be able to become both source and stream.

The day on which a believer takes the decision to produce, through cloning, his genetic double from the nucleus of a cell taken from his own organism, like the sheep named Dolly, is the day which his reverence for God the Father may fail to survive. Putting aside the (provisional) bans of bioethics, the broadening of the possibilities of human reproduction *will relativize*, at the very least, the absolute subtending our civil law and our moral theology. We are supposed to honour (since love is not mentioned in the Ten Commandments) the father God gave us (or the God that our father manufactured to measure and in his own image). Yes, to the extent that one is needed. But a progenitor is no longer indispensable. Will a man who can duplicate himself at will be inspired to 'bend his knee in the presence of the Father from whom all paternity, on heaven and on earth, derives its name'? Will the self-administrator of his own posterity be susceptible to fear and trembling? The technology of procreation (for children), like that of creation (for works), has brought Creation itself into the realm of fabrication. How will the spiritual Father, who initiates life according to the spirit, survive the Father according to the flesh, whose technical surrogates are already in place?

An elite subject, domineering and sure of himself, is what the Father no longer is in a feminized world in which the point of reference has changed gender. It is altogether insufficient to say that paternalism is getting a bad press. The chieftain of the horde, the first link in the monotheistic chain, has abdicated before our very eyes. Childhood is no longer guilty; it is a victim. 'I believe in God, the Father Almighty.' The obligatory *Incipit*. And the universal murmur. For many years there had been debates concerning just how to understand that paternity, and that power. Was it the arbitrariness of the omnipotent Patriarch, who gives and withdraws as he pleases (the Jansenist or Lutheran thesis of predestination)? Or the equitable benevolence, open to all, of the 'Father of mercy and all consolation' (the Wisdom mystery of the tradition)? An old debate. Let us be satisfied in this context with Tertullian's *Nemo tam pater*: no one is more a Father than He. Nor more of an Author. Whether frightening, august, or familiar (the Aramaic *abba* used by Jesus), he was the *pater familias* to the nth power. Only a great-grandfather in our day – given the life expectancy – could aspire to equivalent generational prestige.

Will God at least make Himself 'parental', even if He insists on remaining single? The word would provide an excuse – the only authorized one. Compatible with the transition from the extended to the nuclear family, and with the advent of the child-king, the appropriate counterpart to the current depopulation. From whom would they be taken, those rights of the child (who will soon no longer be obliged, should he so wish, to bear the name of his father), if not from his progenitor? Would the Heavenly Father retain His rights of discipline when His earthly counterpart has long since lost his? Would the civil code exercise no influence? In 1970, 'parental authority' replaced the 'paternal power' of the Napoleonic Code (1804). The monopaternal family makes no distinction between Father and Mother. All roles blend – as in the homosexual adoptions of the future. Officially unisex, the humanitarian West, even in the domain of arms, tends in its inner recesses towards the *feminitarian* (a humanitarian war being a war in which women have their place, one which they can watch on television). What is to be done with a more or less intractable Patriarch when what is desired above all is to be mothered, and the angular is replaced more or less everywhere by the ovoid: in the design of cars, computers, pencil-sharpeners – even in our heads? Send Him to a retirement home. Shaving His beard would not be enough. The neutral, in French, is no longer accepted. One is *écrivain* [a writer] or *écrivaine*; *maire* [a mayor] or *mairesse*. The handsome greybeard (Victor Hugo decked out in hydrophilic fibres) could set Himself up as a bisexual, embracing masculine and feminine. It would be an insult to gender studies. Was the celebrated comment of the American emerging from a coma ('I met God and She's black') an anticipation of the divinely correct of tomorrow? Failing which, we could make do with a genuinely *nice* organizer, whom we might feel free to treat as a pal. But in that capacity, it's the Son who excels, not an Almighty endlessly keeping His distance. The truth is that we no longer have a right to indebtedness and duty.

No doubt that situation is not viable in the long term, and we can predict, in a future phase, a re-establishment of the – symbolic as well as fleshly – father (in accordance with the jogging effect of technical progress) (*l*). Pacts of civil solidarity between equals will not be able to conceal for very long the fact that beyond the question of homo- or heterosexual conjugality, there is the bond of filiation, which, for its part, cannot be a contractual matter. One cannot but agree with the Protestant Federation of France when it evokes 'the duration that precedes and exceeds individual consent', since subjects 'necessarily emerge from childhood and engage with a world more lasting than themselves'. For that indeed is the question: 'How is one to articulate the autonomy of the subject and the institution of filiation? It is consequently the very meaning of institutionality that we must together rediscover, redefine and reinvent.'[6]

For the moment, a failing Father and an evanescent Author. Are we all creators (a generalized *creativity*)? No further need for a Creator. Are we all originals? No further need for an Original. What god would be able to see the difference, in our computerized networks, between an original and a copy? The Web has no further need of a demiurge. Weaving will produce our work. How is one to identify the author of an electronic text or a screen-visual? It is possible to determine who is the author of a painting or a silver-image photo. But to whom, juridically, might we attribute a pool image, an interactive setup, or the simple retransmission of a soccer match on television (five cameras, cameramen, and the producer has the last word)? The author function, with its privileges, no longer leaves its imprint on a world engorged with traces, proliferating diversions and fusions, and crossing all registers. Postmodernity is no more subject to the 'authorities' than modernity was to the centre. But if man is no longer at the centre of the living, and the earth is no longer at the centre of the universe, can God remain at the centre of our concerns? A geocentric universe was naturally theocentric. The Church did not condemn Copernicus and Galileo for the pleasure of it. Why would I put at the centre of my life some-One who did not put me at the centre of the solar system? For how might one imagine that He would place anywhere other than in the middle of the cosmos the creature charged with accomplishing His plan of love and salvation? At the time of the great cosmological decentralization, the invention of pictorial perspective was no doubt a compensation for that narcissistic wound. By recentring visual space on man, the image of God, centre and source of the painting, one re-established below what was being lost on high. But that space, too, has had its day, turning man as it did into a miniature god, deploying the avenues of the visible from the pupil of his eye, as Velásquez did in *Las Meninas*.

The human chameleon is a good sort. He is no longer even surprised by what would have scandalized or depressed him in another setting. The deposing of the Author of things visible and invisible is not unduly troubling to those who profess the Messiah. The most lucid of them wonder, with understandable disquiet,[7] about the place of Christian reality in society at large, but not about the place of God within that

---

[6] 'La famille, la conjugalité et la filiation', Bureau de la Fédération protestante, September 1998.
[7] René Rémond, *Le Christianisme en accusation* (Paris: Desclée de Brouwer 2000).

Christian reality. A discredited religion has more or less blinded us all to the demotion of God by that very religion. Eschatology (the theory of final ends and the end of days) has vanished into a sociology of our present misfortunes.

It is possible, to be sure, to forget the history of God in that of his consecrated intermediaries. To insist on the temporal trials of the latter in order to conceal the vicissitudes of the Former. That division in the labour of lamentation is all the more tempting in that the wounds of the Bride of Christ are visible to the naked eye. What Catholic has not heard it said, or repeated himself on occasion, ever since Vatican II, that 'the Church is going to hell'? Latin, auricular confession, the cassock. The family jewels auctioned off. The portable throne, the giant ostrich-feathered fans with gold embroidered handles: all consigned to museums. And what if the complaint already contained its own balm? In order to avoid plunging the Eternal back into the harshness of the times? It is true that the fate of the institution is not necessarily tied to the Institutor to whom it appeals. As is demonstrated by the fact that a cult can happily survive its alleged object. Jesus retains his ambassadors, and in America, Poland and Korea they are quite prosperous, even though their residual relations with the primordial *Auctor* are simple matters of courtesy. Outside the Orthodox sphere, in which the dogma has been retained intact and the rights of the Father, along with those of the Holy Spirit, are ostensibly preserved, the modern Christian has renewed his lease on Heaven. He deals directly with the Son, a partner who is always accessible and on the point of returning. He whose 'humanity survived the death of God' allows the best-intentioned of the children of the Holy Trinity to take a third for the whole.

From Galaxy to Galaxy

The Eternal, too, must live with his own time. The powers that be apologize for their existence by presenting themselves to their citizens with the alluring traits of the Seductive State. Why not call on the same gimmicks (vibrato, demagogy, youth cult, emotional overkill, etc.) for a Scourge now recycled as a seducer? The communications experts of the Churches have proceeded along these lines by zooming in on Jesus, even more so than in the days of the various messianisms of 1848. He can be 'communicated' as a psychoanalyst, a guerrilla fighter, a 'French doctor', a bigger-celebrity-than-the-Beatles. And even as a pot-smoker (for ravers). To suit the audience. The Father is less malleable or more cantankerous. The change of technocultural attractors (to the audiovisual) incites – or requires – a relegation of His Rigidity considerably far behind His Plasticity in actual catechesis, if not in the catechism. Manifold are the forms taken by the updating of 'Arianism' (Jesus the man, not God). They all apply pressure in the same direction. Leading if not towards *a heathen France* (Monseigneur Hippolyte Simon, Bishop of Clermont) at least towards a cool and likeable Jesus deserting his annoying churches.

An about-face. 'Keep on moving; there's nothing to be seen here,' said the Judaean to the heathen occupier. 'All you've got to do is interpret.' 'Keep on moving', says the comfortable neo-pagan to today's harried Judaeo-Christian. 'There's nothing left to interpret. But open your eyes wide; there's lots to see.' An exhaustion of the *imprimatur* (that it be printed in order to exist) and the emergence of the *videatur* (that it be looked at in order to exist). The first procedure (the authorization to print a text deemed to be in keeping with Church teaching) was not ideal, but all things considered, it was not particularly maladjusted to a Supreme Being who was an impenitent bibliophile. On the other hand, the 'let it be seen if it would exist' contradicts Jesus remonstrating with Thomas: 'Blessed are those who have not seen and yet have come to believe' (John 20: 29). There is a hiatus between a God who emerged, with the Hebrews, from an aversion for the excessively visible, and a videosphere in which what is not seen is not believed, in which visible means credible (it's true, I saw it on TV). To wit: the very equation of idolators. 'For the glory of immortal God,' said Saint Paul, 'they have substituted images representing mortal man, birds, quadrupeds and reptiles.' Add on dinosaurs and E.T., and one can replace *they* with *we*.

The reascendancy of idolatry is a phenomenon comparable to global warming. There is a component of inertia that cannot be manipulated at will, with sarcasm or a sermon. From the handwritten God to the God of print, the Reformers had channelled the *flow* (one was still in the same system of apprehension of the world, and of apprenticeship). A similar continuity in means of locomotion between Ramses II's chariot and Napoleon I's covered carriage. There is less of an ambulatory distance between the Pharaoh and the Emperor than between the horse-drawn coach of 1900 and the Model-T Ford of 1930. In both written supports and hippomobile transports, in the course of three millennia, there were remarkable innovations, but not inventions in the strong sense of the term. Let us distinguish between the two forms of hiatus. *Innovation* renovates, and thus reconnects with the old; *invention* dislocates, and thus renders the old obsolete. In the sixteenth century, the printing press renewed bookbound Reason, without firing a shot but, as it were, from within, remaining inside the (linear, discrete, symbolic) Word. The mechanical reproduction of Scripture did not call the tradition of the Book into question. It accentuated it. The Wars of Religion were a true civil war between the offspring of a common womb. Whence their relentlessness. All this had nothing in common with the estrangement of the children of advertising and channel-surfing from the line of Abraham. In the course of its first three generations (Hebraic, Catholic and Protestant), the God that one read changed, but His readership grew. Until the end of the eighteenth century, devotional and theological works constituted the lion's share of what was published (during the Enlightenment, in France, two-thirds of legal production). As for religious broadcasts, they occupy one per cent of air time. God has exchanged His readers for viewers. The latter can always comfort themselves with the possibility of grasping Him in the Jesus mode. In keeping, if you like, with Orthodoxy, since Jesus was already the Father in the 'image mode'. Except that we are no longer dealing with the same image. Our images 'strip the object of its veil, destoying its aura,' Benjamin had warned, adding: 'Techniques of reproduction detach the reproduced object from the realm of tradition.' Stable photos and animated images get us out of the habit of the double vision that comes from superimposing ritual meaning on those palpable figures. They dispel the distance of the faraway. Even if we are talking about images in both cases, a photo inhabits a reality from which the icon takes its leave. That being said, computerization may bring them back together again. By surmounting the opposition between trace and sign, it will grant the collectors of imprints the wherewithal to free themselves from crude things.

The trustees of the Tradition find themselves, for the moment, in a world in which the image imposes its order on the text – a bit like museum curators, but in reverse. It is up to them to render the *readable visible*, whereas the official guardian of a collection effects 'restorations' intended to make the *visible readable*. And, in so doing, to resensitize the wide general public to the work of art. The museums of France freshen up a number of decaying surfaces; this has the merit of encouraging tourism and an inflow of foreign currencies (through exhibition-events). Their laboratories do daily combat against the entropy which mucks up and obscures works of art. For oil painting, strong solvents are used to remove varnish, which darkens with time, and accumulated surface dirt (religious art, in particular, has been ravaged by candle smoke), in order to make paintings better defined and more luminous. Like boxes of chocolates. So that they can be identified by non-experts at a first glance. Accessible, especially to those who have no notion of art history. Churches, too, have a mission to keep certain deposits of meaning alive, and to proceed in such manner that those deposits should not be a dead letter in the eyes of video-generations that have never seen or listened to the Angel Gabriel, Saint Bernard, or Loyola. Those responsible for Scripture, like the lab workers of the Louvre, also do daily battle. The difference between the two restorative tasks is that one is expected to transcode one language into another, and the other to prepare subtitles or freshen up colours without changing them.

Michelangelo, in the Sistine Chapel, is certainly more 'readable' than he was in 1950, before the restoration of his frescos. Recoloured, the message can be seen better. With one hitch: when they are excessively or poorly revived, the colours denature the work. Such is the problem of restoration: the colouring that kills what it would restore. But here we are not dealing with the removal of a subsequent layer of paint, the lightening of varnish, or the reduction of fly-deposits. We are not rectifying unstable materials so much as effecting a shift in space–time.

11 Every Man For Himself

He converted from Catholicism to the Baha'i religion in college. To his parents, he kept framing his new orientation as part of a continuum with his childhood faith. Jesus was undoubtedly a Manifestation of God, but there have been some others . . . .
(The Reverend Scotty McLennan, *Finding Your Religion*)

With the change in technical milieu, and the change in credibilities which ensued as a consequence, belief in God, which had been spontaneous, became intrepid. It is no longer a reflex or a heritage, but a personal commitment or act of will. The transcendent, which once inhabited words, has been evacuated from recorded images, the new touchstone of reality, and we deal with our fears differently. This defection has led to a decathecting of history as the site of human accomplishment. The reascendancy, in place of the Cross, of the Wheel and the Labyrinth, emblems of circular time, are particularly auspicious for the contemplative and abstentionist mysticisms of the East. It is an era of spiritual resourcefulness. Far from the great void that had been feared, the age has proliferated in virtual traffic jams of meaning. The re-enchantment of the world is already well underway . . . .

With the advent of agriculture, particularly in mountainous regions without irrigation, subsistence became dependent on rainfall, and the god of storms relegated the former god of the Heavens to obsolescence. Zeus, Uranus, or even Hadad, Anu. Tell me what your survival depends on, and I'll tell you what your pantheon is. In what industrial society can it be said that it's God outside, the way we say it's daylight outside? Or that it *whales* for the Eskimos and *bears* for the Samoyeds – the supreme (because most reinvigorating) gods of the ice-bank and the tundra? It availed the totalitarian Christianity of the Inquisitors and the Crusades little to turn its back on Jesus' words ('my kingdom is not of this world'); for it, the Eternal Father was non-negotiable. Its earth and its sun: what was most trustworthy. Faith was ingested with mother's milk, and the divine 'stuck' to the instruments of hand and mind. Just as 'health is life in the silence of one's organs', credibility is a trust in the silence of one's surroundings. One's God does not hurt, and there is no reason to change Him so long as the *pressure of selection* of one's mediasphere does not compel one to do so.

The Law of the Milieu: Change or Death

Penicillin and medicine have loosened the iron grip of natural selection, but for all that we are not free to dream or believe whatever we like, since our artificial environment is no less selective than the other (in which a flu epidemic was enough to eliminate the weakest members of the group). It is that environment, no doubt, that a Darwin of the competition for symbolic survival would put under the microscope. And his task would be no less arduous than that of the botanist and zoologist, since even if humans have succeeded in placing their imagination under glass, interposing a double pane between nature and themselves, they have too much pride to admit that their ideas and images might owe something to the air they breathe, even if it be conditioned. This disdain can take the form of an explicit rejection. Has not an intransigent and attentive Christian like Jacques Ellul denounced technological society as a humiliation of the divine Word and a forgetting of the virtue of Hope? Without rolling of papyrus, scraping of hides, or casting of lead characters, yesterday's techniques, would evangelical Hope have been capable of making its way to Him? Such is the ingratitude of the human mind and the power of our myths. One hypostasizes Technique as an evil subject, graces it with a capital letter, and behold the pseudo-modern Devil, or the prolongation of Sin by the Machine. The new Antichrist to be pursued. In point of fact, the rituals that bind mortals to the Intemporal are essentially *rhythms of life*. The latter evolve with the delays that separate us from each other, and the *tempo* of our agitations. The frenetic individual who goes from Paris to Marseille by train in three hours and keeps abreast of the news twice daily by plugging in his radio and television cannot have the same approach to the Eternal – that time without duration, without either before or after – as a seventeenth-century peasant without a daily newspaper, and whose horizon goes no further than the nearby mountain.

The sacralized Book matured in the cocoon of human memory. Only recently have we begun entrusting it to computers, whose memory capacity doubles every two years (Moore's Law). Numerical memory has grown vertiginously, but our own faculties for memorization have diminished (according to numerous studies of the evolution of the historical, literary and geographical knowledge of both adults and the young). We manage to store information so well that the concept of 'by heart' has disappeared from our schools, and the faithful can no longer recite their *Pater noster*. What Plato had feared from the written auxiliary has been confirmed, and well beyond. The collective brain has become superpowerful, and as a result our heads are less effective at storing. Religious information cannot be deposited in silicon chips. It is up to us, through deeds and words, to activate the temporal extasis that allows us to leave our present life and rejoin the extremely distant events to which our holidays and sacraments make lightning-fast trips. Passover, at the beginning of spring, has us rejoining the exodus from Egypt, with the Seder, a memory-meal in which all is allusion: the bitter herbs to the years of misery, the dates with honey to the mortar of the enslaved builders, the syrup to the sweetness of Canaan. The Christian Eucharist takes us back two thousand years in a single leap, just as Good Friday projects us on to Golgotha. Thus it is, through ritual reiteration, that we deny the time that would deny us. The external supports of memory cannot accomplish this in our place. We can regret that fact, seeing how much it costs men of God not to know how to forget. Witness the endless squabbles over attribution that fill the headlines of our newspapers. What indeed are the 'God-maddened' if not hypermnesiacs? But God, too, has His sages, who keep watch over our 'memory' and save us from mortal oblivion. *Schmor*! Observe, conserve! *Zakhor*! Remember! Yet archiving and anamnesis, those two wellsprings of piety and its practices, cannot emerge intact from our consignments to machines, and from the inner inertia that ensues as a result.

The Bouvard-and-Pécuchet formula ascribed to Malraux (who deserved better), 'the twenty-first century will be religious or it will not be', will not illuminate the future. Which of the twenty centuries of our era (including the century of the Enlightenment) will not have been religious! We might as well prophesy that the twenty-first century would use language. Now that would be a novelty: men symbolize things and venerate fantastical beings. But what then? If the virtual world is already their oldest conquest (in the decorated caves of the Palaeolithic, wall-painters were already virtualizing brute reality), it is only at present that they have succeeded in digitalizing all data and putting satellites into orbit. The interaction of two trivialities – one spiritual, one digital – will give us a God that is anything but trivial.

Especially in so far as the Eternal is no longer in nature, but in our culture. To the simple souls of the past, He dwelled in the accidents, catastrophes (which are still called 'acts of God' in the United States), and hierarchies of the village. In order to encounter Him, more decisiveness than negligence is what is called for from now on, and more anticonformism than docility. Panurge had the gods of his needs, and the needs of his means. But what tangible need does our service civilization have of a barely serviceable Saviour – our culture, with its increasingly effective means of allaying our fears and sources of distress? More utilitarian, but less vulnerable than previously to the assaults of the natural environment, we are less and less 'capable of God', since invoking His Name because He could be useful will apparently no longer do. The old contractual obligations have been taken over by others. Mere faithfulness is no longer profitable. We can do without . . . .

God: What's in it for Me?

What will the functions of the Invisible have been for fifty generations of users? Going off to war without misgivings, for starters, mobilizing cool young things, making sure they confront death while blinded by the light, failing to perceive the abyss in front of them. The Almighty tends to awaken in besieged cities, when the Turk is at the gates, when the Black Death breaks out and the country is invaded. It was when Enlightenment France was encircled and attacked, in 1793, that the anticlerical Jacobins burned the statue of atheism and paraded before the Supreme Being, that unifying ghost.

God, it used to be said, visits three scourges on sinners: hunger, war and pestilence. And now here He is among us, endangered by peace and prosperity; we who are bereft of exemplary punishments, despite AIDS, the last of the divine castigations. The privileged celebrate Gay Pride and war with zero deaths. What need do we have for a chaplain? The pacification of the West by supermarkets, leisure activities and holidays has resulted in an abandonment of the school of sacrifice that a Christian upbringing used to be. As well as of the very idea of sanctifying oneself by shedding blood, as Moses and Jesus did. 'Moses took the blood and dashed it on the people, and said, "See the blood of the covenant that the Lord has made with you in accordance with all these words" ' (Exodus 24: 8). Or: 'Jesus took the cup of wine and said: "This is my blood of the covenant shed for the multitude." ' The State no longer requires of the civilian a tax in blood, and military service already appears to us to be incongruous. The North of the planet is losing its seminarians, but the South is unaware of our crises of religious vocation, and churches prosper wherever life, health and peace are not yet regarded as one's due. Where death lurks at every street corner, and the future seems random. As in the France of Saint Vincent de Paul. God served to allow one to endure great physical and moral suffering. We, on the other hand, have analgesics and therapists. Despite the emphasis placed by some morose individuals on the values of renunciation and death to the self, the Christian, who likes to sing with a joyful heart, is not exactly a Narcissus of pain. Hair shirts, fasts, mortification and abstinence none the less provided an excellent training for a life of hard knocks.

God was above all something that helped to expiate, to pay for one's sins in tears and sweat. The entire dramaturgy of grace and salvation rests on a presumption of guilt. Fault in divorce has been eliminated, and in the case of a car accident, the victim's being at fault does not deprive him of his right to a payout. On the road, every vehicle is in the wrong, every pedestrian in the right. Legal responsibility has been cut off from morality. Which should certainly be enough to discourage our appetite for wax candles and rosaries. To redeem us from what, if the idea of original sin makes us smile? Devotion, abnegation, penitence: what for? Our annual exercises in repentance, political responses to political embarrassments, have no effect on a cornerstone that has quite simply vanished. Genesis stages in a few extremely dense pages an idea that was simple, and has become opaque to us: for every sin, its appropriate punishment. Adam and Eve were ignominiously expelled from the Garden of Eden because they disobeyed. Who these days would not congratulate them for it? Nonconformists, rebels, they dared to say no. Was it Cain who had to wander endlessly because he killed Abel? An unhappy childhood, an awkward radicalism; but he, at least, was someone who pushed things to the limit. Did a Flood inundate the earth because humanity allowed itself to be carried away by violence? With-it liberal freedom consists of every man having his Colt, and let the best man win. Did the language of men become confused because they dreamed of a skyscraper that would beat all records? A high-tech feat, a foretaste of Faustian daring that honours the avant-garde and would have earned a place in the Guinness Book of Records for our architects. Apart from the fact that we consider as good (or a mere peccadillo) things our ancestors considered disastrous – for instance, sexual curiosity (they knew that they were naked) or the desire to penetrate the mystery of things (the Tree of Knowledge). A guiltless anomie could not care less for the Law, which, it may be noted, lost its sacred dimension in losing its fixed material support, becoming the 'legal data' that stream across our screens. In a society in which it is forbidden to forbid, what is hereditarily unpardonable, the fatal apple, the 'guilty but not responsible' that seizes on us in the cradle, border on the unthinkable, somewhere between the barbaric and the frankly droll. The compassionate protocols of the hospital have voided the ceremonies of penitence. The church confessional has emptied out, to the benefit of couch or camera. If one bares one's soul these days, it is for one's psychiatrist, an agnostic priest, or in front of ten million TV viewers, in a loft.

God used to be what served to designate the guilty in a trial by ordeal, or even to torture him into telling the truth. Genetic imprints are more economical (of the blood of the guilty and of judges' time). Above all, God served to neutralize the randomness of life, to 'reassure and protect'. As a call for help when there was none. The sprinkling of holy water, the words of exorcism, the procession of the Holy Sacrament. Every ritual is a source of reassurance: one is less afraid in a group than alone. But what is the point of a benediction when one has one's insurance sticker? The highways no longer have bandits. The wolves have disappeared from our forests, the dead sleep in their graves, vampires have become discreet, and Hugo's *Cour des miracles* has become a parking lot. We are no longer in a vale of tears. What our forebears asked for at Candlemas, at the Feast of Saint Anthony, on Rogation Days, in collective processions around town or field, is now provided by no-fault insurance, the weather forecast, and social security. The bureaucracy of precaution has changed, and protection against a variety of damages, for which religion, our first system of civil security (life insurance for third parties, illness and old age), was a kind of preamble, is organized differently. Our talismans and aspergilla are now the emergency numbers on our telephone. Police, fire station, lifeboats, and so on. The 'Believe in the saving God and you will be saved' has lost some of its urgency as a result. Moreover, it is by no means certain that we have gained out of the exchange. Year in year out, science channels our quest for security, but quite apart from the fact that it is not as certain as one might have thought, it does not give meaning to life, but, rather, removes it. *How* does not suffice for the anxiety-prone mammal, who needs a *why* for his happiness, as well as for his misfortunes. When a car accident, the loss of a child, or hail in one's vineyard no longer *mean* anything, then he becomes *bad*. He starts recriminating and filing suits – against the doctor, prefect, mayor or neighbour. Such is his reflex action. Science and technology have played an all-too-dirty trick on us. They have rationalized our environment and desymbolized life. Which causes a loss of equilibrium. Whence the communicating vessels: fewer people in the churches, more with lawyers; fewer candles lit and votive offerings hung in crypts, more forms filled out and petitions for government action signed. Divine Providence, undoubtedly, cost society less than the Providential – or Welfare – State. And the repercussions affect everyone. The disappearance of the final cause in which, in the last analysis, rationality consists, means that we are more cosseted. Less adventurous, less capable of bearing hardship – less courageous, perhaps. More impatient as well, and more legalistic.

We deal less well with pain, fire and catastrophe. We are less inclined to accept. Physical anomalies are experienced as intolerable, and a handicap is compensated for as one might compensate an injury. Has not a court just recognized the right of every individual to receive a payout for a deformity? Suffering has become 'pointless', and a reversal of fortune is grounds for suicide. With no one to answer for it. No more impenetrable designs. Nothing that 'makes sense' – a good or evil eye. The empty orbit on high, it is true, has not produced *only* unhappiness here below. Our technocracy and the judiciary are, rather, thriving as a result. The principles of precaution (guaranteed minimum risk) and the scapegoat (find me the responsible party) have absorbed the spoils of the Most-High. Experts in civil safety and judges of civil and criminal courts are at least two social categories that have little to complain about in the consignment of Providence to the rubbish heap.

The Three Crowns

The space and time of our lives are less and less stark and invariable givens – always assuming that they ever were. They expand or contract as a function of the mediasphere in which we are circulating, physically or mentally. The public use of reason is 'what one engages in as a *scholar* for the entirety of the reading *public*' (Kant). The private use of the *irrational* is what one makes, as a *believer*, of the very provisional space–time in which one strives to form a community. An *environment of belief* makes for several concentric circles of constraint. At the outer limit, *the social environment*, or the average state of customs and morals, whose evolution can provoke a crisis of the *institution*. There is – less ostensibly but equally significant – the *intellectual climate*, a function of the scientific awareness of a period, which reshapes, at every stage, the division between the credible and the unbelievable. This climate can engender a crisis of *dogmas* and *certitudes*. Finally, there is the material culture, whose changes affect *practices* on a daily basis. This third circle, inscribed at the centre of the other two, is not much to look at. Its banality makes it transparent to us, and virtually innocent. It is not, however, without effect, at first sight, on our description of the divine. Let us simply consider the steeples and towers of cathedrals. Once they dominated the skyline. Now they are abased, brought down, by the superelevation of numerous civilian edifices (thanks to the technology of electric lifting). So much for the chime of the church bell, which reminded the faithful of the time of Mass, now that everyone has a watch. And what becomes of crosses on tombstones, intercessory prayers for the dead, catafalques, temporary altars and mortuary chapels, once urban overcrowding and considerations of public health lead to an acceptance of cremation (which is materially in contradiction with the resurrection of bodies, but which the ecclesiastical authorities were obliged to endorse, through force of circumstances)? What calvaries are conceivable on the verges of motorways?

At the outer circle, the malaise of Catholics is palpable. A hypersexualized, individualistic, hedonistic and mercantile environment clashes a bit too glaringly with the celibacy of priests (which has its social cost), the rule of priestly poverty, the exclusion of women from the priesthood, and the minimally collegial monarchy of the Vatican. Pastoral missions are already entrusted to lay personnel. But how can we, on the one hand, praise democracy and joint decision-making and, on the other, endorse the concentration of power in the Pope's hands, reducing diocesan synods to a merely consultative role? Refuse the ordination of both sexes, make of it a dogma involving the infallibility of the Church, because sexual impurity would prevent one from administering the Eucharist? Forbid the priesthood to married men, which was not the case in the days of the early Church? A striking contradiction, to which Protestants and Anglicans have already given their answer, and one which will result, sooner or later, in a change of structure. The Eucharist has its exigencies, but diverse modes of modernization have theirs as well. A 'gospel of prosperity for American millionaires' has been forged, and choreographed Masses for the villages of black Africa. Maronite rituals in Libya and those of Malabar in Kerala have been integrated into the Roman liturgy. And these are just some examples. Such developments will ultimately cause the theologian to lose ground, and the Holy Spirit to list in the direction of the century. But that is not our concern here.

The progress of knowledge, in the second circle, has plainly diminished the believability of the articles of faith. Aristotle's physics gave an understandable meaning to disputes over the real presence of the body of Christ in the Communion wafer (which led to numerous deaths in the sixteenth century), but the entire idiom of transubstantiation (or not) becomes utterly incomprehensible in an age of nuclear physics. Granted, but it is acknowledged that the Trinity, the Immaculate Conception, Infallibility, and other truths of the faith are not inseparable from the Word of God. They were 'additions', and the Reformation bears ample witness to the fact that one can reject hell and purgatory, and retain transcendence – which seems to be doing all the better as a consequence. An explanation in terms of the culturally archaic serves to excuse whatever seems unbelievable in a literal reading of Scripture (the creation of the world in a week, walls tumbling down at the sound of a trumpet, etc.). 'Demythologization', which separates kerygma from myth by cleansing the sacred text of its fables and primitive dross, proved an effective defence. The faith-bound intellectual clears the ground around the vital core in order to protect it from the surrounding fire. That operation falls to philosophers and virtuosi of the concept. Historians and the literarily inclined are reluctant. For them, myth is inseparable from the theological construct. And its division into separate levels (an imaginary ground floor for children, higher symbolic floors for adults only) would cause the whole biblical edifice to topple. This quarrel is above all the concern of exegetes. It is beyond us.

Our focus, which is more modest, will be on the small circle of trivialities. Not on its contents (at least in an initial phase), but on its *modus operandi*, the gymnastics of faith. Gestures are not the lesser counterparts of sacred words. It is often the other way round, and this or that grandiose myth may be no more than the facilitator of a staged sequence, or a plot improvised from the liturgy. As Father de Tarragon has noted, on the subject of Canaanite worship: 'Myth inscribes the ritual in time; in a reconstructed history, the symbolic function of ritual is the point of juncture between myth's attempt at systematization and the moment of the ritual's effectuation.'[1] In every country in the world, year in and year out, communitarian rituals survive the mythical systems which are their justification, and which the observant would have a tough time remembering.

It is somewhat wounding to our intellectual pride, but it may well be the case that *orthopraxies* carry more weight than orthodoxies in the transmission of faith. And even for a variety of Eastern modes of wisdom, meditation partakes of a discipline. For what one believes is less important than what one does with one's belief. Now the meeting-places of faith are as refractory to the encyclicals of authority as to the wishes of the faithful. The administering of sacraments in depopulated country parishes, Sunday Mass, and the map of dioceses are not questions to be resolved at a stroke of the pen by a democratization of Catholicism or a more inspired Sacred College. In so far as His presence in earthly cities is concerned, God appears to be far more threatened by driving habits and electrons than by the abandonment of Gregorian chant and the marriage of priests.

Our social statisticians keep tabs – indeed, charts, point by point – on rates of baptism, the percentage of religious observers in relation to those going to confession, the declining curve of religious vocations. The resulting quantitative data are quite useful in detecting ongoing changes. It is not insignificant that fewer than half of eighteen-to-twenty-four-year-olds affirm a belief in God, as opposed to four-fifths thirty years ago. That in 1950 there were a thousand priests ordained every year, and in 2000, a hundred. That the average age of our clergy has risen to seventy. That a third of the French population went to Mass in 1945, and a tenth in 2000. But beyond statistical *indicators*, anyone who is interested in isolating *factors of mentality* finds himself obliged, alas, to enter into murky areas that the purists of the divine and the societal have agreed to exclude from the realm of serious matters, as so many mere interferences. Yet the murkiness into which the essential has fallen, quite precisely, owes more than a little to *an interference of the accessory*.

---

[1] Jean-Michel de Tarragon, 'Le Culte à Ugarit', *Cahiers de la Revue biblique*, 1980, p. 19.

Cars, Commotions and Light Bulbs

Such as the new mobility of bodies, jobs and addresses induced by that formidable break in time (to which our historians pay scant attention), the *transport revolution*. Insufficient mobility asphyxiates a collective; too much dissolves it. The railway and the car accelerated urbanization, which had as a corollary de-Christianization, since our Church was rural in its structures (diocese, province, parish), and its rituals were based on agrarian rhythms. With the combustion engine, we are all wandering Jews; Abraham again becomes the norm, a nomad among others, and Babylon, become suburban, spreads like oil. Our vehicles have congested 'sin zones' (the over-population of our metropolises) and emptied regions of 'moral salubriousness' (the rural exodus). Take a brief look just at the car, which entails individualized loco-motion (as opposed to the railway) and itineraries (from point to point, without unloading). Mass motorization has unsettled the most established of neighbour-hoods and played its role in the problematic triumph of what Grace Davie has called 'believing without belonging'. More miles travelled, fewer relationships maintained. Beacons and buoys afloat.

Let us begin with the most elementary: the breakup of the parish setting, and the unsettling of proximities induced by urban dispersion and the pleasures of taking to the road. Weekend trips to the 'country' have resulted in a desertion of Mass and Sunday-morning worship. Parallel with a 'farewell to social class', the century of movies and the car will have seen a farewell to the parish. The falling costs of individual travel affect areas delineated on the basis of travel on horseback (*départements* and dioceses), whose size no longer corresponds in any meaningful way to the capacities of the four-wheeled inhabitant of the West. If car drivers, entirely caught up in the unilateral exercise of their autonomous wills, have already become incapable of constituting a society, how would they constitute a church, which is an even more intensive society? The *autoyen*, the car-driving citizen, is a drifter, a shirker of civic responsibility and a notorious abstentionist (civic space being pedestrian and walkable, on the model of the Greek *polis*). He is haunted by an indifference to place, a spirituality of escapism, and a constantly hurried faith. He is no longer the walker along side roads, the slow man of Péguy's 'cities of flesh', which are 'the image and beginning and body and draft of the house of God'. He *chooses* his points of anchorage, makes his groupings an expression of his will. More subtly, a dependence on the car, the unbelief machine, strips the space of *homo viator* of its drama, diminishes the penitential sense of *peregrinatio*. The Christian pilgrimage, which was – until the nineteenth century in the West – the great motive (and one of the only motives) for travel, like the holy cities, their principal points of destination, transforms 'motion into a unifying undertaking'. It is not a displacement, but a slow advance. And even so, one must avoid taking the coach or special train, the predetermined circuits for collective travel, in order to benefit from the sweat of expiation, a victory over oneself, a transformation by ordeal. Mechanized transport is damaging to pedestrian sublimation. No doubt the train in the nineteenth century and the coach in the twentieth renewed the practice of going on pilgrimages, but the car shortens one's stay (a few hours) and makes of the sanctuary no longer a recompense for one's asceticism, but an agreeable place to visit in itself.[2] From the Scout jamboree to the eschatological ascent to Jerusalem, Christianity is linked with walking on, not with overflights or speed merchants. In Egypt, President Sadat had plans to install a cable car on Mount Sinai, which is difficult to climb, to attract tourists. It would have been the ultimate desacralization. Unless one were intent on converting Mount Athos into Disneyland, it is hard to imagine little electric trains buzzing up and down the Holy Mountain taking pilgrims from one monastery to another (separated by a few hours on foot). Or an escalator on the side of Mont Saint-Michel (where monks once had an arm-activated device for hoisting cargo, as the hermits of Mount Athos raised their wicker containers attached to balloons). Or a stations-of-the-Cross ceremony on Good Friday by conveyor belt, with Coke dispensers – *lite*, please – at every station. Even if places of worship are built at a certain altitude, electrical elevation turns out to be injurious to that of the sentiments, which takes pleasure in combining physical exercise and spiritual satisfaction. Just as its elevator is inseparable from the Eiffel Tower, and the Duo-Lift from the Arche de la Défense, to that very extent arriving atop the towers of Notre-Dame by lift, without panting one's way up the spiral staircase, would complete its transformation into just one more ancient monument among others. The gods no longer dwell on peaks which anyone can reach in a flash by funicular railway or cable car. Let us not forget all that binds, in our culture, the sacred to sacrifice (whence the moral embarrassment of our aerial crusades: can a war without sacrifice still remain sacred?). What precisely is the point of going to a sanctuary that does not require one to make one's way there with one's whole self, body and soul? When, beyond a certain velocity, the land disappears too quickly beneath one's feet, it is to the detriment of that striving towards elsewhere that makes the desert traversable and a God plausible. Physical ubiquity and mystical transport don't go together. The Popemobile is a remarkably ambiguous sign of the times.

To the burning of fuel, we would do well to add *noise pollution*. For the spiritual coefficient of an era is also made of decibels. God, we have seen, breathes better in deserts sheltered from greenhouse emissions (less CO_2 and CH_4, whereas there is methane in swamps). Similarly, we sense His presence when canticles – or silence – can be heard. Just as He prefers candles to flashbulbs, He chose murmurs as opposed to shouts, and music against noise. Can we imagine a monastery – a library or school – on the edge of a motorway or a ring road? How would the service take place, or the meal shared in common – and in silence? The fact that there are fewer

[2] See Michel Lagrée, 'Dieu et l'automobile', *Cahiers de médiologie*, 12 (Autumn 2001).

Speed, light, and cathedral, Cologne, 1974

escapes from noise (a third of Europeans complain about the ambient noise) is no less damaging to apprenticeships of the spirit than to the ruminations of grace, which are caught up in an ever tighter acoustical mesh. Electric saws, jackhammers, horns honking, sirens, plane engines, motorbikes. Without saying that the chime of the steeple is the equivalent of the tinkling of snowbells, or underestimating the din of the horse-drawn vehicles of the past (iron-rimmed wheels on city pavements), we can affirm that the noise level in the major cities of the West appears to have augmented considerably since the nineteenth century. The physical levitation of Gospel and organ would appear to be all the more appreciated as a consequence, certainly, as a moment of happiness or an interlude of repose (the 'jogging effect'). For fans of statistics, we could say that the life of the believer with God, like that of the agnostic with thought, flourishes within a range situated between twenty-five and sixty deci-

bels. Between the hidden-valley-at-twilight level and the small-neighbourhood-street-in-the-middle-of-the-day level. Anything less, and panic ensues. Anything more, as well. A suitable acoustical level would be midway (as in the comparable case of kinetic motion, between the wheelbarrow-wagon and the racing car – say, the priest's *deux-chevaux*). The din (a return of the chaos reigning before the *fiat lux*) is to remain outside the enclosure of church, temple or synagogue. They are sites not of communication but of transmission, like our schools, universities and theatres, where turning off mobile phones is obligatory.

And why not mention, since we seem to be broaching serious matters, the tricks played on us by the imp of electricity? God's eye was like a lamp lit in the dark. If everything is illuminated, He will be less visible. The filament bulb has diminished the range of Satan (darkness being evil), but also that of the Father. To be sure, it had already begun with the fixed lantern, then with gaslights at the end of the eighteenth century. With the light switch, click: no more need for the Creator of heaven to let there be light. He suddenly encountered competition on his own terrain: a negative theology of kilowatts. In all languages, the supreme god is related to a root meaning *to shine* (Greek *Zeus*, Sanskrit *Dyauh*, Latin *Jupiter*, Hittite *sius*). Ours, too, is day and light, but *lumen* (the unit of measurement of lighted surfaces) is not *lux*. 'The light that shines in the shadows' (Saint John) finds its predestined partner in the stained-glass window, the filtering of gold and bronze, a silent murmuring of candles, causing the darkness itself to dream. Indirect lighting. Reverberating. The *Magdelene in a Flickering Light*. The muted lantern of gatherings in the wilderness. The shepherd's quivering wick on the plain, at night. The pensive flame on the threshold of the abyss. The trembling torches when the prehistoric hour arrives. Georges de La Tour, Rembrandt, Caravaggio: the shudder of twilight. Artificial lighting has diminished the terrors of the urban night, and in the countryside as well, and so much the better for us, but a pity for Marian apparitions. We should not conclude from this that the less *lux* there is in the cellar (*lux* equivalent to a square metre receiving a flow of one *lumen*), the more the straw lights up the vent. Nor that the statistical diminution of supernatural visions is due solely to an improvement in public lighting. (Seoul is a city of believers that radiates every night with rooftop crosses.) Let us recall, however, Thomas Jefferson's remark, in a related area: 'When, at the end of the eighteenth century, the Argand [gas] lamp arrived in New England, it was noted that conversation at dinners, which had been previously illuminated by candles, became less brilliant.' Expose a high altar (or a boudoir) to neon lighting, and see what happens to the Mass for the dead (or a late-night dinner).

Light sculptures and projectors bring the architecture of religious monuments into fuller view, by emphasizing shapes and details. But in so doing, they do not spiritualize the aesthetic, they aestheticize spirituality. Dousing with 'sound and light', *son et lumière*, causes stone to sing and prayer to remain silent, replacing meditation with astonishment. Subjected to the same sodium lamps as the Hôtel de Ville or the Palais de Justice, plunged into the same luminous casing as any other 'architectual jewel', the church, in the various prospects it offers, figures as just more décor in the urban landscape. Man's mastery of energy has placed light in the service of the Enlightenment, while diminishing the shadows borne by the mystery of our streets. With a concomitant retreat of the Hugolian pathos of shadows and abysses (building façades illuminated, the Unknown reduced to grey). A laser-based removal of visions. As enlightening as a comparative examination of world religions in terms of their respective *shades of sound* (muezzin, bell, gong, horns, etc.) would be a history of the Absolute in terms of its various modes of radiance and flame, from the oil-lamp in baked clay to the incandescent bulb, by way of the wax candle and the candelabra. In recent times, there would no doubt be a reversal of luminous trajectories. When one travels in the countryside after nightfall, one can assume that a church illuminated from without is a state-certified monument. If the halo filters through from within, one can bet that it is a place where Mass is still celebrated. Depending on whether the light floods the square in front of the church or emerges through the stained-glass windows, lights up the cornices or flickers in the aisles and cloisters, the building will be the province of the Ministry of Culture [*Direction du Patrimoine*] or the Minister of Cults. It is not easy to burn and to illuminate at the same time . . . . And it may be the same with people as it is with chapels. Those who are most in view may have rather limited vision. As though the sizzle of flashbulbs would have the effect on an individual of extinguishing his inner vision . . . .

All this, it will be objected, is no reason to become Amish. However prosperous and respectable that Anabaptist community – founded in 1693 in Alsace by Jacob Amman and since then fled to North America (where it has never stopped growing in number and prestige) – may be, we would rather not. A member of the Amish community of Ohio or Pennsylvania lives in the country, uses only oil-lamps and horse-drawn buggies, is forbidden to listen to the radio, and bans television. We shall not deem the combustion engine, hi-fi amplifiers, and nuclear-power plants injurious to the honour of God. Let us simply thank them, liberated from an extra-worldly approach to questions of faith, for reminding us of the silent battle that has for thirty years pitted visionaries against *voyeurs* and, for a half-century, pilgrims against compulsive travellers.

Planet Circus

A very ordinary set of cross-purposes: reviving traditions and inducing breaks. Wanting to make the break, and to reconnect with tradition. Such was the surprise of the Reformation. The evangelists, resolute partisans of the past, innovators despite themselves, wanted not to modernize but to regenerate the faith by returning to the authenticity of origins (or to what they imagined to be such); and a new man emerged from the old. We see the same rigmarole today with the clichés of the avant-garde and the official cult of the *novum*, but in the opposite direction, since the same pieties, once said to be pitiful, are making a forceful comeback. Nothing is more like pre-Christian times than our postmodern era. The most insignificant squeak is presented as the *dernier cri*; and the return to 'products of natural origin' is dizzying as we walk around our herb emporia. We wanted the new no matter what the price, and a return to the Great Pan of families. Gaia. The queen of clouds. In place of All Saints' Day, Halloween, the Celtic festival of ghosts. Death to history, all honour to nature, to everything that can be regarded as innate. Our sex, our ethnic group, our province of origin. Heredity tightens its grip, and we celebrate the chain that fastens us to our contingency: here we are, women, gays, Bretons or Corsicans, Jews or Gentiles, condemned for life to the hand we were originally dealt.

Laureti Tommaso, 'The Triumph of Christianity or the Exaltation of Faith', Stanze di Raffaello, Vatican City

Laureti Tommaso's painting *The Triumph of Christianity or the Exaltation of the Faith*, follows this process in reverse. The Mediator, at the apex of the central cone, breaks apart; Mercury, cast down, glues himself together again and will take the place of his vanquisher. The God of earthly paths surrenders to the patron of aerial space. The winged helmet again trumps the crown of thorns.

Our time is losing its vector. We no longer have any signs to orientate us. As did the Cross, through which the vertical aspiration of a faith sustained the horizon. 'Christ's Cross saves us from the circular labyrinth of the Stoics,' observed Saint Augustine. The liturgical cycles, of Advent or Christmas, turned on themselves like the seasons, but it was in order to have us await the Last Judgement, which would come only once. With the Cross broken, here come the labyrinths. The arts of the circus and games of the stadium. Everyone on the track, beneath the capitals. Everyone on the wheel, like squirrels. The solar wheel, of which the swastika was a subfranchise. And the Wheel of Fortune, a moneyed version. Or the luminous wheel of amusement parks. Ancient Christianity celebrated its jubilee with the great wheel, the great London Eye and the wheels of the Champs-Élysées. The round space of arenas, stadia and motor races. The signs of the Zodiac. Astrology and the horoscope. Nature is a matter of cycles, ellipses and rotations. The original Eternal comes back: a perpetual present. Great Pan is back at the wheel. And the word revolution reassumes its astronomical sense, the return of a circle to its point of departure .... A curious advance indeed.

Pythagoras professed the eternal return, and chose not to write. A justified abstention. Linearity appears to be alien to oral societies, which are incapable of reducing the dimension of becoming to lists of unusual events or facts. Our writings model themselves on orality, our images circle in on themselves, and the laws of perspective no longer give depth to our present. Our lives become 'tachiste', without guidelines. We can sense all this on our screens and posters, which seem to offer us so many days in the country, holidays from the sombre tunnels of line, paragraph and chapter. To learn how to read and write is necessarily to enter into a series of one-way processions. Written words oblige me to proceed in single file. Just as Christian life imposes a unilinear sequence of sacraments. I am not sole master on board a printed sheet. If 'language is fascist', as Barthes used to say, what shall we say *a fortiori* of that tube which pre-empts my gaze, imposes a direction, makes me go from left to right, or the reverse, without asking my permission? By that standard, the line-by-line of a written page, compared to a video-game, is at the very least Nazi. Nothing could be less libertarian. One enters an image wherever one likes. Through an optical sweep exercised at will. No unidirectional constraints – indeed no direction at all. Wherever and whenever I like. There is something euphoric about moving from a rail to a circle. No more straight line attaching an Annunciation to an End, and enjoining me to fill up the space in between in accordance with a calendar determined in advance. It is with this 'prefabricated' quality of the book that the electronic feast has broken. For that protracted holiday, nothing is written in advance and every law is a dead letter. Not only does it claim the right to do away with such abusive markers as schedules and programmes, with any need to declare in advance to any authority whatsoever its intentions to fix a closing time for its 'free parties' ('what the young ravers are intent on conveying is that their pleasure has no need of a benediction'), but it possesses the means of its happiness: the jolt of its rhythms, the remixing, the lurching suddenness. Unless it has now acquired the mentality of its apparatuses. Our pleasures change with our panoplies.

Believing without Reading?

A sign of the times, and not just anywhere. Anyone who makes the trip – in Jerusalem, the capital of memory – to the Shrine of the Book will find a site that is sublime and virtually deserted. Should he go, as a follow-up, to Yad Vashem, he will find a place that is sublime and mobbed – with civilians and young soldiers. In the heart of the biblical world, the memory of the genocide is winning out over that of the Book. And what could be more natural? Qumran is distant; Auschwitz is yesterday. A focus for identity in the various diasporas and a centre for civic and military inculcation, the Holocaust memorial, like the day of mourning (the 27th of Nissan) and its accompanying liturgy, has become the mainspring of a civil religion common to the secular and the religious. It is no longer a religion of the Book. One federating centrality has given way to another (and there is no incompatibility between them – on the contrary). The reasons are obvious. But the mediologist cannot help observing that at Yad Vashem, however austere the site, there is much to be seen and heard – images and sounds, strikingly present – whereas in the magnificent underground space of the Shrine of the Book there is nothing to do but decipher – or attempt to.

Change or die: such is the dilemma specific to every natural or supernatural being transplanted into an environment that is foreign to its habits and physiology. Fundamentalism is suicidal. Every tradition is a machine for killing time, and is in that sense vital, but it cannot function without consenting to a few transactions with the ambient flow. Tele-evangelism, for example, is a form of folklore, but one which is eloquent as to the instinct for survival through which a religion of the written adapts to the videosphere.

The features of that strange – and yet very much *our* – mediasphere have been described a hundred times over: the primacy of the emotive over the discursive, the instant over the process, the individual over the group, the authentic over the true, parataxis (passive juxtaposition) over syntax (constructed organization), scandals over mysteries. We will not revisit that terrain for the nth time. The adaptive response, coming from the 'old Churches': a change of vehicle from the doctrinal to the charismatic and a transposition into the pastoral realm of the 'sacredness of the moment' – trips with maximal trappings, continent-wide ceremonies, prayer conventions. Without privileged moments, no information. And no info, no existence. Protestant Pentecostalism and Catholic mysticism have a bright future in a world of communicators, and in all probability it is they who will be increasingly setting the tone to Christians under siege. If one wants to be no longer up to date, but on line and in the swing, one has to become interactive and contextual – and sacrifice one's writings to background music (guitar, drum, saxophone). Audio doesn't demand the same attention as reading in private, on which a suspicion of antisociability weighs. As a result, instituted religions are no longer called on to set forth *truths* (deposited in minuscule characters in texts and encased in boxes), but to offer *values* (sensory and participatory *frissons*). Make way for 'strong signs' that 'give meaning'. From the event that it was, the Resurrection has become a vague allegory (Drewermann).

What fate does the post-literary era have in store for the religions of the Book? They worship a God that is to be deciphered, and not stared down ('no one shall see my face without dying', He warned in the beginning, speaking to Moses). And maintain that the image of God, when authorized, is never God, who is the Word set down, Bible or Koran. Will our meta-book retain its exceptional status in relation to ordinary books? With its imaginary capital in meltdown, our commonplace paper brick has taken refuge in a minimally innervated recess of the social body. If its patina still makes it an obligatory stop in the trajectory of heroes of the image – entrepreneurs, actors, singers and politicians – for whom a duly authored volume serves as an auspicious calling card, its ability to command a public, in depth and breadth, diminishes every day (as we can easily see if we compare the different degrees of prestige and ways of life found in the book-, sound-, and image-producing communities). Our ability to read, our sensitivity to the mimetic continuum of literary reworkings, rivalries and parodies which haunts an author's every text (as the history of painting inhabits the most minor sketch of Goya or Picasso), is gently being extinguished. The promoters of literary broadcasts, as a form of exoneration, and also to attract a young audience, talk about defending 'the written in the broad sense'. Would the literal sense frighten them away? Complaints and sermons are useless. The law of the milieu: *dura lex sed lex*. Our new information and communication technologies unsettle simultaneously the mode of reproduction of texts, their support, and our ways of reading (which the printing press, in its time, had modified only slightly). With the dematerialized (and, into the bargain, desacralized) book begins an a-biblical world, invaded by 'culture' and deserted by the practice of reading. *A-biblical* may be said of a world in which writing circulates more cheerfully than it did before, but in which the book, transformed into a database manipulable at will, has lost its symbolic centrality, which now accrues to utilitarian printouts and selective reappropriations. The book in fragments. God in pieces?

The French term for computer, *ordinateur*, is a word out of church Latin, designating the person who presides over an ordination, confers the sacrament. Christ was called the 'ordainer' in the thirteenth century, a term that Malebranche also applied to God. He who disposes of things in an order, a rank of succession (the ordinal, as opposed to the cardinal), and to whom we are all subordinated. The word *ordinateur* has prospered, but our computerized Babel juxtaposes without ordering. The new dance of traces and bodies shakes the columns of the temple while awakening the wanderlust of both. For the digital attacks the fixity of words (the problematic copyright of websites). The sign overflows, scurries off, takes flight in every direction. It may be assumed that the Bible will not be too out of place on the Web, since it was already, with its hypertextual links and mirrorings, an 'electronic text' *avant* the byte: a book never closed but prolonged by commentaries, malleable, indefinitely annotated, without a recognized author, in which one can navigate from book to book, and which would have eluded the bourgeois rules of literary property had they existed. Incommensurability and polyphony are the characteristics of Holy Scripture, but they were obscured by the physical unity of the collection (in its paper version), which extended its unity to its putative author, God. The computerized edition, particularly well adapted to our millennial miscellanea, comes too late to broach the canonical integrity of the collection. The Bible will remain what it is, for a practice of reading that already is no longer such, but 'a book changes by virtue of the fact that it does not change while the world changes' (Roger Chartier). The establishment of correspondences between everything and everything on the Web, the effacement of narrative, can only deprive it of its overriding eminence. But far more compromising for the higher Authority than the dispersion of His traces is the risk entailed by that of His faithful.

What is the original *Ordinateur* to do in the face of our contemporary *ordinateurs*? Transform Himself, of course. The correlative of libraries without readers, where people come for the Internet, is religions without dogmas, and priests without cassocks. From the networks of tomorrow, we can expect an e-God just in time – commutable, telecommandable, and without copyright.

A good for an ill. Every new machine generates one form of servitude while liberating us from another. The alphabet of the desert delivered us from mother-goddesses and entrusted us to a people of a unique cast, a link between the Lord and the nations. The handwritten *codex* delivered that written God from His confinement to a holy land, making Him universal and shareable, not merely in theory but in fact. The hand press shattered the ecclesiastical confinement, opening Him up to the polyglot free will of all. It freed the only God from the only Church, and the believer from the Latin of the clerics. From what will digitalized reproduction and the realm of telepresence currently deliver us? From the notion of integrity. From the notion of an integral whole. Hence the emergence of a divinity in kits, atomized, in modules, optional, amenable to tinkering, collages and deviations (like an installation in contemporary art). Religions without God are the most detotalized, deconfessionalized, deregulated and, consequently, the most competitive. The spiritual no longer broadcasts on a frequency – or, rather, every denomination has its own, one among others, it being up to us to surf channels. From the Pope to the Dalai Lama, by way of His Beatitude and the self-appointed Patriarch. A veritable bouquet of grand sorcerers competing freely.

What emerges from all this, for the Eternal of old, is a new kind of governance. The pastor of his flock is now the CEO of a series of social-service industries (baptisms, marriages, burials). With a clientele to be seen to. What is a customer? A *user who has a choice*. Not a believer: a member. Of a club or an association, with a considerably expanded margin of freedom. Now when it comes to the goods of salvation, a globalized consumer has an *embarras du choix* with which to load his supermarket cart. A bit of Zen, a session of transcendental meditation, a dose of reincarnation, a touch of Talmud – not forgetting an emergency ration of the angelic, just in case. The most confident can round things off with the X-Files or an extraterrestrial conspiracy. The result: in the market of beliefs, as in that of votes and brands, the firms of the Lord are obliged to adapt to the desires of the customer-surfer-king. Such obligatory marketing is known euphemistically as 'the obligation to respond to the expectations of society'.

From the deliberations of the radio-photo prize committee, Walter Benjamin observed in the 1930s, there emerged two winners: the dictator and the vamp. Ferocity and Allure. From the Hertz-Byte committee, which has taken over from the first, the singer and the guru emerge on top. In order to counter the *aestheticization of politics*, which peaked with Nazi Nuremberg's cathedrals of light, the German philosopher proposed that we *politicize aesthetics* (which did not work out). To counter *the aestheticization of the spiritual*, with shows on superscreens, one might be tempted to *spiritualize aesthetics*, but the result would hardly be more convincing.

The Mediator at Risk in the Media

The unstable sociabilities of the Net and individualist underestimation strike at the heart, and thus at the spirit, of consecration rites (a priest does not say Mass alone). It is the gathering that ensures the sharing of Word and Bread, *in praesentia*. And the two meanings of communion cannot be dissociated. Real telepresence, in this respect, remains an aporia, and the teledistribution of the Eucharistic species remains a square circle. If the mystical body becomes a random assemblage of believers, to what extent will it remain mystical? Such is the *embarras des projets* for virtual churches, and already, it may be anticipated, of televised Masses. Someone who attends a service in front of his TV is no longer an agent but a receiver, prey to aesthetic passivity (the Mass as a beautiful spectacle), and deprived of the thrill of being together, in the same space. The screen does not institute a site – or, rather, it transforms the sonorized and filmed nave into a non-site, like petrol stations, toll booths and supermarkets, all substitutable for each other. By distancing me from my fellow man (or by bringing me closer to what is distant), the tele-totality helps to atomize the people of God just that little bit more, which is not much help to the Eucharist. Non-soil-grown tomatoes are edible, though they're a bit tasteless; but liturgies? Can there be a telesacrament as there is telelabour? There is a threshold in the scale of disembodiment beyond which transmission fails and the Spirit takes off at a tangent, so consubstantial is Incarnation to it. Losing the ceremonial site as well as the Book which holds its readers would be tantamount to deactivating grace. In sixteenth-century Northern Europe the mobile character of type shattered the mediation of the ecclesial body. If on-line and off-line procedures were to shatter, along with the *in-situ*, the body itself, it would no longer mean a renewal but an implosion. God can do without a Sovereign Pontiff – but not without a physical assemblage of celebrants.

The technologies of live broadcasting do not tolerate what has been recorded (which amounts to everything charged with conveying what has been consigned, entrusted – faith, knowledge or rules). As a result our various institutional bodies have been laid waste one after another: State, School, Justice, Army. And the Christian Churches, starting with the most constrained and constraining, the Roman Apostolic, are in the firing range of immediacy. Jesus himself, our first mass-medium, is not really at ease in the mass media, and his servants even less so. Let us pass over the matter of holy icons. Visual messages, Valéry used to say, concern the most men possible only because they 'demand the least Man possible'. The Son of Man, in the movies or a photograph, no longer prompts one to lower one's eyes or raise one's head. The slippage from vision to 'the visual' (when the image of the divine no longer corresponds to an experience of the divine) – iconoclastic out of an excess of idolatry – has seen the advent of a way of looking that is detached, even excited, but from which all value of transcendence has been banished.

It is the inelegance of conviction, the awkwardness of faith, that currently provoke the gibes of good taste. 'Angelism' and pious kitsch satisfy our thirst for mockery. A concern for the other world, when the reign of pleasure calls on us every other minute in this one? The suggestion is laughable. Catholics feel the most derided, and are prepared to see themselves as the sacrificial victims of the ambient collapse of deference, even as they try, in a thousand ways, to find their own niche (through the celebrity system, media events, sensationalism). Protestants would be most justified in protesting, but there are too few of them in France to attract derision. Judaism is sacralized by the Shoah, Islam by antiracism, and evangelism by its low profile. But Protestants, the pioneers of the modern revolution, have not reaped any dividends for their efforts, and this is surely unfair. Lack of an emblematic leader (no photo-ops), limited doctrinal authority, complexity of positions, negligible folklore: the Reformed have suffered the greatest penalty, not only because they lack glitz (without an identifiable head, there can be no attractive body), but because of the massive return of magic and the occult to the airwaves. In addition to a depressing past (in brief: the Inquisition, the Saint Bartholomew's Day Massacre, Galileo, Pétain), Catholics – at least in France – have the disadvantage of being numerous and, worse still, middle-of-the-road. The media sieve is better at retaining ostentatious minorities, histrionic and aggressively promoted identities. Emotional and pathos-laden attitudes thus benefit from a bonus, when it comes to exposure, which the centrists of God are denied. In the competition among victims, Catholics, however, are not at the greatest disadvantage, inasmuch as cameras and microphones, drawn to the powerful, are reserved for Eminences. Whence an over-exposure of the (otherwise unattractive) hierarchy. If we add to the picture, for France, the rumours of paedophilia (19 priests out of 25,000 found guilty as of 2000), we can agree that this is not an auspicious moment for members of the faith. There will be better ones.

Saturation of Space, Evacuation of Time

The refrain of the 'end of history' is borrowed from the same European author, Hegel, who first announced to us, in his *Faith and Knowledge* (1802), 'with infinite pain', the death of God. A romantic tremor which he endowed with speculative breadth. It will be maintained that History has never stopped ending, nor God dying. There remains, none the less, an undeniable correlation between expectation – the fact that we no longer anticipate (from any future) something essentially different from our present – and – in tandem – the fact that we no longer peg our felicities and griefs to a suprahuman design. The more Europe de-Judaeo-Christianizes, the more it depoliticizes. It was the unconscious remorse of Abraham's forward thrust that impelled us towards the forum, the secular theatre of the sacred Promise. In which context François Mauriac is succinct: 'My vocation is political to the precise extent that it is religious. I am engaged in problems here below for reasons from on high.' Impossible to have faith without having hope. And hope without wanting to do things. 'Is a faith that does not act a sincere faith?', asked Corneille. The salvation *in* history of the Christian is not the salvation *through* history of the militant, but our late religions of temporal salvation were the tails of the comet of our mother-religion. What will our revolutionary militancy turn out to have been, when the verdict is in, if not Judaeo-Christian hope less *contemptus mundi*? It is naive to oppose point by point the dependency on the past of religiously governed societies to the orientation towards the future of political ideologies. Societies that are anterocentric and those that are futurocentric. The alleged transition from religion to ideology (to use particularly crude terms) was effected in and by way of the religious. The radiant future of 'scientific socialism' rediscovered humanity's infancy, primitive communism, and the inception of Christianity was the thrilling announcement of Joy at the end, the Resurrection. Who can fail to see that the believer's past is a loan taken out on the future? The socialist and the Christian each had a *destiny* to accomplish, in opposition to the *fate* which is the lot of every Eternal Return. We were here to suffer, to be sure, but we did so in order to precipitate the end of days, clearing the way, taking the intitiative. No question of slacking. The Reformed – in whose view original sin was too crushing for our own merits to be able to save us from it, counting as they did on grace alone to redeem us – were by no means the last to put their hearts into the effort and their money aside. Defining the world, with Calvin, as 'the theatre of God's glory' could arouse only a desire to take to the stage. No doubt the founding event – Judaic revelation, Christian incarnation – had something limiting about it. Mass was already said. What might occur could only take up anew, repeat, confirm what already was. Despite such rehearsals, a redemptive project staked out the path (on which nothing was determined in advance), which, as a result, ceased to be a random collection of anecdotes, a museum of horrors. There was a period of incubation, a trajectory, and a finality. With a launching point (Sinai, Golgotha) and a vanishing point (the Millennium, the earthly Jerusalem). The Eternal spiritualized the ephemeral. We would not have idolized the course of things under the name of Progress if an extrovert God had not, from the time of His Hebrew birth, inhabited and unsettled it. Western morality recognized itself in action because our share of eternity realized itself in history. That militancy stemmed from that destination. The design of salvation degraded into a craving for 'still more'? A contraband millenarianism, a sacrilegious caricature, 'Christian ideas gone mad' – as has been said over and again – but it conveyed the dimension of a future prospect: the International Brigades, and the Commission for the Plan. 'And all to me was promise ... .' Once upon a time, young people wanted to *do something*; these days they want to *be someone*. Right away. Currently, when everything takes place in the present, we can breathe in the fresh air on the edge of the lapping waves. Events are noisier; the melody is gone. Squeaks, for lack of a theme. Whether endearing or unhealthy, reading the newspaper is no longer our morning prayer. To whom are we to speak? The lack of suspense makes the world of the news simultaneously stupefying and unappetizing. Everything comes to us directly – but of what use is synchrony if the marrow of becoming has vanished? The Word has silently fled, and the flesh of catastrophes sinks into itself, a wobbling, witless cellulitis that makes one want to look the other way. After *allegro con brio*, *syncopation*. Techno. The electro-Bacchic fury of our raves; the mesmerizing rhythms of techno-paganism. Ecstasy for all.

Our ferocious innocence, our thirst for purity, our obsession with evil have prompted us to flee – via the occult and our various highs, with or without 'acid' – the labor of the negative and the anxiety of the furrow. Which is not – far from it – the morose contemplation of what is condemned to disappear or the conventional melancholy of ruins, but the fear provoked (not merely among virtue-trippers) by the compromises of action and the deviations entailed by any journey through time. The reduction of shouts to written form frightens us. Fleeing reality towards principle, history towards intentionality, and duration towards the moment are three aspects of a common movement – of withdrawal. Everything is coherent. The current fashion of moralism would be less, from this perspective, a sequel to Christianity than the shell left by its ebbing. We no longer know how to articulate the Infinite with the finite. Nor yesterday with tomorrow. Nor words with deeds. We have lost the instructions. Jehovah was not a prize for virtue, and for a Judaeo-Christian there is no universal without a particular (translate: no morality without a politics). At least, not if sermons are to commit us to anything. It was all too uncomfortable and risky, the Incarnation. It plunged us into dubious battles, more bitter than sweet. With the abstract universal, we felt sheltered, on the side of Good, and free to withdraw our stake from the game. Handsome in the mirror.

It is rare to be able to escape the innocence of inaction without substituting time for space in the hierarchy of official values. Such was the exploit of Judaism. The authors of the Bible (who have accustomed their descendants to subordinate geography to history) recount far better than they describe. The plot, in the Law and the Prophets, blinds us to the setting. Men of God have eyes only for the end and the origin. Excellent genealogists and mediocre landscapists. Good predictions, but rather imprecise surveys. Such was no doubt the artistic and literary price to be paid for the transition from repetitive myth to active history, or from the magic of places to obsession with an aim. And now, curiously, we appear to be backtracking. We no longer await our salvation from a tomorrow (nor tomorrow as salvation), but from an *elsewhere*. We have replaced messianism with tourism, and expect more precious secrets from interstellar space than from our origins. Space is again becoming the criterion of bliss. Do Egypt in a week. We are in seventh heaven when we have gone from one point to another in the shortest possible time. Formula 1, ritual of the century, *nec plus ultra* of temporal ecstasy.

  We have mastered distances so effectively that we replace temporal substance with time-as-distance (subway-minute, train-hour, light-year). We flee 'dead time' like the plague. In the blink of an eye, the 'short twentieth century' – separating the bicycle from the supersonic plane – has inverted its parameters: distances travelled are of little concern, but the slightest delay has become unbearable (for us, who are no longer painters or gardeners). The sacredness of records broken, commando operations, and flash sequences is what has been left to us, in His retreat, by a distant and slow God, who would take time to keep His promises and was not particularly fond of any jostling at the gates. Our happiness is no longer in the patience of the road, advancing together, 'forward march!' – but in the immediate and egotistical occupation of an exclusionary space, our lifeless 'living space'. Every man for himself – preferably in his own home.

The Revenge of the East

The obsolescence of the media of the alphabetical God is of no small consequence in this shift from a conquest of time to a conquest of space. Specifically: from a culture of collective *accomplishment* to a culture of personal *fulfilment*. The man without a calling can regard his debt to history as liquidated. Which means that our saints will no longer be heroes – those of medieval and classical Christianity often wore two helmets – nor our monks soldiers. In the West the decline of the militant, an intimate of Becoming, serves the cause of the champions of renunciation. The servants of the sacred, in the public squares in front of derelict cathedrals, will soon be sitting in the lotus position, bestowing flowers on tourists.

Kipling, in the end, got it wrong. The 'twain' – East and West – are indeed meeting, as the West becomes Easternized. It has lost its cardiac stimulator and is in quest of serenity. The former Author of its days had made it anxious about redeeming its sin, and out of that anxiety it had forged its signal virtue: salvation through action. A violent virtue laden with crimes against humanity, if we take into account the Crusades, colonization, the slave trade, and the destruction *manu militare* of 'strange gods'. But a *dynamic* virtue. Western man was reputed to be active, concerned, enterprising. He took things in hand. He wanted to become master and possessor of nature. He had a will to organize. He called that impatient asceticism activism. The model was provided by the Only God, who filled our calendar day by day without leaving anything to chance. A strange Absolute for the West, who did not live self-enclosed, like those Eastern gods whose attributes are more easily apprehended than their noble deeds. They do not get overly involved in our petty affairs, do not conjugate verbs in the future tense, are not interventionist by nature, and are frankly apolitical (Eastern Christianity being already more static and contemplative). No winged couriers to facilitate their work. Our God, prescribing engagement, did not surround His throne with assistants in order to escape boredom, but to change the course of the world. His altogether angelic militarism helped Him to militate. In brief, along with God the Father, it is a bit of the specificity of the West which has left the scene. A kind of levelling has occurred, by way of macrobiotics, between the tranquil East and the industrious West, a progress in the globalization of souls. Abraham's mentor was too great a departure from the absentee deities of calmer times. His dismissal will make the 'dialogue of cultures' easier (a net gain for UNESCO conferences).

We have long opposed History to Nature. A rhetorical seesaw? Perhaps, but also a springboard for finding a 'way out'. That spring is about to lose its tension: human history is in the process of becoming zoological again. The biological is winning out. Volcanic eruptions, tsunamis, floods, heatwaves, cold waves and earthquakes have always existed, but for a little while – two or three centuries – we thought they had receded into the background. And here we are again with air, water and fire at the centre of the news. Parliamentary life, party directives, are disappearing in the face of an unleashing of the elements, accidents that we might see as forming a circular sequence. Storms, droughts, shipwrecks, pandemics, avalanches, pollution, land-slides, illnessess. The history of wills, for which we had been prepared by 'salvation through works', is coming to a gentle close. It was a mere interlude. And the history without history of an animal species, reverting to its low-water mark, the struggle for life, begins anew. A species for which the climate, viruses and other domestic species, mad cow and scabby sheep, are the source of many a misfortune, but which muddles on, from one catastrophe to the next. Surviving is already quite enough.

One of the ironic and rather sympathetic features of climate change and the mutation of species is the revenge – indeed, the triumph – of cultural formulae that had previously been considered marginal, because they were out of place. In Dahomey, the young goat, thick of fleece, runs less rapidly than the others because its muscles get overheated. The hyena, descending on the flock, will devour it first. 'Having disappeared early on, it will not reproduce', notes Bernard Stiegler, the inventor of this little mediological fable. But let the climate drop a few degrees, and the isothermal handicap will fall to the other members of the flock, with their insufficient coat of fleece, whose turn it will be to serve as nourishment for the predators. With the ensuing re-emergence, in full glory, of the thick-fleeced goat. Traits which begin as negative become positive according to whether the thermo-meter rises or descends. Unadapted to the military–industrial society of yesterday, a variety of Buddhisms show themselves to be well adapted to the bio-informational age of today. A world of networks is a world whose beginning is everywhere and whose end is nowhere. That is well suited to the grand cosmic cycles (regeneration/ destruction) of the spiritualities of the East. Thus, from having been mere philo-sophical curiosities in Schopenhauer's day, the Eastern schools have been broadly acclimatized. Non-violence, the priority of working on oneself in polite indifference towards the other, the absence of a stable and closed corpus, ignorance of sin, individual death as a recycling not in the beyond but right here on earth – all these features, which had previously been irritants because they ran against the grain, have become harmonious corrective responses in our denatured and chlorophyll-starved sphere. Such is the case for techniques of psycho-corporeal well-being, such as Yoga or certain forms of secular Zen.[3] Hindu Atman, the Upanishads or the *Bhagavad-gita* are also looking less archaic. An undifferentiated Absolute – alien to time, inviting a non-dualism, transplanted into a post-Cartesian world in which man seeks to reintegrate himself into the long chain of living creatures and surrounds himself more than ever, in the city, with pets – suddenly seems more 'modern' than our Gospels. Closer to the gentle green symbolism whose nostalgia moves us. Communing with the cosmos, losing oneself in the All, no longer being locked into the human: these vegetarian formulae resonate better and better with the East of our soul, and that East is moving into our homes. A reversal of poles.

Twilight of God, Morning of the Magicians

Here, then, is our current excess placed in perspective. The nocturnal face of man can turn in every direction. Christianity is becoming Easternized, but Hinduism is being Westernized, like Zen. Centre and periphery have changed positions. The globalization of beliefs has crossed the cardinal points of cultures.

What is clear – to remain within the Western perimeter – is that the closing of the literary cycle similarly concerns belief in heaven – or not. Is the transmission of the religious legacy fading? That of the literary legacy as well. Is Saint Thomas leaving us, along with Pascal and Saint Teresa? But so is Virgil, along with Montaigne and Diderot. The humanities are undergoing the same disasters as the catechism; the literary competition the same abandonment as the sermon. Fewer literary texts, newspaper articles and iconographic documents in French class. No more grammar, but 'creativity'. The patrimonial catastrophe of the Eternal begins, for us in France, with the difficult apprenticeship in reading and writing in primary school, the collapse of the language a few years later, the consignment to the rubbish dump of the Letters curriculum in lycées, and the organized mockery of the teaching of philosophy in the final year. Our God is made of the same textual fabric as our secularity. Which might have issued in a joint programme. For communicating the archives of the Eternal to a dyslexic younger generation would be of interest to neither one nor the other. But beyond the alphabet, which bound (though they were unaware of it) those *frères ennemis*, the believing Christian and the secular humanist, it appears that either of them would be surprised by a bizarre result that contradicts the contrary expectations, fears or hopes, common to both spiritual families: the death of God has not meant, as had been feared or hoped, the birth of a man wholly and only man. Which gives our late modernity an Alexandrine air of

---

[3] See Éric Rommeluère, 'Un Zen à l'occidentale est-il possible?', *Voies de l'Orient* (Brussels, July–September 2001).

late Antiquity (we, too, have our great libraries and museums). The disenchantment of the world through its rationalization – a short-term prediction, with my apologies in advance to received opinion – just will not do. The juxtaposition of a God in peril and believers in full bloom invites us to reconsider several all-too-convenient presuppositions.

When a majority of young Europeans declare that they no longer believe in God, but in 'something after death'; when two out of three French citizens are anxious to have a religious burial, whereas only one in ten goes to Mass on Sunday; when the notion of reincarnation convinces a third of eighteen-to-twenty-four-year-olds, who more or less confuse it with the Resurrection, what do we discover? That our ancestral God is perfectly separable from modes of supernatural life, which have no need of Him in order to regain their ascendancy. The social and therapeutic functions assumed by Christian churches lead us to wonder whether God was not ultimately a *burdensome accessory* for collective credulities. 'Sire, I had no need for that hypothesis.' Might not a prosperous and syncretic market of individual salvation, with an eschatological offer reduced to the affective, adopt as its own Laplace's celebrated reply to Napoleon, who asked him where he had lodged the Creator in his celestial mechanics?

When we witness the rise of spiritualities drawn from the East, in which 'everything is God except God': the surge of Katmandu-style cults which teach that 'the gods circulate among men and that they live in each of us'; and the neopaganisms of *cybermagic*, not to mention the various Solar Temples which have been hauled into court, what do we find? That the decline of the traditional religions of the West marks a *return to the long tradition* of the species. The God who was to the world 'what an inventor is to his machine, what a prince is to his subjects, and even what a father is to his children' (Leibniz) is again becoming the good old cosmic torch 'whose flies we are'. A return to the fold of the prodigal son, to the blindness of high noon: the cult of the Egyptian and Canaanite sun from which the children of Israel had been able to extricate themselves only with great difficulty.

When we see the fortune, now officially academic, of astral fluid (the subject of a doctoral degree granted by eminent sociologists at the Université René-Descartes), of homoeopathy, parasciences and 'paranormal' phenomena (sorcerers, alchemists, healers, parapsychologists, exorcists, bone-setters, etc.), without mentioning the Princeton 'Gnostics' and Paolo Coelhos of the moment, what do we find? That the absence of religion has resulted not in incredulity, but in superstition. As though the aberrant obsession with security, once freed from the yoke of dogmas and institutions, could at last give itself free rein (the efforts at channelling have failed, and things are beginning to overflow). Not only have our systems of explanation not eliminated 'irrational fears', but by putting an end to the universe's rotation around the human navel, they have, rather, aggravated them. We knew that 'la pensée sauvage', as Lévi-Strauss called it, duplicated the other, but it was never said that it would succeed it. Scientific prudence, the self-limitation of bodies of positive knowledge, and a concern for rigour leave fallow a number of vital areas (death, origins, the beyond) that abhor a vacuum. The dispellers of uncertainty, emerging from the Neolithic, are staging a return (Victor Hugo, an anticlerical of impeccable credentials and a practising spiritualist, was already consulting ghosts, just as a certain socialist president consulted his clairvoyants ...). Are we so certain that the nocturnal declines when the educational level rises? Has it not been established that atheist individualists are more prone to phone their fortune-tellers than practising believers prudently integrated into their parish? The Catholic Church (and *a fortiori* the Protestant Churches as well) forbid all forms of divination, horoscope or Tarot, occult influence or the wearing of amulets, etc., since 'the proper Christian attitude consists in placing oneself with trust in the hands of Providence and abandoning all unhealthy curiosity regarding such subjects'.[4] He who would know the future ahead of time would expropriate God's prerogatives. A sacrilegious will to power. This anecdotal example serves as a reminder that before Reason, the Only God had already disenchanted the cosmos. His imitations, or his metastases, might soon find us missing the Original.

---

[4] *Catéchisme pour adultes*, The Bishops of France, pp. 497–8.

12 The Eternity of the Eternal

The skeleton alone is eternal.
(Anna de Noailles)

The idols revolve, but the axis on which the carousel turns, the incurable believer, remains perpetually ready for one more round of faith. Our ways of belief change with our contrivances, but not our disposition to believe. Why? Because of an incompletion, which does us great wrong but which eludes our will, we cannot come together with our fellow creatures to construct durable and distinct collective personalities without opening ourselves up to 'something that transcends us'. Pascal already observed as much: 'Man transcends man infinitely.' The immanence of a social system is incapable of thwarting on its own the forces of death and division that were once called diabolical without an extrinsic point of reference which cannot belong to the system which it grounds, and which that system can in no way justify. This is the handicap within which, in our view, the invariant of religious variations dwells. The resurgence of mysticism – and there is no way of foreseeing its end – would thus appear to be ineluctable. The progress of science and technology will no doubt impede neither the vital impulsion to believe nor the concomitant violence.

A warning. At this point in the itinerary, the philosopher takes over from the mediologist, and the questioner from the investigator. That change of designation is not in order to draw the moral of the story – a moral we do not know, and a story that is not over (if the Apocalypse, despite massacres, comes neither today nor tomorrow). But out of a simple concern for honesty, as when one reveals one's cards. 'Where is he speaking from, anyway?' The investigator, up until now, had been walking in the footsteps of a Fugitive, without overly distancing himself too far from his visible tracks. The questioner will ask whose prints they are, and why people run after the Infinite so tirelessly. Where does our demand for saviours and mysteries come from, and how are we to explain that the effacement of God as a proper noun gives rise to so many demigods – taken as a common noun? Such are the probably insoluble questions one can broach only indirectly, and at one's own risk. As a dreamer, an idler or an adventurer.

'I Advance Masked'

But first of all, just who is this Shadow you've been telling us about for three hundred pages? Would it not be simple courtesy to show us his papers? And identify the universal Sphinx? No. Impossible. Were there a clear answer, there would no longer be a question. There would be no subject. Nor any interest. Nor foundation. It is the characteristic of a foundation is to be unfounded. If it could be deduced from a founding principle, it would not found anything. The guarantor is never guaranteed, which is precisely what the professionals sense when they 'avoid the subject' or 'refrain from definitions'. Consult the authorities. 'Of God,' said Saint Thomas, 'it is easier to say what He is not than what He is.' He searched for rational proofs of God's existence (*An Deus sit ...*), out of academic obligation, but in spite of himself. When one truly believes, one keeps silent. *Cordon sanitaire*: keep out. Woe unto whosoever speaks of God! Whence the whirligig of indifference in which the universal Creator has been caught ever since He entered the lists, and which confronts Him alternately with either blind prostration or a shrug of the shoulders. He cannot be the object of critical discussion in the societies over which His shadow is cast, which consider the slightest distance taken from Him a form of sacrilege. But when they no longer believe in him, the discussion would be regarded as idle and pointless (we've moved beyond all that). Such is the misfortune of the Father. He excites either too much interest, or none at all. The result: the joker in the pack has become the ace.

Rationalists should not rejoice too quickly over the adversity of their Rival, since we ourselves are victims of a similar aporia. A scientific theory cannot furnish an absolute justification of the principles on which it rests, since only one of two situations can apply. Either such justification would presuppose the introduction of additional principles which would than have to be demonstrated in turn, and we are confronted with an infinite regress. Or the theory demonstrates its principles through the consequences whose foundation they enable, and we have lapsed into circular reasoning. We are thus obliged to call a halt at some point – arbitrarily. At that postulate or axiom beyond which it has been decided (or requested) that we should not go. The Eternal, in this perspective, is the *postulate* of Judaeo-Christian systems. Such is the stroke of genius in Revelation: to assume to the limit the aporia of a beginning by inscribing it into a history as brute fact. There was a break at a specific moment, an interruption in the course of things, and nothing can be done about it. The 'no need to look any further' puts a halt to sterile regression *ad infinitum* (what is the source of the source? And the genesis of Genesis?, etc.). God justifies and explains because He is inexplicable and unjustifiable. *Credo quia absurdum*. Wherever it may be, the first principle remains 'up in the air'. In a more down-to-earth idiom, the most fragile stone in a building is its cornerstone. Which is precisely what the inhabitants of an edifice of faith understand when they declare it untouchable: let us not run the risk. *Branlante* [tottering] means decisive and undecidable, without obvious or univocal answer. A contemporary example, between the political and the religious: Israel defines itself as 'a Jewish state in the land of Israel'. Every Jew throughout the world has the right to immigrate. Whence the practical question: what is a Jew? There is no clear and definitive, unanimously accepted answer to that question of definition even in Israel itself. Everyone has his own. Better, then, to leave the cornerstone aside. Everywhere what is most vital, socially, is what is least certain, logically. The institutive process is what the Institution bans as a topic for discussion (*m*). Scientific activity avoids speculating as to what, basically, a scientific result is, and active mathematicians spend little time wondering about the status of mathematical idealities (creations of the mind or realities in themselves, pre-existent to our calculations?). One no more discusses God in a monastery than one discusses truth in a laboratory (or rope in the home of a man who has been hanged). And one is right not to: wherever one may be, conventions are required, and they are arbitrary. Don't press the point.

As it happens, the definitional weakness of the Principle makes for its organizational strength. God would lose His capacity to unite the dispersed if He were obliged to weigh Himself down with attributes and properties. As with Constitutions: the shortest ones are the best. Brevity may be the soul of governance, or even absence. 'God is cruelly lacking to me' indicates a profound goodness on His part: He saturates with His absence. Insane? Yes, which is why it works. For the real world cannot find the sources of its value in itself. Our buildings need domes or cupolas, and when they collapse, we are obliged to rebuild. The strength of the Absolute is to be relational. There is no God in Himself, but always for someone. Therein lies His usefulness: to serve as the wholly Other for the Same, to bring air into our closed precincts.

The fact that a scientific theory cannot exhibit a principle with absolute validity does not prevent it from producing interesting results. A monotheist has no need to furnish proofs of the existence of God in order to 'do his work' and give rise, here and there, to imaginary and experiential coherences. Similarly, the fact that the idea of God has a history, as have mathematics and even ethics, is not proof that it is without validity (and, even less, without utility). Religious belief has its strong reasons, which are not those of Reason. It can be demonstrated that it constitutes a valid choice in its own realm, which is not that of logical argument but, rather, of the *conatus*, the tendency of every being to persist in its being. It is thus understandable that the monotheistic innovation could, wherever it was proposed, be selected (and not rejected) by the evolution of the species. It was not imposed by force alone. Nor by a conspiracy of the priestly party, intent on abusing the credulous masses. Physical violence lasts only for a time. As does social conditioning. They alone do not explain a survival this long. It may be legitimately imagined that the synthetic proposition was adopted and re-exported because its effects, upon experience, revealed themselves to be positive for the physical health of communities thus joined, as well as for individuals. Or at least positive enough to balance out, in the long term, its negative effects, and to compensate for the costs of its adoption. Bergson was of the opinion that in order to find religion, it was enough to 'resituate man within the realm of the living and psychology within biology'. He would have been happy to learn from contemporary neurology that 'transcendent unitary states' have a beneficial effect on the hypothalamus and the autonomous nervous system. 'Studies have shown that participation in spiritual activities such as prayer, services or meditation can reduce blood pressure and heartbeat, lower cortisone levels and produce improvements in an individual's immunological system.'[1] Believers can hope for a better life, fewer heart attacks and less heart disease

---

[1] Andrew Newberg and Eugene d'Aquila, *Why God Won't Go Away: Brain Science and the Biology of Belief* (New York: Ballantine 2001), p. 6.

than other people (all things being otherwise equal). Dr Koenig of the Duke University Medical Center reports that a lack of religious commitment has an effect on mortality equal to forty years of smoking one pack of cigarettes a day. America has succeeded in reconciling apologetics and physiology, and why indeed reject the raw data accumulated by physicians and psychiatrists from across the Atlantic?

And man said let the Eternal be, and man saw that it was good. And he kept Him above himself. More or less concealed by the clouds, depending on latitude and weather conditions.

Futuristic and Archaic?

The divine weather forecast is not as bleak as we may have suggested. Our historical sequences could have been deployed differently, and it would not have been the chronicle of a death foretold, but the oblique fulfilment of the great Promise. As though our heavenly Houdini had more than one trick up his sleeve. As though the history of His doubles were not part of His own. Once the illusion of an immobile Eternal – like a porcupine rolled up in a ball to resist the assaults of secularization – has been dissipated, the itinerary of the Only One in the West turns out to support a reading not in terms of decline, as we have done, but of ascent. In the three levels we have descended, corresponding to three millennia, an optimistic child of Abraham will be able to sort out as many phases of an unrelenting ascent towards a universally acknowledged Mount Sinai, from which a vigorous Moses would shine forth, having drawn on the best of all worlds. That culminating point might almost be called an *atheistic monotheism*. It would be the mix of ingredients successively gathered in the course of its advance in order to correct one local accent by another. Yahweh would have supplied the basic foundations, with the dogma of the Law. Christ would have fulfilled them, sweetening them with the notion of the person and inner morality. Mohammed, observing Christianity abandoning its original project of radically reforming fundamentally unjust societies, would have added a strong dose of social equality (hence his contemporary success). And a Buddha, arriving in our latitudes out of curiosity, saddened to see how little place monotheisms give to living nature, would have poured into the mix a measure of compassion for all animate beings. Into the multicultural shaker, our agnostic piety, not wanting to be left out, spiced the mixture with the universal Declaration of the Rights of Man, the Geneva conventions, humanitarian interventions, a touch of spiritual tourism, and a pinch of astrology. By now there is something for every taste – or rather, as in the films and meals known in French as *avionables*, fit for aeroplanes, the brew would be sufficiently insipid not to upset any palate, and thus fit to be served to all passengers, of whatever origin, opinion or religion.

What we are thus caricaturing is a process of moral industrialization whose reality no one would seek to deny and which began within our theologies. Each god used his local predecessor as a step on the ladder that allowed him to climb higher and embrace more widely. He extracted what was most exportable or generalizable. The Yahweh of the Jews appropriated the cosmic and ethical virtues of El, principal god of the Canaanites, who also struggled against the underground god of the great waters (the god Moth, who became our Behemoth), cutting 'flames of fire' and 'making the wilderness tremble' (as is repeated in Psalm 29). Christ, when his turn came, took from the national religion what was already universal in it – as we find, for example, in Isaiah, when the prophet sees 'all the nations' streaming to Jerusalem and 'numerous people on the march' (Isaiah 2: 3). For there are always two lines leaving Mount Zion. One, which is generous, calls out expansively; the other, which is circumspect, demands that one should not mix with others (or sit at the same table as a goy; that one should avoid intermarriage, not live in the same neighbourhood, etc.). The first Christians took up the *extrovert* tendency and left the *ethnocentric*. Each new circle is rediscovered inscribed in the next, which frees it of its particularisms (thus the Catholic, still inserted in the Roman Church and becoming the universal individual in the Protestant mode), and will itself be relieved of its ballast by its successor. Up until the quasi-pantheistic embrace of Gaia, the Earth Mother, for whom the sacred includes animals. And rivers. And plants. And the ozone layer. The cosmos finally as beautiful as a god .... .

In that happy globalization, the history of the Eternal would open from native soil to the Earth itself, like the diaphragm on a camera. Close-up, medium, wide-angle. The henotheism of a local divinity becoming, after Babylon, the monotheism of a chosen people. Extended subsequently to all the peoples of the inhabited world by Christian evangelism. Then broadened to the planet by the proselytism of the Reformers. And finally given back, in the course of the twentieth century, to most civil societies through a 'secularization' that disseminates sacred values in the profane world. Thus did the Decalogue gradually become the law of nations. The circle closes. The opening credits: midway into the first millennium BCE, in a minuscule bit of the Near East, a sheaf of village myths is bound together with the all-purpose notion of a universal Creator. Closing credits: at the beginning of the third millennium, the original One, having been exported in the interim under numerous denominations as far as the antipodes (Pacific included), returns to Himself in the form of a normalized world consciousness, but without any label of origin.

In the light of that happy end, the ill becomes a good. The loosening of the grip of the churches, for example. It ought to make the various clergies happy, since it serves their ultimate end by allowing a planetary creed to transcend denominational boundaries. Forgetting that a concept's extension is the inverse of its comprehension (what one gains in breadth is lost in depth), the malcontent will object that our cult of human rights, a highly accommodating religion, is to the Abrahamic revelations what Esperanto is to the universal language, or the G8 to the peoples of the world. Our answer to him will be that it is the asymptote that counts. Consider the vanishing point, not the sham appearances of transition. And let us rejoice together that our century has seen the emergence of the 'catechism of the *honnête homme,* the gentleman', as dreamt by Voltaire. Shall we call this greatest common denominator the Christianity of the poor in spiritual values? Or the Lord's prayer of the de-Christianized, rich in dollars and euros? What is important is that the One should belong to everyone, and everywhere: in Jerusalem as in Cairo, in Washington as in Moscow. In that perspective, the 'death of God' would be the sinister version of an ongoing process of cloning (and which does honour to the genetic genius of the species). Western consciousness has removed from its ageing organs, the instituted Churches, the nucleus of a monotheistic cell, and implanted it in the egg cell of a brand-new organism, our hemispheric Directorates, the United Nations and the international tribunals, in order to produce reinvigorated moral tissue, genetically identical to the old and universally graftable.

Let us flesh out the scenario. The spiralling movement towards a religion in which we all unwittingly partake, atheists above all, and for which a common paternity in God would have been no more than a necessary detour on the journey towards the brotherhood of mankind, did not transpire in the clouds. It was borne, conveyed and implemented by the constantly intensifying contest between various logistics of meaning that we have attempted to follow at a gallop. The ascent began with *writing*, which ensures an autonomous memory for language (no more need for a present and live speaker in order to transmit). Was pursued with the *alphabet*, which universalizes access to that memory (being the same for all). Then with the *printing press*, which permits its automatic reproduction (no more need for a man to recopy). And culminates with the *computer*, which gives the language thus reproduced an autonomous productivity (software works on its own; language becomes robotic). In externalizing his nervous system, man has finally succeeded in innervating the planet itself (by placing his data-retrievers beneath, on, and above the terrestrial surface); this allows him to take charge of the globe. Cabling, for informative and scientific ends, has given him the ability to extend 'being-together' to the biosphere as a single whole. Transcendence in that case becomes evolution as it occurs: Saint Thomas plus Darwin. And that ascent, at the very heart of the industry of signs, allows us to broaden our sense of responsibility to the non-human. From the alphabetical character to the World Wide Web, from the papyrus scroll to the third-generation laptop, by way of the in-12, lithograph and offset, each 'revolution' has responded better and better to the overall design of a mnemotechnical Providence: more numerous, less expensive and lighter (multiply resources, lower costs, facilitate distribution). Frightened spectators intent on getting off before the cosmoplanetary last station has been reached will at least be able to console themselves with having passed from a niche God, in a very specialized market, to a standardized mass-public God, whose prefiguration – a colourless but panoptical Eye, certificate of moral conformity and guarantor of institutional efficiency (hence the

Supreme Court, 1952: 'We are a religious people whose institutions presuppose a supreme Being') – will have been the God of America.

'They seem to be dispensing with my services a bit rapidly in this corner of the solar system; the cemeteries are chock full of irreplaceable people, but all the same ... .' The Almighty would be wrong to be vexed at seeing our carousing, trade-based societies turn their backs on Him with a certain indelicacy. The fact that the moral authority of His Churches, above all in Europe, no longer rests on any -logy (theo-, soterio- or eschatology) would of course meet with his displeasure. But history, the young Marx might tell Him as a consolation, always advances by its bad side. Is not the conversion of a religious revelation at one point in time (Thou shalt not kill, thou shalt not steal, etc.) into a code of good diplomatic and political conduct invokable against any miscreant a mark of fabulous success? Such would be the ultimate ruse of the Eternal (as was the case with Reason), just before His efface-ment from the tablets, in order to continue reigning in our forgetful hearts: the Father passing Himself off as dead in the interest of His large family. Is His memory no longer of interest to very many people? Let us admit as much. Has He lost his enemies along the way – the versions of Prometheus intent on taking heaven by storm (all of them dead, shot or decorated) – whereas one lives and is esteemed only by virtue of the number and quality of one's enemies? Granted. But what does it matter if the value of values for Christians – to put it simply: the victim is always right – has become the official doctrine of the family? Its point of honour. Some-thing that never could have been carried off had the doctrine been presented under its original trademark, with an imprint of cross or star. The logo has vanished before the *Logos*. Abnegation to the end. 'Good job too,' He might say. 'I've done my work so well that they no longer need me. This business can take care of itself. Let's take a look elsewhere (millions of remaining galaxies). End of episode Earth.'

The triumphal scenario holds. On paper or on the screen. We would like to subscribe to it. But anyone who sticks his nose outside to take in the air of our villages (and particularly the monotheistic ones) will soon, alas, encounter a pan-demonium far removed from our idyll.

What a Teilhard-style ascent towards some endpoint of planetary reconciliation failed to take into account was the unexpected stubbornness of our various insu-larities. Worse still: it is the insurrection of local memories, stirred up by techno-economic dislocation, which revives and exacerbates the need for palpable and ostensible purity. And remobilizes the gods who keep watch over the ramparts.[2] The vernacular rears up beneath and against the global. Re-Judaization of Israel (where

---

[2] A process analysed in detail in my *Critique de la Raison politique: sur l'inconscient reli-gieux* (Paris: Gallimard 1981) / *Critique of Political Reason*, trans. David Macey (London: New Left Books 1983).

the rabbis have never had as much power since independence). Re-Islamization of the Arab countries and campuses (where Allah has never been so present since decolonization). Re-Christianization of Eastern Europe. Charismatic renewal in Latin Europe. Return of Pentecostalism in the Americas. Retreat of secularism in France itself. 'The revenge of God' gives the prefix *re* a plethora of opportunities, inverting past and future, high and low.[3] While placing in the saddle the *reincorporating* and *indemnifying* function of confessional safeguards (between Poles and Russians, Irish Protestants and Catholics, Armenians and Azerbaijanis, Hungarians and Romanians, Serbs and Albanians and Croatians, Tamils and Hindus, Palestinians and Israelis ...). Identity-based retrenchment is a many-coloured thing: the saffron wave in the Indian Union, green in central Asia; Buddhist in Eastern Asia (Sri Lanka, Thailand, Burma), neo-Buddhist in Japan, Methodist in Melanesia. Modernizers who look down on these 'regressions' would do well to turn to their holy land, America the great, held together by a fusion of the national and the religious. Would what is praiseworthy at the top of the ladder be unacceptable on the lower rungs? Ought not every collective to have the right to persist in its being? Moreover, they have no hesitation in so doing. The angels may have a bit of lead in their wings, but Thanksgiving Day and *kashrut* are doing just fine, thanks. Ramadan is increasingly well observed, and Lourdes is never empty. Every community, be it national or any other kind, that preserves a ritual, even if it does not quite grasp its meaning, is preserving itself, a sign that it does not want to be gobbled up by others that are more advantageously situated. Gestures, we have noted, traverse the centuries better than dogmas. Is not the sustaining and relaunching of collective aspirations tantamount to serving the polymorphous cause of life itself, whose colour has always been that of the rainbow? We are free to interpret things in such manner, if we don't want to lose Hope in the divine plan, but if we take a second look, there is enough to make Candide despair: the Symbolic, which binds us, operates by way of the Diabolic, which tears us apart. *Janus bifrons*: fraternity on one side, hostility on the other. No use betting everything we possess on a toss of the divine coin. It will land on its edge and bounce from one side to the other, from oppression to liberation and vice versa (democratic Spain freeing itself *from* the Church, and Poland *through* the traditionalist Church). Undecidable.

Esprit de corps and its Blind Spot

In identifying demarcations many see an obstacle, a brake applied to the soaring of Spirit. In the face of the idea of the body-as-corset, we would prefer that of the

---

[3] See Gilles Kepel, *La Revanche de Dieu* (Paris: Seuil 1991) / *The Revenge of God: The Resurgence of Islam, Christianity, and Judaism in the Modern World*, trans. Alan Braley (Cambridge: Polity 1994).

body-as-spring, which does not invalidate the first, to be sure, but is its corollary. It seems incongruous, since it is from the unfinished and borderless that we traditionally expect the mystic's secret to come. Partisans of the 'exigencies of the soul' turn towards the indeterminate. Hence Romain Rolland and his 'oceanic feeling', which would be the sensation of the boundless become perceptible. It seems to us, on the contrary, that wherever the physical persists, there is a hint of the mystical in the air. A need for the sacred plagues us not out of some soulful vagueness, but out of our need to escape the indefinite by bringing precision to our assorted vaguenesses. As Jacques Derrida has recalled, in the Bergsonian tradition of two sources, the religious is an ellipse with two foci, just as the word itself has two etymologies (*relegere* and *religare*), to re-collect and to bind together.[4] On the one hand, what partakes of the fiduciary, faith, belief; on the other, of what is healthy, undamaged, our *own*. We shall ask later on whether it is not possible to establish a logical connection between those two poles, but it may be noted that the search for the undamaged, separate and intact is at the core of the notion of the sacred [*heilig*]. Sacral activity (prayer or sacrifice) aims at avoiding harm and prejudice for oneself and one's own. There is a geopolitical translation of the auto-immune reflex, which says to the other: don't touch me; don't contaminate me. Such is the heterogeneous or sacralizing character of borders, and the boundary-driven character of fundamentalisms. As a general rule, the group in contact (with others-than-oneself) is more fanatical than those protected in the interior. The shock troops of identity-combat, the 'soldiers of God', are most often recruited not in the central zones of (Islamic, Hindu, Christian or Jewish) civilization, but from the physically and mentally exposed outposts of a believing collective, near its outlying fortifications, in its buffer zones. Fanaticism appears to be *friction-induced behaviour,* a pathology of the interface between an 'us' and a 'them'. The skin disease of societies.

The appeal to a God-of-our-own to resist everything that can dissociate, disassemble, dislocate the integrity of a tradition has something all the more paradoxical about it in that the Supreme Principle is posited as a Justice of the Peace. As a means of erasing all spats and divisions. This is an illusion, but it appeals to us. It has recently been taken over by two secular messianisms, proclaiming the universal republic – once by the soviets, once by market capitalism: the classless society and proletarian internationalism, on the one hand, or the myth of a history without geography; and, on the other, the market without creeds or languages, or the myth of an economy without cultures. Has not the smoothing away of differences served as a common platform for those two hostile perspectives on the world, in spite (or because) of the fact that they share an identical fundamental optimism?

---

[4] Jacques Derrida and Gianni Vattimo, *La Religion* (Paris: Seuil 1996), p. 51 / *Religion* (Stanford, CA: Stanford University Press 1998).

Break the Tablets of the Law and smooth down all the edges. Proclaim the end of the symbolic, in the name of a 'pure exchange of ephemeral wills', and the end of singularities, in the name of the interchangeable: the religious illusion of the moment is a world without religion. The blurring of affiliations and the broadening of the contractual sphere are too flagrant not to give proclamations of a grand trade-based reconciliation a certain allure. A number of cybergospels are, in fact, exalting.[5] Public opinion and celebrated thinkers maintain that democratic society, self-administered and managerial in spirit, has invented an entirely new form of being-together, in which everyone would be free to live and think in the indicative, rather than the optative or subjunctive. Was that not the perspective that had already inspired the announcement, in the nineteenth century, that the government of men would soon be replaced by the administration of things – with the help of the Suez Canal and the railways? And is it not what we can detect lurking behind the will to arrive at a zero-institution, by reducing School, the Courts, the Army, the Republic, and the new Euroland to so many functionally meshing gears, without capital letters or external basis of belief, without 'sursum corda' (lift up your hearts!). Where the whole of each thing would lie wholly *within* its wholeness.

It is a great question, that of determining whether the advent of democracy does or does not constitute an exception to the constraints joining religion and security. Whether it partakes of a different grammar of civilizations, still in search of itself, from yesterday's societies, alienated or subjected to external powers; of another way of crystallizing that might do without 'the bishop from without' (as the miracle-working king was known in Christian times). That exceptional status has been evoked in finely lyrical terms by the Mexican writer Octavio Paz: 'Other political systems', he says, 'are based on principles alien to men: the mandate of heaven of the Chinese emperors, the divine right of absolute monarchs, the will of history and the proletariat of Communist leaders. Democracy founds the people in the name of the people; it is the law that men give to themselves. It is neither a fate promulgated from on high or from beyond history, nor a law dictated by blood and the dead. It is not a faith and it proposes nothing absolute ... .' Such is indeed the hope of our liberal democracy, its imaginary relation with itself, what it believes and wishes to be. But leaving ideological habit aside, the fundamental question is one of determining whether one can forge an *inter* without the help of a *meta*. A dynamic regrouping without a gleaming point of darkness suspended over our heads (*n*).

The self-creation of a *we* by itself ('order by noise') would indeed be the Good News of our era, allowing us to relegate to the Dark Ages our: 'Kill them all. God will recognize his own.' It would be inseparable from the proclamation of a village global at last, which our information highways are attempting to infuse with life.

---

[5] See Pierre Lévy, *World Philosophie* (Paris: Odile Jacob 2000).

And it is probable that a totally open collective, without filtration or selection, could do without untouchables, *the sacred being precisely what closes*. A society without entrance fee could indeed send the Ten Commandments and Liberty, Equality and Fraternity, not to mention Pantheons and their great and good, packing, but it has only one drawback: it has no possible geographic and historic translation – on earth, under heaven. As was true of all civilizations until now; the historian Fernand Braudel, who has studied their systems, has shown that however permeable and welcoming they may be, however nourished by exchange and borrowing, caravans and ports; however hesitant and slow their customs procedures may have been, they all had their secret mechanisms of closure or rejection (Byzantium closing up to the Latin world, Italy to the Reformation, the Anglo-Saxon world to proletarian Marxism, etc.) 'A civilization is generally reluctant to adopt a cultural good that puts one of its deep structures into question. Such refusals to borrow, such secret hostilities, always lead to the heart of a civilization.'[6] Thus a certain amount of prudence is called for in welcoming the idea that we will be immune to the fragilities of incompletion as soon as we enter into the 'universal without totality' (Pierre Lévy): a world of infinitely ramifying interconnections, that of the ubiquitous circulation of *data*. With the unlimited circularity of servers and the commutative nature of digital encodings, in an a-centred and infinitely extensible Web, our petty folkloric localities would commune in a cybercommunity in which commonality would no longer depend on an origin, a myth of redemption or a creed to be shared, but on the experience of sharing itself. With universalized cabling and eddying acceleration of the exchange of information effecting a process that is inherently religious in itself, the horizontal would be able to do without verticality, with no further need of an external reference point.

Is it not precisely the fact of being without contours, 'untotalizable', that prevents 'virtual communities' from being grounded, and establishing themselves? A digital space with neither centre nor circumference gives everyone a feeling of being liberated, more inventive and knowledgeable, but that ease in circulating is paid for with an accelerated evanescence (if we may judge from the feeble life expectancy of Internet sites). Our new cognitive tools allow for a formidable expansion of knowledge, in my opinion, but we cannot superimpose the homogeneous space of a scientific Republic (which is unlimited in theory and practice, and everywhere equal to itself) on the polarized and divided territory of communities of memory and projects, which enter into relations of friction and confrontation with each other over pre-eminence, language, norms or turf. One does not have the feeling, travelling from east to west, that such communities are prepared to disappear as a result of a higher level of education and consumption.

Let us not extrapolate, as our scientists do, from knowledge to consciousness, and

---

[6] Fernand Braudel, *Grammaire des civilisations* (Paris: Arthaud–Flammarion 1987), p. 61 / *A History of Civilizations*, trans. Richard Mayne (New York: Penguin 1994).

from scientific acquisitions to modes of behaviour. Reason is not value; technique is not praxis. Auguste Comte would undoubtedly have seen in the confusion of the two terms one more 'insurrection of the mind against the heart'. He was one of the very few to have announced a twentieth century simultaneously scientific and religious, religious because scientific. If he ventured to imagine the religion of a single indivisible Humanity, capable of burying 'the corpse of war' and establishing universal peace, it is because – contrary to the misinterpretation of the word positivism – he was fully aware of science's inability to forge the spiritual unity of a people. The failure of his grandiose project testifies to the fact that a stroke of the philosophical pen will not do away with the bond between the *ascendant* and the *persistent*. Humanity (or the set of beings past, present and future) which worships itself is a serpent biting its tail. The immanence of Comte's Great Being to itself, without break or disruption of level, nipped in the bud the idea of directly erecting sociology into a theology. Such is the common fate of 'horizontal religions'. They are like the legendary Baron von Münchhausen, who, having been unlucky enough to fall into a pond, was intent on rising to the surface by lifting himself up by his own hair. It is an economical idea, a salvaging operation billed to one's own account, less costly than a discount accorded by a questionable creditor, but one whose efficacy is, alas, subject to doubt.

Astonishment Would Be More Appropriate

The expansion of the world and the sphere of communications have stimulated rather than impeded the 'return of the religious'. Had it ever really left? We should be full of admiration for the fact that legends and gestures invented thousands of years ago have managed to remain ours for so long. All the technological, scientific and political disruptions that have ensued since the invention of firepower have not succeeded in breaching that core of credibility. The unbelievable but stubborn fact remains that delusions, tales dating from before year zero and the windmill, are still alive and sources of inspiration for hundreds of millions of individuals whose life-equipment and life expectancy are at the mercy of 'big science'. If these cock-and-bull stories were no more than stopgaps for our ignorance, who would still care about them? The cosmology, physics and medicine of Saint Augustine's time are of interest only to historians of science; its swing-ploughs and millstones only to historians of technology. Their expiry date came and went ages ago. Who today would prefer fifth-century potions and infusions to antibiotics? But *On the Usefulness of Believing* by the same Augustine, written in the year 392, has not dated at all. It could be brought out today. If we changed the date and author's name, and cut a few of the minor arguments with the Manichaeans (which means all of them), we would end up with a text that could have been written yesterday. The familiar examples invoked by the Bishop of Hippo to show that being a believer does not mean being credulous, and that one cannot get by in everyday life without an act of faith in things one can't see, or without placing one's trust in authorities concerning which one has reason to think that they know no more than we do (Church State, Family, Newspaper), are all quite understandable today. The friendship for me that I attribute to my friends, with no guarantee that they actually feel it with any depth, or my firm belief that my father sired me because he declared as much on official documents, and took me under his roof (which would not prevent my mother from having taken a lover) – none of this has aged, and it never will.

What does that difference in reception indicate if not that belief and knowledge are not in competition? They do not occupy the same hemispheres of the brain; each has its function. It is the same with the keys to human behaviour as with the keys to works of beauty: time has nothing to do with them. Belief is not from *before* science, and epic fiction cannot be assigned to a *pre*-rational stage of thought that would have vanished as soon as we had rules of calculation and thermometers at our disposal. If that were the case, the Bible, after Kepler and Copernicus, would be no more than a curiosity for scholars of Inscriptions and Belles-Lettres, to be studied for what it is (from a 'positive' point of view), a jumble of tales and foolishness. The emanation of a number of obsolete imaginations. And similarly, Saint Mark or Saint John would speak only to Hellenists and specialists of Judaeo-Roman Palestine. If their meaning is decontextualizable, if they can still command attention and give us some basis for understanding society and ourselves, it is because those fictive contraptions serve as a cipher for a truth that transcends them. They disguised a memory as a myth, but that myth would not be such a solid point of reference if it did not in turn shed some light on actual history for us. Figures of origin are universal and, for that very reason, always topical, far beyond the initial breadth of their audience. Such is the case of Prometheus, Oedipus, Ulysses and Hermes. But also of Adam, Cain and Joseph (the eye, as Hugo put it, is in the grave, and continues to shine). Those sharply contoured sketches, characters and emblematic roles reverberate through the centuries in that they prefigure, as if in outline, a more articulate representation of the existential drama. That drama did not wait for the arrival of the human sciences to find expression, and all its fantasies have a symptomatic (or harmonic) value. Does the proliferation of religious fantasizing incline us to scepticism? But the fact that there is a multitude of languages, and no universal language, deprives our thousands of idioms neither of meaning nor of the ability to impose order on our common muddle.

Some speak to us more than others. A matter of latitude, or of habit. In France, with our school curricula and family agendas, we understand Jesus better than Zeus, Joan of Arc better than Hercules. Beyond the fact that an ethnocentrism that is acknowledged is already half excused, it is by no means absurd to posit that the trajectory of a Great Obstinate One brings into more readable focus what the mythologies of Antiquity disperse over a plethora of tales. The advantage of the

Judaeo-Christian concentrate over more profligate and heady solutions, such as the Graeco-Roman legends constitute, is to distil for us an essence of what is at stake before it is diluted for analysis. Our corpus of biblical legends may be read as the early stages of an anthropology in the rough, reduced to its essence and cast in dramatic form. The myth of origin is an anticipation of our analytic procedures, which are undoubtedly more rigorous, but also less evocative. The sacred gave utterance to the profane, but without skewing or concealing matters. With more brutal honesty than our partial models and scholarly jargons. *Revelation*, for instance, does not skirt the impossibility we encounter in rationalizing an origin; it registers it in unadorned terms and legitimates its intrinsic arbitrariness, to be received as an incomprehensible rent in the fabric of history. The Christian *mystery* is also valiant in the face of the inherently illogical: it asks us to believe without any wish to explain. Our foundation narratives combine sagacity and ingenuousness. A felicitous freshness, which brings to the epic staging of a repetitive chaos of carnage and iniquity a symbolic charge laden with promise, which a more coldly precise historiography would have been unable to give us. The Old Testament, the Gospels, the Apocalypses confer on our feature-length film a feeling of luminosity and joy that its actual occurrence, to be sure, never had. And that is because a supernatural dimension exercises its good will by intervening in history at every difficult pass – Egypt, Babylon, Golgotha – in order to set *in extremis* the altogether compromised course of things aright. In those blessed times, God offered humanity the guarantee of a *good ending*, much as in our day an insurance underwriter might before the first scenes of a big-budget film are shot.

Incompleteness and the Placebo Effect

What universals of the human condition does the monotheist narrative allow us to perceive, if not grasp (for it is not certain that we are able to intervene in it with any practical effect)? If a clerk of the court, just prior to the end of the hearing, may be permitted to answer the traditional 'and you, how do *you* understand it?', here is the interpretation he would like to propose of the enigma of a God who is dead and continues to resonate. The theme, the refrain, of the Bible might be summarized in trivial terms as follows: human beings will not be able to pull through on their own. Every time they imagine they can muddle through without the Other above, the result is catastrophic. Adam and Eve, Cain and Abel, Joseph and his brothers. At some point in time, they decide they don't need anyone; they cook up their mess of pottage together, without the assistance of a Third Party – and bang! It all falls apart. Similarly, when there's a conflict or threat of disintegration within a community, be it small or large, someone invokes the Absent One, or encounters Him unexpectedly, and a *we* is reconstituted. The Hebrews in flight. David and Jonathan. The pilgrims of Emmaus. In less figurative and poetic terms, we might translate:

every *among (us)* presupposes an *above*; and when the *meta* level caves in, the *inter* is dislocated accordingly. When the Symbol (etymologically, what joins pieces together) fails, the diabolic reappears (the devil being he who does the opposite: divides couples, clubs, teams, nations, and ultimately humanity against itself). Thus salvation is not in the dollar but in the federating impulse – love, friendship or sharing. In *in God we trust*. For God and the devil, substitute negative entropy and entropy; for 'resurrection', the triumph of the former over the latter, and you have a prosaic scheme for the way things function. If such fabulations are still capable of emerging from their traditional Sunday context and affecting even miscreants, it is because they resonate with a principle that may (fortunately for us) be open to modulation and negotiation in its conditions of implementation, but concerning which it may be wondered whether it is not constitutive of human assemblages – elsewhere we have called it *incompleteness*.

Or the hypothesis of a principle effecting the formation of stable groups and articulating, through an unconscious mechanism, the *closure* of a territory – be it ideal, or spatial, or both at once – and its *openness* to an extrinsic point of cohesion. Far from being opposed, as Bergson imagined, the two functions would entail one another, internal consistency being obtained by way of external reference. Since no system is able to 'enclose' itself solely by virtue of elements internal to the system, the crystallization of a collective would thus entail the placing of its members in relation with a given that is never given *per se* in experience, the object of an act of faith, deposed in a myth. It is the *nail* on which the picture is hung. One is needed or the picture will fall and break. This point of attachment, our blind spot – and each collectivity has its own – is decreed unavailable to technical or critical manipulation, an interdiction characterizing the *sacred* (for us, Holocaust denial is sacrilegious and, as such, punishable by law). What could be more comprehensible for an intrinsically precarious organism, as is every collective culture, even an atheistic one, than to declare inviolable and 'sacred' what impedes its dislocation into utter randomness? Every transcendence would thus be the index and instrument of an incipient and unconscious will-to-live. This prerequisite of coalescence may take many (more or less grotesque) forms, all of them none the less conveying through their folklore an *a priori constraint of communitarian viability*. The constitutive lack – what Lacan called the lack-of-being [*manque-à-être*] – of societies renders impossible in practice the national self-sufficiency brandished in our various agendas (of self-institution), in which the present would owe nothing to the past, nor what is to what might or should have been. It confers on human assemblages an irreducibly delusional context, since it subordinates them to electrifying mirages, optical and tonic illusions, which iconoclasts may (and indeed should) ridicule. If no set of relations can persist solely in relation to itself, it means that when three men meet, they are obliged to agree on a point of convergence on which to focus their gazes, lest they (sooner or later) come to blows. Robinson Crusoe can resort to evasions, but the arrival of Man Friday makes the imagining of a myth on which their tiny community depends imperative. As soon as there are two or more, the social organism tests 'positive'. Drugs are compulsory. Individuals may, with some heroism, be satisfied with what they are, without any outside additive, but straggling villages worry and search for some point of escape towards which they can raise their eyes. Lest they melt like ice in sunlight, they are obliged to 'mobilize themselves' – on whatever questionable pretext. Drawn by a promise, maybe a political one; or by nostalgia for a golden age, even if it be a complete fabrication.

This regrettable dependence of the consistent on the delusional and the resistant on the fabulatory allows us to understand the impotence of the analytic spirit in dissipating the enchantments that continue to move crowds, as though the sovereignty of reason were obliged to stop short, not *de jure* but *de facto*, in the face of the inherently unreasonable functioning of collective entities. The vertical axis escapes the control of intelligence, yet it is what secures and binds human aggregates. We can and should impose on such delusions proper manners – or, at least, manners that are as proper as possible. But unidimensionality is unattainable. There are always two dimensions. When you see a rampart, you can be pretty sure that there is a tower behind it – minaret, steeple or cupola. When you encounter the relative, look for its Absolute. If you're in a sacred place, look for the altar. If you're near an altar, look for the sacred place. As soon as it is circumscribed, a flat terrain requires something like an *elevation*, or a totem come from above, if it is intent on distinguishing itself from the surrounding flatlands. Like the *Kaaba*, the black stone of Mecca, the heart of Islam, gift of the Archangel Gabriel to Abraham, and concerning which it is tacitly agreed that it fell mysteriously from heaven at precisely the right spot.

'Set limits around the mountain and keep it holy', said the Lord to Moses (Exodus, 19: 23). And Saint Paul takes up the theme: 'The Lord allotted the time of their existence and the boundaries of the places where men would live' (Acts 17: 26). The roots of words in other cultures attest to the geographical function of divinity, in the first and violent sense of the term: to inscribe in space what the facts of history exhibit. *Templum*, the temple, comes from the Greek *temno*, to divide. And the Romans called *templation* the gesture by which the augur apportioned in the sky with his baton, his *skeptron*, a square to be observed. Similarly, *rex*, the priest-king, is linked to *regere fines*, tracing limits on the ground. ('It is a matter', according to Benveniste, 'of delimiting the interior, the realm of the sacred and the realm of the profane, national territory and foreign territory.') The Roman *urbs* was born when Romulus traced the furrow which delimited, within the limitless land of Latium, the *pomerium* (the sacred space where neither building nor the cultivation of crops is permitted), an enclosure whose sacrilegious violation or forced entry was deemed punishable by death (it was not the twin in Remus who was sacrificed by Romulus, but the leaper of the ditch). Zeus was said to be *orios*, protector of limits. And to introduce the worship of a god was called, in Greek, *oreizon theon*: to delimit a territory consecrated to that god. 'The first,' said Rousseau, 'who having enclosed a plot of land took it upon himself to say: this is mine, and found people simple enough to believe him, was the true founder of civil society.' And by virtue of the simple act of enclosing itself, that society ceased to be civil. It entered into the dimension of the politico-religious.

Yahweh, Jehovah, the Lord of Hosts, King of Kings, Father, Supreme Being: so many codenames given by the lineage of Jerusalem to a universal constraint shared by other civilizations (under their own colours), because giving a name and a face to what one cannot prevent is a way of domesticating, acclimatizing the ineluctable. That is to say: if there is to be a specific bond among random individuals, they must be *bound* by a reference on high which precedes them in time and is expected to survive them. It may be that the ego, in its cell, is less exposed (or not to the same extent) to this predicament, which concerns, above all, *men* (in the plural). An *individual man* manages to stand on his two legs, provided he is given something to eat. But *men*, as a group, lack *consistency*. They scatter in every direction as soon as they find themselves free to pursue their petty manias and quarrels. The whole mess just won't stand up straight without a steep slope to slow down the inevitable relapse of the singular into the random. What the biblical patchwork gives us advance warning of might thus be formulated as follows: 'Do you want a bond among yourselves? Then find a transcendence. Call it Jehovah, if you find that more impressive. But I warn you: if you don't make a hole in the ceiling, you'll suffocate. It doesn't matter what you put there; what counts is the opening to the air.'

The placebo effect designates a positive physiological change induced in a patient by a neutral substance without any active principle. He thinks it's medicine, it isn't; and a clinical improvement is observed (in the case of Parkinson's disease, it has been shown that the brain, under the influence of belief, actually produces dopamine, the necessary molecule). Why would the unconscious of collective entities not proceed in like manner with what might be considered the placebos – each with its label, as it were – known as religions? It would be no more than a return to sender, since the terms comes from church Latin, in the service for the dead (*Placebo Domino in regione vivorum*: I shall please the Lord in the land of the living). Translated in reverse: The Lord is pleasing to us because He delays the forces of degeneration, and thus the day of the service for the dead. Just as God is the superlative figure, and a perfect stand-in, for the Reference that turns a pile into a whole ('Hell is living in the absence of God', Cardinal Ratzinger, the Roman prefect of Catholic doctrine, *rightly* says, if we immediately specify that 'God' is one among other keystones that might be envisaged), so does 'religion' designate the archetypal, but by no means exclusive, form of a structural configuration in which the relation among places is more important than the nature of their contents.

'Religion' is both a simple and a confused word. Cicero's definition in *De inventione* has the merit of sobriety: 'Religion is the fact of being concerned with a certain *higher* nature which is called divine and to which one dedicates a cult.' The Romans, who were not given to grandiloquence, were rather matter-of-fact; they had their feet firmly on the ground. Higher (or upper) should be understood here in the commonplace spatial sense of a floor, a lip, the flow of a river or the deck of a boat. Meaning what is to be found above, higher than the level on which one is oneself (the level of immanence). The Old Testament lies upstream from the Jewish people, and the New from the Christian people. The Constitution, from the American people, and the Koran, from Islam. And so forth. The superstition to which each human aggregate dedicates its parades, ceremonies, harangues, public squares, airports, national holidays, and so on, can take on a variety of names. The tonic and ascendant effect can be worked by a prophet, heavenly being, battle, general, sage, motto, Declaration . . . . Each will have his preferences. In France, the patronage of Saint Louis, the fourteenth of July, Sacré-Cœur, and the Declaration of the Rights of Man are certainly not of identical value or effect. But formally, the act of dedication or the shared taking of the going collective placebo, which is translated as a day off or a national holiday, persists. It requires the interruption, at a regular rhythm, of our works and days in the name of a regeneration or recharging from above. With an entering into relation, ritualized in a ceremony or speech, between the super-real that binds and the reality to be bound, the operation is entrusted to *High Priests*. Justices of the Supreme Court. Ideologues of the Politburo, Tribunes of the Republic, Nobel Prize winners, when one finds oneself in an officially post-God era, or within the limits of reason alone. Cardinals, pastors, reverends, mullahs, ayatollahs, chief rabbis and other holy men, in the preceding phase. The division of labour between the consecrated dispensers of consecration, bearers and guarantors of ultimate legitimacies (high priests), and the random, colourless folk (you and me) whom they edify traverses the ages – of faith or disbelief – without the slightest hitch.

Apparatus Variable, Disposition Invariable

We are thus under an obligation to 'believe in something' in order to remain 'someone', speaking from 'somewhere'. Here we encounter the Freudian notion that religious *illusion* is not of the same nature as *error*, in that it is defined not in terms of its relation to effective reality but in relation to the wishes that give rise to it. The secret of the strength of illusion is the strength of the wishes motivating it. Error is refutable; illusion is not. But Freud, inspired by the scientist outlook of his day (even as he overlooked the genius of Auguste Comte), characterized those wishes as infantile, and advanced the notion (perhaps out of simple politeness) that as the result of immaturity they would soon be surmounted. In his opinion religion was a mass delusion, a universal neurosis, born of our narcissistic wish to overcome our infantile helplessness and inventing for itself a fantasied Father – but it was only an unfortunate phase to be left behind.[7] Ensuing events have tended to show that this alleged past of humanity has had a hard time 'passing'. Should we dare press the criticism of founding fables to the point of speculating why they continue to be invented, over and again, the question would appear to be somewhat clarified by the hypothesis of incompleteness, which makes of subjective illusion the indispensable correlate of collective cohesion. It renders the 'neurosis' unelimbinable – indeed, salutary – under forms which are, it is true, subject to modulation according to ethnic grouping, technological generation and social class, and exceed the bounds of the revealed religions (o).

The man of belief appears to be endowed with immutable properties, whereas the man of knowledge (his *alter ego*) changes ceaselessly. If an astrophysicist from the year 2002 were to meet a cosmologist from 1402, they would not have very much to say to each other. A dialogue of the deaf would be inevitable. But a Christian, Jew or Muslim of today, discovering his fellow believers of times past in paradise, would have no trouble finding areas of agreement with them, since global codes of meaning would allow them, in this case, to understand each other. This is not to say that systems of belief have not varied, even as the domains of the believable have.[8] Belief [*croyance*], like religion, is a word that lies as soon as it is preceded by the (singular) definite article. As it is in French: *la religion, la croyance*. Has 'believing in God' always meant the same thing, under Ezra, Henri IV, Louis XIV, and Henry Ford? Surely not. With the exception of ideological uses for comfort purposes (from one camp or the other), we cannot be satisfied with catch-all generalities and categories. As we have seen: with all that it implies of acknowledged uncertainty and assumed subjectivity, belief, in the current usage of the term, came to us with the Christian notion of conversion. The Old Testament shows no knowledge of the word. One has no need of 'believing in God' to be part of strictly observant Judaism; one lives with it. Greeks and Romans, the most religious of men, had no need of a creed, or sacred books, or heresies in order to fulfil their civic duties (any more than we do in relighting a flame or laying chrysanthemums on a grave). We are aware of how laden with traps the word is in Christendom. 'The Western Middle Ages proved much and believed little,' a medievalist has observed.[9] The builders of cathedrals were undoubtedly less credulous than we are inclined to believe. They observed, reasoned, believed they knew, and, moreover, trusted in authority: the Church as

---

[7] Sigmund Freud, *The Future of an Illusion* (New York: Norton 1989).
[8] Jean Wirth, 'La naissance du concept de croyance XIIᵉ–XVIIᵉ siècle', *Bibliothèque d'Humanisme et de Renaissance*, vol. 45 (1983), pp. 7–58
[9] Alain Boureau, 'L'Église médiévale comme preuve animée de la croyance chrétienne', *Terrain* (March 1990), pp. 113–18.

the concrete and historical incarnation of truth. We baptize 'beliefs' propositions that formerly passed for knowledge. In sum, our classifications (knowledge/opinion/belief) are in no way foundational or permanent – no more so than the modern debate pitting 'belief' against 'disbelief'. Scholasticism was content to oppose true (authorized doctrine) and false beliefs (fables, unendorsed superstitions). 'Held to be true' is a rainbow of infinite subtleties that has us moving imperceptibly from probability to faith, by way of supposition, opinion, conviction, support, certitude, and so on. Saint Thomas himself was careful to distinguish. *Believing in God*, or giving oneself over to Him heart and soul, by joining love to knowledge (*credere in Deo*), is not *believing what God advances*, or adhering to it solely with one's mind (*credere Deo*), and even less *believing God*, which does no more than coldly recognize that He exists (*credere Deum*).

The examination of the interactions between man and his various milieux (which is what mediology consists in) would do well to take, as its name suggests, a median path between two all-too-simple-minded formulations: the superstition of technical apparatuses, which forgets the unaltering character of dispositions; and the superstition of the permanent, which forgets the efficacy of various apparatuses and the crises of confidence that the transition from one to the other can provoke. For there is a history of the plausible, according to the reliability, at a specific juncture, of one or another type of simulacrum. A miracle, for example, is told, a utopia written. 'Worthy of faith' depends on the eminently variable powers of certification and authentication connected with our diverse ways of grasping reality. Each of them establishes with its user a certain contract of belief. In the order of images, for example, we do not expect the same type of truth from a painting or a photograph, from a news clip or an image in a televised film. Someone who watches a fictional film believes in what he is seeing (otherwise he gets bored and leaves the cinema), but not in the same way he believes in a documentary. An unverifiable representation (say, a comedy) does not call for the same kind of credibility as an allegedly verified sampling of reality (say, in a 'wildlife' film). The nuances one does well to insist on within the visual sphere are even more imposing when one changes mediaspheres. In the graphosphere, the handicaps of written abstraction are no less serious or virulent than the current nihilism of images. They are simply different (or the same in reverse). The censoring of the body, the emotive and the sensory, the individual, factual, and particular, of the present in its immediacy, has been paid for dearly (our perpetually future happiness). And our videosphere can be interpreted as an inevitable consequence, the bill to be paid for the liabilities incurred by the Book (with its humiliations and zones of desiccation that had previously gone unnoticed).

At this juncture the most flagrant opposition would pit the *orality* of myths, tales and legends against the *written* character of theological systems. The exception proves the rule: the myth of Atlantis, the only popular tale to be penned by a philosopher, Plato, with all the subsequent extra-academic, novelistic and political tribulations.[10] It remains, none the less, that the ear is more credulous than the eye, and – unfortunately and maddeningly for us – enjoys a certain priority. Is not *to obey* in Greek *to listen* (*upakouein*)? There is a reserve of passivity in hearing, of autonomy in vision. One can skip the pages of a book, but not the sequences of a film in a cinema, which imposes its progress and rhythm on the viewer. Visual perception is inherently distanced; sonorous perception tends towards fusion, if not towards the tactile. It has no knowledge of the separation between subject and object, nor, on occasion, between individual and group; nor, perhaps, if we retrace in the history of a body, the separation between pre- and postnatal either. The foetus hears its mother's body as an omnipresent din, and the as yet blind baby listens. Descartes: 'In so far as we have all been children … ,' we remain susceptible to Grandmother's stories, Santa Claus and werewolves. The sonorous immersion of fable comes from deeper, and further away, than proofs of the existence of God, forged, pen in hand, by the knights of dialectic, erudite scholars and other adepts of the arts of the Sorbonne.

These remarks remain brief in that they articulate a specific mode of belief with a specific apparatus, restricting the play of credibility to the order of mental representations. Now belief is not primarily a state of mind. It is a disposition to *act*, which is to be evaluated in terms not of the truth values or logical propositions according to which I would accord, upon reflection, my assent as a function of their degree of plausibility (as in the cognitivist models currently in fashion), but of ongoing or projected actions. When I say: I believe in something, I link *saying* with *doing*, by signifying that I commit myself to act on behalf of that thing (through a promise, a proclamation, a prayer, an order – in sum, a speech act). I take a vital risk. I open myself to an other and to a future. I establish a contract with the future. I affirm my conviction, and when I do so, my expectation reinforces the bonds of solidarity within the group to which I belong. Believing, Michel de Certeau so accurately observes, 'creates a network of debts and rights among the members of a group. It underwrites a sacral character grounded in a duration.'[11] The question of belief binds the question of time (which knowledge, like seeing, does not heed) to that of the other. Now all mediaspheres do not accord the same opportunities to duration and sociality. Our own is inhospitable to deferred temporalities, such as those of belief and hope (losing a present for a future), because it gives everyone the keys to immediacy and directness. Wherein it offers as little encouragement to political commitment as to religious observance, two forms of collective anticipation which share a practice of taking out a loan on the future by rejecting the present. With our technical equipment granting a semblance of self-sufficiency to

[10] Pierre Vidal-Naquet, 'Athènes et l'Atlantide', in *Le Chasseur noir* (Paris: La Découverte 1983).
[11] Michel de Certeau, 'Une pratique sociale de la différence', in *Faire Croire* (École française de Rome, 1981).

the *here and now*, become palpable and jubilatory, the messianic referral from present to later, be it of this world or the next, does not find our videosphere a particularly auspicious environment.

That being said, it is impossible for us not to inscribe the relation with one's fellow being within duration, in the shared expectation of *novissima tempora*. We mutualize our anticipation (to believe is to believe in the belief of the other, each serving as a respondent of the other). The granting of credit gives shape to every social fabric, however unresistant and unprotective. It is always prudent to ask an enthusiast of the faith by virtue of what authority, witness or document he believes what he believes. But 'technical' precaution ought not to prevent us from wondering about the source of his (or my) need to believe. The apparatus [*dispositif*] is more than a point of application, but *it* is not what invents the mental *disposition*. Where does it come from? Philosophers have been debating the matter for twenty-five centuries, grousing all the while, since belief is the bugbear of all reflection enamoured of truth. From Plato to Heidegger, they prefer *thinking* or *knowing*. Believing remains their great enemy. They did all they could to ridicule or diminish it. In vain. Such meritorious efforts slide off collective entities like water off the proverbial duck's back. In their humdrum existence there continues to reign an 'I know, but all the same', and even Madame du Deffand's 'I don't believe in ghosts, but I'm afraid of them'. The Devil and the Good Lord are resolutely indifferent to professorial words of caution. Their concern is with life, not intelligence. And their business is with Hippocrates, not Socrates. The latter should at all costs retain his right to examine the former; no one can forbid him to apply the blade of his criticism to all subjects, including taboos. But let him have no illusions: the therapist, in his realm, is sovereign. His charge is to allow wounded or suffering bodies to live, and if placebos help, the final word remains with the practitioner, not the chemist. Health comes first. 'Error, mother of the living,' acknowledged Nietzsche (who, moreover, knew how much we who are interested in truth 'still remain pious'). Repairing the damage of intelligence in order not to die of the truth is a labour that collective exaltation takes on rather effectively, if we are to judge from all the human congregations still holding fast, who 'want and believe', from the local rugby team to nations struggling to retain a place in the sun. Who would advise them to give up the psychical benefits of faith, which moves mountains, in order to make up for their 'intellectual backwardness'?

The Acts of the Apostles, chapter 17: 'Then Paul stood in front of the Aeropagus and said: "Athenians, I see how extremely religious you are in every way. For as I went through the city and looked carefully at the objects of your worship, I found among them an altar with the inscription, To an unknown God."'

The Greeks, who invented geometry, philosophy and democracy, were cautious people. They had a strong suspicion that there were many gods beyond their horizon, past or future, and that at least one might be missing from their temples. Dedicating an altar to the forgotten deity was a way of calming his wrath in advance.

Paul preached, convinced that his own God was the unknown deity that the ancient world anxiously awaited. If he had been in less of a hurry to proclaim his own certainties to the Athenians gathered to hear him, perhaps he would have taken a moment to observe that provident altar. Then, he would have been able to see a public square with empty arcades and extended shadows, one of those enigmatic chalky premonitions of the sort that the painter De Chirico liked to compose in his youth, in order to restore for us, as his friend Apollinaire put it, 'the fatal character of modern things'. And in the middle of that esplanade where the clock of the centuries had come to a stop, he would have discovered a composite effigy, quite different from our mental image of imperilled colossi: feet of granite, face of clay, precariously propped there. The municipal services would replace the head, from time to time, the identity of the central idol being deemed a matter of relative indifference by the sages. Only the pedestal was made to last.

Postscript: 'Please accept my apologies. In the end, my biography was better than my definition. My all-too-famous: "I am that I am" turned out to be unworthy of my future. I should have said to Moses: I am He who dies and becomes. I am the Being whose essence is to play hide-and-seek, to veil my face and sneak up on you from behind, to surprise you. Millennium after millennium. Fundamentally, I was poetry itself: a myth that tells the truth. And the truth is that you cannot do without a poem, a collective dream, a spark from elsewhere, if you want to *live*, not merely to subsist. You are too negligible to get there on your own. Forget numbers. You can be five, six, ten billion on this earth, and still not make up for your insufficiency of being. You will remain lacking. I suggested that it was your fault with the story of original sin, because the image was effective and I could make you feel guilty into the bargain. It was, you should be aware, only a manner of speaking. Find another if you like, but you will never escape the vertical. We'll meet again. Me or an Other … Farewell.'

Giorgio de Chirico, 'The Anguish of Waiting', Magnani Rocca Foundation,
Corte di Mamiano

Complementary Notes

(a) p. 1.

This instruction, made all the more imperative by the disintegration of channels of transmission, raises several difficulties of organization and conception. Its absence in institutions of secondary education raises a number of problems that are more serious still. Proposing, for example, 'art education for all' without beginning with what informs our visual and cultural heritage, and alone allows access to it, is rather surprising. It goes without saying that a secular history of religions requires a scientific (rather than sectarian or moralizing) approach. The caricature counter-model in this respect is offered by Spain, where bishops appoint teachers. Such instruction should be entrusted to the teachers themselves, historians trained in the field, not to external intermediaries or representatives of various clergies, in order to avoid proselytism and sectarianism. Failing which, there is a risk that the young will turn away from our lay schools in order to gain access to the sources of our culture and history. The Republic, quite properly, does not *recognize* any religion. Should it, for all that, fail to take *cognizance* of them? One might very well, as a consequence, in the name of tolerance and a commendable concern not to introduce religious divisions and conflicts of civil society into our schools, ultimately exacerbate them, by favouring a drift towards private (and aggressively sectarian) establishments. The 'perverse effect' has more than one trick up its sleeve.

(b) p. 2.

See, in particular, *Critique de la raison politique ou l'inconscient religieux* (Paris: Gallimard 1981); *Cours de médiologie générale*, fourth and fifth lessons, 'Le mystère de l'incarnation' and 'L'expérimentation chrétienne' (Paris: Gallimard 1991); *L'Incomplétude, logique du religieux* (Bulletin de la société française de philosophie, Paris: Armand Colin 1996); and *Croire, Voir, Faire* (Paris: Odile Jacob 1997).

(c) p. 35.

Territorial surface, in the animal world, is relative to the density of sources of nourishment. It entails certain defence costs, and ought thus to bring benefits which exceed them in terms of survival (limiting predators, facilitating reproduction, acquisition of food and social organization). In general, animals defend their territory only against members of their own species (each species possessing its own vital domain). The delimiting of respective niches may be achieved, in the case of birds, through signals of an auditory (song) or visual (exhibitionist) sort. In mammals, marking by smell, through deposit of urine or faeces, takes precedence. In order mutually to keep their distance from each other, human groups, which are more highly evolved, seem to have recourse to patently religious (sonorous, alimentary, vestimentary and architectural) markers.

(d) p. 50.
The pagan world at its best exudes a certain felicity of finitude appropriate to an Apollinian character – from which a specific geographical dimension should not be excluded. Zero and infinity were not Mediterranean inventions, and no one has suggested that the Greeks, however athletic they may have been, ever undertook to scale Mount Olympus. To what extent did landscapes – without vanishing points, featuring clearly defined shapes, lumps and bumps (which might also be qualified as Apollinian) – contribute not only to classical Antiquity's logical and geographical propensity for definition, but to its scrupulous realism of line and contour? A model of landscape and a model of thought: academic ideology's rejection of the work of Taine will not facilitate the study of this kind of intersection. On this subject, see *Paysage méditerranéen* (Milan: Electa 1992), the catalogue for the Seville World's Fair of 1992.

(e) p. 51.
From a religious point of view, there is nothing aberrant in the case of the United States. Need we recall that for twenty centuries the Catholic Church constantly supported the death penalty, which, despite a few recent and localized cases of rejection, has still not been the subject of formal condemnation *urbi et orbi*? The notion that exemplary redemption occurs by way of blood – according to the ancestral logic of sacrifice – is undoubtedly not alien to this longstanding approbation. All the more so in that the worst of earthly punishments cannot be considered supreme, from the Church's perspective, since the supreme instance of appeal is situated in the beyond.

(f) p. 148.
Before the Apostles' *Didascalia* (the 'set of instructions given by the apostles to the bishops' [c. 380]), whose Greek original has been lost, there was the *Didache* (or doctrine of the twelve apostles), from the end of the first century, which was still quite Judaic in spirit, and accorded primacy to apostles, prophets and doctors. Then the *Apostolic Tradition*, a Greek text attributed to Hippolytus of Rome (between 197 and 218, translated into Latin *c.* 375–400), which establishes the *paradosis*, or

the apostles' way of transmitting their teaching. The *Apostolic Constitutions* designate a compilation of eight books in Greek in which the author has the apostles speak.

(g) p. 151.
Canonical Communist congresses respected the same rule of unanimity as Catholic Councils. Since the spirit of social class can no more contradict itself than the Holy Spirit can, final decisions cannot be taken on a majority basis. With the aim of obtaining unanimous consent from Church or Party, a final resolution commits the deliberating body, whether mystical or proletarian, in its entirety. Unanimity thus becomes the sign whereby one recognizes the 'supernatural' or 'scientific' character of the proceedings of the assembly of believers.

(h) p. 156.
We should not forget, however, that Voltaire, an anti-Christian deist, was extravagantly and viscerally hostile to Judaism. Under 'Tolerance' in the *Dictionnaire philosophique*, we read that the Jews are 'the most intolerant and cruel people of all Antiquity'. And, under 'Chinese catechism': 'Woe unto a people sufficiently imbecilic and barbarous to believe there is a God for its province alone!' His *Essai sur les mœurs* contains a precise calculation of 'Jews exterminated by their brothers or by order of God Himself, from the time of their wandering in the desert to the time they acquired a king chosen by chance': he ends up with 239,020 victims. Later, he would talk about more than a million men. Every occasion is deemed appropriate for blackening the picture. Extreme right-wing thought can enlist the services of Voltaire, who was both anti-Semitic and anti-black. Diderot, on the other hand, is of no use at all.

(i) p. 178.
We should recall that in Saint John's day the word *Ioudaios*, had three possible meanings. (1) Geographic: an inhabitant of the Kingdom of Judah, a Judaean. (2) Ethnic: a member of the Jewish nation, enjoying a specific cultural and juridical status anywhere in the Empire. (3) Religious: the follower of a specific monotheistic cult.

(j) p. 181.
In a 1936 text entitled 'L'Élasticité américaine', Paul Claudel, before evoking the 'enormous provision of space and emptiness furnished by a continent rich in desert', notes: 'There is in the American temperament a quality which is conveyed by the word *resiliency*, for which I cannot find a precise equivalent in French, since it combines the ideas of elasticity, suppleness, resourcefulness, and good humour.' Has anyone put it better? (*Œuvres en prose*, Paris: La Pléiade, p. 1205).

(k) p. 192.

La Bible enfin expliquée par plusieurs aumôniers de sa Majesté le Roi de Prusse
(complete title) was published in 1776. Voltaire accompanies the text of the Bible,
centred on the page, with extremely harsh marginalia concerning the fictionalizing
excesses and the atrocities of the Pentateuch narrative. The New Testament is
treated more indulgently.

(l) p. 227.

In mediology, the 'jogging effect' designates a reactivation of the old by the new, or
the return of the culturally archaic in the wake of technological progress. Now that
city-dwellers travel by car, they run more, because they walk less.

(m) p. 265.

The materialist militants of the last century did not escape the rule which forbids
discussion, in a group, of its reason for being. Thus Rosa Luxemburg: 'The class
struggle cannot be freely criticized within the Party.' The stronger the vital investment, the more pronounced the rational taboo. Kautsky, at the end of his life: 'Were
it one day to be revealed that the materialist conception of history and the conception of the proletariat as guiding force of the coming revolution had become
obsolete, I would have to admit that everything was over for me, and my life would
no longer have any meaning.'

(n) p. 273.

The 'emergence from religion' prepared by the Christian distinction between God
and Caesar, sacred and profane, priesthood and empire, as hypothesized by Marcel
Gauchet, would concern only society. For Gauchet, religion would continue to
speak to individuals, as a residual sentiment. It will be understood that I am supporting the opposite thesis: that it is easier for individuals to take leave than it is for
their group of affiliation, by virtue of the 'religious' structuring of collective entities.

(o) p. 282.

If one wanted to systematize the attempts of critical thought, from Epicurus to
Freud, to explain the irrational rationally, thereby according it a certain positivity or
consistency, the outlines of three genealogies – three families of interpretation, to
oversimplify – would emerge: the advocates of sociogenesis, who read religion as the
effect within consciousness of social relations, evolving with them, and indeed
capable of being rectified like them (at least for Feuerbach and Marx); the advocates
of biogenesis (Nietzsche joining up with Bergson here); and the advocates of psy-
chogenesis, of whom Freud remains the best known. In *The Future of an Illusion*,
for example, he extrapolates from individual pathology to social normality. No
doubt these three rival lineages are not incompatible; in any event, each of them is
ignorant of its neighbour.

Bibliography

I have listed, chapter by chapter, only books, journals and articles which will allow the reader to pursue the theme treated.

Chapter 1 A Reader's Guide

Andreas-Salomé, Lou, *Création d'un Dieu* (French translation by Maren Sell).

Dagognet, François, *Philosophie d'un retournement* (Fougères: Encre marine 2001).

Gilbert, Pierre, Jourjon, Maurice and Bourgeois, Henri, *Sens chrétien du monothéisme* (Faculté de théologie de Lyon, undated).

Leroi-Gourhan, André, *Le Geste et la Parole: Technique et langage* (Paris: Albin Michel 1964).

Leroi-Gourhan, André, *La Mémoire et les rythmes* (Paris: Albin Michel 1965).

Leroi-Gourhan, André, *Les Racines du monde* (Paris: Belfond, 1982).

Parrot, André, 'Le Temple de Jérusalem', *Cahiers d'archéologie biblique* (Neuchâtel: Delchaux 1954).

Ricœur, Paul, *Lecture 3. Aux frontières de la philosophie* (Paris: Seuil 1994), especially 'Entre philosophie et théo: La Règle d'or en question'.

Trigano, Shmuel, *Le Monothéisme est un humanisme* (Paris: Odile Jacob 2000).

Vattimo, Gianni, *Éthique de l'interprétation* (Paris: La Découverte 1990).

La Naissance des dieux, collective volume, ed. Suret-Canal, Vernant, Chesneaux, *et al.* (Paris: Les Éditions de l'Union rationaliste 1964).

Philosophie et religion, collective volume, Centre d'études et de recherches marxistes (Paris: Éditions sociales 1974).

Chapter 2 An Endpoint Called Origin

Albright, W. F., *From the Stone Age to Christianity: Monotheism and the Historical Process* (Baltimore, MD: Johns Hopkins University Press 1957).

Anati, Emmanuel, *La Religion des origines* (Paris: Bayard 2000).

Bottero, Jean, *Naissance de Dieu: La Bible et l'historien* (Paris: Gallimard 1986).

Bottero, Jean, Ouakkin, Marc-Alain and Moingt, Joseph, *La plus belle histoire de Dieu, Qui est le Dieu de la Bible* (Paris: Seuil 1997).

Brown, Raymond E., *Que sait-on du Nouveau Testament?* (Paris: Bayard 2000).

Husser, J.-M., 'Entre mythe et philosophie. La relecture sapentielle de Genèse 2–3', *Revue biblique*, April 2000, pp. 232–60.

Lys, Daniel, *Treize Énigmes de l'Ancien Testament* (Paris: Cerf 1998).

Mimouni, Simon C., 'Les órigines du christianisme. Aux XIXe et XXe siècles en France. Questions d'épistémologie et de méthodologie', in *L'Orient dans l'histoire religieuse de l'Europe* (Paris: Brépols 1999).

Mohen, Jean-Pierre, *Les Rites de l'au-delà* (Paris: Odile Jacob 1995).

Nodet, Étienne, *Essai sur les origines du judaïsme: De Josué aux Pharisiens* (Paris: Cerf 1992).

Ségal, Abraham, *Abraham, Enquête sur un patriarche* (Paris: Plon 1995).

Thompson, Thomas L., *The Bible in History: How Writers Create a Past* (London: Random House, 1999).

Vallet, Odon, 'L'héritage des religions premières', in *Une autre histoire de la religion*, 6 vols (Paris: Gallimard 2000).

Les millénaires de Dieu. Une vieille histoire pleine d'avenir, ed. André Julliard (Grenoble: Musée dauphinois 2000).

Le Monde de la Bible, texts presented by André Lemaire (Paris: Gallimard 1998).

Chapter 3   High Atop the Dune

Berque, Augustin, *Écoumène, Introduction à l'étude des milieux humains* (Paris: Belin 2000).

Comblin, Joseph, *Théologie de la ville* (Paris: Éditions universitaires 1968).

Deleuze, Gilles and Guattari, Félix, *A Thousand Plateaus: Capitalism and Schizophrenia*, trans. Brian Massumi (Minneapolis: University of Minnesota Press 1987), ch. 12.

Durand, Jean-Pierre and Froger, Jean-François, *Le Bestiaire de la Bible* (Paris: Destris 1994).

Hari, Albert, *L'Écologie de la Bible: l'eau, les animaux, les humains* (Paris: Édition de l'Atelier 1995).

Lacarrière, Jacques, preface by Lawrence Durrell, *Les Gnostiques* (Paris: Albin Michel 1991).

Loti, Pierre, *Le Désert* (Saint-Cyr-sur-Loire: Christian Pirot, 1923).

Mathiex, Jean, *Civilisations impériales, Kiron* (Paris: Éditions du Félin 2000).

Miquel, Dom Pierre, *Dictionnaire symbolique des animaux, zoologie mystique* (Paris: Le Léopard d'or 1991).

Montagne, Robert, *La Civilisation du désert, Nomades d'Orient et d'Afrique* (Paris: Hachette 1947).

Rodinson, Maxime, *Mahomet* (Paris: Seuil, 1967).

Wunenburger, Jean-Jacques, 'La forêt ou le sacré sauvage', *Le Beffroi*, revue philosophique et littéraire, September/November 1990.

Traverses / 19, 'Le Désert' (Centre Pompidou–CCI, June 1980).

'Le Désert et la Quête', *Cahiers de l'Université Saint-Jean de Jérusalem*, 8, 1982 (Paris: Bery International Éd. 1982).

Chapter 4   Alphabetical Liftoff

Bottero, Jean, *Mésopotamie, l'écriture, la raison et les dieux* (Paris: Gallimard 1987).

Briquel-Chatonnet, Françoise, *Les inscriptions protosinaïques. Le Sinaï durant l'Antiquité et le Moyen Âge* (UNESCO Colloquium, September 1997, Paris 1998).

Chrysostome, Jean, *De l'incompréhensibilité de Dieu, Homélies 1–5 contre les Anonéens* (Paris: Payot, 2000).

Dagognet, François, *Écriture et Iconographie* (Paris: Vrin 1973).

Dorandi, Tiziano, *Le Stylet et la tablette, dans le secret des auteurs antiques* (Paris: Les Belles Lettres, L'âne d'or 2000).

Fitzmyer, Joseph A., *Responses to 101 Questions on the Dead Sea Scrolls* (New York: Paulist Press 1992).

Glassner, Jean-Jacques, *Écrire à Sumer, L'Invention du cunéiforme* (Paris: Seuil 2000).

Goody, Jack, *Entre l'oralité et l'écriture* (Paris: PUF 1994).

Goody, Jack, *L'Homme, l'écriture et la mort* (Paris: Les Belles Lettres 1996).

Ouaknin, Marc-Alain, *Invitation au Talmud* (Paris: Flammarion 2001).

Perrier, Pierre, *Évangiles de l'oral à l'écrit: Le Sarment* (Paris: Fayard 2000).

Piveteau, Jean-Luc, *Temps du territoire* (Geneva: Zoé 1995).

Puech, Émile, 'Origine de l'alphabet, Documents en alphabet linéaire et cunéiforme du IIe millénaire', *Revue biblique*, April 1986, pp. 161–214.

Schmandt-Besserat, S., *How Writing Came About* (Austin: University of Texas Press 1996).

Sirat, Colette, *Écritures et civilisation* (Paris: Institut de recherche et d'histoire des textes 1976).

'L'Écriture, ses diverses origines', ed. Annie Berthier and Anne Zali, *Dossiers d'archéologie*, no. 260, February 2001.

Chapter 5   Portable Yet Homebound

Adéoussi, Claudia, 'Le Saint-Siège et la question palestinienne', *Revue d'Études palestiniennes*, 27, Spring 2001.

Barnavi, Élie, *Israël au XXe siècle* (Paris: PUF 1982).

Eco, Umberto, 'La ligne et le labyrinthe: les structures de la pensée latine', in *Civilisation latine. Des temps anciens au monde moderne*, ed. Georges Duby (Paris: Olivier Orban 1986).

Freud, Sigmund, *Moses and Monotheism* (New York: Norton 1939).

Gonçalvez, Francolino J., 'L'exil. Remarques historiques', *Théologiques* 7/2 (1999), pp. 105–26.

Keel, Othmer and Uehlinger, Christoph, *Dieux, déesses et figures divines, Les sources iconographiques de l'histoire de la religion d'Israël* (Paris: Cerf 2001).

Levallois, Agnès and Pommier, Sophie, *Jérusalem, de la division au partage?* (Paris: Michalon 1995).

Leibowitz, Yeshayahou, *Israël et judaïsme, Ma part de vérité* (Brussels: Desclée de Brouwer 1993).

Moubarac, Youakim, La question de Jérusalem, 1 et 2', *Revue d'Études palestiniennes*, 6, Winter 1993.

Schmidt, Francis, *La Pensée du Temple. De Jérusalem à Qumran. Identité et lien social dans le judaïsme ancien* (Paris: Seuil 1994).

Stern, Ephraïm, 'Religion in Palestine in the Assyrian and Persian Periods', in *The Crisis of Israelite Religion: Transformation of Religious Tradition in Exilic and Post-Exilic Times*, ed. Bob Becking and Marjo Korpel (Leiden: Brill 1999).

La Bible, images, mythes, et traditions (Cahiers de l'hermétisme, Paris: Albin Michel 1995).

'La politique de l'Église au Moyen-Orient', *La Documentation catholique*, no. 2203, 2 May 1999.

Chapter 6   One For All

Celsus, *Contre les chrétiens* (Paris: Phébus, 1999).

Coutin, André, *La Vie du Christ après sa mort* (Paris: Philippe Lebaud–Éditions du Félin 1998).

Dodd, Charles-Harold, *La Prédication apostolique et ses développements* (Paris: Éditions universitaires, 1964).

Duquesne, Jacques, *Jésus* (Brussels: Desclée de Brouwer, Flammarion 1994).

Ellul, Jacques, *La Parole humiliée* (Paris: Seuil 1981).

Grant, Robert, *Le Dieu des premiers chrétiens* (Paris: Seuil 1971).

Imbert, Jean, *Le Procès de Jésus* (Paris: PUF 1980).

Lamour, Denis, *Flavius Josèphe* (Paris: Les Belles Lettres 2000).

Peña-Ruiz, Henri, *Dieu et Marianne, Philosophie de la laïcité* (Paris: PUF 1999).

Renan, Ernest, *Du judaïsme et du christianisme* (Paris: Desclée de Brouwer 1995).

Les Origines de la chrétienté (Cahiers Histoire, 76, 1999). Specifically Sachot, Maurice, 'Les origines du christianisme au crible de la médiologie.

Bible et Christologie, Commission biblique pontificale (Paris: Cerf 1984).

'Jésus dans l'Histoire', *Dossiers d'Archéologie*, 249, December 1999–January 2000.

Chapter 7   The Mediating Body

Badiou, Alain, *Saint Paul, La Fondation de l'universalisme* (Paris: PUF 1997).

Balthasar, Hans Urs von, *Qui est l'Église* (Preface and translation by Maurice Vidal. Paris: Éditions Parole et Silence 2000).

Boismard, Marie-Émile, *À l'aube du christianisme. Avant la naissance des dogmes* (Paris: Cerf 1998).

Daniélou, Jean and Marrou, Henri, *Nouvelle Histoire de l'Église*, I, *Des Origines à Saint Grégoire le Grand* (Paris: Seuil 1963).

de Diéguez, Manuel, *Et l'homme créa son Dieu* (Paris: Fayard 1984).

Faivre, Alexandre, *Ordonner la fraternité. Pouvoir d'innover et retour à l'ordre dans l'Église ancienne* (Paris: Cerf 1992).

Jacques-Jouvenot, Dominique, *Choix du successeur et transmission patrimoniale* (Paris: L'Harmattan 1997).

Mimouni, Simon C., 'Paul de Tarse. Éléments pour une réévaluation historique et doctrinale', in *Le Judéo-Christianisme dans tous ses états* (Paris: Cerf 2000).

Pomeau, René, *La Religion de Voltaire* (Paris: Nizet 1956).

Savart, Claude, *Introduction à l'histoire de l'Église* (Cahiers de l'École Cathédrale, Paris: Mame 1993).

Taubes, Jacob, *La Théologie politique de Paul* (Paris: Seuil 1999).

Vallin, Pierre, *Histoire politique des chrétiens* (Paris: Nouvelle Cité 1987).

L'Église: Institution et foi, collective volume (Brussels: Faculté interuniversitaire Saint-Louis 1984).

Chapter 8   Salve Regina

Bechtel, Guy, *Les Quatre Femmes de Dieu* (Paris: Plon 2000).

Mondzain, Marie-José, *Image, icône, économie. Les sources byzantines de l'imaginaire contemporain* (Paris: Seuil 1996).

Prigent, Pierre, *L'Image dans le judaïsme, Du IIe au VIe siècle (Collection Le monde de la Bible,* 24, Paris: Labor et Fides 1991).

Prigent, Pierre, *L'art des premiers chrétiens. L'héritage culturel et la foi nouvelle* (Paris: Desclée de Brouwer 1995).

Quenot, Michel, *L'Icône* (Paris: Cerf et Fides 1997).

Tertullian, 'La toilette des femmes' (Sources chrétiennes, no. 173, 1971).

Toubert, Hélène, *Un art dirigé. Réforme grégorienne et iconographie* (Paris: Cerf 1990).

Vallet, Odon, *Femmes et religions* (Paris: Gallimard 1994).

Vallet, Odon, *Le honteux et le sacré. Grammaire de l'érotisme divin* (Paris: Albin Michel 1998).

Vircondelet, Alain, *Je vous salue Marie, Représentations populaires de la Vierge* (Paris: Éditions du Chêne 1996).

Wirth, Jean, *L'Image à l'époque romaine* (Paris: Cerf 2000).

Les Ailes de Dieu. Messages et guerriers ailés entre Orient et Occident, ed. Marco Bussagli and Mario d'Onofrio (Exhibition Catalogue, Silvana Editoriale, 2000).

Byzance et les images ('Conférences et colloques', Louvre, 1994).

L'Image et la production du sacré, ed. Françoise Dunand, Jean-Michel Speiser and Jean Wirth (Paris: Méridiens-Klincksieck 1991).

L'Interdit de la représentation (Montpellier Colloquium, 1981, Seuil, 1984).

'Observatoire de la parité entre les hommes et les femmes. Procès-verbal des auditions', *Religions et franc-maçonneries*, March–September 1996.

Chapter 9   The Last Flame

Baroni, Victor, *La Contre-Réforme devant la Bible. La question biblique* (Lausanne: La Concorde 1943).

Chartier, Roger, *L'Ordre des Livres, Lecteurs, auteurs, bibliothèques en Europe, entre le XIVe et le XVIIIe siècle* (Aix-en-Provence: Alinéa 1992).

Colas, Dominique, *Le Glaive et le Fléau. Généalogie du fanatisme et de la société civile* (Paris: Grasset 1992).

Debray, Régis, *Christophe Colomb, Le visiteur de l'aube* (Paris: La Différence 1992).

Dupuigrenet-Desroussilles, François, *Dieu en son Royaume, La Bible dans la France d'autrefois, XIIIe–XVIIIe siècle* (Paris: Cerf 1992).

Gilmont, Jean-François, *La Réforme du Livre, 1517–v. 1570* (Paris: Cerf 1990).

Gilmont, Jean-François, *Jean Calvin et le livre imprimé* (Geneva: Droz 1997).

Johannet, Yvonne, *Tourner la page, Livres, rites et symboles* (Paris: Jérôme Millon 1988).

Marienstras, Élise, *Les Mythes fondateurs de la nation américaine* (Paris: Maspero 1977).

Martin, Henri-Jean, *Histoire et pouvoirs de l'écrit* (Paris: Perrin 1988).

Wunenbuger, Jean-Jacques, 'De la terre promise à l'Ouest américain: les transformations d'un espace–temps mythique', in *La Bible, images, mythes et tradition* (Paris: Albin Michel 1995).

Le Livre et l'Historien, Études offertes en l'honneur du professeur Henri-Jean Martin (Paris: Droz 1997).

La passion des manuscrits enluminés, Bibliophiles français: 1280–1580 (Catalogue of the exhibition at the Bibliothèque nationale, 1991).

Le pouvoir des bibliothèques. La mémoire des livres en Occident, ed. Marc Baratin and Christian Jacob (Paris: Albin Michel 1996).

Chapter 10   Parricidal Christ

Baschet, Jérôme, *Le sein du père, Abraham et la paternité dans l'Occident médiéval* (Paris: Gallimard 2000).

Batut, Jean-Pierre, *Dieu le Père Tout-Puissant* (Paris: Cahiers de l'École Cathédrale, Parole et silence, 1998).

Boespflug, François, *La trinité dans l'art d'Occident, 1400–1460, Sept chefs-d'œuvre de la peinture* (Strasbourg: Presses universitaires de Strasbourg 2000).

Boureau, Alain, *Théologie, science et censure au XIIIᵉ siècle, Le cas Jean Peckham* (Paris: Les Belles Lettres 1999).

de la Brosse, Olivier, 'L'Église de France face aux problèmes de communication', *Revue d'éthique et de théologie morale*, no. 210, 1999.

Coutin, André, *La Vie du Christ après sa mort* (Paris: Philippe Lebaud 1998).

Delumeau, Jean, *Le Christianisme va-t-il mourir?* (Paris: Hachette 1977).

Delumeau, Jean, *La Peur en Occident, XIVᵉ–XVIIIᵉ siècle* (Paris: Fayard 1978).

Delumeau, Jean, *Rassurer et protéger* (Paris: Fayard 1989).

Rémond, René, *Le Christianisme en accusation* (Paris: Desclée de Brouwer 2000).

'La Paternité', *Melampous, Revue de l'Association française des magistrats de la jeunesse et de la famille*, no. 7, 1997–98.

Chapter 11   Every Man For Himself

Babes, Leila, *Les Nouvelles Manières de croire* (Paris: Éditions de l'Atelier 1996).

Dery, Mark, *Escape Velocity: Cyberculture at the End of the Century* (New York: Grove Press 1996).

Ferreux, Marie-Jeanne, *Le New Age: Ritualités et mythologies contemporaines* (Paris: L'Harmattan, 2000).

Hervieu-Léger, Danièle, *Le pèlerin et le converti, La religion en mouvement* (Paris: Flammarion, 1999).

Kepel, Gilles, *La revanche de Dieu, Chrétiens, juifs, et musulmans à la reconquête du monde* (Paris: Seuil 1991).

Lapointe, Guy, 'L'espace liturgique éclaté', *Maison Dieu*, no. 197.

Poulat, Emile, *Liberté Laïcité, La guerre des deux France et le principe de la modernité* (Paris: Cerf/Cujas 1987).

Poulat, Emile, *L'ère postchrétienne* (Paris: Flammarion 1994).

Weber, Max, *The Sociology of Religion*, intro. Talcott Parsons (Boston, MA: Beacon Press 1993).

Chapter 12   The Eternity of the Eternal

de Certeau, Michel, 'L'Institution du croire', *Recherches de sciences religieuses*, LXXXI, 1987, pp. 61–80.

de Certeau, Michel, *La Faiblesse de croire* (Paris: Seuil 1987).

Derrida, Jacques and Vattimo, Gianni, *Religion* (Stanford, CA: Stanford University Press 1998).

Freud, Sigmund, *The Future of an Illusion* (New York: Norton 1989).

Lévi-Strauss, Claude, *Tristes tropiques* (New York: Modern Library 1997), Chapter XXXIX, 'Taxila'.

Saint Augustine, *La Foi chrétienne, Œuvres*, vol. 8 (Paris: Desclée de Brouwer 1951).

Schmitt, Jean-Claude, *Le corps, les rites, les rêves, le temps. Essais d'anthropologie médiévale* (Paris: Gallimard 2001).

Wirth, Jean, La naissance du concept de croyance (XIIᵉ–XVIᵉ siècle), Bibliothèque d'Humanisme et de Renaissance, vol. 45, pp. 7–58 (1983).

'La croyance', *Nouvelle Revue de psychanalyse*, no. 18 (Paris: Gallimard, Autumn 1978).

'Le religieux et le politique: Dieux en sociétés', *Autrement*, February 1992.

'Qu'est-ce que croire?', *Agone*, no. 23 (Marseille 2000).

Index